UNDERSTANDING COMMUNICATION THEORY

A Beginner's Guide

Stephen M. Croucher

Routledge
Taylor & Francis Group

NEW YORK AND LONDON

First published 2016
by Routledge
711 Third Avenue, New York, NY 10017

and by Routledge
2 Park Square, Milton Park, Abingdon, Oxon OX14 4RN

Routledge is an imprint of the Taylor & Francis Group, an informa business

Library of Congress Cataloging-in-Publication Data
Croucher, Stephen Michael, 1978–
    Understanding communication theory : a beginner's guide / Stephen M.
Croucher.
        pages cm
    Includes bibliographical references.
    1. Communication—Study and teaching. I. Title.
    P91.3.C733 2015
    302.2—dc23
    2015005975

ISBN: 978-0-415-74803-2 (hbk)
ISBN: 978-0-415-74804-9 (pbk)
ISBN: 978-1-315-79671-0 (ebk)

Typeset in Classical Garamond
by Apex CoVantage, LLC

UNDERSTANDING COMMUNICATION THEORY

This book offers students a comprehensive, theoretical, and practical guide to communication theory. Croucher defines the various perspectives on communication theory—the social scientific, interpretive, and critical approaches—and then takes on the theories themselves, with topics including interpersonal communication, organizational communication, intercultural communication, persuasion, critical and rhetorical theory, and other key concepts. Each theory chapter includes a sample undergraduate-written paper that applies the described theory, along with edits and commentary by Croucher, giving students an insider's glimpse of the way that communication theory can be written about and applied in the classroom and in real life. Featuring exercises, case studies, and keywords that illustrate and fully explain the various communication theories, *Understanding Communication Theory* gives students all the tools they need to understand and apply prominent communication theories.

Stephen M. Croucher is Professor in the Department of Communication at the University of Jyväskylä in Finland. With Daniel Cronn-Mills, he is co-author of *Understanding Communication Research Methods*.

CONTENTS

ACKNOWLEDGMENTS

There are many people I want to thank for helping me complete this project. First, I want to thank the students and co-authors who contributed their works. Without these valuable contributions this project would be incomplete. Second, a big thank you goes out to my mother and father for always supporting and believing in me. Third, thank you to Shawn, my love . . . there are not enough words to express my feelings.

PART I

INTRODUCTION AND APPROACHES TO THEORY

1 INTRODUCTION TO COMMUNICATION THEORY

Chapter Outline

- History of Communication
- What is Communication?
- Why Study Communication?
- The Communication Discipline
- The Structure of this Textbook

From the cave paintings of Tassili n'ajjer, Algeria to social media today, how we communicate has dramatically evolved over the past 130,000 plus years. What has remained constant is the ever-present role and importance of communication in our lives. In this book we will treat communication as an essential part of the human experience. In doing so, we will explore the various ways in which communication has been, and is, studied. It is impossible to examine all of the ways that communication is understood from a theoretical and/or practical way; however, this book attempts to explore some of these many ways.

History of Communication

In its earliest forms, communication has taken place since Homo sapiens have been on the Earth, in the form of unorganized, and/or organized signs. It was not until about 130,000 BCE that humans began to develop cave paintings/ drawings. The exact purpose of these paintings is not known; theories abound. Some theorists claim that some paintings were made to show other humans which animals and foods were safe and not safe to eat. It is believed that humans started to "speak" roughly 90,000 to 100,000 years ago (Corballis, 2002). It was not until 3,300 and 3,100 BCE that writing was invented in Iraq and Egypt. Egypt was also the first place to have a courier service, which facilitated the delivery of messages (2,000 BCE). A standard alphabet was soon established in 1,600 BCE in Israel and Lebanon. After the development of an alphabet the first "postal system" was established in Ancient Persia (modern day Iran and Iraq) in 500 BCE, which had a profound impact on the spread of communication across the Persian Empire.

While the Chinese invented paper in 200 BCE, this knowledge was not used for mass communication (news, etc.) for many years to come. It was not until 131 BCE that the first public notices were published in Rome, *Acta Diurna* or "Daily Acts." The *Acta* (in 59 CE) were initially just for government affairs and legal issues, but then became more public and open, though often censored. The *Acta* were published on stone slabs. The next major step in printing for the masses was by the Chinese in the sixth century CE, when the Chinese invented printing with blocks. The first known printed book was the *Diamond Sutra* in 686. This technology slowly spread to Europe. In fact, for the next 800 years handwritten books, or manuscripts, were the norm throughout the world. In fact, the word manuscript comes from the Latin term "libri manu scripti," which means, "book written by hand." Most of the manuscripts were of a religious nature and few people could read the manuscripts, as most people were not literate. However, in the thirteenth century non-religious (secular) books were produced for the first time as a result of the development of universities. These texts (communication) brought increased knowledge and education to the masses. As the demand for religious and secular manuscripts increased, one printer invented a way to speed up the printing process: Johannes Gutenberg. Gutenberg's press was invented in 1450, and it revolutionized the printing world. With this press, manuscripts (now books) could be mass-produced at a cheaper price for the masses. Shortly after Gutenberg's press the first newspapers appeared in Belgium, France, and Germany (in the 1600s). In 1702 the first daily newspaper began, London's *Daily Courant*. In 1833, the *New York Sun* began printing the first mass-circulated penny press newspaper.

In 1837 the first telegraph message was sent. This was a breakthrough in communication, as the message was sent over a wire, and not through print. Then in 1876, Alexander Graham Bell made the first telephone call; how we were communicating was growing at a rapid rate. Soon film was developed (1884), motion pictures made their debut (1894), and the first radio message was sent (1895). In the twentieth century, broadcast media has dramatically evolved into more advanced formats: cassette tapes to CDs, VHS to DVD, network TV to cable to digital television, etc. An additional way in which our communication has developed is through the Internet. The first email message was sent in 1971. Today it would be very difficult to imagine a world of communication without email. In 1992 the first text message was sent; imagine life without texting, particularly since more than 8,000,000,000,000 texts were sent in the United States in 2011. In 2014 communication is ever connected with the Internet. Americans spend on average 40 minutes a day on Facebook communicating with others in some way (Constine, 2014), and we send on average 500 million tweets a day (internetlivestats, 2014).

WHAT DO YOU THINK 1.1

Thinking back to the development of communication, how do you think communication would be different today without the Internet?

What is Communication?

Clearly, communication in one form or another has been all around us for thousands of years. But, what is communication? There is not one definition of communication that researchers and practitioners all agree on as *the* definition. Littlejohn (1999) said, "communication is difficult to define. The word is abstract and, like most terms, possesses numerous meanings" (p. 6). To better define communication see Figure 1.1, which offers some various definitions of communication.

Each of these definitions—and there are many more out there—offer differing views of "communication," with some sharing and some overlapping

1. A verbal interchange of thought or idea. (Hoben, 1954)
2. A process through which we try to understand individuals and have them understand us. The process is dynamic and continually changing in response to the situation. (Andersen, 1959)
3. An act through which we reduce uncertainty. (Barnlund, 1964)
4. The transmission of ideas, information, emotions, skills, etc. through symbols, words, pictures, etc. (Berelson & Steiner, 1964).
5. A process that links discontinuous parts of the world together. (Ruesch, 1957)
6. A process of sharing meaning with others. (Croucher & Cronn-Mills, 2015)
7. The means of sending and receiving messages via couriers, radio, telegraph, telephone, etc. (*The American College Dictionary*, 1964).
8. The central interest of communication is to transmit a message to a receiver with conscious intent to affect the receiver's behavior(s). (Miller, 1966)
9. "All of the procedures by which one mind can affect another." (Weaver, 1949, p. 95)

Figure 1.1 Definitions of Communication

elements. A few of the definitions take a very broad or a very narrow approach to communication, which is not suitable for this textbook. For example, Hoben's (1954) definition of communication only considers the verbal exchange of thoughts and/or ideas. As you will find in the following chapters, communication involves much more than verbal messages. Barnlund's (1964) definition of communication is that communication is the reduction of uncertainty. Once again, you will find in the following chapters that yes, communication does do this, but also much more. Similarly, Ruesch's (1957) definition, focusing on linking discontinuous parts of the world, is just one of the many things that communication can do. *The American College Dictionary* (1964) offered more of a description of means of mass communication, which is discussed more in Chapter 10. Miller's (1966) assertion that communication has a conscious intent is something we will talk more about in a moment. However, for now know that intent to communicate has been a key issue of debate for communication researchers. Weaver's (1949) definition, unlike the others just discussed, is a bit too broad. Following this approach, if I think I want some coffee and someone else is in the room with me and I get up to get coffee, I could possibly have communicated to them my intent to get coffee without ever speaking or gesturing toward coffee. My thoughts about coffee and moving *could* communicate my desires. Most researchers today do not follow this approach to defining communication. Most researchers would follow a combination of Andersen, Berelson and Steiner, and Croucher and Cronn-Mills. There are various elements of each of these definitions that we will discuss to understand the similarities and differences in how we conceptualize communication.

Similarities in Communication Definitions

The first area of similarity for many researchers and across many definitions of communication is that communication is symbolic. Communication comprises sharing symbols via **signs**. A sign is essentially an object (e.g., word, letter, phrase, action, event, etc.) that represents something else. To understand the word sign it is essential to define two linked terms: **signifier** and **signified** using the example of a mobile phone. The signifier is the word "mobile phone." The signified is the physical object that is the "mobile phone," the metal and electronic parts that physically make up the "mobile phone." The relationship between the signifier and the signified is the sign. This relationship is often clearly understood, but not always. In most cases people have their own mental concepts of what an object is, this is called the **referent**. Ogden and Richards (1927) took this one step further and explained how we associate meanings from symbols with the semantic triangle. When we see a symbol ("dog") we associate it with a referent (a four-legged creature with a tail . . . I imagine my miniature dachshund), and at the other point of the triangle we have thoughts to describe the symbol, such as barking. Thus, the process of communication for Ogden and Richards was a process of meaning generation and understanding of symbols. Different theories throughout this book, such as those in Chapter 11 and 12, will delve deeper into the significance of meaning building in communication.

> **KEY TERMS 1.1 AND 1.2**
>
> **Sign** – an object (e.g., word, letter, phrase, action, event, etc.) that represents something else.
>
> **Referent** – a mental concept of what a sign is.

For example, let's think more about the word "dog," the word is the signifier. A dog is typically a four-legged animal with hair and a tail, which comes in many varieties and sizes—the signified. However, the mental concept (referent) we all have for "dog" differs. Many of us consider a dog to be man's best friend, or a nice pet to have. Others consider a dog to be food. I knew a person who was attacked by a dog when they were young, so "dog" to them meant a scary creature who attacks. The mental concept we have in our minds to explain the signified (the physical object of the four-legged creature with fur and a tail) is the referent. A key to communication is that when we communicate signs to others we hope the other individual(s) shares the same meanings as we do. While some degree of shared similarity exists in the same language families, for most signs expressed through verbal language, misunderstandings over meaning may still occur. In this text we talk about ways in which to reduce uncertainties in communication and promote shared meanings in communication.

The second area of similarity is that communication is viewed as a process. Essentially, communication is ongoing, ever-changing, and all of the components are connected to one another. Consider the following example. A married couple is having an argument over household chores. If communication is viewed as a process, we realize this interaction is rather complex. The interaction is affected by past interactions and behaviors of the individuals (e.g., Does one partner habitually not do one chore? Does one partner "nag" the other? Does one partner believe the other does not treat them as an equal?), and by the situation surrounding the interaction (e.g., the in-laws are arriving in 30 minutes, or one spouse just lost their job and is under a lot of stress). Moreover, this interaction will affect future interactions, as we do not forget past interactions. All in all, our communication is influenced by our past and present situations when we realize communication is a process.

The third area of similarity is that communication is widely seen as transactional. From a transactional point of view, communication is regarded as a back and forth between sender and receiver. In this sense, feedback is critical to communication. However, a transactional view of communication goes further than emphasizing feedback. As Burgoon and Ruffner (1978) noted, participants in the communication process consistently influence one another in the process:

> People are simultaneously acting as source and receiver in many communication situations. A person is giving feedback, talking, responding, acting, and reacting continually through a communication event. Each person is constantly participating in the communication activity. All of these things can alter the other elements in the process and create a completely different communication event. This is what we mean by transaction. (p. 9)

To better understand the transactional approach to communication let's look back at the married couple's interaction over household chores. When thinking about this interaction look to Figure 1.2 below as a model of communication. Each of the individuals is a sender of messages, while at the same time being a receiver of messages. Both communicators are **encoding** (processing messages to send out), and **decoding** (processing messages received). In this particular case their communication channel is verbal and non-verbal communication (voice, talking, eye contact, and gestures). However, they could also have this interaction over another communication channel, such as Facebook, or via texting for example. No matter what communication channel they use the other person receives their messages and gives them feedback, more than likely in the same communication channel. However, as we all know from communicating with people, we often misinterpret communication messages, we can decode messages incorrectly. This can be attributed to many things, one being noise. Noise is any physiological, physical, psychological, and/or semantic thing that interferes in our understanding of a communication message. Physiological noise includes hunger, fatigue, headache, depression, medications, and other issues that affect how we feel. Physical noise includes things that physically disrupt the communication, like loud sounds and bright lights. Psychological noises are the issues within us that limit our abilities to decode properly, such as prejudice, being defensive, being bored, being in love, etc. Semantic noise is when words cannot be understood. This transactional approach to communication considers the complexities of communication. All of us have had a hard time getting our message across at one time or another, look to the model below, considering how communication is symbolic and a process, and hopefully you will have an improved understanding of communication.

KEY TERMS 1.3

Noise – any physiological, physical, psychological, and/or semantic things that interfere in our understanding of a communication message.

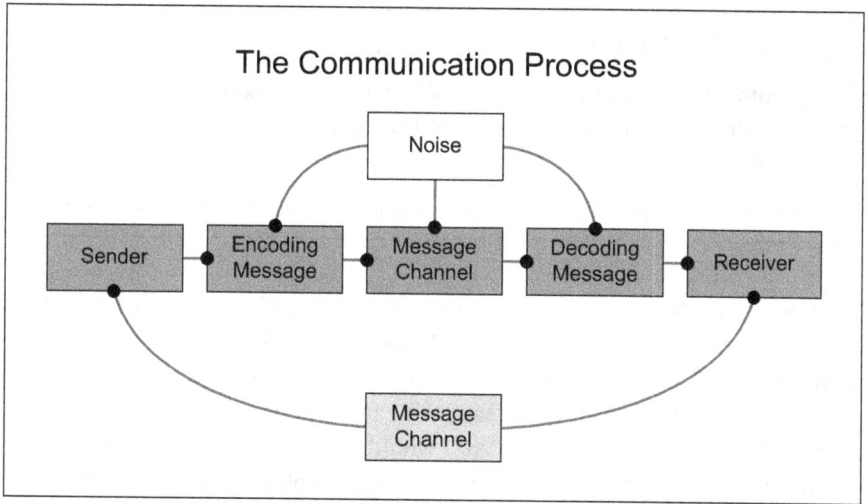

Figure 1.2

Differences in Communication Definitions

While most communication researchers and teachers agree on communication being a process, symbolic, and transactional, there are some points of disagreement in defining communication. Two points have the most disagreement: does communication need to be intentional or not, and is communication a social activity?

Watzlawick, Beavin, and Jackson (1967) wrote that you cannot not communicate. Essentially, every behavior is communication; it is impossible not to communicate. Even when one tries not to communicate, they are still communicating according to Watzlawick et al. (1967). "Communication" such as facial expressions, being silent in one's physical presence, not responding to a Facebook or email message, can all be considered communication under this theory. Not all researchers have supported this view of communication. Miller (1966), stated that the central interest of communication is to transmit a message to a receiver with conscious intent to affect the receiver's behavior(s). From this point of view, communication involves conscious intent on the part of the sender. Andersen (1991) and many others have continued this debate, arguing that any behavior or communication received is communication.

Other researchers such as Motley (1990) and Andersen (1987) have differentiated between controllable physical actions and uncontrollable physical actions, and their communicative effects. **Symptomatic behaviors,** or observable autonomic responses (e.g., stomach growls, yawns, etc.) have a source whose purpose is not to influence receivers. **Analogic behaviors** on the other hand are imitations of symptomatic behaviors (e.g., faking a yawn). In these cases you are trying to communicate that you are tired, unlike when you yawn naturally. The difference is that with an analogic behavior you consciously communicate to a receiver a message: you are tired or bored.

KEY TERMS 1.4 AND 1.5

Symptomatic behaviors – or observable autonomic responses (e.g., stomach growls, yawns, etc.) have a source whose purpose is not to influence receivers.

Analogic behaviors – imitations of symptomatic behaviors (e.g., faking a yawn).

Think about this as an example. You are in class and your teacher is lecturing. While your teacher is lecturing you are texting. Are you communicating anything to your teacher? You are clearly communicating something to the person you are texting to: the messages you are sending. However, what about your teacher? Watzlawick et al. (1967) would say that you are communicating to your teacher: disinterest, disrespect, and any number of other feelings since you are not paying attention to him/her. However, Miller (1966) would argue that your intent is the key. Do you intend to communicate any of these feelings to your teacher? If the teacher feels any disrespect, etc., Andersen (1991) would argue that you have communicated to the teacher. Thus, this debate is still not resolved as to the intentionality of communication.

The second point of disagreement is about whether or not communication is a social activity. Does communication need more than one person to take place? Interpersonal communication (Chapter 5) discusses communication between two or more people. However, what about communication within one individual or **intrapersonal communication**. While some researchers prefer to label intrapersonal communication as cognition or psychology, some researchers study this as a form of communication (Honeycutt & McCann, 2008; Stacks & Andersen, 1989). Even researchers who see communication as a social activity also recognize the intrapersonal processes at work in communicating. We will discuss in this book theories related to emotion (Chapters 5 and 11), discourse (Chapters 10, 12, and 13), and the processing of messages (Chapters 5, 9, 10, and 11). More importantly, seeing communication as a social activity is seeing communication as a practical means to do something, to share information. When we communicate with others (as a social activity) we are sharing information, thoughts, emotions, and behaviors. We are trying to reach mutual understanding. Ultimately, we are not negating the intrapersonal if we consider communication as a social activity. In fact, we are emphasizing the fact that through communication we influence those around us.

Why Study Communication?

Now that we have gone through the definitional similarities and differences in defining communication, it is probably clear that defining communication is not an easy task. People will probably be debating for years on how to define the term. Such disagreements have existed for years, and will persist. As you progress through this textbook you will need to develop your own definition of communication. So, with the field in disagreement over a definition of the term "communication," why should you study communication? Littlejohn (1999) said, "communication is one of the most pervasive, important, and complex aspects of human life" (p. 3). There are various reasons to study communication, particularly communication theory. We will talk more in Chapters 2–4 about what "theory" is. One reason to study communication is because communication is an integral part of our lives. We communicate every day, in a variety of ways. Thus, it is vital to understand what communication is, how it affects our lives, and how to better communicate. Second, studying communication helps us to see the world differently. I have had many students tell me that after studying communication theories they have looked at the world through completely different eyes. The study of communication opens our eyes and ears to different ways of knowing and seeing things. In each of the chapters you will be introduced to theories and concepts that will help you to understand the world around you. Apply these theories and concepts and see how they might help you to see the world differently. Third, employers are increasingly looking for employees who understand communication. The United States Bureau of Labor Statistics reported promising job and income growth for communication majors, while the American Association of Colleges and Universities listed communication skills as one of the six main learning outcomes that employers look for (National Communication Association, 2014).

The Communication Discipline

Communication as a standardized discipline in colleges and universities is a relatively new phenomena. Although the study of communication dates back thousands of years, it was not until 1879 at Curry College in Milton, MA that the first "communication" program was founded: the School of Expression. The National Communication Association (NCA), originally the National Association of Academic Teachers of Public Speaking, was founded in 1914 to advance communication as a discipline in all its forms. Up until the 1940s many communication researchers were working in English, Political Science, Sociology, Psychology, or other humanities and social science departments. Other communication departments would soon emerge, primarily in the Midwest at the University of Illinois, Michigan State University, Purdue University, the University of Iowa, and at other schools. In 1950, the International Communication Association (ICA), originally the National Society for the Study of Communication, was formed.

Over time the discipline has grown exponentially with hundreds of universities and colleges offering a communication degree of some sort in the United States alone, with many more developing around the world. With this growth has also come division or fragmenting of the discipline. Departments of communication define themselves in many ways, ranging from Departments of: Speech Communication, Communication, Communications,

Human Communication, Communication and Media, Communication Studies, and the list continues. Within each of the major international associations various divisions or interest groups have developed that focus on specific areas of communication research. These areas focus on different levels of communication (e.g., interpersonal, intercultural), contexts (e.g., political, health, feminist studies), and/or processes (e.g., communication apprehension, technology). Even though these divisions may seem defined, they often overlap; intercultural communication can be both a level and a context, for example. Figure 1.3 shows some of the associations affiliated with the communication discipline, and Figure 1.4 shows the divisions and interest groups from the NCA and ICA. These figures are not comprehensive, as it is impossible to have comprehensive lists of all of the communication associations in the world, as associations come and go each year. Moreover, it is impossible to list all of the divisions and interest groups in communication, as such a list would be too extensive for a textbook.

American Association for Public Opinion Research
American Communication Association
American Rhetoric Communication Association
Association for Business Communication
Australian & New Zealand Communication Association
Baltic Association for Media Research
Canadian Communication Association
Center for Communication Research
Central States Communication Association
Chinese Communication Association
Communication Association of Japan
Eastern Communication Association
European Communication Research and Education Association
International Communication Association
International Visual Communications Association
Israel Communication Association
Journalism Education Association
Korean Communication Association
National Communication Association
National Research Foundation
New Zealand Communication Association
Nordic Information Centre for Media & Communication Research
Religious Communication Association
Russian Communication Association
Sociedad Argentina de Informacion
Sociedad Española de Periodística
South African Communication Association
South Asian Journalists Association
Southern States Communication Association
Western States Communication Association
World Communication Association

Figure 1.3 Communication Associations

Activism and Social Justice Division
African American Communication and Culture Division
American Studies Division
Applied Communication Division
Argumentation and Forensics Division
Asian/Pacific American Communication Studies Division
Basic Course Division
Children, Adolescents and the Media
Communication and Aging Division
Communication and the Future Division
Communication and Law Division
Communication and Sport Division
Communication and Technology
Communication Apprehension and Competence Division
Communication Assessment Division
Communication History
Communication as Social Construction Division
Communication Ethics Division
Communication Law and Policy
Communication and Social Cognition Division
Critical and Cultural Studies Division
Environmental Communication Division
Ethnicity and Race in Communication
Ethnography Division
Experiential Learning in Communication Division
Family Communication Division
Feminist and Women's Studies Division
Freedom of Expression Division
Game Studies Division
Gay, Lesbian, Bisexual, Transgendered, and Queer Communication Studies
Division
Global Communication and Social Change
Group Communication Division
Health Communication Division
Human Communication and Technology Division
Information Systems
Instructional Development Division
International and Intercultural Communication Division
Interpersonal Communication Division
Instructional and Developmental Communication
Intergroup Communication
Journalism Studies
Language and Social Interaction Division
Latino/Latina Communication Studies Division
Mass Communication Division
Nonverbal Communication Division
Organizational Communication Division
Peace and Conflict Communication Division
Performance Studies Division
Philosophy of Communication Division
Political Communication Division

Figure 1.4 Communication Divisions and Interest Groups

Popular Communication
Public Address Division
Public Dialogue and Deliberation Division
Public Relations Division
Rhetorical and Communication Theory Division
Spiritual Communication Division
Sports Communication
Theatre, Film, and New Multi-Media Division
Training and Development Division
Visual Communication Division

Figure 1.4 Continued

As demonstrated in Figures 1.3 and 1.4, the field of communication is vast, with numerous associations and fields of inquiry. It is impossible in one textbook to cover all of these fields of interest. The diversity in the field offers a chance for individuals from different theoretical and methodological perspectives to all work together under the large umbrella of "communication."

The Structure of this Textbook

This chapter has focused on discussing the different ways that communication is defined. As you may have noticed, there are many ways to define communication. Furthermore, there are hundreds of communication theories, particularly when you consider the fact that many communication researchers borrow theories from other disciplines like sociology, psychology, anthropology, and other fields. When writing this textbook it was difficult to choose which communication theories to include and exclude. The purpose of this book is to provide students with a foundational, in-depth, and state-of-the-art coverage of the key theories in communication. Thus, the theories included in this textbook need to be described in detail. Therefore, it is impossible to include all theories that may be of interest to students, researchers, and/ or practitioners, and it is also difficult to review all relevant literature about the included theories. Choices were made based on the following criteria.

First, only theories that can be relatively considered theories of communication were included. When you read through Chapters 2 through 4 in the textbook you will be introduced to the different approaches to theory: social scientific, interpretive, and critical/cultural. The remaining chapters, Chapters 5 through 13, all include theories that are overwhelmingly considered communication theories. While communication researchers often use theories from other disciplines, these theories have not been included in this textbook as there is simply not enough room in one textbook to review *all* theories used by communication researchers.

Second, throughout the textbook social scientific, interpretive, and critical/ cultural theories are incorporated. While the majority of the theories are social scientific, many are interpretive, with some theories coming from the critical/cultural approach. This is not to discount the critical/cultural approach. In fact, Chapter 13 showcases various critical/cultural theories. The diversity of theoretical approaches highlighted in the textbook shows the diversity of the communication field itself.

The remainder of the first section of the textbook describes the three theoretical paradigms. Chapter 2, "The Social Scientific Approach to Theory" defines the social scientific paradigm, traces the development of the paradigm, discusses the significance of the scientific method to the paradigm, and answers metatheoretical questions. Chapter 3, "The Interpretive Approach to Theory" defines the interpretive paradigm, traces the development of the paradigm, explores the significance of rationalism and subjectivity, and answers metatheoretical questions. Chapter 4, "The Critical Approach to Theory" defines ideology, oppression, and power, overviews the development of Marxism and critical theory, discusses postmodernism, and answers metatheoretical questions.

The second section of the textbook (Theoretical Contexts) reviews key communication contexts and theories. This section contains the remaining nine chapters of the textbook. Within each chapter you will find a case study and a student paper. The case studies are applications of one of the theories from each chapter. For example, in one chapter a case study links organizational identity and culture to working at Google. In each chapter (at the end) you will also find an example student paper. This paper is included to show one way you could write a theory paper about the theories discussed in that particular chapter. These papers were written by real students who were taking a communication theory class. The assignments differ in complexity and length, to show the variety of tasks you could accomplish.

Chapter 5, "Interpersonal Communication" defines and discusses the development of interpersonal communication, and reviews social penetration theory, self-disclosure, the dialectical theory of relationships and conflict, relational partner characteristics, couple types, and relational dissolution. Chapter 6, "Organizational Communication" defines organizational communication, discusses the different approaches to the study of communication within organizations, and reviews organizational socialization/assimilation, organizational identity and culture, and organizational dissent. Chapter 7, "Intercultural Communication" by Stephen M. Croucher, Diyako Rahmani, and Mélodine Sommier defines intercultural communication, discusses its development, describes sub-fields, discusses dimensions of cultural variability, and reviews anxiety uncertainty management theory, face negotiation and ethnolinguistic identity theories, cultural adaptation theory. Chapter 8, "Small Group Communication" defines small group communication, discusses the different components of groups and the various kinds of small groups, and reviews structuration theory, the functional approach to small groups, groupthink, and symbolic convergence theory. Chapter 9, " Health Communication" defines health communication, discusses the place of theory within health communication, examines research on patient-provider interactions, reviews the Comprehensive Model of Information Seeking (CMIS), the Theory of Planned Behavior, and the Health Belief Model. Chapter 10, "Mass Communication" focuses on two theoretical aspects of mass communication: media effects on society, and how media influence public opinion. The chapter defines mass communication, and reviews social cognitive theory, uses and gratifications theory, agenda setting theory, and spiral of silence theory. Chapter 11, "Persuasion" defines persuasion, discusses the essential elements and outcomes of persuasion, and reviews cognitive dissonance theory, the elaboration likelihood model, and inoculation theory. Chapter 12, "Rhetorical Theory" by Jansen B. Werner and Daniel Cronn-Mills discusses the primary characteristics of rhetoric, examines Aristotle, describes the rhetorical situation, demonstrates how the classical view connects the past and the present, explains the imagined audience and how it changed our understanding of rhetoric, defines genre and metaphor, and discusses the work of Kenneth Burke. Chapter 13, "Critical Cultural Theory" by James P. Dimock and Kirsti K. Cole defines critical theory and discusses the different components of class by discussing the philosophy of Karl Marx, describes ideology, explores critical race theory, critical gender theory, feminism and queer theory.

Chapter Summary

This chapter is an introduction to the numerous ways in which we can understand communication. Communication is not an easy term to define, which may frustrate some, but I hope the variety of definitions and approaches you encounter in this textbook pique your interest as budding communication theorists. In the chapters that follow (Chapters 2 through 4) you will be introduced to "theory" in its many forms. Each of these chapters offers different conceptualizations of theory, which guide how researchers define and study communication theories. After reading these chapters you will be better prepared to delve into Part II and discover some of the communication theories that help us to understand human behavior.

Key Terms

Analogic behaviors	Decoding	Encoding	Intrapersonal communication
Noise	Referent	Signified	Signifier
Signs	Symptomatic behaviors		

Activity

1. Google two of the communication associations listed in the chapter. Find out how they define "communication." How are the definitions similar and different?

2 THE SOCIAL SCIENTIFIC APPROACH TO THEORY

Chapter Outline

- The Social Scientific Paradigm
- Theoretical Foundations of the Social Scientific Paradigm
- Metatheoretical Questions for the Social Scientific Paradigm

We have all been faced with choices in our lives. The ability, or sometimes being forced, to take a different approach to solving a problem is an advantage, but it can also be confusing. What is the best approach to take? Is there a best approach to take? Why do some people like one approach over others? These are common questions people ask when approaching communication theory. The one thing you will soon learn is that there is no one way to approach communication theory. In fact, there are numerous ways to approach communication theory. The different theoretical approaches, or paradigms, are the very foundations of what make up theory itself.

In this chapter we will explore the first of three approaches or paradigms that guide scholarship in research: the social scientific paradigm. In the first section we will define the social scientific paradigm and trace the development of this paradigm. In the second section we will discuss the significance of the scientific method to the social scientific paradigm. In the third section we will answer metatheoretical questions associated with this paradigm.

The Social Scientific Paradigm

Social Science

The social scientific paradigm is one of the three theoretical paradigms discussed in this text. **Social science** is an organized method of research that combines empirical observations of behavior with inductive and deductive logic to confirm and test theories that are then used to describe and/or predict human behaviors and activities. For theorists who subscribe to this paradigm, describing and/or predicting human behavior through the testing of theory is of key importance to theory and research. To better understand this appreciation/devotion to empirical observation and logic let's briefly trace the development of the social scientific paradigm. As we trace this development we will introduce some key terms for the social scientific paradigm and this approach to theory.

KEY TERM 2.1

Social science – an organized method of research that combines empirical observations of behavior with inductive and deductive logic to confirm and test theories that are then used to describe and/or predict human behaviors and activities.

Inductive Reasoning

Social scientific thinking dates back to the ancient Greeks, Romans, and Egyptians. Philosophers during these periods combined empirical observations of behavior with deductive logic when testing, confirming, and discovering theories to describe and/or predict human behaviors and activities. Hippocrates (the father of the Hippocratic Oath) for example collected large amounts of empirical (scientific) data on issues and wrote about his observations. Over time, as data collection and research methods advanced, researchers continued to develop the social scientific paradigm.

European philosophers/researchers further developed the social scientific from the 1700s to the 1900s. David Hume (1711–1776) for example in his *Treatise of Human Nature* (1739–1740) outlined how human nature (behaviors, emotions, etc.) affects scientific research. John Stuart Mill (1806–1873) (known for his "Social Contract"), in *A System of Logic* (1840), outlined the relationships between logic and scientific research; specifically he delineated five principles to inductive reasoning. Let's review these principles, as they are essential to basic argumentation.

1) Direct method of agreement. In this method of reasoning, Mill argued that it is beneficial to look for a common factor that is present in all cases in which an effect occurs. Take the following example. Person A has red hair, and has studied hard for a statistics exam. Person B has black hair and has also studied hard for the exam. Both did well on the exam. We can conclude that studying well on the exam caused the result on the exam, since it is the only constant between the two people.

2) Method of difference. In this method of reasoning, Mill argued that one should take away a causal factor, holding all other factors constant and see whether the effect still happens. Take the following example. Person A has red hair, glasses, studied for the statistics exam, and passed the exam. Person B has red hair, glasses, didn't study for the statistics exam, and failed the exam. A method of difference approach

would argue that studying or not directly affected whether the Persons passed the statistics exam.

3) Joint method. In this method, the direct method of agreement and difference are combined. Consider the following example. In the football (soccer) matches that Messi plays in Argentina, the team wins, and when Messi is absent the team loses. Other circumstances being the same, the playing of Messi is the cause of the winning of the team. The joint method proves the causal relation in an indirect way. The method of agreement suggests a causal relation through a positive set and the joint method confirms the suggestion through another set, the negative set.

4) Concomitant variation. In this method a quantitative change in something is associated with quantitative changes in a given factor. Take the following example. How many of you have ever heard your brakes squeak? You may hear them squeak so you take your foot off the brakes to see if the noise stops (method of difference). You may however vary the amount of pressure on your brakes to see whether the noise varies depending on how much pressure you put on your brakes; this is concomitant variation.

5) Method of residue. In this method, Mill argued that we already know the presence of certain factors, X and Y, before we measure Z. Thus, we can calculate the effect of Z based on what we know from X and Y. Consider the following example. A veterinarian weighs 175 pounds. He picks up a dog to weigh it. The scale then reads 215 pounds. We know that the dog weighs 40 pounds. The residual effect is due to the weight of the dog.

WHAT DO YOU THINK 2.1

Mill's forms of inductive reasoning are a key part of common sense and scientific reasoning. Can you think of any situations where you have used one of these arguments recently?

Positivism

Emile Durkheim argued that science should be value free in *Rules of the Sociological Method* (1895). Philosophers such as Auguste Comte and members of the Vienna Circle also began to further a concept known as positivism during this time (1800s to 1930s). **Positivism** is the scientific philosophy which asserts that the only legitimate or valid kinds of information come from mathematical, statistical, or scientific explanations of reality, and that truth can be revealed only through science. The overwhelming majority of researchers have moved past positivism, and accept many aspects of positivism while at the same time acknowledging that the researcher can influence the research process. This amended version of positivism is **post-positivism.** Two types of positivism emerged, which have had a profound impact on social science: classical positivism and logical positivism.

KEY TERM 2.2

Positivism – a scientific philosophy that asserts that the only legitimate or valid kinds of information come from mathematical, statistical, or scientific explanations of reality, and that truth can be revealed only through science.

Auguste Comte (1798–1857), a French philosopher, is one of the most known classical positivists. **Classical positivism** is the belief that knowledge comes from verification and that all true knowledge assumes only scientific observation/study. Essentially, the emphasis for classical positivists is the relationship between scientific inquiry and "true" knowledge. In his *Cours de Philosophie Positive* (*The Course of Positive Philosophy*) (1830–1842), Comte defined key principles of social science. He argued the natural sciences were being studied properly, but the social sciences were not, and should be. He further outlined three stages of knowledge that human thought must pass through toward development: theological, metaphysical, and scientific or positive. According to Comte, theological knowledge limits mankind's ability to think logically because people accept "facts" or "doctrines" without scientific evidence. The acceptance of a God for example without empirical proof for Comte and other positivists is problematic and against logic, as such a "belief" lacks evidence. In the metaphysical stage individuals still do not rely on science, but instead rely on rationalism, or logic, which is a weaker form of knowledge. In this second stage, individuals are more likely to question existence itself and how to interpret it. In the final stage, which Comte predicted would occur in the future, individuals will turn to science for "facts" and "truth." Essentially, Comte, and other classical positivists like Henri de Saint-Simon (1760–1825) and Pierre-Simon Laplace (1749–1827), asserted that the only way to find "truth" is through scientific inquiry.

We can see much of what Comte and others predicted coming true in the twentieth and twenty-first centuries as many societies rely heavily on "facts," such as medical and scientific data. If you read the news online, or watch television you will increasingly see more and more attention paid to terms like "evidence," which show society's increasing reliance on "fact" and "truth." However, theological and metaphysical knowledge are still very powerful in today's society. In many pockets of global society, faith and devotion to the theological has increased, which might trouble the likes of Comte.

KEY TERM 2.3

Classical positivism – the belief that knowledge comes from verification and that all true knowledge assumes only scientific observation/study.

Logical positivism emerged as a reaction to classical positivism. **Logical positivism** asserts that knowledge comes from verification and that all true knowledge includes scientific observation and rational thought. In this way, logical positivism adds the component of rationalism as an essential element of human inquiry. Philosophers connected to the Vienna Circle[1] included Moritz Schlick (1882–1936), Hans Hahn (1879–1934), and Ludwig Wittgenstein (1889–1951). Schlick in his *General Theory of Knowledge (Allgemeine Erkenntnislehre)* (1918–1925) argued that all statements of fact must be verified by scientific evidence and logic. This assertion was a departure from the classical positivists, who only emphasized scientific evidence. Wittgenstein, who often disagreed with his fellow Vienna Circle philosophers and with his own work, in his *Tractatus* (1921) explained an inseparable relationship between science and language. Many researchers had previously ignored such a relationship between science and language, except for Galileo. Galileo centuries earlier recognized the necessity of description in measuring and describing scientific values/quantities. He asserted that the only true language available to describe the world was mathematics. Philosophers like Wittgenstein recognized this need to use the proper language to describe what is happening, the real, and to even transcend it. Thus, the language of some science (particularly some social scientists) today has become more scientific to more engage with the observed world.

KEY TERM 2.4

Logical positivism – the idea that knowledge comes from verification and that all true knowledge includes scientific observation and rational thought.

The philosophies of positivism were not without their critics. Karl Popper (1902–1994), an Anglo-Austrian (1934), argued that theories and knowledge "can never be proven or fully justified, they can only be refuted" (Phillips, 1987, p. 3). His argument is based in the notion of **falsification**, or the refutability of a statement or theory. For Popper, it is necessary to have statements that are not 100 percent improvable. For example, can we disprove the theory of evolution 100 percent? Thus, it is necessary to keep testing the theory to gain a better understanding of it, which for Popper would make the theory a more logical theory. Researchers like Popper continue to call for value-free, logical, empirical, and predictive social scientific research, but with slight modifications (we will see some of these modifications below). The need to modify positivism and post-positivism led to the development of the theoretical foundations of the social scientific paradigm. In particular, social scientists today rely on the scientific method, with an acknowledgement of researcher presence (logical positivism).

WHAT DO YOU THINK 2.2, 2.3 AND 2.4

What is the difference between positivism and post-positivism?

What is the difference between classical and logical positivism?

Can you think of any examples in the news where modern science (positivism) and theology clash regarding "truth"? Why do the two clash? Can the two co-exist?

Theoretical Foundations of the Social Scientific Paradigm

Developing out of logical positivism is a reliance on the scientific method with an acknowledgment of researcher presence. The **scientific method** is a four-step process in which a researcher conducts "research," which can be done in various ways. The scientific method has four basic steps: a theory is proposed or presented, predictions are made (hypotheses), observations are made, and empirical generalizations are generated.

The first step in the scientific method is proposing a theory. A theory (review from Chapter One) is a conceptual representation or explanation of a phenomenon. Theories are attempts to represent processes. There are eight key things to know about theories (Craig & Tracy, 1995; Littlejohn, 1999):

1) theories organize and summarize knowledge;
2) theories focus attention on specific variables and relationships between those variables;
3) theories clarify what is observed;
4) theories permit prediction of human behavior;
5) a "good" theory should generate further research;
6) a theory cannot reveal the whole truth about anything;
7) people create theories; and
8) some theories are meant to challenge existing life and generate new ways of life.

KEY TERM 2.5

Scientific method – a four-step process in which a researcher conducts "research," which can be done in various ways.

The second step in the scientific method is developing predictions about the relationships between things. Predictions usually come in the form of hypotheses. A **hypothesis** is a prediction about what a researcher expects to find in a study. Hypotheses are educated guesses/predictions about the relationships between variables. When conducting research, the purpose of a hypothesis is to help researchers to make predictions based on the theories under analysis.

Examples of hypotheses include: 1) Childhood obesity is related to the amount of sugar eaten daily. 2) Worker satisfaction is positively correlated with organizational identification. 3) If I close the windows in my apartment the temperature will change.

KEY TERM 2.6

Hypothesis – a prediction about what a researcher expects to find in a study.

The third step in the scientific method is testing hypotheses. Testing can happen in multiple ways (if you take a method course you will learn all about research methods). When testing hypotheses, social scientists are interested in empirically observing variables (think back to positivism). For social scientists, the idea that a researcher can only research what they can observe, or **empiricism** is key. Things you can't observe are not scientific, but theological or metaphysical according to Comte. For example, could you observe the existence of God? The existence of God is a matter of faith, and something you cannot empirically prove, or disprove 100 percent. Another key concept related to testing hypotheses is **objectivity**, or the need to be sure that researcher emotions and personal feelings do not interfere with research and/or predictions. For a positivist, research is 100 percent objective. However, post-positivists, which are most social scientists today, recognize some level of researcher subjectivity in research. The goal then is to take steps to minimize the effects of subjectivity on the theory generation and research process.

KEY TERMS 2.7 AND 2.8

Empiricism – researchers can only research what they can observe.

Objectivity – the need to be sure that researcher emotions and personal feelings do not interfere with research.

The fourth step of the scientific method is making empirical generalizations. This is where you describe a phenomenon based on what you know about it from your research. Generalizations should build on and/or refine the theory/area of study in some way.

WHAT DO YOU THINK 2.5 AND 2.6

Why do you think social scientists hold onto the scientific method?

Is it possible to be 100 percent objective in our research?

Metatheoretical Questions for the Social Scientific Paradigm

Based on the development of the social scientific paradigm, the following questions underline the social scientific paradigm. Each of these questions is based in issues of axiology, epistemology, and/or ontology. To help you understand these metatheoretical questions, they will be applied to a key social scientific theory in communication, inoculation theory (Ivanov, Parker, & Pfau, 2012; Pfau, 1992; Pfau & Burgoon, 1988; Pfau, Kenski, Nitz, & Sorenson, 1990). We will talk more about inoculation theory in the Persuasion Chapter of this textbook.

First, what is the purpose of research? For social scientists the purpose of research is the discovery of, or the testing of, theories that explain and predict human behaviors and activities (Lindlof & Taylor, 2002). Social scientists empirically collect and test data. Collecting and testing data is an endless process, as knowledge discovery itself is an endless process. For Michael Pfau (a key inoculation theorist) and associates, the crux of this line of research was to develop a model to explain how an individual could be inoculated against negative messages by giving them a small dose of the message before they encounter the full message. In essence, this is a persuasive form of a flu shot. Over numerous years, Pfau and associates collected empirical data.

Second, what is reality? For social scientists reality can be observed because it is out there. Social scientists have a realist ontology; there is a reality out there that is made up of physical and social objects. If we can see, touch or hear something, we can observe/study it. Moreover, reality is fairly stable; this means our behaviors and traits do not change much over time. Thus, we can make predictions about human behaviors, activities, and traits because such aspects of life do not change considerably over time. Pfau's research (Pfau, 1992; Pfau & Burgoon, 1988; Pfau et al., 1990) focused on predicting human behavior over time, and how they would respond to inoculatory messages.

Third, what is human nature? Social scientists do not forget that human beings are still mammals. We are self-interested and take steps to avoid pain and seek pleasure (Neuman, 2011). Durkheim (1938) stated, "[s]ocial phenomena are things and ought to be studied as things" (p. 27). As human beings are essentially animals, our nature can be observed and empirically measured. In each of the studies on inoculation, empirical data was collected and primary experiments were conducted to ascertain if inoculation techniques were effective or not.

Fourth, do humans have free will? Social scientists subscribe to the belief that humans and human actions are primarily caused by identifiable external factors and internal attributes; this is called **determinism**. Ultimately, a lot of our decisions are caused by external stimuli we cannot control, such as culture (media, family, language, politics, economics, etc.). How such factors influence our lives makes up a bulk of social scientific inquiry. For example, research into agenda setting theory (McCombs & Shaw, 1972; Rogers, Dearing, & Bergman, 1993) has shown how the media (external actor) create images in our minds of issues, which in turn influence how we (the public and policy makers) think about issues. Inoculation research shows how, if you give an audience the right amount of a persuasive message, you can inoculate them against a future persuasive message (e.g., Ivanov et al., 2012; Pfau, 1992; Pfau & Burgoon, 1988; Pfau et al., 1990).

KEY TERM 2.9

Determinism – humans and human actions are primarily caused by identifiable external factors and internal attributes.

Fifth, what is theory? Social scientific theories are, first of all, descriptive, predictive, and/or causal in their explanation. Second, a theory sets boundary conditions or situations under which the theory operates/applies (Dubin, 1978). Third, a theory typically has axioms, postulates, and/or theorems. These statements about how the tenets of the theory work, and the relationships between the different tenants add to the testability of the theory. Fourth, a theory is generally testable in various cultural situations, unless otherwise specified as such in the boundary conditions. Inoculation theory is descriptive, predictive, and causal. The theory is intricate in its boundary conditions and theoretical statements.

Sixth, how do social scientists determine good or bad claims? Claims are weighed based on our knowledge of empirical evidence and theory. Popper asserted knowledge claims cannot be proven or entirely justified 100 percent, "they can only be refuted" (Philips, 1987, p. 3). Therefore, refuting claims is a neverending quest that social scientists consider testing theory. Researchers of inoculation theory are regularly building this line of research with new studies that try to show the effects of inoculatory messages on viewers.

Seventh, what is the role of values in research? Social scientists try to be as free of value in their research as possible. The belief is that research should be as free of religious, political, and other personal influences/values as possible, which may affect the objectivity of the research process and findings. While value-free research is a goal, it is impossible to achieve. Condit (1990) said that the goal of social scientists is to recognize the place and impact of researcher values on their research. With such recognition the researcher can recognize and accept the role of inevitable values in the research process. Inoculation researchers take numerous steps to remove value from their research. The use of intricate experiments with control and experimental groups helps to increase validity and reliability in their studies.

WHAT DO YOU THINK 2.7 AND 2.8

Why do we conduct research?

The idea that humans are just mammals can be a dangerous proposition. Can you think of historical or current examples where this proposition (philosophy) has caused ethical dilemmas for science?

Chapter Summary

The social scientific approach to research is an organized method of research that combines empirical observations of behavior with inductive and deductive logic to confirm and test theories that are then used to describe and/or predict human behaviors and activities. The three sections of this chapter offer a glimpse into the social scientific paradigm. The first section defined the social scientific paradigm and traced the development of this paradigm. The second section discussed the significance of the scientific method to the social scientific paradigm. The third section answered metatheoretical questions associated with this paradigm.

Key Terms

Classical positivism	Determinism	Empiricism	Falsification
Hypothesis	Logical positivism	Objectivity	Positivism
Post-positivism	Scientific method	Social science	

Activity

1. Apply the seven metatheoretical questions to another theory that you believe to be social scientific. Is the theory social scientific according to the questions?

Note

1 This group of researchers were called the "Vienna Circle" because the first group met in Vienna before WWI and subsequent groups met between WWI and WWII.

3   THE INTERPRETIVE
APPROACH TO THEORY

Chapter Outline

- The Interpretive Paradigm
- Development of Interpretive
  Theory
- Rationalism and Subjectivity
- Metatheoretical Questions for
  the Interpretive Paradigm

In the previous chapter (Chapter 2) we talked about how there is no one way to approach theory. There are different theoretical approaches, or paradigms. Chapter 2 discussed a paradigm that has the scientific method at its heart. This chapter describes a paradigm that has a slightly different approach. When you look at the picture above you may see many things: it is an abstract painting. Abstract art is open for interpretation by the viewer. What do you see in the painting? Each of us has our own interpretation of what the painting means. These individual interpretations of what the painting means are the essence of the interpretive paradigm.

The interpretive paradigm is the second theoretical paradigm described in this textbook. For interpretivists, the purpose of theory is to better understand or explore different meanings within/about social phenomena. How we interpret or understand social phenomena offers a great deal of information about who we are and about social phenomena. Thus, in this chapter we will explore this approach to theory. In the first section we will define the interpretive paradigm and trace the development of this paradigm. In the second section we will explore the significance of rationalism and subjectivity. In the third section we will answer metatheoretical questions associated with this particular paradigm.

The Interpretive Paradigm

Interpretive research, sometimes called humanistic research, emphasizes the significance of subjectivity in constructing individual perceptions of reality. Unlike theories from the social scientific paradigm, which focus on describing and predicting human behaviors and activities, theories from the **interpretive paradigm** seek to describe individual meanings and social constructions of reality/realities. For these theorists, it is essential to be two things: rational in science and inseparable from the research/theory process. **Rationalism**, or the idea that we can gain knowledge, and learn and describe the world through a variety of logical means is essential to interpretive researchers. While a social scientist would not dare explore a study on the existence of God, an interpretivist might, as we can describe in various ways how people experience "God." Moreover, interpretive researchers embrace **subjectivity**, or the belief that they are inseparable from the research context. Interpretive theories allow for/encourage more research involvement in data collection, writing, and analysis. To better understand the appreciation/devotion to rationalism, subjectivity, individual meanings, and social constructions of reality let's trace the development of this paradigm. As we trace this development we will introduce some key terms for the interpretive paradigm and this approach to theory.

KEY TERM 3.1

Interpretive paradigm – a research paradigm that seeks to describe individual meanings and social constructions of reality/realities.

Development of Interpretive Theory

Interpretivism was a response to social scientific inquiry in the 1800s and the 1900s. As increased calls for social scientific inquiry from researchers/philosophers like Emile Durkheim (1858–1917) and Auguste Comte (1798–1857) began to grow, researchers criticized the social scientific calls to study human behavior from what they saw as a natural science perspective. Scholars like George Wilhelm Hegel (1770–1831), Edmund Husserl (1859–1938), Ferdinand Töennies (1855–1936), Max Weber (1864–1920), and Georg Simmel (1858–1918) advanced ideas such as *verstehen* (the interpretive approach to social science). These researchers argued that the natural sciences were an inappropriate means for studying human behavior as such means/methods did not consider culture and social processes (Weber, 1991). Töennies asserted that two flaws of social science were that it did not consider the influences of the community (*gemeinschaft*) or the society (*gesellschaft*) on human behavior (Cahnman, Maier, Tarr, & Marcus, 1995). The interpretivist paradigm developed into various research fields widely used today (e.g., hermeneutics, phenomenology, and symbolic interactionism to name just a few).

Hermeneutics

An interpretive field of study, **hermeneutics** is a theory of textual interpretation. This line of theoretical inquiry was originally only for interpreting sacred texts, such as the Bible, Talmud, or other such texts. However, in the late nineteenth century this line of inquiry expanded to include other kinds of texts. Wilhelm Dilthey (1833–1911) emphasized the importance of hermeneutics in understanding the "individual" spiritual experiences of others (de Mul, 2004). With this theory of textual interpretation, a researcher is able to reveal something about themselves (the researcher/author), the social context in which the text takes place, other observers of the text, and then provide a shared experience between the creator(s) of the text and the observer(s) (Gadamer, 2003). For hermeneutic theory, three points are important to remember. First, subjective understanding is key. We all understand a text differently. Second, a variety of things or objects can be considered a text for analysis. Third, it is impossible to separate the observer from what they are observing (subjectivity). Hermeneutics is the very essence of interpretive theory, the search for individual meanings and social constructions of reality/realities.

KEY TERM 3.2

Hermeneutics – a theory/method of textual interpretation, which at first focused on interpretations of religious texts.

Let's consider the following brief hermeneutic analysis. In 2014 the United States Supreme Court in Burwell v. Hobby Lobby decided 5–4 to allow for-profit corporations to be exempt from federal government regulations requiring employers to cover certain kinds of contraceptives for female employees. As soon as this decision came down the American people started debating the future of American women and American religious freedoms. However, as Fish (2005) argued, interpretations of the United States Constitution and US laws are flexible, with two main camps: intentionalists and textualists. Intentionalists believe they must try to interpret what the Founding Fathers and other writers of laws had in mind when laws were written. Textualists on the other hand claim that the Constitution and other laws are open to interpretation. In the case of Burwell v. Hobby Lobby, the majority opinion stuck to a strict interpretation of legal text in interpreting the Religious Freedom Restoration Act (1993). A hermeneutic analysis of this case would examine the differing opinions from the justices and scrutinize their varying levels of subjectivity in how they came to a decision on this case.

WHAT DO YOU THINK 3.1

Can you think of any examples where a "text" was interpreted one way by one person and a different way by another person? How did the different interpretations impact communication between the individuals?

Phenomenology

A second broad interpretive theoretical area to emerge is **phenomenology**, or the systematic explanation and study of conscious and subjective human experience. Phenomenology is the study of the meanings that things have for us in life (Husserl, 1970). Key phenomenological theorists include Martin Heidegger (1889–1976), Edmund Husserl (1859–1938), Jean-Paul Sartre (1905–1980), and Alfred Schultz (1899–1959). For many phenomenological theorists, activities/experiences have structure to them, which is often taken for granted or overlooked. Thus, the purpose of phenomenological theory is to analyze the structure of those activities/experiences. In Leonard's (2013) analysis in Greenland of a Polar-Eskimo language, he explored the relationship between culture and language. The author examined how speaking and knowing a language are often taken for granted. Think about this notion for a moment. We all speak at least one language, but we often take this knowledge for granted, and it becomes second nature. When we are in the midst of learning another language we can reflect better on the language learning process and how intricately linked language and culture are.

KEY TERM 3.3

Phenomenology – the systematic explanation and study of conscious and subjective human experience; the study of the meaning that things have for us in life.

Here's a phenomenological example of having a great meal. Having a great meal may sound trivial or silly, but this is an experience that each person does and remembers differently. When describing a meal most people would not include a list of the basic ingredients, how many calories were in it, or how the amount of fat in the meal is going right to their thighs. Instead many people's descriptions would include some details about what was served, but most details would revolve around the flavors, colors, textures, smells, etc. (which differ for each person). In essence, people don't generally talk much about what appears, but instead about the way things appeared. The experience of the great meal is the way it happened, and this way is different for each person.

WHAT DO YOU THINK 3.2

Each time you interact with your teacher you do it often without even thinking about the interaction. Think about one of your most recent interactions with a teacher and ask yourself how the structure of that interaction was formed.

Symbolic Interactionism

A third broad interpretive approach to theory is symbolic interactionism. **Symbolic interactionism** emphasizes the relationships between symbols, social interaction, and the social world. While George Herbert Mead (1863–1931) is credited with the phrase "symbolic interactionism," he probably never even used the phrase. The basis of symbolic interactionism is that human thought (mind) and social interaction (others and the self) help us to understand the world where we live (society). Essentially, our thoughts and interactions with others shape how we understand society. Three key principles guide symbolic interactionism and help us to understand how people create an image of self and socialize within a community. The first principle is meaning, which states that people act toward others according to the meanings given to those people. The second principle is language, which is the medium through which people communicate via symbols. The third principle is thought, which is the mental conversation people go through to interpret communication. It is through meaning, language, thought, and interacting with others that we define ourselves and understand the world around us.

Consider the following example some college-aged students may be able to relate to. John and Christine are in the same communication class. Both students have been talking to each other for the whole semester. John asked Christine to go to a movie with a couple of friends, Christine agreed, and so the four went. Christine thought they were going out as friends, since there were four people going to the movies; John had a different *meaning* intended for the night as he thought it was a chance to go on a "date" with Christine. John wanted to have a quasi-romantic night with Christine in the dark of the movie theater, but this was not communicated (*language*) to Christine. The two students clearly had different thoughts going through their minds before and during the evening, or date, depending on whom you asked.

WHAT DO YOU THINK 3.3

Think about a recent social interaction you have had (a conversation with friends, family, teachers, an interaction at a store, etc). How did the language used and the culture of the participants affect the interaction?

Now that we have gone through a discussion of what the interpretive paradigm is, how it developed, and some of the starting theoretical approaches, the next section of Chapter 3 discusses the significance of rationalism and subjectivity to the interpretive paradigm.

Rationalism and Subjectivity

The discussion about rationalism is rooted in epistemology, the study of what knowledge is and how it is created. Essentially, rationalism views reason, not evidence, as the primary root to knowledge. Rationalists follow one of the following three propositions. First, the induction/deduction thesis asserts that some propositions in a subject area (X) are only knowable to us by intuition; while others can be knowable through the process of logical deduction. In essence, there are some things we just know to be true (even if they are not). There are other things we must deduce, and evidence is not necessary. The assertion that knowledge can be "known" or deduced without empirical evidence is a departure from the social scientific paradigm (Aune, 1970). For many rationalists the belief in God is something people just know to be "true" and later believers deduce it to be true. However, a strict social scientist would demand hard evidence.

KEY TERM 3.4

Rationalism – the belief that reason, not evidence is the primary test of knowledge.

Second, the innate knowledge thesis asserts that as part of our rational being, we have knowledge of some truths about a particular subject (X). This means that we have knowledge of a subject independent of experience, but through our nature and history (Casullo, 2003). Some rationalists for example would argue that we gain such knowledge from our very existence, for example from God or culture (Carruthers, 1992). For example, a culture may teach a person about what Jesus Christ looked like, and this image becomes accepted. However, without any 100 percent evidence of what Jesus Christ looked like, these depictions are imagined images based on historical, oral narratives.

Third, the innate concept thesis argues that as part of our rational nature/being, we have concepts that we use in a particular area (X). For these rationalists, some experiences are not gained by experience. Instead, some of our understanding of the world is rational and experiences trigger our rational/irrational understandings. When individuals go through traumatic experiences many are likely to turn to religion for spiritual guidance. The traumatic experience may affect how they rationalize "religion." As you progress through the chapters in this textbook you will find various communication theories based in a rationalist perspective. Such theories emphasize reason and experience over empirical evidence.

WHAT DO YOU THINK 3.4

Apply the rational theses and the scientific method to the following two situations; which philosophy works best for each situation: 1) ghosts exist, and 2) gravity exists.

A second epistemological issue to consider with the interpretive paradigm is subjectivity. For interpretive researchers, the social world is relativistic, in that it is inseparable from the researchers studying it. Such researchers believe in studying a phenomenon from the inside while social scientists believe the better way to understand a phenomenon is to study it from the outside (objectivity). Through such theoretical inquiry, interpretive theories encourage the generation of knowledge that is situated, individual, and emergent. For example, an interpretivist and a social scientist could both study language and cultural adaptation among immigrants. The social scientist would more than likely use methods with the goal of generalizing to the broader immigrant community. Moreover, the theory chosen by the social scientist would better facilitate such an inquiry. The interpretive research would more than likely use qualitative methods with the goal of describing the individual experiences in the particular situation(s). The theory chosen by the interpretive research may be the same as the social scientist, but they would approach it differently, or they may choose a theory that permits more subjective inquiry.

KEY TERM 3.5

Subjectivity – the belief that a researcher is inseparable from the research process.

In a 2006 piece analyzing external pressures to conform to Canadian culture I employed cultural adaptation, a predominantly social scientific theory along with language ideology, an interpretive theory (Croucher, 2006). Language ideology (Silverstein, 1979, 1985) describes how language is ideological. Using language ideology allowed me to better understand how individual Chinese shopkeepers in Montreal felt like their language was being oppressed by the Canadian government. This study, like other interpretive studies, was not meant to generalize but to show individual meanings and subjective understandings of language policies and immigration experiences. For this particular project, and for other interpretive projects, a strength of this approach is that the researcher is able to show individual perspectives. We will talk more about some strengths/limitations shortly.

WHAT DO YOU THINK 3.5

Why would a researcher choose subjectivity?

Metatheoretical Questions for the Interpretive Paradigm

Based on rationalism and subjectivity, the following questions underlie the interpretive paradigm. Each of these questions is based in issues of axiology, epistemology, and/or ontology. To help you understand these metatheoretical questions, they will be applied to a key interpretive theory: speech codes theory (e.g., Carbaugh, 2007; Fitch, 2006; Katriel & Philipsen, 1981; Philipsen, 2000; Ward Sr., 2010). Speech codes theory examines how groups communicate differently based on cultural, societal, gender, or other factors. These factors have a strong influence on individuals within a community and how they communicate.

First, what is the purpose of research? The purpose of research for interpretivists is to "understand, explain, and demystify social reality through the eyes of different participants" (Cohen, Manion, & Morrison, 2007, p. 19). These researchers emphasize understanding social reality, rather than predicting or explaining it. For researchers interested in speech codes, the emphasis of their studies is on understanding symbolic action, interactions, and communication through speech. For example, Ward Sr. (2010) explored the unique conversion testimonies of American fundamentalists for four years in seventeen states. In this analysis, Ward Sr. showed the diverse experiences of individuals who are "saved."

Second, what is reality? For the interpretivist researcher, reality is socially constructed, is based on individual interpretations, and is subjective (Neuman, 2011). When people interact with one another they create their own meanings for events and actions, thus events are distinct and cannot be generalized. Speech codes research focuses on the individual communicative meanings that individuals create while interacting with one another (e.g., Fitch, 2006; Katriel & Philipsen, 1981).

Third, what is human nature? Like, the social scientists, interpretivists do not forget that human beings are mammals. However, human nature is not something that can easily be observed and measured as reality is socially constructed/created (Neuman, 2011). In interpretivist studies researchers are keen to focus on individual experiences. To this end, great attention is paid to observing human behavior, understanding thoughts, and interpreting actions and experiences. The majority of such studies employ interviews, ethnography, or a plethora of other qualitative methods to gather their data.

Fourth, do humans have free will? While social scientists subscribe to the school of determinism, or the notion that human actions are caused by identifiable external factors, interpretivists subscribe to free will or **voluntarism**, the idea that people are able to make conscious choices based on reason (Neuman, 2011). Interpretivists must be considerate of their subjects' individual feelings, and decision-making processes. Such processes and feelings can often reveal how participants understand phenomena (phenomenology), or interact with society (symbolic interactionism). Thus, interpretive theories take into consideration the decision-making nature of human beings.

KEY TERM 3.6

Voluntarism – the belief that people are able to make conscious choices based on reason.

Fifth, what is theory? An interpretivist theory is hard to define, as there is no one definition. These theories, as previously mentioned: "understand, explain, and demystify social reality through the eyes of different participants" (Cohen et al., 2007, p. 19). To do this, interpretivist theories: 1) embrace subjectivity and rationalism; 2) accept free-will; and 3) do not presume to generalize. Unlike social scientific theories, interpretivist theories are less likely to have boundary conditions, axioms, postulates, and/or theorems. However, the theories, will still have statements or propositions to help users/readers understand how the theory functions. Speech codes theory for example was developed out of the Ethnography of Communication by Philipsen. There are six main propositions that guide speech codes theory (Philipsen & Albrecht, 1997):

1) Speech codes are distinct to a given culture.
2) Multiple speech codes exist in a given speech community.
3) A speech code has a distinct psychology, rhetoric, and/or sociology.
4) The speech community understands and assesses the meaning of the speech codes.
5) The rules of the speech codes are linked to speech.
6) Speech codes affect life.

Sixth, how do interpretivists determine good or bad claims? Explanations should provide in-depth description of phenomena, and offer coherent interpretation of experiences. A goal is to provide what Geertz (1973) called "thick description." Interpretive researchers detail the experiences of others by providing a "thick" or rich description to support the analysis. As previously mentioned, reading an article about speech codes will provide thick description of what participants were experiencing. In Ward Sr.'s (2010) analysis of the speech codes of fundamentalists, he found numerous conversion testimonies. The following is one passage from his piece, which provides a "thick description" of the conversion process for fundamentalist high school and college students:

> I had the privilege of growing up in a Christian [i.e., fundamentalist or perhaps Evangelical] home. I was saved at an early age [usually between four and seven years old] after I heard a sermon [or Sunday school lesson] at church about heaven and hell, and asked my mom [or dad] about it when we got home. My mom [or dad] took the Bible and showed me how I could be saved, and I prayed to accept Jesus into my heart. But there wasn't really a change in my life. I knew how to follow the rules at church and [my fundamentalist] school. But I wasn't serious about God and never had devotions or told anyone about Jesus. I wasn't on fire for God and was living for myself and the world. Then we had a preacher come to my school [or fundamentalist summer camp or college or church] and I came under conviction that I needed to get things right with God. I realized that

I had never really been saved [or I was never really sure] after I prayed my prayer as a kid. So I talked to my parents [or fundamentalist pastor or friend or mentor] and prayed to receive Christ [or to make sure of my salvation]. Since then God has given me a hunger for His Word and a desire to tell my friends about Christ. Now I'm praying about what God wants me to do, whether it's going into the ministry or into missions, or to witness where I work. My "life verse" is [recite Bible reference and verse]. (p. 123)

Seventh, what is the role of values in research? Interpretive researchers embrace their position in the research process. Separating values and morals from research decisions/outcomes is not encouraged, if not impossible. An interpretive researcher should not be a disinterested, objectivist who reports on phenomena. An interpretive researcher is a subjectivist who is actively involved. For interpretivist researchers, it is not necessary to remove value from research. As the research is part of the research process, subjectivity and rationalism are an integral part of the process.

WHAT DO YOU THINK 3.6 AND 3.7

Voluntarism or free will differs significantly from determinism (discussed in Chapter 2). Which do you subscribe to and why?

Is it possible to remove values from the theory building and testing process?

Chapter Summary

The interpretive approach to research seeks to describe individual meanings and social constructions of reality/realities. For these theorists, it is essential to be rational in science and inseparable from the research/theory process. The three sections in this chapter provide a glimpse into the interpretive paradigm. The first section defines the interpretive paradigm and traces the development of this paradigm. The second section explores the significance of rationalism and subjectivity. The third section answers metatheoretical questions associated with this paradigm.

Key Terms

Hermeneutics   Interpretive paradigm   Phenomenology   Rationalism
Subjectivity   Symbolic interactionism   Voluntarism

Activity

1. Apply the seven metatheoretical questions to another theory that you believe to be interpretive. Is the theory interpretive according to the questions?

4 THE CRITICAL APPROACH TO THEORY

Karl Marx

In Chapter 2 we discussed a paradigm that focuses on the scientific method. In the previous chapter (Chapter 3) we talked about the importance of individual interpretations, and that how we interpret the world influences our theory construction. Chapter 3 discussed a paradigm that has how we interpret or understand social phenomena at its heart. The current chapter discusses a paradigm with a vastly different approach than the previous two chapters. The paradigm we will talk about in this chapter, the critical paradigm, borrows heavily from philosophers like Georg Wilhelm Friedrich Hegel (1770–1831) and Karl Heinrich Marx (1818–1883) (pictured above).

The critical paradigm is the third and final theoretical paradigm discussed in this textbook. For critical researchers, the purpose of theory is to understand power, ideology, and oppression in society. Specifically, researchers and theories in this paradigm look for ways to change power relationships and overcome oppression. How we define and overcome these terms is key to critical theory. Thus, in this chapter, we will explore these terms and more as they relate to critical theory. In the first section we will define ideology, oppression, and power. In the second section we will overview the development of Marxism and critical theory. In the third section we will briefly discuss postmodernism. In the fourth section we will answer metatheoretical questions associated with this paradigm.

Ideology, Oppression, and Power

At its most basic level, an **ideology** is a doctrine or belief system that guides a person or group of people. We all, whether we know it or not, have ideologies that guide us in our thinking about the world. However, who determines or creates an ideology is important to consider. Philosophers like Marx and Friedrich Engels (1820–1895) stressed how the ideas of the ruling class are in every essence the ruling ideas/ideologies. There are various kinds of political and cultural/social ideologies. Examples of political ideologies include political parties (Republican, Democrat), communism, Marxism, and Liberalism. Examples of cultural/social ideologies include environmentalism, racism, feminism, and all religions. Each of these ideologies stresses the importance of one particular worldview over another.

KEY TERM 4.1

Ideology – a doctrine or belief system that guides a person or group of people.

WHAT DO YOU THINK 4.1

Can you identify one or more ideologies that influence your way of thinking?

As societies became more and more industrialized, the significance of the dominant ideology controlling other ideologies became more evident. Antonio Gramsci (1891–1937) expanded the notion of ideology to include **hegemony**, or the supremacy/domination of a cultural or political group over other groups. In the nineteenth century writers like Gramsci described how the political and military influence of the German and French Empires heavily influenced European politics. In the twentieth century the Soviet Union and the United States politically and culturally influenced different spheres of the world, spreading their hegemonic influence through film, politics, economics, and culture. In the twenty-first century, US cultural and political influence has been spread throughout the world via films, music, and other means of entertainment. Many nations such as France and Germany in fact limit the number of English language films and dub most if not all English language films shown in the nations to preserve their own media and language. This is also an attempt to limit the powerful effects of American cultural hegemony in these and other nations.

KEY TERM 4.2

Hegemony – the supremacy/domination of a cultural or political group over other groups.

WHAT DO YOU THINK 4.2

What is the relationship between ideology and hegemony?

Hegemony, like ideologies, are all about power. The people or groups with the power are generally the ones who dictate the dominant ideologies, and thus dominate other groups (hegemony). Critical theorists are concerned with understanding power, particularly **oppression**, or the exercise of power, by one entity (e.g., a person, group, or organization) for its own benefit over another entity. For critical theorists, the goal of theory is to develop/find ways to change power relationships and overcome oppression. Critical theorists have identified various approaches to power or influence.

KEY TERM 4.3

Oppression – the exercise of power, by one entity for its own benefit over another entity.

Power is understood as the ability to perform an act that will lead to a change in another person (Cartwright & Zander, 1968). Power is both a thing (an object people have and use) and a performance (an action people carry out). This means that power is located in the consciousness of the people with power and in the consciousness of the people over whom power is exercised. There are four types of power generally identified by researchers: coercive, reward, legitimate, and persuasive power. **Coercive power** depends on fear, threats, or punishments. In this case, a person gets power by threatening harm to another. **Reward power** is when someone has the right to deny others something tangible for not doing an act. For example, a child is given an allowance for doing their chores or not given the allowance when chores are not performed. **Legitimate power** is when a person has authority because of some social norms/rules that give them an appointed, selected, or elected position of authority. For example, the leader has legitimate power. **Persuasive power** is when a person is able to use communicative abilities to compel someone to do something. Politicians and lawyers often persuade people to do things with their communicative abilities.

WHAT DO YOU THINK 4.3

How are coercive, reward, legitimate, and persuasive power different?

A key philosopher interested in power dynamics was Hegel. The next few paragraphs offer a brief glimpse into Hegelian thought, which is rather dense. Hegel believed that the way people think determined how they approached power and their living conditions. Hegel believed in a philosophy of change. Mechanical physics was a key philosophy of the European Enlightenment. Everything in the universe functioned much like a pocket-watch. The universe was seen as a closed system in which matter in motion caused other matter to move. However, rationalism (discussed in the previous chapters) could not explain how things changed. In mechanical physics, change only comes from the outside. As a pocket-watch winds down, an outside force—a hand—turns it and makes it run again. For mechanical physics, there is nothing outside of the system to lead to a change. So what leads to a change in society and life?

Hegel proposed the notion of dialectic, a tension between an idea and its contradiction. For most of us the idea of contradiction means opposite; this is not the case for Hegel. He saw contradiction as beginning. Here is an example from Gasper (2010). Within every caterpillar is the potential to become a butterfly. At the point where the butterfly exists, the caterpillar no longer exists, and the butterfly cannot become a caterpillar. Therefore, within every caterpillar is its own negation. If you negate the caterpillar, you also negate the butterfly though. For Hegel, the key is movement from one stage to the next. Hegel called this **dialectic**, or contradiction between an idea and its negation.

For Hegel, to better understand the role of power, and the self in society, one must analyze themselves and their surrounding environment. This analysis is called critique. Critical philosophies/theories from this time focused on initiating change and freedom in society, which were of the utmost importance to Hegelians. Other theorists did not agree with Hegel's thoughts on the idea that the nation was a manifestation of a particular idea, which could often lead to oppression, and could not simply vanish through revolutionary actions. One of the outspoken critics of Hegel was Karl Marx.

WHAT DO YOU THINK 4.4

What is dialectic?

Marxism and Critical Theory

A key area in critical theory is the thinking of Karl Marx. His works have greatly shaped critical theory. The following section reviews Marxism and discusses how it relates to modern critical thought.

When Karl Marx was young his father, Heinrich, gave a speech in which he suggested that a benevolent ruler should support social and political reforms. These statements caught the attention of the Prussian police, and Heinrich was forced to recant his statements. This event, and others, left strong resentment in Marx toward the aristocracy and the growing capitalist society. This resentment is clearly visible in the writings of Marx. For Marx, and later Marxist theorists, the defining aspect of human beings was labor. Labor power is the "aggregate of those mental and physical capabilities existing in a human being, which he exercises whenever he produces a use-value of any description" (Marx, 1978, p. 336). Labor continually transforms and eventually leads to the formation of classes in society, who then divide the labor.

Division of labor appears as far back in philosophy as Plato. The notion that particular classes focused on certain tasks (labor) was key to the economic theories of Adam Smith. Durkheim (1955) theorized that the division of labor defined civilization itself when he asserted that this division regulates our inter-actions lest conflicts "incessantly crop out anew" and "mutual obligations had to be fought over entirely anew in each particular instance" (pp. 5–6). As Marx saw it, there were two classes, the ruling class (the bourgeoisie), and the work-ing class (the proletariat). Class has little to do with how much money a person makes, but with the means of production. In an agricultural society, production is the land. The bourgeoisie own the land and the proletariat work the land. In an industrial society, production is goods from factories. The bourgeoisie own the factories and the proletariat work in the factories. For Marxists, labor is what defines a person. A worker has no choice in what is made, the conditions under which it is made, how it is sold, etc. The factory owner on the other hand has numerous options: they can choose to hire whomever they want, close or open a factory, make a new product, and so forth. A non-Marxist theorist, like a capitalist, would argue that the worker can choose to not work, or to work somewhere else; but the worker will still never be 100 percent in control of working conditions. This is the start of Marxism.

Mass production of goods further separates the bourgeoisie from the pro-letariat. In mass production, workers only produce a small part of a final product, as much of the production is mechanized and divided among multiple workers. The deskilling of labor alienates and dehumanizes workers and reduces them to nothing more than a tool. This alienation extends to the greater social system where workers compete with others for resources. The bourgeoisie are also alienated and dehumanized because they see workers as tools, furthering their need to purchase things.

Think of the following example to understand the differences between the classes, alienation, dehumanization, and production. In the 2014 World Cup teams from around the world went to Brazil to compete. Even though many of the players make millions of dollars a year, they are the proletariat (working class). Their bodies are put on the line every game to produce a win for their nation. The players really have no say in the line-up or scheduling, they really are tools for the "team." While a player may have personal objections to the poverty, working conditions, heat, or other issues in Brazil, that player really cannot decide not to play a game without serious repercussions. The rules within each team, and the FIFA rules are set up to benefit the tournament and FIFA. It really is all about money, and where one is positioned in the relationship determines their class. In this case, FIFA, the governing body of the World Cup is the bourgeoisie.

 WHAT DO YOU THINK 4.5

Think about Marx's notion that a worker has no choice in labor. Do you agree with this argument? Why or why not?

Marxist thinking is highly ideological. For Marxist thinkers, ideology is a kind of false consciousness, or an illusion that is hard to see and understand because it is shrouded in power. Power from a Marxist perspective is maintained/held in one of two ways. The first way is through state repression. In this case, the state is not subject to any other power and exerts power over its subjects. The state (e.g., the United States, Finland, China, New York) is a machine or apparatus of repression that empowers the ruling class to dominate the working class (Althusser, 1989). The state makes laws and rules to protect the ruling class, maintain production, and exploit the working class. Weber (1991) explained how actions generally regarded as illegal for others are regarded as legal for the state, such as the use of force or violence to control the masses. The state for example can tell you what you can, cannot, and must do. If you refuse to accept the rules, the state can fine you, put you in prison, or in extreme cases execute you. From a Marxist perspective, this use of power is not legitimate and favors the bourgeoisie.

The second way in which power is held from a Marxist perspective is through ideological means. While state repression means directly controlling the working class through the state, ideological means is where control happens through **interpellation**. This is where the state apparatuses impact the way in which the public sees and understands the world around them. The public consciousness is shaped through a variety of ways: communication networks (television and the Internet), cultural institutions (cultural performances like opera or theater), educational institutions (school curriculum), political institutions (political parties and governments), religious institutions (religious groups), etc. From a Marxist perspective, each of these institutions/networks provides information to the public that is in some way filtered or controlled to favor a particular worldview favored by the state or controlling bourgeoisie.

KEY TERM 4.4

Interpellation – a form of control where the state apparatuses impact the way in which the public sees and understands the world around them.

For example, we partially learn our ideologies from the media we consume, as the media shape our understanding of the world. If you are only a consumer of Fox News, MSNBC, or CNN news, you will receive a slightly biased view of the news. This view will be affected by an ideological worldview (political, religious, and communication). Your viewpoint of world events will differ from a viewer of another news channel and from a person who views numerous news channels, or reads various news outlets from different ideological perspectives.

WHAT DO YOU THINK 4.6

Think about your upbringing and the different institutions you were and still are exposed to (cultural, educational, political, religious, etc.). How have these institutions influenced you and how you look at the world? Also, how are these ideologies at all influenced by the "state"?

Postmodernism

Marxism has declined in public acceptance for a number of reasons. In Marx's time (the nineteenth century) Germans working in factories and on farms made up the proletariat. Since then the world has gone through two world wars, colonialism has ended, civil rights continue to improve for many groups, communism has all but fallen, and numerous other world events have changed the face of politics, economics, and society. The economic booms after both world wars also increased the standard of living for much of Marx's proletariat in Europe and other parts of the "developed" world. Thus, less attention was paid to the working class. Moreover, the establishment of the Soviet Union after the 1917 Russian Revolution brought forth an extremely modified version of Marxism called Bolshevism, which favored a top-down approach to socialism and power. The Soviet Union supported such movements with their Russianization efforts. While Vladimir Lenin (1870–1924) borrowed greatly from Marx in his ideas to form the Soviet Union, Marxist ideas were not very closely followed, particularly after Lenin died in 1924 and Joseph Stalin (1878–1953) took over as leader. Once the Soviets were in power many other governments and revolutionaries strived to model themselves after the Soviet model; none of these governments followed Marxists ideas, but the new form of government: communism. In twentieth-century politics, economics, and the academic world, Marxism retreated to the realm of ideas rather than reforms.

What has emerged from the remains of Marxism is postmodernism. For postmodern thinkers, there is no definitive reality of singular truth, or meta-narrative. **Postmodernism** is "a movement of thought which rejects totalities, universal values, grand historical narratives, solid foundations to human existence and the possibility of objective knowledge" (Eagleton, 2003, p. 13). This is not an easy definition to understand, I know, but the following paragraphs break it down further, do not worry. There are four concepts that are essential to understanding postmodernism: materiality of discourse, discourse as performance, polysemy, and identity.

KEY TERM 4.5

Postmodernism – a movement of thought which rejects totalities, universal values, grand historical narratives, solid foundations to human existence and the possibility of objective knowledge.

Similar to Marxists, postmodernists are interested in the material world. However, unlike Marxists, all of our language use, or discourse, is material in three ways. First, discourse influences the material world. How we talk about the world influences how we see the world and interact with it. For example, in 2014 there was a conflict in the Crimea. When the President of the Ukraine called troops in the Crimea rebels he was trying to convince European powers and the US to help him in a conflict with Russia. Second, discourse is material because it serves the material interests of those in power. In an election the candidates or campaign donors like Political Action Committees (PACs) in the US design the advertising because they have the power to do so. Third, discourse does more than influence us (and the world); it is material.

For postmodernists, power is not something one has but something one does. Power is discourse performed repeatedly. Thus, there are some things we can do and some things we cannot do. For Michel Foucault (1972), knowledge, a product of discourse, is "controlled, selected, organized and redistributed according to a certain number of procedures, whose role is to avert its powers and its dangers, to cope with chance events, to evade its ponderous and awesome materiality" (p. 216). In essence, power and knowledge are inseparable. When someone is denied needed information about something, that denial is an act of power, which would be of keen interest to a postmodernist.

Since postmodernism rejects universal values and grand narratives, representations of discourse (a conversation, book, speech, movie, advertisement, etc.) are fragmentary (part of a larger whole) and intertextual (made up of parts of other texts). Thus, it is impossible to find one truth about any discourse, as discourses are fragmentary and interextual. The fact that a discourse has many truths and/or meanings is what postmodernists call **polysemy**. The concept of multiple interpretations for the same concept should remind you of the previous chapter (Chapter 3) where you read about the interpretivists.

KEY TERM 4.6

Polysemy – the notion that a discourse has many truths and meanings due to it being fragmentary and intertextual.

Postmodernists, like Marxists, are interested in issues of identity. However, while Marxists focus on class identity (the proletariat and the bourgeoisies), postmodernists' view of identity is broader. Identity is instead something that we perform. As power has many forms, so too does identity have many forms that we can perform. For example, postmodernists are interested in issues related to gender/sex, and race/ethnicity. A postmodernist for example would argue that the struggles faced by a working class white male are different than those faced by a working class Hispanic male.

WHAT DO YOU THINK 4.7

Can you think of a discourse that has been understood one way by one entity (a person, group, or nation) and understood in a completely different way by another entity? What effects has this difference in understanding had on power between the groups?

Metatheoretical Questions for the Critical Paradigm

Based on a basic understanding of the role of power, oppression, ideology, and varied interpretations of discourse, the following questions underlie the critical paradigm. Each of these questions is based in issues of axiology, epistemology, and/or ontology. To help you to understand these metatheoretical questions, these questions will be applied to a key area of research influenced by the critical paradigm: feminist studies.

First, what is the purpose of research? For critical researchers, the purpose of research is to understand power, particularly oppression by one entity for its own benefit over another entity. Then to develop/find ways to change these power relationships and overcome oppression. For example, Antony (2010) explored how the bindi serves as a performance of resistance and identity in India. While she showed the bindi was once a form of womanhood and oppression, her discursive analysis revealed how the bindi has evolved through women to now be "chic" and is now a representation of feminism.

Second, what is reality? For a critical research, reality is socially constructed with power dynamics always present in relationships (Neuman, 2011). When entities interact with one another, varied interpretations of discourse are created, which can drastically affect the interactions and the relations between the entities. Feminist research for example focuses on the assertion that gender is one of the most defining aspects of social life. In social interactions, gender affects the way entities interact, particularly since society is inherently patriarchal (male dominated) (Foss & Foss, 1991; Penelope, 1990).

Third, what is human nature? Like the interpretivists, critical researchers do not see human nature as something that can be easily observed and measured, as reality is socially constructed/created and influenced by power dynamics (Neuman, 2011). In critical studies researchers focus their attention on how power relates to human nature. To this end, great attention is paid to understanding human behavior, thoughts, and interpreting actions and experiences, and then offering ways to improve human conditions. The majority of feminist research examines, through a plethora of methodological means, how gender affects individual's lives and offers ways to liberate individuals from patriarchal oppression.

Fourth, do humans have free will? Critical researchers see humans as having free will. In fact, critical researchers believe that through self-reflection, historical constraints and oppression can be realized. This is the process of critical emancipatory cognitive interest, where these constraints and oppressions are self-revealed. It is through free will that we are able to reveal the entities that oppress us and then reveal the means to our own liberation (Mumby, 2000). For feminist researchers this means that members of an oppressed gender should reflect on the means of their oppression to fully liberate themselves from the oppression.

Fifth, what is theory? A critical theory is a social theory directed toward critiquing and changing society in some way. To do this, critical theories: 1) recognize the influence of power, ideology, and oppression on society; 2) accept self-revelation as part of free-will; 3) promote liberation from oppression; and 4) do not presume to generalize. Often critical theories may read more like a philosophy, and much less like a social scientific or interpretivist theory. Or, a critical researcher may interpret a theory from a different paradigm from a critical perspective. For example, Hyams (2004) combined feminist scholarship with group scholarship to explore how the attention given to voices in group discussion dismisses meaningful silence in discussions.

Sixth, how do critical researchers determine good or bad claims? The key issue a critical researcher considers when evaluating claims is whether or not their research emancipates entities from oppression. Accomplishing this task is difficult, as it is hard to "measure" whether or not an entity has been liberated from oppression. To account for this difficulty, critical researchers therefore focus on reflexivity. Reflexivity begins with the notion that the researcher must be accountable for themselves. In this way a researcher cannot conclude that no conclusions are valid. If no conclusions are valid the conclusion that no conclusions are valid is not valid itself. So some conclusions must be valid. Reflexivity goes even further when critical researchers turn criticism on itself. Critical theorists often ask others to critique their work: only by having others critique their work can a critical researcher be more certain they have not been too subjective or too objective (a process of reflection). Feminist researchers have regularly critiqued Marx's work, as did postmodernists. Such critiques have led to the evolution of critical theory to where it is today.

Seventh, what is the role of values in research? Critical researchers believe we "live amid a world of pain, that much can be done to alleviate that pain, and that theory has a crucial role to play in that process" (Poster, 1989, p. 3). This assertion shows how values are to guide the research process because critical researchers are change agents. Feminist scholars for example act to reveal and liberate the oppressed. The notion that a researcher believes it is their right to reveal and liberate another shows value in the theory and research process.

WHAT DO YOU THINK 4.8 AND 4.9

Think about the feminist idea of a patriarchal society. Can you give examples of how your society is patriarchal?

How can critiquing work (reflexivity) improve its logical basis?

Chapter Summary

The critical approach to theory is concerned with understanding power, particularly oppression, or the exercise of power, by one entity for its own benefit over another entity. For critical theorists, the goal of theory is to develop/find ways to change power relationships and overcome oppression. Critical theorists have identified various approaches to power or influence. The four sections of this chapter demonstrate how critical theorists theorize. The first section defined ideology, oppression, and power. The second section overviewed the development of Marxism and critical theory. The third section briefly discussed postmodernism. The fourth section answered metatheoretical questions associated with this paradigm.

Key Terms

Coercive power	Dialectic	Hegemony	Ideology
Interpellation	Legitimate power	Oppression	Persuasive power
Polysemy	Postmodernism	Reward power	

Activity

1. Apply the seven metatheoretical questions to another theory that you believe to be critical. Is the theory critical according to the questions?

PART II
THEORETICAL CONTEXTS

5 INTERPERSONAL COMMUNICATION

Chapter Outline

- What is Interpersonal Communication?
- Interpersonal Communication in Developing Relationships
- Communication in Relationships
- Romantic Relationships and Interpersonal Communication
- Relational Partner Characteristics (Cognitive and Affective)
- Student Paper

When many people think about interpersonal communication they think about two people communicating with one another in some kind of relationship. This is one of the many components of interpersonal communication—at least two communicators "communicating with one another." When we start to look at interpersonal communication more deeply we can see that it really involves much more. Each of us is involved in interpersonal communication on a daily basis, no matter how outgoing or shy we may be. Whenever we communicate with at least one other person that person influences us in some way. *Interpersonal communication* is the study of how at least two communicators intentionally influence one another's behaviors and actions through the communication process.

In this chapter we will explore interpersonal communication or the study of how individuals communicate with others. The issues discussed in this chapter vary considerably and, like many other chapters, choices had to be made as to what could be included in the chapter due to space restrictions. In the first section we will define and discuss the development of interpersonal communication. In the second section we will discuss interpersonal communication in developing relationships with attention paid to social penetration theory and self-disclosure. In the third section we will describe interpersonal communication in developed interpersonal relationships with a focus on the dialectical theory of relationships and conflict. In the fourth section we will analyze romantic relationships paying particular attention to relational partner characteristics, couple types, and relational dissolution. Within this section you will find a case study illustrating how relational dissolution takes place. In the fifth and final section you will find a student paper. This paper is an interpersonal communication student paper that is included to serve as an example of the kind of writing assignment you *could* do for an interpersonal communication theory assignment.

What is Interpersonal Communication?

The field of interpersonal communication has a long and diverse history: from its early origins with the work of Simmel (1908 [1950]) on rituals, secrecy, lies, and truth; to its further development with the work of Elton Mayo and colleagues on human productivity in corporations (Roethlisberger & Dickson, 1939); to the growth of symbolic interactionism (Blumer, 1969); to a shift in psychiatry, focusing on interpersonal relations to explain adult schizophrenia (Chapman, 1976); to Hall's (1959) work on nonverbal communication; to Goffman's (1963) work on analysis of social behavior; to the 1970s and 1980s when the study of interpersonal communication became one of the most established areas of communication study in the United States. This historical development of the field (very briefly outlined here for space purposes, see Knapp, Daly, Albada, & Miller, 2002 for a more in-depth historical review) details how interpersonal communication became what it is today. The researchers and studies of the past shaped the field into what it is today.

Interpersonal communication is the study of how at least two communicators intentionally influence one another's behaviors and actions through the communication process. This is just one of many definitions of interpersonal communication, as the researchers who study this field each approach it from a slightly different angle. However, there is *general* consensus on the following perspectives regarding how we understand or define interpersonal communication: it is a process of interaction, context is key, interpersonal communication involves behavior, intent is integral, and the construction of meaning is important.

KEY TERM 5.1

Interpersonal communication – the study of how at least two communicators intentionally influence one another's behaviors and actions through the communication process.

Interpersonal communication is a continual process of interacting between two individuals to understand interaction. For both listeners and speakers in an interaction it is essential to understand the purpose of interactions within an interpersonal relationship, no matter what type of relationship it might be. This process of building understanding is integral to social interaction, discourse, interpersonal skills, and building long-lasting relationships.

The context in which interpersonal communication takes place is also a point to consider. Bateson (1978) stated that "without context words and actions have no meaning at all" (p. 15). Context has been studied in many ways regarding communication: social settings (e.g., school, work, home, etc.), disciplines in communication (e.g., interpersonal, organizational, intercultural, etc.), and types of relationships (e.g., work, family, etc.) to name a few.

The bulk of interpersonal communication research analyzes and describes verbal and nonverbal behaviors that influence interpersonal communication in one way or another. When we interact with another person our behaviors have an effect on their behaviors; the extent of which is explored in various interpersonal communication theories, such as those in this chapter.

For many interpersonal researchers intentionality is essential to communication. A key question is, do communicators intend or not to communicate? While researchers do not agree fully on intent when it comes to communication, there are some things that most researchers tend to agree on: there are varying levels of intent in communication, we can have different intentions when we communicate, and our intentions can change during communication.

Finally, the construction of meaning in interpersonal communication is a vital piece of the puzzle. Knapp et al. (2002) asked the following questions: "How do we conceptualize meaning in interpersonal transactions? How is meaning created? Is meaning something that can be 'located' in a particular place?" (p. 15). When researchers explore interpersonal communication these kinds of questions guide their theoretical and methodological paradigms.

All in all, the field of interpersonal communication is made up of many issues that guide students and researchers alike. It is because of these many issues and its long history that the field has developed diverse approaches and theories to understand human interaction. The next section of this chapter begins our discussion of interpersonal communication theories by exploring theories that examine interpersonal communication in developing relationships.

WHAT DO YOU THINK 5.1

Considering all of the different perspectives on interpersonal communication (interaction, context, behavior, intent, and the construction of meaning), how would you alter the definition of interpersonal communication provided earlier in the chapter?

Interpersonal Communication in Developing Relationships

There is a plethora of research studies and theories linking interpersonal communication and relationships. In fact, for many the two may seem synonymous. How individuals develop relationships, how relationships function (or are dysfunctional), and how relationships end are a mainstay of interpersonal communication scholarship. It is evident that communication is an intrinsic part of how relationships develop, grow, and in some cases end. In this section two theoretical constructs are presented that help us to better understand communication during relational development: social penetration theory, and self-disclosure.

Social Penetration Theory

Altman and Taylor (1973) developed **social penetration theory** to describe how communication develops from a more shallow level to more intimate levels as people become more acquainted. Essentially, as a relationship develops, individuals who first communicated about superficial concepts then move on to more personal (deep) topics, which slowly penetrates a communicator's public persona. **Penetration** is the disclosure of self-information to others to develop a relationship. We will talk more about self-disclosure in a few pages. Altman and Taylor (1973) at first thought social penetration was a continuous process through which relationships always became deeper. However, research now shows this process to be cyclical and dialectical, which means our social penetration can go back and forth as our relationships go back and forth in intimacy (Taylor & Altman, 1987). As we learn more about another person our relationship does not always get better or deeper, as we often have to work through conflicts or tension in a relationship, a dialectic which we will talk more about later in this chapter. At some points in time a relationship may be very open while at other times it may close down and penetration may cease.

KEY TERM 5.2

Social penetration theory – a theory that describes how communication develops from a more shallow level to more intimate levels as people become more acquainted with one another through various stages of development.

There are four main stages that relationships go through, which were outlined in the original explanation of social penetration:

1) Orientation – In this first stage individuals are tentative in how they interact with one another. Little information is shared between individuals and most social interactions are rule or norm governed. For example, we only share superficial information about ourselves with other people and generally just have small talk and share pleasantries.

2) Exploratory – We start to relax a little bit and we slowly start to share more information about ourselves. We begin to move past small talk.

3) Affective Exchange – In this third stage most of the barriers to more open communication have been broken down and people are likely to openly communicate about intimate (personal) issues. This is when people develop closer friendships and may even develop romantic or intimate relationships.

4) Stable Exchange – This is where people in a relationship understand one another deeply through continual interaction with one another. Often at this stage individuals are even able to understand one another nonverbally.

WHAT DO YOU THINK 5.2

Think about a current interpersonal relationship you are in and how it has developed. Can you identity the different stages of social penetration in that relationship?

A key part to the stages of social penetration according to Altman and Taylor (1973) and Taylor and Altman (1987) is the breadth and depth of communication on specific topics. As individuals get to know one another they begin to discuss a greater variety of topics, and not just "getting to know one another" topics. Thus, during the social penetration process the **breadth** of topics refers to the discussion of generally superficial topics and how the discussion of these topics tends to increase, as people are more comfortable talking about a variety of topics with one another. However, during the process of social penetration topics also increase in their **depth**, or become more specific, focused, or intimate with the topics they share. When people become more comfortable with one another they are more likely to share intimate information with another person; this deep sharing is part of the social penetration process.

Altman and Taylor (1973) and Taylor and Altman (1987) developed an onion metaphor to explain breadth and depth of communication during social penetration. See Image 5.2 for a further explanation of the onion metaphor.

As shown in Image 5.2, breadth involves surface level topics, while depth is going further into the layers of the onion, which can take time. A modern example of the onion metaphor is 2001's *Shrek*. In this film Shrek, the ogre, tells Donkey that ogres are like onions. Here is how the dialogue went in which Shrek tells donkey that there is more to him than people think, but his true self is hidden under layers (which people can only learn through social penetration):

Shrek:	For your information, there's a lot more to ogres than people think.
Donkey:	Example?
Shrek:	Example . . . uh . . . ogres are like onions!
Donkey:	They stink?
Shrek:	Yes . . . No!
Donkey:	Oh, they make you cry?
Shrek:	No!
Donkey:	Oh, you leave 'em out in the sun, they get all brown, start sproutin' little white hairs . . .
Shrek:	NO! Layers. Onions have layers. Ogres have layers . . . You get it? We both have layers.
Donkey:	Oh, you both have LAYERS. Oh. You know, not everybody likes onions. CAKE! Everybody loves cake! Cakes have layers!
Shrek:	I don't care what everyone likes! Ogres are not like cakes.
Donkey:	You know what ELSE everybody likes? Parfaits! Have you ever met a person, you say, "Let's get some parfait," they say, "Hell no, I don't like no parfait."? Parfaits are delicious!
Shrek:	NO! You dense, irritating, miniature beast of burden! Ogres are like onions! End of story! Bye-bye! See ya later.

A key way to break through the different layers of the onion, or to better understanding another individual is through self-disclosure. In fact, social penetration theory is often discussed in tandem with self-disclosure. Thus, the next section discusses self-disclosure and then explains how self-disclosure aids in the development of interpersonal relationships through social penetration.

Self-Disclosure

When we are uncertain in our interpersonal relationships we take steps to reduce that uncertainty. Such steps include "getting to know" other people (social penetration). One way in which people do this is through self-disclosure (Allen, Long, O'Mara, & Judd, 2003). Self-disclosure is important for relationships; the kind of relationships we have with another plays a role in our self-disclosure decisions. Research on uncertainty reduction theory and on self-disclosure has shown increased intimacy and decreased uncertainty are correlated with increased amounts of communication in relationships

(Berger & Calabrese, 1975). **Self-disclosure** is verbal communication that reveals something private about the self to someone else. It is multi-dimensional, consisting of (a) Intent to Disclose, (b) Amount of Disclosure, (c) Positive-Negative Nature of Disclosure, (d) Honesty/Accuracy of Disclosure, and (e) Depth Control of Disclosure (Wheeless & Grotz, 1976). We can view self-disclosure as an intrapersonal-interpersonal dialectic where the intrapersonal element focuses on individuals' cognitive and behavioral processes and the interpersonal element highlights relationship processes (Dindia, 1994).

Through self-disclosure individuals are able to share personal information and develop a deeper interpersonal relationship (social penetration). Self-disclosure typically involves reciprocity, interpersonal relationships become more intimate. **Reciprocity** is when one person shares something about themselves and another person shares something about themselves in return (Dindia, 1994). As sharing increases a relationship normally becomes more intimate (Chen & Nakazawa, 2012; Derlega, Winstead, Wong, & Greenspan, 1987; Dindia, 1994; Gudykunst, 1989; Tolstedt & Stokes, 1984).

KEY TERM 5.3

Self-disclosure – verbal communication that reveals something private about the self to someone else.

Developments in Social Penetration and Self-Disclosure

Social penetration theory is a theory about long-term relational development. Thus, it is rather difficult to *really* test the whole theory, as you would need to measure, test, or follow the development of a relationship over a long period of time. However, Taylor and Altman (1987) did confirm numerous hypotheses from their original 1973 work regarding how penetration works concerning intimate versus non-intimate partners and how the process responds over time: "progressive development in exchanges over time, with less rapid development in intimate than non-intimate ones, and a general slowing down of the process at later time periods" (p. 261).

A further development has been exploring social penetration and self-disclosure among intercultural friends (Barnlund, 1989; Chen, 2002; Chen & Nakazawa, 2012; Kudo & Simkin, 2003). Intercultural friendships face different challenges in relational development than intracultural friendships (Orbe & Harris, 2008). Cultural differences hinder the development of intercultural friendships, as individuals often do not know how to self-disclose to culturally unlike individuals (Gareis, 2000).

WHAT DO YOU THINK 5.3

Think about a current relationship you are in. How did self-disclosure in the relationship help to further the development of the relationship?

Communication in Relationships

Once we get past the first development stages of a relationship (peeling back the layers of the onion), it is time to communicate in a relationship. We have moved past the first stages of getting to know someone and now we "know" them. In this section we turn our attention to friendships, and family relationships, and how we communicate within these interpersonal relationships. Specifically, we address two concepts related to these relationships: the dialectical theory of relationships, and interpersonal conflict.

Dialectical Theory of Relationships

Relationships are made up of **dialectics,** or tensions inherent in relational contradiction where some issue defines a relationship and helps that relationship to endure. For example openness/closeness is one kind of dialectic in a relationship. In any kind of relationship members show a level of openness with the other partner and expect openness from the partner in return. However, both partners also keep some things private. The tension is how much openness and closeness each person and the relationship should have; this is dialectic.

There are four concepts critical to dialectics: contradiction, totality, process, and praxis. Contradiction is the idea that opposites exist at the same time. In an intimate relationship you can be open and secretive at the same time. Totality refers to the joining of the contradictions, as they cannot be understood separately. A person's openness and their desire for secrecy affect one another. Dialectical contradictions happen and are interpreted through social and interpersonal processes such as conversations and/or discourse. As a relationship progresses the partners better understand one another's desire(s) for openness or secrecy through prior conversations about these wishes. Finally, praxis is the idea that a relationship progresses as we experience and interact to realize our needs. An analysis of praxis would show what choices we make in a relationship to realize our desired levels of secrecy and/or openness.

Based on this notion of dialectics, Baxter and Montgomery (1996), Baxter (1990, 2004), and Rawlins (1983, 1989, 1992) each devised a series of relational dialectics (tensions/contradictions) in interpersonal relationships, particularly in friendships. Baxter (1990) specifically outlined three dialectical tensions in relationships: certainty–uncertainty, connection–autonomy, and openness–closedness. The certainty–uncertainty dialectic focuses on the amount of uncertainty present in a relationship. In any relationship there is a level of uncertainty (anxiety, nervousness, excitement, the unknown). The management of uncertainty is crucial to a "successful" relationship. When you have too much uncertainty in a relationship the relationship will likely fail, while at the same time if you have too little uncertainty in a relationship you will likely get bored and the relationship will also more than likely fail (Baxter, 1990; Rawlins, 1983). A second relational dialectic is connection–autonomy. A major part of any relationship is the tension between wanting to be with another person (connection) and also wanting our independence (autonomy). Baxter (1990) said: "No relationship can exist unless the parties forsake individual autonomy. However, too much connection paradoxically destroys the relationship because the individual entities become lost" (p. 70). A third relational dialectic outlined by Baxter (1990) is openness–closedness, or the extent to which private and public information is shared within the relationship. In any relationship, particularly with friends and loved ones, we need to communicate openly and know how to communicate. Baxter (1990) said that "[r]elationship well-being requires the parties to display both candor and discretion in the information that they disclose to one another" (p. 228). How we balance these three dialectics has an effect on the communication within a relationship and can influence the longevity and level of intimacy of a relationship (Baxter & Montgomery, 1996).

WHAT DO YOU THINK 5.4

Consider Baxter's three relational dialectics: certainty–uncertainty, connection–autonomy, and openness–closedness in regards to your closest friend. How have you negotiated these tensions? How has your negotiating of these tensions affected your friendship?

Research into relational dialectics has been conducted on numerous kinds of relationships in different contexts, and has added extensively to our understanding of relational development and communication. Researchers have explored relational dialectics among married couples and how marriage rituals help married couples to manage relational dialectics (Baxter, 2004; Braithwaite & Baxter, 1995). Long-distance relationships, and how couples in these relationships negotiate relational dialectics has added to our understanding of how such relationships function (Sahlstein, 2004). Research has also shown negotiating relational dialectics is key for parents who experience the death of a child (Toller, 2005). In a different relational context—healthcare—Apker, Propp, and Zabava Ford (2005) examined the relational/role dialectics of healthcare workers and identified the communication strategies that nurses use to manage team interactions in medical settings.

Interpersonal Conflict

Along with dialectical tensions, there are many other ways to explore communication within relationships. For example, the development and expression of conflict is an important part of communication within a relationship. Hocker and Wilmot (1991) defined **conflict** as an "expressed struggle between at least two interdependent parties who perceive incompatible goals, scarce resources, and interference from the other party in achieving their goals"

(p. 12). Essentially, a conflict is when two or more parties believe they are in competition for the same thing and they are each interfering with one another's goal of achieving said thing. Conflict is an inevitable part of everyday life in relationships. While many people think that conflict is negative, in fact, if managed well conflict can have a positive effect on interpersonal relationships (Canary & Messman, 2000).

There are three components to conflict: affective, behavioral, and cognitive. The affective component relates to the negative emotional aspects of conflict. For example, you may experience sadness, anger, frustration, or other emotions when you get into a conflict with your boy/girlfriend. The behavioral component is when you interfere with the objectives of another person. For example, you may get jealous of your boy/girlfriend spending too much time with their friends, so you get angry with him/her whenever the friends want to go out and do something. The cognitive component is a disagreement between you and your spouse that shows your competing objectives and interests. For example, you and your spouse may argue over how to discipline your child. Your spouse may believe in spanking a child while you do not. This disagreement shows how the two of you have conflicting opinions on child raising.

KEY TERM 5.4

Conflict – expressed struggle between at least two interdependent parties who perceive incompatible goals, scarce resources, and interference from the other party in achieving their goals.

We manage, or try to resolve, conflicts in different ways in our interpersonal, organizational, and intercultural relationships (Blake & Mouton, 1964; Chau & Gudykunst, 1987). Rahim (1983) developed five styles of interpersonal conflict management to explain how we try to manage conflict. These five styles take into consideration how much emphasis we place on the self-versus-other in a conflict situation: avoiding, accommodating, competing (or dominating), collaborating, and compromising.

Researchers have explored how our approach to conflict is related to relational, situational, and cultural variables. Studies have shown that conflict style preference differs based on whether an individual is more individualistic or collectivistic. For example, Cai and Fink (2002) found that individuals from collectivistic cultures tend to prefer the compromising and integrating (collaborating) styles. Research has also shown that context is related to conflict style. Individuals from high-context cultures are less likely to approach conflict, as conflicts can be seen as damaging to face and relationships (Chau & Gudykunst, 1987; Ting-Toomey, 1985). Conflict has also been studied extensively in relation to how our interpersonal relationships influence our approach to conflict. The intimacy levels within a relationship have been

Avoiding – There is low concern for self and low concern for other as no direct communication about the conflict takes place. This style is indirect or passive, little information exchange, which means it is generally less effective in managing conflicts. Example – You ask your boss for a raise and do not get one. Instead of telling your boss you are angry about not getting the raise you ignore him/her and glare at him/her poorly until they ask you what is wrong. You then respond by saying, "you should know what is wrong."

Accommodating – There is low concern for self and a high concern for others. It is often viewed as being submissive. Often people accommodate because they are obeying or being generous. Example – You ask your boss for a raise. Your boss responds by explaining how your division's low productivity is linked to your ineffectiveness as a leader, and asks if you deserve a raise. Your response is "I guess I agree." Inside you really disagree and think you still deserve a raise.

Competing – There is high concern for self and a low concern for others. We want to win the conflict at the expense of the other. Competing conflict style is not the same thing as being competitive, as competition is not always at the expense of the other. Often coercive tactics are used to get the other party to bend to change their behavior. Example – You ask your boss for a raise. Your boss responds by explaining how the company is not profitable this year and the biggest part of the loss is from your division. Your boss says if you want a raise you need to perform better. You explain how your division has done better than last year but your boss responds with a discussion of how if you want the raise, or to keep your job, your division needs to perform even better.

Collaborating – There is high concern for self and a high concern for others. High investment in the conflict situation normally. Typically this is a win–win situation. Example – Imagine the same conversation with your boss. In this case, your boss offers a raise that is linked to higher division performance. While this negotiation may be fruitful for the company and you, it has disadvantages. It can be time consuming and often only one party will push for it as one party normally pushes their own agenda to some extent.

Compromising – There is moderate concern for self and others. Often there is low investment in the conflict and/or the relationship. This is not always a win–win situation as the conflict may get solved in the short term but both parties may not be entirely satisfied. Example – Imagine the same conversation with your boss. In this case your boss offers a short term raise contingent on your division increasing productivity 20 percent within three months. If after three months productivity is not increased by at least 20 percent you lose the raise and an additional 5 percent of your current salary. You both give up something in this scenario.

Figure 5.1 Five Interpersonal Conflict Styles

shown to lead to more in-depth and heated conflicts (Buss, 1989; Cloven & Roloff, 1994; Stets, 1995). Research has explored how spouses demand and withdraw in conflicts/arguments (Gottman & Levenson, 2000; Johnson & Roloff, 1998). Also, research has shown that the issues of a conflict often repeat themselves and range from what we may consider mundane (food/ errands) to more personal (sex and relational maintenance) (Buss, 1989; Surra, 1985). These lines of research have drawn in-depth attention to the complexities of how conflict develops, grows, and is difficult to manage and resolve in interpersonal relationships.

WHAT DO YOU THINK 5.5

Look to the descriptions of the five interpersonal conflict styles. Which style do you tend to favor in your interpersonal relationships? Why do you think you favor this style over other conflict styles?

Romantic Relationships and Interpersonal Communication

Many relationships develop past the friendship stage and become more intimate. These kinds of relationships can be categorized as romantic relationships. When individuals first meet one another how they communicate can determine if there is a future or not for a romantic relationship. Our communication before and during a romantic relationship defines our relationships (Knapp, 1984). When looking to our romantic relationships there is an abundance of research and theories to consider. However, for time and space considerations, three areas of research are discussed below to aid our understanding of how romantic relationships develop, function, and terminate: the characteristics of relational partners, couple types, and how we end relationships.

Relational Partner Characteristics (Cognitive and Affective)

Romantic relationships are dynamic and interactive, as they are based on consistent interaction between the partners. The cognitive and affective characteristics (of the partners and of the relationship) that emerge during these interactions influence the relationship and are influenced by the relationship. How we think about a potential romantic partner affects whether or not we initiate or want to be in a relationship with that person. People who think a potential partner is dangerous are more likely to avoid that person, unless they want danger in their life. The research into cognition about relationships has focused on three aspects: relational schemes, beliefs and standards, and attributions and accounts. The research into affective aspects of relationships has focused on negative and positive behaviors in relationships, and the relationship between affective expression and gender.

Cognitive Aspects of Relationships

Relational Schemes

Planalp (1985) defined **relational schemes** as "coherent frameworks of relational knowledge that are used to derive relational implications of messages and are modified in accord with ongoing experience with relationships" (p. 9). Relational schemes define how and what a person is like in relationship to others ("I am a good lover." "He is a nice person." "She is a good listener."). Our knowledge structures about our self and the other person in the relationship are interdependent: each influences and is influenced by the other, and these structures have an effect on how we behave in romantic relationships. For example, individuals with high levels of self-doubt tend to underestimate their partner's love for them (Murray, Holmes, Griffin, Bellavia, & Rose, 2001). Also, individuals with low self-esteem report less rational love, and also perceive their partners more positively than those individuals with higher levels of self-esteem (Dion & Dion, 1988). Extending this line of research into relational schemata, researchers have found that how we perceive ourselves and our partner in an intimate relationship shapes our attachment as adults (Bartholomew & Horowitz, 1991; Collins & Read, 1990). Each of us has positive and negative views of ourselves and our partner, and when combined these views lead to various attachment styles: *secure* (positive view of both parties); *dismissing* (positive view of self and negative view of partner); *preoccupied* (negative view of self and positive view of partner); and *fearful* (negative view of both parties). Individuals who have a more positive attachment style (generally secure) tend to have more positive relationships with better outcomes (Baldwin, 1992; Palomares, 2009). Think about yourself, or any friends of yours in a romantic relationship; can you identify their attachment style and how they frame their relationship? Have you seen the trend happen where the people in a *secure* relationship tend to have a more long-lasting, generally happier relationship?

KEY TERM 5.4

Relational schemes – frameworks of relational knowledge that are used to define how and what a person is like in relationship to others.

Beliefs and Standards

Baldwin (1992) argued that we all have standards and beliefs we use to evaluate our relationships with others. When our standards or beliefs are not met in a relationship we tend to be unhappy, unsatisfied, and/or uninterested; on the other hand when our standards or beliefs are met we are more likely to be satisfied, happy, or interested in our relationship and partner (Vangelisti & Daly, 1997). We often have unrealistic beliefs and standards about relationships though. Research shows many of us may expect too much from our partners, which could be related to the high rates of divorce in the United States in particular. More and more individuals believe their relationship is "better" or "healthier" than other relationships, which may have led to heightened perceptions of what a relationship should or can be (Baker & Emery, 1993). This perceptual change has been led partially by television images of what the "ideal" relationship should and can be (Segrin & Nabi, 2002). Once again think about yourself or any friends of yours in a romantic relationship; where did you or they get their standards or beliefs about what makes a "good" romantic relationship?

Attributions and Accounts

While standards and beliefs help us to evaluate and frame our relationships, the attributions or reasons that people provide for others' behaviors, and the accounts or stories that people give about events in their relationships are important to romantic/intimate relationships (Surra, Arizzi, & Asmussen, 1988). Pyszczynski and Greenberg (1981) explained how in intimate/romantic relationships we often seek reasons for negative behaviors, or things we disagree with to try to understand those behaviors. We may say things like, she got angry and yelled at me because she was having a bad day, or he did not call as promised because he was busy. Research has shown the more satisfied we are with our relationships the more likely we are to choose positive attributes to explain our partner's behaviors (Grigg, Fletcher, & Fitness, 1989). Moreover, our willingness to forgive our partners for a sexual transgression (cheating on us) is related to the levels of blame and forgiveness, and to the reasons why we think they cheated (Boon & Sulsky, 1997).

WHAT DO YOU THINK 5.6

Why do you think we are more likely to attribute our partner's behaviors to positive attributes when we are in a more satisfying relationship?

Affective Aspects of Relationships

Negative and Positive Behaviors in Romantic Relationships

Cutrona's (1996) research supported the notion that positive behaviors in a relationship improve the overall quality of the relationship and heighten satisfaction with the relationship. This line of research goes back to Jacobson, Waldron, and Moore (1980) who found that couples rated their relationships as better when the relationship had more positive behaviors in it than negative behaviors. In essence, the presence of negative behaviors in a relationship has been shown to effectively (emotionally) hurt a relationship.

Affect Expression and Gender

Research has consistently shown that women are more emotionally expressive in romantic relationships, showing both positive and negative emotions (Burleson, 2003; Gonzaga, Turner, Keltner, & Campos, 2006; Trobst, Collins, & Embree, 1994). While wives and female partners tend to express more emotions in relations, the expression of particularly negative emotions in romantic relationships has not been shown to have a detrimental effect on romantic relationships. Huston and Vangelisti (1991) for example found that wives' negativity did not have a negative effect on a husband's marital satisfaction. Ultimately, the research shows that women tend to simply be more emotionally expressive.

WHAT DO YOU THINK 5.7

Why do you think that women tend to be more emotionally expressive in relationships?

Couple Types

Not only do the cognitive and affective aspects of relationships impact the duration and satisfaction we feel toward relationships, but also the type of relationship we are in is a critical question to consider. Fitzpatrick (1977), when analyzing married individuals, described four different types of couples: traditional, independent, separate, and mixed. Further research has supported Fitzpatrick's typology (Fitzpatrick, 1988; Gottman, 1993). He asserted that this typology considers the beliefs and behaviors reported by the partners in the marriage. A **traditional couple** is one that has more conventional ideologies regarding marriage and relationships. These individuals prefer to spend time together (activities and such). Individuals in this kind of relationship prefer to avoid marital/relational conflict. **Independent couples** have more nonconventional ideas about marriage and relationships. The individuals tend to be more independent, often keeping separate physical spaces (separate homes or bedrooms), and do not mind marital/relational conflict. **Separate couples** do not have strong feelings about conventions on marriage/relationships; they typically have less companionship and share less than other couples. They also tend to avoid conflict. The final couple type is a **mixed couple**. In this kind of couple each partner has a different idea/definition of the relationship; one may prefer a separate, while the other prefers a traditional. Gottman (1977) was keen to point out that these types are not all inclusive, as some couples may not fit in one type, and some couples will overlap types. Look to any of your family or friends (or yourself) who are married; what kind of couple types are they in?

Ending Relationships

The previous sections of this chapter have discussed how relationships, no matter what kind, develop. However, as we all know, many relationships end.

Mastekaasa (1997) stated that relational dissolution is a stressful process. Often after a romantic relationship ends individuals have health problems, depression, and higher risks of death (Kurdek, 1993; Murphy, Glaswer, & Grundy, 1997; Slotter, Gardner, & Finkel, 2010). It is important to note that ending a romantic relationship, whether the couple are dating or married, is not a one-time event. Ending a romantic relationship is a process that takes a long-term toll on all parties involved (Amato, 2000; Knapp, 1978).

Knapp (1978) outlined a five-stage process of relational dissolution, emphasizing the process aspect. In this model Knapp (1978) described the levels of and kinds of communication between partners (Cupach & Metts, 1986). The first stage is the differentiating stage. In this stage the partners start to differentiate themselves from one another through disengaging each other. The partners may start to do more things apart from one another. Conflict happens more regularly in this first stage. The second stage is the circumscribing stage. In this stage the individuals talk mostly about safe topics, or issues that are not sensitive. Very little intimate information is shared at this stage of dissolution. The third stage is the stagnating stage. In this stage communication has almost stopped entirely. Even safe topics are not discussed as the partners see even these topics as useless to the relationship. While the couple may be in the same physical space, emotionally they are distant from one another. The fourth stage is the avoiding stage. In this stage the partners take all available steps to avoid contact with each other. The fifth stage is the terminating stage. In this stage one partner or both individuals will have a conversation about ending the relationship. If neither party openly discusses ending the relationship then eventually it will just end by itself through avoidance. Unfortunately, as Knapp (1978) and Koenig Kellas, Bean, Cunningham, and Cheng (2008) pointed out, many individuals in relationships do not openly terminate the relationships. Thus, many relationships end with fade, with communication messages that "suggest" a termination.

WHAT DO YOU THINK 5.8

Consider Knapp's five stages of relational dissolution. Can you apply them to a romantic relationship you have been a part of? How would you describe the different stages? What happened in each stage? How did the relationship and how did you feel affectively (emotionally) and cognitively?

Relational Dissolution Example

John and Susan were dating for four years. In that time the two individuals moved from being friends, to close friends, to a romantic (sexual) couple, to an ex-couple. The couple had spoken about getting married at one point. However, one year ago the two started to spend more and more time apart from one another. John and Susan were both spending more time at work and traveling. When the two of them were together they talked mostly about their jobs, how different their jobs were, and they started to talk about how different they were becoming. In one conversation John said, "You know Susan, I never noticed how we really have so little in common." They also started to argue more about the lack of time together, travel schedules, and other "small" things.

About six months ago their communication really changed when they quit talking about their feelings with one another. While they used to try to talk about the impact of their travel schedules on one another and their relationships, this has ended. Now when they see each other they talk about bills, the pets, and other logistical items around the house. Sometimes talking about these matters is even too difficult and the two rarely speak at all. When Susan returned home from one trip she saw John in the living room and said, "I am too tired to deal with you tonight, I am going to sleep in the spare room." Susan has avoided even having contact with John. Over the last six months of their relationship John and Susan have interacted with each other in this way, when they are not traveling. They take as many steps as possible to avoid one another.

John came home from a business trip and waited for Susan in the living room. When she came home from work he told her, "This is not working for me, and I don't think it is working for you either." This one sentence started the termination of their relationship. They talked it over. The discussion included arguing (conflict), and was emotional. In the end, the two decided it was best to dissolve the relationship.

WHAT DO YOU THINK 5.9

Can you identify the five steps of relational dissolution in the case study?

Chapter Summary

Interpersonal communication or the study of how at least two communicators intentionally influence one another's behaviors and actions through communication is a rich field of inquiry. The four sections of this chapter offer a glimpse into how this process takes place. The first discussed the development of interpersonal communication. The second section described interpersonal communication in developing relationships, paying close attention to social penetration theory and self-disclosure. The third section outlined interpersonal communication in developed interpersonal relationships with a focus on the dialectical theory of relationships, and conflict. The fourth section analyzed romantic relationships, specifically relational partner characteristics, couple types, and relational dissolution.

The issues and concepts outlined in this chapter demonstrate the nature of interpersonal communication, particularly in relationships. As relationships develop from start to sometimes dissolution, we must consider the various issues that affect relationships. The final section of this chapter is a student paper from the University of Jyväskylä by Lauwo George and Cheng Zeng. This paper is a review of literature on social penetration theory. This paper, like with the other chapters, is included to show you one of the many ways you can write about/research interpersonal communication.

Key Terms

Breadth	Conflict	Traditional	Dialectics
Independent	Interpersonal	couple	Penetration
couple	communication	Depth	Separate
Reciprocity	Relational	Mixed couple	couple
Social penetration	schemes	Self-disclosure	
theory			

Activities

1. Apply social penetration theory to a movie. Describe the ways in which the main characters share information with one another to further develop their relationship.
2. There are three components to conflict: affective, behavioral, and cognitive. In a group, identify at least three examples of each component not listed in the book. Then discuss with your group how these components of conflict could be constructive or beneficial to a relationship if managed properly.

Student Paper

The following paper is from a Communication Theory Class at the University of Jyväskylä. Stephen Croucher taught the class. This is the assignment for the paper:

The final paper is a review of literature of a communication theory discussed in the readings. This paper must be:

1. Written in APA style (6th edition).
2. Must be 10–15 pages in length not including references and title page. The paper does not need to have an abstract.
3. You must work with a partner on this paper. You may work in a group of up to three people on this paper. You cannot work alone on this paper.
4. You must have your theory approved by the Professor.
5. The purpose of a review of literature is to "review" a theory. This means many things. You can review the development of a theory, you can review how scholars have studied a theory, you can topically review a theory, chronologically review a theory, etc. . . . There are many ways to approach a review of literature. I will discuss some

ways to do this in class. If you have questions about your structure or paper . . . talk to me as soon as possible. The paper is worth 200 total points.

Literature Review Assignment

Social Penetration Theory

Lauwo George & Cheng Zeng
University of Jyväskylä

Introduction

Social relationships are strongly facilitated and held together by channels of communications. There are innumerable theories of communications which have been developed already, and many more are still being developed in response to new emerging social interaction phenomena. The past few decades have witnessed scholars tirelessly trying to figure out how interpersonal interactions are developed. These scholars study social interactions patterns in different settings of our societies and propose a paradigm (theory) to substantiate their observations.

A theory is something that can be likened to a map (scale drawing), that is, a representation of a landscape on the ground (Kim, 2001). So we use a map as a tool for orienteering on a physical landscape, and this map (a theory) pointed us toward the direction we were headed to. Theoretically, a map should be able to provide precise details of a physical landscape. The same applies to communication theories, although in social interactions there are new phenomena emerging every now and then due to inevitable social changes that are happening all the time. Landscapes can stay the same over a hundred years but social interactions are frequently altered by social, economic, and political influences.

This is a literature review that discusses social penetration theory, a theoretical framework that dwells mostly on the issue of communication in developing relationships. The literature in this review

> This is a really nice introduction to what a "theory" is from a social scientific point of view.

(Continued)

It is always good to provide a preview of the review of literature or any other paper for the reader. Such previews frame the paper.

One thing the authors could try to do is try to find and use the original source and not a theory textbook. Original sources are generally better.

explains in brief how social penetration theory was developed and its weaknesses from the perspectives of communication theories critics. A great deal of discussion revolves around how other scholars have studied and used this theory in trying to understand and explain relationship development situations.

Social Penetration Theory

Knapp (Katherine, 2004) asserted that theory is more or less the experiences of a theorist, as an effort to understand and definitely explain daily happenings in life. Altman and Taylor developed social penetration theory in the early 1970s. In their theory they tried to explain the concept of sequential development stages in relationships by pointing out four significant stages, ranging from orientation to stable exchanges of personal information. The stage "process" can be summarized by the following statement: a relationship progresses from a superficial level to deeper layers of human personality (Honeycutt & Godwin 1986; Katherine, 2004). An example mostly cited with regards to the above social penetration stages is a university setting, in which you have a freshman joining the campus to start a new academic life with total strangers (Griffin, 2009; Katherine, 2004). In trying to make acquaintances with his new social environment, the freshman orients him/herself toward others, who are unfamiliar to him/her, by sharing as little information as possible. This is the orientation stage, the first of the four stages of social penetration. As the information exchange process continues, the freshman enters the second stage of social penetration—exploratory. This stage is characterized by interactants loosening their guard a bit and socializing in a relaxed, friendly manner, by exchanging experiences through small talk. This interpersonal communicative attempt leads to the third communication penetration stage of affective exchange. Remember, interactants have already oriented themselves to each other, they have loosened their information disclosure guards through

(Continued)

friendly small talk, and now they are on the basis of establishing close a friendship/romantic relationship by exchanging information openly. If this openness occurs continuously to nonverbal extremes then the interactants will reached the final stage of stable exchange, in which interactants understand each other well.

Altman and Taylor asserted that the process of social penetration is a complex one as depicted in the onion model. The onion model represents a cross-section of human personality as a multilayered structure, that's why in Altman and Taylor's theory people are compared to onions (Griffin, 2009). There is the surface part of an individual, visible to everyone, but as communication gets deeper with that individual one discovers that there is another layer of personality underneath, and more layers layered beneath each other. Based on this fact, social penetration theory has come to be known as the onion theory of personality (Baack et al., 2000). These human personality layers are penetrable through closeness and self-disclosure depending on the level of reciprocity between interactants. On the contrary there are situations where friendship deteriorates and information sharing ceases to occur, a process termed as depenetration, whereby interactants slowly withdraw from the level of deep disclosure to surface talk disclosure. This depends on how a relationship develops: if it develops in such a way that interactants are not satisfied with each other, then there is no point maintaining the closeness between each other. Social penetration theory explains this point on the basis of rewards and cost. Interactants expect rewards in the form of satisfaction in a relationship, but if exchange of information exposes them to a greater risk of vulnerability (cost) then interactants tend to withdraw from the process. In other words, the amount and nature of the rewards and costs are the determining factors of the development of relationships (Tang & Wang, 2012).

Self-disclosure is the process of making oneself known or accessible to others through revealing

This is a really nice description of the stages of social penetration.

(Continued)

personal information. Jourard and Lasakow (1958) identified seven factors involved in self-disclosure, which are depth, amount, breadth, valence, timing, targets, and social values. It begins with breadth of discourse and moves deeper over time (Altman & Taylor, 1973). Self-disclosure has been shown to be one of the major facets of relationship formation, maintenance, and development (Chen & Nakazawa, 2009). It is central to the social penetration process, since it upholds liking and rapport between partners regardless of the depth of a relationship (Sprecher et al., 2013). With more quantity and quality self-disclosure taking place, more liking and closeness are generated, thus advancing the relationship.

A desire for privacy in human personality seems to refute social penetration theory, no matter how much we want to socially penetrate towards others and vice versa (Griffin, 2009). Petronio (2013) brings to our attention the concept of privacy boundary—the line between private and public information. Petronio's argument is that social penetration theory did not consider the privacy boundary, Petronio cited cultural factors such as the level of openness of North Americans as opposed to Southeastern Asians. She went on to mention that women are known to disclose more than men, and when men prefer to disclose they do it with a woman, etc. What Petronio is trying to tell us is that personal privacy boundaries differ, and this factor plays a big role in the social penetration process. This argument is supported also by Altman, the architect of social penetration theory. Altman began considering privacy as a factor in an intimate relationship, and went on to propose a dialectical model, a concept that incorporated privacy and intimacy in a relationship. Apart from Petronio's critiques on social penetration theory, other scholars have questioned the selfishness aspect of the theory, that humans are motivated by self-interests, that we enter into an interaction if there is something to gain. This factor is refuted by an argument that not all relationships are driven by self-centered interests. For example, positive things happening to friends can be considered a

(Continued)

reward (pleasure) to the other friend. In a different aspect, an individual may wish to self-disclose to another person simply for expressing his tension in life without expecting any reward or desire for connection with the other person.

Theory Application

When a communication theory is developed, scholars use it from different social standpoints to explain social phenomena in their immediate surroundings. Researchers applied social penetration theory in the 1970s, after it was first developed, predominantly focusing on face-to-face relationships. Many variables were examined, such as age, gender, ethnicity, shyness, and toughness (Bruch & O'Brien, 2002; Dhariwal et al., 2009; Hammer & Gudykunst, 1987; Zacchilli et al., 2009). Since technology has dramatically changed the way people communicate, online channels of communication have become a crucial part of everyday life (Bronstein, 2013). Consequently scholars have also shifted the way in which they study and apply social penetration theory into computer mediated communications studies (Pennington, 2008). Recently, especially, social penetration theory has been employed predominantly in online studies, such as sexual self-disclosure, online friendships, and online social networks (Tang & Wang 2012). However, anonymity, privacy, and other personal issues make communication in cyberspace vastly different from conventional communication. For example, sexual disclosure with a partner should positively correlate with relationship intimacy in real life while the intimacy of the relationship has little influence on sexual self-disclosure in online communication (Mu-Li et al., 2010). Therefore, the validity of social penetration theory in online communication has been questioned frequently.

Gender has been one of the most studied topics in social penetration theory. Morman et al. (2013) found that masculinity negatively correlates with willingness to self-disclose. On the other hand, both femininity and androgyny associate positively

---

Overall, the discussion of social penetration is sound. The authors define the key aspects of the theory and also discuss the different components of the theory.

This is a nice overall discussion/preview of the different ways in which social penetration theory has been studied. In a review of literature it is essential to not only define the theory but to also explain/review the different ways in which the theory has been studied, a review.

(Continued)

with willingness to self-disclose. In other words, males revealing personal information and emotion would appear more feminine and less masculine. Masculine individuals tend to disclose less and be less receptive to disclosure from others, by providing less sentimental support. Females disclose more to females than to males. For males, the receiving partner's sex has little impact on disclosure.

Social penetration theory has been used as a viewing glass to examine ethical reasoning and behavior in the business sector (Baack et al., 2000). Ethical decisions and moral dilemmas on an individual and organizational level with regards to management issues have been a key issue (Baack et al., 2000). According to Baack et al., social penetration on an organization level is a factor in patterns such as hiring, promotion, discrimination, and financial decision, etc. The same applies to individual ethical issues in behavioral patterns, such as stealing, gaining promotion, and getting others fired. Baack et al. (2000) argued that an individual behaves in a malicious way at work (stealing, vandalizing, mismanaging) based on his/her intimate connection with the workplace. This intimacy is determined by a satisfying relationship between an employee and the workplace (reward/cost outcome). In other words, according to the layers of personal moral dilemma (in reflection to layers of personality in social penetration theory), aspirations for the workplace are a peripheral layer of an employee, therefore malicious intent to the workplace does not affect his/her deepest moral dilemma. Therefore, an employee does not feel guilt for stealing or for vandalism in the workplace, thus his/her self-esteem remains unaffected. On the contrary, if this person is a user of social media, let's say Facebook for instance, his/her self-esteem may be vulnerable based on how much information he/she discloses for acknowledgement from friends and other users within the social media circle. Human personality online and offline do not seem to differ much any more, based on how human life has embedded itself in today's online culture (Olson, 2013). The other side of the argument

(Continued)

asserts that information presented in cyberspace could be different from the one communicated in real life (Yang, Yang, & Chiou, 2010), and interactants in one-on-one settings tend to disclose more as opposed to unseen strangers (Keiser & Altman, 1976). So to put social penetration theory in perspective with social media (Facebook), when a person posts something on Facebook it could be a way of expressing his/her wishes of what he/she wants to be. He/she is socially trying to penetrate other media users by disclosing wishes. It is possible that he/she might be supported and complemented, which will boost self-esteem and facilitate relationship development. At the same time he/she might also be refuted and rebuffed rendering him/her vulnerable by bruising his/her self-esteem. Olson (2013) argued that the sharing of information online to facilitate developing relationships happens in layers. When the initial post of information has been positively acknowledged, a person will disclose much deeper details later.

One of the newest areas that scholars tend to explore with social penetration theory is online blogging. The traditional limits of real life could be of little importance when blogging. Additionally, the comments, sharing and liking make blogs more interactive than fixed personal homepages. A mass number of bloggers voice their opinions and share their feelings with other Internet audiences by posting texts and photos. Blogs are often seen as places where high amounts of self-disclosure occur (Bronstein, 2013). However, there is a chance that bloggers may self-disclose to unknown or unexpected audiences. As for bloggers, they could choose to be anonymous, pseudonymous, or identifiable. The concern of exposing information to unwanted audiences and the extent of anonymity of self-identity have profound impacts on how bloggers express themselves. Tang and Wang (2012) reported that most bloggers are highly aware of the risks of disclosing online. Therefore, the topics mentioned on blogs are mostly related to personal hobbies and experiences rather than personal information or money issues.

This is a nice discussion of a new and relevant issue, blogging, which is then related to social penetration theory.

(Continued)

The social penetration theory model is also useful to theory-building researchers. The factors studied in social penetration theory, personal characteristics, reward-cost assessment and situational context, have profound impacts on decision-making. Baack et al. (2000) developed an ethical decisions model based on social penetration theory.

Future Research Directions

Altman and Taylor's (1973) social penetration theory was developed based on their observations among modern urban and suburban Americans. Therefore, the impact of culture on the theory is not known. Many cross-cultural studies have discovered and confirmed there is a difference in self-disclosure between Eastern and Western individuals. More cross-cultural research needs to be conducted in order to validate the theory (Chen & Nakazawa, 2009). In addition, since social penetration is an ongoing and relationship-long process, Griffin (2009) argued that the real-life relationship scenarios, like breaking up, feeling angry, and feeling pain, are very complicated and chaotic, a process which the theory fails to explain well. Researchers should collect data over an extended period of time to better understand the dynamics between interactive partners (Sprecher & Hendrick, 2004).

More and more research on social penetration is emerging in the context of computer-mediated communication. However, this research is largely text-based; to validate these research results more video and audio web communication should be studied as well. Moreover, studies should look at the interplay between online identities and life in real world, and analyze the influences on relationships (Tang & Wang, 2012). Furthermore, there are two roles in the self-disclosure process: discloser and recipient. In real-life interactions, these roles are rapidly and constantly changing. In other words, each interlocutor is receiving and giving messages all the time during a conversation. However, the dynamic of the changing of roles and its impact on the

(Continued)

self-disclosure process is not known. Future studies should focus on these issues (Sprecher at al.,
2013).

Conclusion

Social penetration theory was developed in the
1970s. Researchers have used it since then as a tool
to understand relationship development changes.
Before the advent of computer technology, online
channels of communication and social media, scholars focused mostly on face-to-face encounters to
understand relationship development behavior. There
are a myriad of studies on cyberspace and the process of social penetration and self-disclosure. Even
though social penetration theory was developed when
cyberspace was not yet active, or rather immature,
scholars have not hesitated to utilize it in understanding trending cyber social phenomena. The theory
defines development stages of social penetration to
the level of building a stable relationship between
strangers. It has undergone some developmental
changes since it was first developed. Communication
researchers have critiqued in an attempt to see if
it is a falsifiable framework. Literature suggests
that social penetration theory has its weaknesses,
like other theories, and there are a lot of areas of
interest suggested for future research.

The authors point out the strengths of the theory and the lines of research. However, the authors also point out how the theory has areas of further development.

References

Altman, I., & Taylor, D.A. (1973). *Social penetration and the development of interpersonal relationship*. New York, NY: Holt, Rinehart & Winston.

Baack, D., Fogliasso, C., & James, H. (2000). The personal impact of ethical decisions: A social penetration theory. *Journal of Business Ethics, 24,* 39–49.

Bronstein, J. (2013). Personal blogs as online presences on the Internet explor-ing self-presentation and self-disclosure in blogging. *Aslib Proceedings, 65,* 161–181.

Bruch, M.A., & O'Brien, K.M. (2002). Shyness and toughness: unique and moderated relations with men's emotional in expression. *Journal of Counsel-ing Psychology, 49,* 28.

Chen, Y., & Nakazawa, M. (2009). Influences of culture on self-disclosure as relationally situated in intercultural and interracial friendships from a social penetration perspective. *Journal of Intercultural Communication Research, 38,* 77–98.

(Continued)

Dhariwal, A., Connolly, J., Paciello, M., & Caprara, G. (2009). Adolescent peer relationships and emerging adult romantic styles: A longitudinal study of youth in an Italian community. *Journal of Adolescent Research, 24,* 579–600.

Griffin, E. (2009). *A first look at communication theory.* New York, NY: McGraw Hill.

Hammer M. R. & Gudykunst W. B. (1987). The influence of ethnicity and sex on social penetration in close friendships. *Journal of Black Studies, 17,* 418–437.

Honeycutt, J. M., & Godwin, D. D. (1986). A model of marital functioning based on an attraction paradigm and social-penetration dimensions. *Journal of Marriage and Family, 48,* 651–667.

Jourard, S. M., & Lasakow, P. (1958). Some factors in self-disclosure. *Journal of Abnormal and Social Psychology, 56,* 91–98.

Katherine, M. (2004). *Communication theories: perspectives, processes, and contexts.* Boston, MA: McGraw Hill.

Keiser, G. J., & Altman, I. (1976). Relationship of nonverbal behavior to the social penetration process. *Human Communication Research, 2,* 147–161.

Kim, Y. Y. (2001). *Becoming intercultural.* Thousand Oaks, CA: Sage Publications, Inc.

Morman, M. T., Schrodt, P., & Tornes, M. J. (2013). Self-disclosure mediates the effects of gender orientation and homophobia on the relationship quality of male same-sex friendships. *Journal of Social & Personal Relationships, 30,* 582–605.

Mu-Li, Y., Chao-Chin, Y., & Wen-Bin, C. (2010). Differences in engaging in sexual disclosure between real life and cyberspace among adolescents: social penetration model revisited. *Current Psychology, 29,* 144–154.

Olson, A. M. (2013). *Facebook and social penetration theory.* Ann Arbor, MI: ProQuest LLC.

Pennington, N. (2008). Will you be my friend: Facebook as a model for the evolution of the social penetration theory. Conference Papers – *National Communication Association,* 1.

Petronio, S. (2013). Communication privacy management theory of Sandra Petronio. Retrieved from McGraw Hill Website: http://highered.mcgraw-hill.com.

Sprecher, S., & Hendrick, S. S. (2004). Self-disclosure in intimate relationships: associations with individual and relationship characteristics over time. *Journal of Social & Clinical Psychology, 23,* 857–877.

Sprecher, S., Treger, S., & Wondra, J. D. (2013). Effects of self-disclosure role on liking, closeness, and other impressions in get-acquainted interactions. *Journal of Social & Personal Relationships, 30,* 497–514.

Tang, J., & Wang, C. (2012). Self-disclosure among bloggers: re-examination of social penetration theory. *Cyberpsychology, Behavior & Social Networking, 15,* 245–250.

Yang, M.-L., Yang, C-C., & Chiou, W.B. (2010). Differences in engaging in sexual disclosure between real life and cyberspace among adolescents: Social penetration model revisited. *Current Psychology, 29,* 144–154.

Zacchilli, T. L., Hendrick, C., & Hendrick, S. S. (2009). The romantic partner conflict scale: a new scale to measure relationship conflict. *Journal of Social & Personal Relationships, 26,* 1073–1096.

6 ORGANIZATIONAL COMMUNICATION

Chapter Outline

- What is Organizational Communication?
- Organizational Socialization/ Assimilation
- Organizational Identity and Culture
- Organizational Dissent
- Student Paper

All of us have been involved in an organization of some kind: job, school (university, college), religious institution (church, mosque, synagogue, etc.), sports team, Greek life (fraternity or sorority), military, and the list goes on. What you will notice about organizations is that every organization is different from the other; however, all organizations share commonalities. For example, many of you may have noticed that organizations are not static entities, they change over time, they develop. Moreover, as organizations are made up of individuals, who have unique personalities, organizations have ups and downs. Think about all the organizations you have been a part of and some of the changes and ups and downs you have encountered in these organizations. Consider all of the different ways in which you and others communicate in organizations, and the different ways in which organizations communicate with members and with outside entities. *Organizational communication* is the study of all of these issues, and more. This chapter addresses the communicative aspects of organizations.

In this chapter we will explore organizational communication or the study of the role of communication in organizational settings/contexts. The theories and concepts, like those in many other chapters, vary considerably. Many of the issues discussed in this chapter come from a very theoretical perspective, while others come from a more practical perspective. Moreover, the issues range from social scientific to critical/cultural. In the first section we will define organizational communication and discuss the different approaches to the study of communication within organizations. In the second through fourth sections we will examine three key theoretical areas in organizational communication. There are a plethora of organizational communication theories that could be included in this chapter. These areas have been chosen because they represent different stages in our organizational development. Therefore, in the second section we will examine the process of organizational socialization/assimilation. In the third section we will discuss organizational identity and culture to understand how people place themselves within/understand organizations. Within this discussion of identity and culture a case study about working at Google is provided to further illustrate the applicability of organizational communication theory. In the fourth section we will describe organizational dissent, which is a form of voicing opposition to organizational policies/decisions. In the fifth and final section you will find a student paper. This paper is an undergraduate organizational communication student paper that is included to serve as an example of the kind of writing assignment you *could* do for an organizational communication theory assignment.

What is Organizational Communication?

Organizational communication is a lively area of research in communication studies. The field originated in the 1930s and 1940s with studies of business and management structures/organization. In the 1960s, the first "organizational communication" theories and studies were conducted. Such studies focused on upward/downward communication within organizations (corporations and governments for example), organizational vocabulary, and channels of communication (Jablin, 1990; Tompkins, 1967). Since those early days, the field and study of organizational communication has grown immensely. **Organizational communication** can be defined in two ways: 1) studying communication as something that exists in organizations (Taylor, 1993); or 2) as the study of communication as a way to understand, describe, and explain organizational settings/contexts (Deetz, 1994). In the first school of thought, the key philosophy is that if you can define it (see it), you can study it. Often questions such as, "What is communication and how does it take place in the organization?" are asked and analyzed. This is the more standard way to look at the study of "organizational communication." In the second, communication is seen as a way of thinking about organizations. While sociologists, psychologists, and economists can explain organizational processes in unique ways, so can communication researchers. In this second school of thought, the focus is not on the theories of organizational communication (like in the first), but more on making *a* theory *for* communication *in* organizations (Deetz, 2001). Organizational communication research is shaped by not only these two definitional approaches, but also by researchers' theoretical and methodological orientations. In organizational communication research, Deetz (2001) identified four main research orientations, which include the bulk of research conducted: normative, interpretive, critical, and dialogic.[1]

KEY TERM 6.1

Organizational communication – studying communication as something that exists in organizations or the study of communication as a way to understand, describe, and explain organizational settings/contexts.

Normative studies "accept organizations as naturally existing objects open to description, prediction, and control" (Deetz, 2001, p. 19). These researchers seek out regularity and generalization in organizations and communication, and the research is typically value neutral. There are three types of normative approaches: covering laws, systems theory, and communication skills. When organizational research attempts to provide generalizations that are "law-like," they fall under the **covering laws** category. Such research strives for generalizations, depends on theory, is largely statistical in nature, and is very positivistic in its approach. Research into supervisor/subordinate interactions (Sias & Jablin, 1995), some conceptualizations of organizational culture (Schein, 1992) and organizational dissent (Croucher et al., 2009), and most strategic management research adopt this covering laws approach. **Systems theory** is similar to covering laws in some ways; however, systems theories focus on understanding the processes that transform/alter communication and organizations. In essence, this line of research explores the process of organizing and not organizations. There is also a great body of research and writing conducted on **communication skills**, or how to be more skillful at communication in organizations. As it is an imperative to effectively communicate in organizations, it is no surprise that organizational communication researchers have tried to develop generalized tips/tools for effective communication. A considerable amount of research in communication competence falls under this communication skills category (Lustig & Koester, 1999; Wiseman, 2002).

Interpretive studies focus on showing how individual realities are socially constructed and maintained via talk, rituals, heroes, and other daily cultural activities within an organization. Think back to Chapter 3 and the discussion of the interpretive approach to theory. These researchers emphasize the metaphor of organizational culture as an individual experience, and are less prone to conduct statistical analyses. More often, such researchers will conduct qualitative research, such as interviews, ethnographic analyses, or focus group research, to name a few. While theory is important for these researchers, it is less important than it is for the normative researchers.

Critical studies in organizational communication focus on developing organizations that are free from control, domination, and inequality; organizations should be places that promote diversity and growth for all members (Deetz, 2001). Researchers from this perspective have tended to focus on ideological critiques of organizational structures. If you look back to Chapter 4 you will see a more in-depth discussion of ideology. Ideologies are conscious or unconscious abstract ideas that guide an individual's thoughts. When specific ideologies are favored over other ideologies in organizations, some individuals will be advantaged, while others will be exploited. Critical researchers explore these sites of potential advantage and exploitation.

The following four sections of the chapter review some of the research that has taken/is taking place in organizational communication. Within each of these sections you will find ways that you can approach organizational communication from the different research orientations reviewed above. Each of these sections is just a snapshot of the depth of organizational communication research. If you want to know more about any of these areas of study, look to some of the provided references, the online references, or talk to your instructor for more details.

WHAT DO YOU THINK 6.1

Which research orientation to organizational communication do you think you prefer? Why or why not?

Organizational Socialization/Assimilation

Organizational socialization/assimilation research has developed considerably over the past four decades. During this time, researchers have developed a variety of theories and models to help describe the processes that individuals take when they prepare to, and then enter an organization, and thus try to become a part of the organization. The research has consistently shown that successful entry and socialization is linked to employee retention, satisfaction, organizational satisfaction, and overall "success" in the organization (Bullis, 1993; Myers & Oetzel, 2003). To understand the process of entering and assimilating into an organization we must look at two broad processes: vocational anticipatory socialization and organizational entry/assimilation.

Vocational Anticipatory Socialization (VAS)

Children learn what it means "to be" or how one "should" behave as a lawyer, a doctor, a teacher, a mechanic, or in any other profession or organization. Parents, family, friends, media, and other outside influences socialize us (teach us formally and informally) to think a certain way about professions/fields and organizations. This is the essence of **vocational anticipatory socialization (VAS)**, the development of beliefs or expectations of how an educational area, profession, and/or organization does or should function (Jablin, 1985, 2001; Vangelisti, 1988). Understanding VAS is essential to organizational communication because we enter an organization with a set of beliefs and expectations, which are explained through the VAS model.

KEY TERM 6.2

Vocational anticipatory socialization (VAS) – the development of beliefs or expectations of how an educational area, profession, and/or organization does or should function.

Think back to childhood; how many of us chose a major or a career partially because of the different influences encountered during our childhood? For example, females are grossly underrepresented in the sciences, technology, engineering, and math (STEM) fields. There are many reasons for this: boys and girls are socialized to prefer different majors/careers, they are treated differently in math and science classes, and historically the media has showed more men in STEM roles (Adya & Kaiser, 2005; Gordon, 2007; Myers, Jahn, Gailliard, & Stoltzfus, 2011).

In a comprehensive review, Jablin (2001) outlined five sources of VAS: family, peers, educational institutions, media, and part-time jobs. We learn a lot about education, careers, and organizations from our parents. Children watch their parents, listen to them, and learn from their parents. In fact, parents are often a determining factor in our career choices (Medved, Brogan, McClanahan, Morris, & Shepherd, 2006). Our peers also influence how we look at our future careers or involvement in organizations. Eccles and Barber (1999) for example explained how conflict resolution between friends/peers is a starting point for future conflict resolution techniques in the workplace. Moreover, Jablin (2001) explained how peers provide positive and negative opinions about organizations and careers. Educational institutions are the first settings where we learn to communicate in a "formal" setting (Jablin, 2001). We learn rules, norms, how to compete, power dynamics, gossip, etc. in such institutions. It is this cultural learning that has a profound impact on how we communicate in organizations in the future. The media also play a role in shaping how we look at careers and organizations (Jablin, 2001), often creating stereotypical images. Media have historically often shown female nurses, male doctors, male police officers, etc . . . (Steinke, 2005), though these gendered roles for careers is slowly changing with some TV series and films. Media have also depicted many organizations as more flat, while others are more hierarchical; for example IT firms are often depicted as flat organizational structures with universities being very hierarchical (in reality it is not that simple). Finally, part-time jobs shape how we look at careers and organizations. Depending on the type of part-time job(s) a person has when they are young, these jobs will influence how they look at a career and the type of organization that career is in. Jobs in a career of interest will often foster motivation to pursue a similar organization or career, while jobs not in a field of interest or menial jobs will not foster interest (Levine & Hoffner, 2006).

Collectively, these five sources shape how we look at careers and organizations before we enter them. However, these expectations and beliefs are not always accurate. We may expect or believe one thing, and the exact opposite happens. Jablin (1984) stated that job applicants often have "inflated" expectations about the organizations in which they are seeking employment. When our expectations or beliefs about an organization are violated we are likely to feel betrayed and identify less with the organization (Jablin, 2001). We will talk more about identification shortly. Thus, while we do develop beliefs and expectations long before we ever encounter an organization, it is essential to be open to possible realities of the organization reinforcing or challenging our socialized expectations and beliefs. We learn such realities during the organizational entry/assimilation process.

WHAT DO YOU THINK 6.2 AND 6.3

Think back to when you were a child. Can you remember anything that led you to choose your major in college/university?

Choose any organization you are a member of and then think about the expectations and beliefs you had about that organization before you joined it. Where did you get those expectations and beliefs?

Organizational Assimilation

Organizational assimilation is the "processes by which individuals become integrated into the culture of an organization" (Jablin, 2001, p. 755). Becoming part of the organization does not mean that one must abandon all aspects of themselves before they entered the organization; rather assimilation in this case is a two-sided process where an individual learns about the organization, becomes part of it, and the organization learns about the individual and the organization may change because of the individual's membership. There are at least three stages to organizational assimilation. The first stage is anticipatory socialization, or all of the things that happen before the person encounters the organization, like VAS. The second stage is the encounter stage, which is where the individual enters the organization and is oriented and begins to learn about the organization. The third stage is the metamorphosis stage. In this stage the individuals transforms into a "member" of the organization. While Jablin (2001) noted that most organizations believe that individuals generally become a "member" within three to six months, this assertion does not consider individuals who naturally adapt/assimilate faster than others (Myers & Oetzel, 2003).

KEY TERM 6.3

Organizational assimilation – processes by which individuals become integrated into the culture of an organization.

Myers and Oetzel (2003) proposed six dimensions, or aspects of organizational assimilation, which further explain the ongoing and interactive process of becoming part of an organization: familiarity with others, acculturation, recognition, level of involvement, job competency, and role negotiation. As you go through these six dimensions, think about how these dimensions relate to a recent organization you have assimilated into, successfully or not so successfully. *Familiarity with others* is getting to know and feel comfortable with the people in the organization. When people know others in the organization they are more likely to develop interpersonal relationships at work, feel at ease speaking out in the organization, and seek emotional support in the organization. *Acculturation* is when members learn the norms, rules, and culture of the organization. Learning the culture of the organization is important, as it helps members know whether or not they "fit" with the organization. *Recognition* is when members of the organization are recognized by others within the organization for their contribution(s) to the organization. Recognition reinforces a sense of belonging and has been linked to higher organizational commitment and satisfaction (Myers & Oetzel, 2003; Pincus, 1986). A member's *level of involvement* is important to the assimilation process because typically members who show a higher level of interest in the organization through things like volunteering or being active in the organization are more likely to understand the organization and feel like they belong. Individuals who know better how to perform their job tasks or roles will have higher *job competency*. These individuals will generally assimilate better into the organization. Finally, linked to VAS, *role negotiation* is when members successfully negotiate their expectations about the organization and the realities of the organization. Jablin (2001) said that we often enter organizations with expectations that do not meet reality, thus we must negotiate these differences to enhance organizational satisfaction and commitment.

Let's consider these six dimensions and how they relate to our own organizational assimilation. Think about an organization you are currently a part of and ask yourself some of these questions:

1) Do you talk to your peers in the organization? Do you think you know them personally/professionally? Do you feel comfortable talking to them personally/professionally?
2) Has the organization, through things like an orientation period, manuals, instructions, etc., adequately taught you the rules? Do you have a good idea of how the organization functions/operates? Do you know the values of the organization? Do you know the official/unofficial ways in which things "get done" in the organization?
3) Is your work appreciated? Are your ideas listened to? Do you think your judgment is appreciated? Would the organization miss you if you left?
4) Do you volunteer for tasks in the organization? Do you feel involved? Are you happy doing the work or tasks you are doing?

5) Do you have the skills needed to do your job(s)? Do you help others do their tasks? Do you feel competent at what you are doing?

6) Do you want to change how the organization operates? Are you surprised at how things are done?

These questions represent your own organizational assimilation audit that can help you to understand the level of assimilation you are going through in your organization. Throughout the entire process, you and the organization will be interacting with one another. For a more in-depth review of these kinds of questions, see Myers and Oetzel (2003) and the following readings on organizational assimilation/socialization, which cover a broad range of topics such as: socialization into the clergy (Forward, 1999), socialization of new communication faculty (Cawyer & Friedrich, 1998), the importance of information seeking for veteran employees to reduce uncertainty about new hires (Gallagher & Sias, 2009), the steps women take to seek out information about nontraditional occupations (Holder, 1996), and the use of technology to seek out information during organizational assimilation/socialization (Waldeck, Seibold, & Flanigan, 2004).

WHAT DO YOU THINK 6.4

Why is organizational assimilation considered a process?

Organizational Identity and Culture

Not only will the organization be teaching you how to do tasks within the organization (required skills at a job for example) during the assimilation/ socialization stage, but organizations also pass on organizational culture and identity to members. As we are socialized into an organization we learn the culture of the organization and the organization becomes part of our identity, even if in only small way. Our sense of self can be dramatically changed through the organizational socialization process (Cheney & Christensen, 2001). Two processes are at work, which can change an individual's sense of self as they are socialized into and become more permanent members of an organization: organizational identity and organizational culture.

Organizational Identity

Organizational identity is formed of the messages about what an organization "is," "stands for," and/or "wants to be." Organizations do not just have one identity, but can have multiple identities (Pratt & Foreman, 2000), which are affected by internal and external forces, actors, and changes. These identity messages are transmitted to internal members of the organization and to the external forces on the organization (Cheney & Christensen, 2001). Most individuals view their membership in an organization as an important part of their personal identity (Cheney, Christensen, Zorn, & Ganesh, 2004). In fact, for many people, an affiliation with an organization can be as significant, or even more significant, of an identity as sexual, ethnic/racial, national, or other identities (Hogg & Terry, 2001). An individual's role(s) in an organization can have a great influence on shaping their level of identification, or buy-in with the organization (Cheney, 1991). Is there an organization you identify with strongly? Why do you identify with it strongly or not? Think about this question as you read on further in the chapter.

KEY TERM 6.4

Organizational identity – the messages about what an organization is, stands for, and/or wants to be, and the extent to which a member of the organization agrees with these messages.

Factors of Organizational Identity

There are various factors that predict the level to which individuals will identify with an organization. Rothwell (1992) identified six factors that influence how much an individual will identify with an organization: 1) interpersonal attraction (physical, emotional, social, psychological, etc.) to individuals in the organization; 2) attraction to organizational activities; 3) attraction to organizational goals; 4) establishment of meaning and identity; 5) attraction to the fulfillment of needs outside of the organization; and 6) demographic characteristics. Ultimately, a wealth of research has shown that both an individual's personal and social identities shape their organizational identity (Sha, 2009; Scott, 2007). Moreover, the creation and maintenance of these identities has been shown to be critical in fostering organizational success and survival (Albert, Ashforth, & Dutton, 2000; Haslam, Postmes, & Ellemers, 2003).

Studies of Organizational Identity

Organizational identity research has primarily been conducted in three settings: the corporate, educational, and non-profit contexts. In corporate settings, employees with stronger organizational identification are typically more likely to devote more energy to the organization's success, have more pride in it, and are more likely to remain with the organization for a longer period of time (Bartel, 2001; Sha, 2009). Similarly, among non-profits, high organizational identification leads members to have a high sense of loyalty and dedication to internal and external stakeholders, which leads to the success of the non-profits (Brilliant & Young, 2004). In the higher education context, research shows identification with an institution, such as a university, equates with increased fundraising abilities and retention of students (Lizzio, Wilson, & Hadaway, 2007; Van Der Werf, 2000).

For a more in-depth review of organizational identity and the variety of ways in which it has been studied please see the following readings, all of which describe organizational identity in a variety of contexts or in relation to other organizational traits/behaviors: low prestige organizations (Frandsen, 2012), faith-based organizations (McNamee, 2011), telecommuting (Fay & Kline, 2012), commercial airline pilots (Ashcraft, 2005), organizational burnout (Lammers, Atouba, & Carlson, 2013), and communication values (Aust, 2004).

Let's look at a university/college as an example of an organization that promotes an organizational identity through the development and distribution of paraphernalia. Take your university/college for example. How many of you wear university paraphernalia (e.g., T-shirts, sweatshirts, etc.)? This is one way the university promotes a collective identity among those who are current students, alumni, staff, and/or "fans" of the university/college. The idea of wearing a T-shirt with the university logo on it is very uncommon in many other nations, particularly in most of Europe like Germany, Poland, and Finland. In these nations higher education is largely government sponsored (free). The universities do not have large bookstores filled with university paraphernalia with the university logo on everything. Students do not generally identify as "an X university student." Instead many simply see their school as stepping-stone to their career. In Finland however, the different faculties (schools or colleges in each university) have different colored overalls that serve the purpose of uniting students. Some of my students have said they enjoy the overalls while they are undergraduates, while others have said they find such things to be trivial and prefer to just go to school. The idea of an identity linked to education is difficult to grasp and create in some nations, which is one way in which culture plays a key role in organizational identity.

The next section discusses the role of culture in identities; specifically it discusses the role of an organization's culture in influencing an organization's identity.

WHAT DO YOU THINK 6.5

Think about your university/college; what steps does it take to foster identification among members (students, faculty, staff, and alumni) and among non-members (fans of the university/college)? Is it successful in building and maintaining an "identity"?

Organizational Culture

Organizational culture is not easy to define because "culture" is not easy to define and **organizational culture** encompasses many different concepts (Alvesson, 2004). Schein (1992, 1999) defined organizational culture as the shared assumptions that a group has learned as it solves problems of external adaptation and internal integration. Witmer (1997) saw organizational culture as a metaphor for how "meaning is constructed in organizations" (p. 325). Pacanowsky and O'Donnell-Trujillo (1982) defined culture in an organization as the sense-making of individuals and identifying how life takes place in organizations. This sense-making and identifying (cultural understanding) occurs partially through learning the stories, vocabulary, and rites/rituals of an organization (Eisenberg & Riley, 2001). Stories typically center around previous members and events in the organization. Such stories serve as a way to create a community for organizational members (Burke, 1945), which bonds members of the organization together. Organizations also have specific vocabularies, or ways of speaking, writing, and/or communicating—jargon for example (Croucher, Long, Meredith, Oommen, & Steele, 2009a). Members learn the vocabulary as they are socialized into the organization. Organizational culture also develops through learning the rites and rituals of the organization. Individuals are taught and learn unwritten rules of an organization, and the way things "should" or are "normally" done, which only insiders know (Eisenberg & Riley, 2001).

KEY TERM 6.5

Organizational culture – a metaphor for how meaning is constructed in organizations. Shared assumptions that a group has learned as it solves problems of external adaptation and internal integration.

Schein (1992, 1999) explained the significance of cultural artifacts to organizational culture. Cultural artifacts include technology (how it is used, and what kinds are used), things we experience with our senses and tangible things (language, stories, and things like published statements/stories), and behavioral patterns within the organization. Cultural artifacts are observable in an organization; however, the artifacts will have different meanings for different members within an organization. Take email for example (an example of technology). Email is one form of communication within an organization. However, is it an appropriate form of communication to use when dismissing (firing) someone? In some organizations email more than likely is. There would clearly be a reason why email is used in one organization as opposed to another to dismiss an employee, and this relates to a variety of other organizational factors, which influence the culture of an organization.

Factors of Organizational Culture

To further understand organizational culture and how it is analyzed/studied in various settings, Glaser, Zamanou, and Hacker (1987) proposed six organizational factors that an organization should foster to promote a culture:

1) teamwork; 2) morale; 3) information flow; 4) involvement; 5) supervision; and 6) communication during meetings. Teamwork refers to the amount of cooperation/competition that is encouraged among individuals. Morale is the level of motivation and feelings about the working or organizational conditions; basically, do people feel good about their organizational environment? Information is important and people like to be informed about what is happening in their organizations. Therefore, effective and adequate information flow is an important element of a "positive" organizational culture. Individuals also like to feel as though they have a say, or have involvement in the decision-making processes in an organization; individual opinions should be taken into consideration. People also appreciate being given feedback on how they are performing and/or meeting expectations in an organization. The act of giving appropriate feedback is essential in providing positive supervision. Finally, people prefer meetings that are productive and not a waste of their time.

Studies of Organizational Culture

There is scholarly debate as to the "place" or influence of culture in organizational culture and its research. Fairhurst and Putnam (2004) offered three different orientations into the study of organizations, which relate to the discourse (things like meetings and/or internal correspondence) and study of an organizations' cultures: 1) object orientation; 2) becoming orientation; and 3) grounded in action orientation. From an object orientation, cultures are measureable, cultures shape discourse, and cultures are fixed. This approach allows individuals to control or alter culture. However, this approach negates the effects of external forces on the organization's system. From a becoming orientation, discourse is an ongoing process that shapes culture, discourse has cultural elements, and culture is not fixed. While communication is focused on more in this orientation, this orientation has a tendency to sometimes focus too much on discourse. From a grounded-in-action orientation, discourse is created and constrained by culture and discourse and culture mutually construct one another. In this orientation, culture and discourse in the past and present shapes the organization. However, this orientation tends to overemphasize past interactions in the organization and it also over-privileges discourse over culture (Fairhurst & Putnam, 2004; Messersmith, Keyton, & Bisel, 2009). Collectively, these three orientations demonstrate the varied ways that researchers can conceptualize the place of "culture" in an organization, which helps to explain the diverse ways in which researchers study organizational culture.

Research has explored the links between organizational culture and a variety of communication traits/behaviors in numerous kinds of organizational settings. Studies have examined: organizational culture and collaboration in consulting firms (Dixon & Dougherty, 2010), employee values in Italian high-tech firms (Morley, Shockley-Zalabak, & Cesaria, 1997), organizational identity among intercollegiate speech and debate competitors (Croucher et al.,

2009a), information adequacy and job satisfaction in dispersed-network organizations (Rosenfeld, Richman, & May, 2004), and sense-making and sexual harassment in academia (Dougherty & Smythe, 2004).

The relationship between organizational culture and identity has received considerable scholarly attention. Hatch and Schultz (1997) called the relationship between organizational culture and identity a dynamic process "involving mutual interdependence" (p. 361). When members are effectively socialized into an organization and learn its culture, the members are more likely to have a stronger sense of identity with the organization (Cheney, 1991; Cheney et al., 2004; Croucher et al., 2009a; Glaser et al., 1987; Hatch & Schultz, 1997). All in all, the learning of and practicing of organizational identity and culture are interrelated processes that individuals go through as they are socialized into an organization.

An Outsider's Inside View of Identity and Culture at Google – Audra Diers-Lawson (Manchester Business School)

Everyone today is familiar with Google—it's a noun, it's a verb, with its over $50 billion earnings each year it's in *Fortune Magazine's* top 100 companies, and it also topped *Fortune's* list of best places to work for 2013 and 2014. However, Google is not the only technology company at the top of this list—in 2014 half of the top ten companies to work for were technology companies.

The technology companies that emerged in the mid-to-late 1990s did more than revolutionize the way we search for information, connect with one another, and do all of that from our smartphones—in a lot of ways they revolutionized the way that organizations operate. Many of these young companies represented a new generation's rejection of hierarchical structure with middle management and an atmosphere more akin to military operations than problem-solving and creative organizations.

Google was no exception—the founders wanted a company that would ". . . organize the world's information and make it universally accessible and useful" and was driven by the value of "Don't be evil." These mission and value statements tell us about an organization that seeks to be democratic, socially responsible, and engaged. But what would that look like from the inside? In Google's case, it means an organization without a lot of hierarchy (i.e., a flat organization), deconstructed office spaces where people are just as likely to sit on a couch and work as they are to sit at a desk, free breakfast and lunch, free drinks, video games at work, the autonomy to create and develop new applications and tools because the idea sounds interesting, and a lot of opportunities to get together at organized activities and events outside of work. It also means being a part of weekly conference calls with at least one of the founders, and a whole lot of team spirit. People do not just work at Google, they become "Googlers." Becoming a Googler is tough—the company is notorious for its interview process because they are not just looking for people who can do the job, they are looking for people who can become Googlers. In short, demonstrating genuine identification with the company is a meaningful part of the interview process.

The interview process is not the only way that people come to work at Google—one of the company's common practices is buying small start-up technology companies and absorbing their offerings and many of their employees into the Google "machine." One such employee—an IT systems engineer named John—shared his experience of being a Googler while the two companies' systems were being integrated. In the first few weeks, John, like most Googlers, raved about the food and drinks—like the Freshman 15, a lot of new employees experience the "Google 15" as the open snack bar and catered lunches are too enticing. He noticed no one leaving for lunch—why would they? The company had created a nearly irresistible opportunity for socializing and these opportunities to get to know and socialize with his peers came regularly with free movie tickets to the latest superhero movie, the barbeques after work, tickets to the dedication of a new part of a presidential library, and the like. The problem was that John, unlike most of his 20-something counterparts, was over 40, married, and had a life of his own, so he just was not as interested in assimilating completely into the very social environment at Google. This environment seemed incredibly natural and comfortable for the majority of his co-workers because it felt a little bit like a college environment—they went to work and they went out with the same people. But John noticed there were few "old guys" like him around.

As someone who preferred working in environments where he could innovate and work at his own pace, the relaxed Google environment seemed ideal. As a systems engineer, John had worked in companies that micromanaged their employees, forcing them to account for every minute of every day; this was not the case at Google. If he needed a break, he could go play some *Grand Theft Auto* on the PS3, shoot some pool, or just relax for a little while in the break room and, so long as he met his project expectations, his manager was happy. The thing was that it was hard for him to sit down and concentrate when he wanted to work because of the deconstructed office environment, the constant socializing, and sounds of video games. For him, it was like trying to work at home with all of the comforts and distractions of his home environment.

In the end, John shocked a lot of his colleagues when he told them that once the system integration was complete, he was not going to be applying for a permanent job with Google because their mouths were watering at the idea of the flexibility, comfort, and a resume line listing Google as one of their employers. John said that Google seemed exactly like it had been sold to him—a flat culture focusing on democratic decision-making and work autonomy—the problem was that he did not feel like there was room for a counter-culture middle-aged metal head amongst the collection of fresh-faced optimist hipsters. In a lot of ways, he just did not care about the free lunches and movie tickets—he simply was not a Googler.

WHAT DO YOU THINK 6.6

What aspects of "culture" have you learned about/from your university/college? How do these aspects of culture influence how you feel about your university/college?

Organizational Dissent

The final area of organizational communication research detailed in this chapter is organizational dissent. Even though individuals are socialized and identify with the culture of an organization, there are times when organizational members may express opposing viewpoints about an organization. **Organizational dissent** is "expressing disagreement or contradictory opinions about organizational practices, policies, and operations" (Kassing, 1998, p. 183). There are some important elements to this definition. First, the dissent must be *expressed* or communicated to someone. Second, the dissent must include disagreement or opposition. Third, the disagreement or opposition needs to be about something within the organization. There are three kinds of dissent, differentiated by the different audiences of the dissent: 1) **articulated,** or upward dissent to management/supervisors; 2) **displaced,** or dissent expressed to individuals outside of the organization such as family or friends; and 3) **latent,** or dissent expressed to individuals at a similar level in the organization (Kassing, 1997, 2000a; Kassing & McDowell, 2008). Think about a time in an organization when you did not support an initiative, or disagreed with a decision. Did you tell someone your opinions? Did you express your discontent about what the organization decided? If you didn't, why not, what held you back?

KEY TERM 6.6

Organizational dissent – expressing disagreement or contradictory opinions about organizational practices, policies, and operations.

Factors Related to Organizational Dissent

The expression of dissent is an individual choice/process and hard to predict. There are a variety of factors that determine whether an individual will dissent, including individual, relational, and situational (Garner, 2009; Kassing, 1997, 1998, 2008). Individuals who have been in an organization longer are typically more likely to voice dissent, because they feel more comfortable in their organizational position than newcomers to an organization. When people feel as though they have more friends in an organization they are also more likely to dissent, because they believe they have the support of their peers. On an organizational level, people are more likely to dissent when they believe their organization promotes free speech, openness, a positive climate, and when people have higher organizational commitment and organizational identification (Croucher et al., 2009; Gronstedt, 2000). Think about any organization you have been a part of and something you opposed. If the organization promotes a climate of free speech, you are more likely to voice dissent to those at the same level as you (latent or to co-workers maybe), and to your superiors (articulated or to a boss possibly). This willingness to dissent is because you believe your dissent will not be met with some kind of punishment. Furthermore, if you identify strongly with your organization you may be more likely to dissent and offer alternative ideas to preserve the strength of the group; however, if you identify too strongly you are not likely to identify because you might be in a state of groupthink (we will talk about this in Chapter 8).

Studies of Organizational Dissent

Over the past two decades research has examined organizational dissent from a variety of perspectives, studied it in different contexts, and explored the relationships between dissent and various communication traits/behaviors. Researchers of organizational dissent have been particularly interested in further exploring the factors that are related to dissent. For example, research has demonstrated, in varying ways, that our tendency to dissent is related to our level of argumentativeness, or our predisposition to "advocate positions on controversial issues and to attack verbally the positions, which other people take on these issues" (Infante & Rancer, 1982, p. 72). Kassing and Avtgis (1999) for example found argumentativeness to be linked to effective articulated but ineffective latent dissent. In essence, individuals who are equipped to advocate for their positions are more likely to be able to effectively dissent upward, but not to those at the same level as themselves in an organization, according to Kassing and Avtgis. However, in a subsequent study, Croucher et al. (2009) found no relationship between argumentativeness and articulated or latent dissent. Croucher et al. (2009) did find argumentativeness was positively related to individuals expressing more displaced dissent though. All in all, this line of research is one example of the growing lines of research into argument and dissent.

Another research area with organizational dissent is the relationship between dissent and workplace freedom of speech. Gorden and Infante (1991) defined the perception of workplace freedom of speech as the degree to which an organization creates/facilitates a climate open to argumentation, dissent, or the open expression of ideas. Organizations with higher levels of freedom of speech are more likely to encourage participatory decision-making and employee equal rights. Individuals who think they are part of an organization with higher freedom of speech are more likely to report things like higher levels of organizational commitment, identification, and workplace satisfaction (Garner, 2007). Such environments are conducive to individuals feeling more involved and liberated in the organization. In such an organization it makes sense then that members would feel more comfortable to voice dissent. Kassing (2000b) reported that individuals in organizations with higher perceived freedom of speech are more likely to dissent because they not only identify more with the organization, but they also feel more comfortable within the organization. All in all, this line of research shows that the relationship between our level of identification with an organization, our perception of the organization's openness of critique, and our willingness to dissent all relate to one another. In practical terms it is helpful for organizations to understand the mechanisms at work for its members regarding such issues, as these issues have a profound effect on how organizations function (Kassing, 2011).

 WHAT DO YOU THINK 6.7

What kind of dissent do you favor in your organizations? Why?

Chapter Summary

Various processes are at work within and outside of organizations that make each organization unique. The four sections of this chapter provide a glimpse into the rich world of what is called organizational communication. The first section defined organizational communication as a field of academic inquiry and discussed different research orientations within the field. The second section described the process of socialization/assimilation. Within this section, vocational anticipatory socialization (VAS) (Jablin, 1985) and organizational assimilation were provided as examples of how we are socialized/assimilated into organizations (Myers & Oetzel, 2003). The third section detailed the relationship between organizational identity and culture—two key aspects of any successful organization. The final section discussed organizational dissent, which is a growing area of research into how people voice contradictory opinions about organizational decisions, policies, or practices (Kassing, 1998).

The concepts discussed in this chapter open a variety of opportunities for future theoretical inquiry. Moreover, these concepts also explain organizational practices, which is helpful in understanding and improving how organizations function. The final section of this chapter includes an undergraduate student paper from the University of Nebraska-Omaha by Kylie Dischler, Matthew Ferrante, and Abigail Stephans. The paper focuses on participation and decision-making in organizations. This paper, like with the other chapters, is included to show you one way you could write about/research organizational communication.

Key Terms

Articulated dissent	Communication skills	Interpretive studies
Critical studies	Displaced dissent	Organizational assimilation
Latent dissent	Normative studies	Organizational dissent
Organizational communication	Organizational culture	Vocational anticipatory socialization
Organizational identification	Systems theory	
	Covering laws	

Activities

1. Look back to the case study on Google in this chapter. If you were to change Google's organizational culture how would you do it?
2. Imagine you work for a company and you disagree with a new initiative. Would you dissent about this initiative? What factors would affect your decision to dissent? To whom would you dissent?

Note

1 As the dialogic is less commonly known in organizational communication research, and is a bit advanced for an undergraduate level text, it will not be reviewed in this text.

Student Paper

The following paper is from an Organizational Communication Class at the University of Nebraska-Omaha. Joy Chao taught the class. This is the assignment for the paper:

Term Paper (100 points) — PCH 4170 Organizational Communication

1) topic needs approval of the instructor by XXX
2) outline and reference list due by XXX
3) the formal paper due on XXX

Purpose:

Each undergraduate student should team up with another two students (three in a group). The overall goal is to find an area or topic in organizational communication that interests all group members (e.g., conflict, group relationships, organizational culture, diversity in organizations, empowerment, leadership, crisis communication, public relations, etc. . . .).

Tasks:

The group will then be charged with three tasks: 1) developing an outline and a reference list of 10–15 sources in APA style; 2) writing a 10–15 page in-depth organizational study paper; and 3) presenting a 15 minute group presentation.

Guideline:

You need to gather data/information by **interviewing at least two members** of an organization **and making observations** as permitted. As a guideline, aim for at least two hours of interviewing and observing to carry out this study.

In your report, you should discuss

1) what you intended to study;
2) how you went about studying what you studied;
3) what you found out; and
4) your conclusions, especially in relation to concepts and theories covered in class.

The purpose of this component is to see how real people in real organizations are dealing with organizational communication issues. Also, your report should include an introduction and be organized according to items 1–4 above. This paper involves **reporting and reflecting** upon your observations and should reveal a technical and not just common-sense understanding of course material. Again, you need to find sources to support your ideas, argument or interpretation throughout the paper and use correct APA style not only for your in-text citations but also in your reference list.

Vertical Versus Horizontal Structures and their Impact on Participation in Decision-Making

Kylie Dischler, Mathew Ferrante, & Abigail Stephans
University of Nebraska-Omaha

Introduction

Participation in decision-making is important to the functioning of an organization on a variety of levels. What it means to each organization and how each

(Continued)

Overall, the
introduction
does a nice
job of
introducing
the topic of
participation
in decision-
making.
However, the
authors
could do
just a
little bit
more to
justify the
topic. Why
write about
it? What
makes this
topic
important?
The paper
could also
use a clear
preview for
the readers.

The authors
spend a bit
more time
here talking
about why
the topic is
important
. . . the
justification.
This is
something
that should
be very
early in the
paper. Often
you will see
it in the
introduction,
but very
early in the
review of
literature
is good as
well.

organization will handle participation in decision-making varies depending on a multitude of factors. The structure of the organization directly impacts the types of participation in decision-making used and how inclusive efforts for participation in decision-making are within the organization. Leadership, trust, and interdependence are also factors in how much and what kinds of participation in decision-making will occur and how these occurrences can impact the functioning of the organization.

Literature Review

Participation in decision-making refers to the involvement and requested influence of a group of individuals in decision-making processes that would normally be handled by organizational superiors (Parnell, 2000). The importance of participation in decision-making was noted in studies by Jackson (1983), which showed that job satisfaction is positively correlated with higher levels of participation in decision-making. Earlier studies (Driscoll, 1978), which assumed this as a potential prediction of job satisfaction, also determined that a congruence between the desire for participation and perceived participation was more important to job satisfaction for employees than simply creating greater participation overall. Thus, it is important to understand how much participation in decision-making is desired by employees to understand its usefulness within an organization. The need for greater participation in decision-making relies on an understanding of what the term itself means as well as the various types of PDM that can be used within different organizational structures.

Types of Participation in Decision-Making and Their Relationship to Organizational Culture and Structure

Types of participation in decision-making range from no participation to pseudo-participative styles, which change according to many factors, such as

(Continued)

cultural determinants, underlying beliefs, and types of decisions made, according to a cross-cultural analysis study done by Sagie and Zeynep (2003). Sagie and Zeynep determined that low or moderate power distances combined with high individualism tend to lead to more face-to-face PDM styles between superiors and subordinates, but for hierarchically structured organizations, the more direct PDM styles are often implemented for improving quality of work output. Still, this type of PDM continues to exclude all employees but those that possess expertise skill or knowledge needed by their superiors in a given task, especially within hierarchical structures (Sagie & Zeynep, 2003).

Collective participation in decision-making is an approach that is often used in low to moderate individualistic orientations of the organizational culture or external culture combined with low to moderate power distances (Sagie & Zeynep, 2003). This type of participation is often found in work councils, consultative committees, and even delegates or representatives. It does not necessarily focus on common goals between employer and employee, but is more employee-centered (Sagie & Zeynep, 2003). This is the type of participation in decision-making seen more in flat or horizontal organizations in the United States and is actively legislated into common practice in countries like Germany and Sweden.

This correlates with findings from other studies that show how much participation in decision-making must be enacted throughout the entire organization (Bess, Perkins, Cooper, & Jones, 2011). "A PDM culture may be associated with greater organizational capacity in terms of structures and processes that promote human resource development and learning" (Bess et al., 2011). The collective participation in decision-making requires these structures and processes.

Paternalistic PDM emphasizes high power distances and low individualism in which the leader's main role in PDM is to make final decisions and share them with subordinates (Sagie & Zeynep, 2003). This type of PDM is typically used to gain commitment and compliance

(Continued)

from employees to their employer, rather than actually grant influence from the employee with their employer. According to Driscoll (1978), this type of participation in decision-making may be enough if the employees or subordinates have high enough levels of trust in their organizational decision-makers, but may not be a conducive type of PDM for more individualistic or low power distance cultures (Sagie & Zeynep, 2003).

This is an interesting finding, as additional research shows one of the main differences in an organization's culture or structure is how much all members of the organization are valued as resources for problem-solving. Those organizations that perceive even lower-status members of the team as being such resources were found to be higher in collaboration, effective communication, and shared resources according to case study by Bess et al. (2011).

Pseudo PDM appears to be the antithesis of most participative decision-making processes: "it implies a directive management covered with a mask of participation" (Sagie & Zeynep, 2003, p. 459). This type of PDM is mentioned as being used in Eastern Europe, where more autocratic managerial processes remain in place with higher frequency and less resistance (Sagie & Zeynep, 2003).

Other types of PDM, such as self-managing teams, which are becoming more and more prevalent in Western culture, show how the interdependency of tasks and mutual responsibility can increase job satisfaction, reduce absenteeism, and improve productivity (Sagie & Zeynep, 2003). These more autonomous groups can be found in both vertical and horizontal organizational frameworks and can be used effectively in both.

Participation in Decision-Making: Obstacles and Outcomes

Various factors present themselves to prevent or create greater participation in decision-making. By reviewing the types of participation in decision-making, one can see how external culture impacts

The authors in this section have provided a clear definition of PDM. The definition is backed up by previous literature (scholarly articles). From this section there should be no doubt for the reader what the authors mean when they say "PDM."

(Continued)

what levels of participation in decision-making are desired or welcomed. How much individual perspectives impact the acceptance of participation in decision-making and how this acceptance alters the functions of organizations must be evaluated to fully understand the complex relationship between organizational structure and participation in decision-making.

Studies show that ethnic and gender similarities between superior and subordinate do not seem to be factors that determine or influence if superiors grant participative decision-making opportunities to subordinates (Singh, 2009). However, the importance of trust is an essential aspect to an employer-employee's interdependency in participation in decision-making. Bosses are more inclined to share decision-making processes with trusted employees (Singh, 2009) while employees are less likely to have job satisfaction if they are excluded from participating in decision-making when they do not trust the key personnel in decision-making within their organization (Driscoll, 1978).

The effectiveness of participation in decision-making efforts tend to fall upon the individual managers as much as the processes and structures within the overall organization. Parnell's (2001) study on participative decision-making found that the individual manager is often the engine that allows or shuts down the process of participative decision-making. Parnell highlights this tendency in creating a scale for management's propensity for decision-making (2001). Those managers who view participation in decision-making as a hindrance to organizational effectiveness and a loss of managerial power are those least likely to promote participation in decision-making from their subordinates (Parnell, 2001).

A study of managers from Peru and Mexico also showed that the perceived loss of a manager's power causes participation in decision-making to be negatively linked to organizational effectiveness (Parnell, 2010). From both of these studies, the perceived loss of power from subordinate participation in

This is a nice transition paragraph as the authors develop their description of PDM further and focus now on the obstacles and outcomes of PDM.

(Continued)

The end of this section nicely wraps up the authors' description of PDM, its obstacles and its outcomes. The authors also bring in some of the concepts discussed in this book, such as groupthink (Chapter 8), and organizational learning (which is part of the socialization process discussed in the current chapter).

decision-making creates a negative perception of organizational effectiveness while using PDM (Parnell, 2001, 2010). These studies help to highlight the impact that managerial perceptions can have on the employment of participation in decision-making in more hierarchical organizational structures.

While the study by Sagie & Zeynep (2003) helped to explore how the different types of participation in decision-making are impacted by power distances and collectivistic versus individualistic orientations within organizational cultures, different outcomes are more likely to occur within low power distance cultures and collectivistic orientations, commonly found within more flat or horizontal structures of organizations. The different cultures and structures of an organization tend to impact aspects of participation in decision-making and their outcomes in three areas: social loafing, groupthink, and organizational learning.

Social Loafing

Participation in decision-making may be impacted by the structure of the organization itself, but research has also evaluated how personal factors mediate the effects of organizational structures as well (Stark, Shaw, & Duffy, 2007). Social loafing is a behavior often found in group tasks, and many studies have been done to discover the individual and external factors that contribute to this negative trend in group work.

It has been found that individuals with high winning orientations may choose to avoid social loafing for either external evaluators' or peer evaluators' to maintain a favorable social image and to protect their ego. Those with negative attitudes towards group work and who are low in winning orientations still tend to avoid social loafing when their behaviors are observable by evaluators, and high-task interdependence also tended to mediate the impact of personal dynamics for social loafing (Stark et al., 2007). Overall, the research suggests that the structure of the organization, the means by which

(Continued)

participation is evaluated, and the interdependency of tasks is more important to predicting whether individuals will loaf or participate in group tasks than the individual or personality dynamics alone.

Peer evaluations were also found to produce higher levels of workload sharing, voice, and cooperation within self-managing teams that have external evaluations (Erez, Lepine, & Elms, 2002). These same higher levels of workload sharing, voice, and cooperation could be found in self-managing teams that rotated leadership responsibilities between the members rather than the self-managing teams who used emergent leaders for tasks within the team (Erez et al., 2002). While social loafing is more likely to occur in flat or horizontal organizational structures, the methods at overcoming these through peer evaluations and shared responsibility through rotating leadership (Erez et al., 2002; Stark et al., 2007) show that the same organizational structure provides greater overall collaboration and participation in decision-making.

Groupthink

Another common occurrence when organizations implement higher levels of participation in decision-making is a tendency towards groupthink. Groupthink is:

> a mode of thinking that people engage in when they are deeply involved in a cohesive in-group, when the members' striving for unanimity override their motivation to realistically appraise alternative courses of action . . . a deterioration of mental efficiency, reality testing and moral judgment that results from in-group pressures. (Janis, 1972, p. 9)

Studies have shown that self-managing teams are more inclined to succumb to groupthink than more vertically defined structures for several reasons (Moorhead, Neck, & West, 1998), some of which include the task assignment, decision-making autonomy, group

(Continued)

The text talks about groupthink at length in Chapter 8. This is a profoundly powerful group process, what really does limit group effective-ness. Take a look at Chapter 8 and its discussion of groupthink for more information.

cohesion, insulation from external authority or experts, and supervision of the team.

Methods at overcoming groupthink can be used to encourage greater participation in decision-making in self-managing teams, and use decision-making pro-cesses that encourage participation while reducing groupthink behavior (Moorhead et al., 1998). Impar-tial leadership style, self-managing teams composed of both genders or of different speech communities, training in technical and self-leadership skills, higher levels of task-based cohesion and lower lev-els of interpersonal cohesion, higher levels of innovation processes, and team norms that promote methodical decision-making processes are effective methods of overcoming groupthink. These steps take place in self-managing teams and create healthier environments for effective participation in decision-making processes.

Organizational Learning

Team-based knowledge work has also been tied to dif-ferent structures within organizations (Erhardt, 2011). Knowledge processes within extremely hierar-chical structures tend to show little interdepen-dence in knowledge processes and thus require little overall decision-making participation, since each process is conducted mainly at the individual level before being passed on (Erhardt, 2011). However, a complex relationship exists between the complexity of the task at hand, the diversity of the knowledge present within a team, and the necessity for a greater interdependency in knowledge processes and thus more involvement in decision-making processes. Thus, a more complex the task and a team with greater diversity of knowledge will more likely recognize the greater group interdependency required, and thus promote higher participation in decision-making (Erhardt, 2011).

On the same note, self-managing teams can promote cohesive or collaborative learning within the team when the tasks are highly interdependent but the

(Continued)

skills required within the team are diverse and complementary to accomplishing the task at hand (Moorhead et al., 1998). Such collaborative organizational learning is more difficult in hierarchical organizations, which tend to promote more individual-based learning based on the solitary roles that employees play in accomplishing their given tasks.

The previous research reviewed here shows how diverse participation in decision-making can be, how it changes between organizational cultures, and how different elements of organizational structure can create different outcomes from participation in decision-making. While management and key personnel positions tend to be a few of the determining factors for participation in decision-making in hierarchical organizational structures, things like groupthink and social loafing become just as important to the process of participation in decision-making in horizontal or flat organizational or team structures.

Method

Stemming from the above mentioned research, this study was conducted to observe these dynamics of PDM through various organizational constructs to gain a more realistic and tangible understanding outside of the academic research. Its focus is to compare the various levels and outcomes of PDM between vertical and horizontal organizational structures. The technique used to gather the information for this study involved a substantial qualitative survey in which one participant representing each organizational structure volunteered to complete this survey via an interview. Two interviews were conducted to gain insight into their organization and its practices relating to PDM.

The vertical structured organization observed in this study was the popular consumer electronics retailer, Best Buy. Sean, a Customer Sales Manager at a Best Buy Store was specifically chosen as he has worked his way up Best Buy's scalar chain over the

Organiza-
tional
learning is
linked to
socializa-
tion. We are
socialized
and taught
the
different
processes
within an
organization.

(Continued)

last ten years. Holding various positions ranging from Best Buy Mascot to Geek Squad Supervisor, he is now placed in a senior management position at that store. Due to this, he is uniquely qualified to understand and discuss many aspects of Best Buy's hierarchal structure. As a senior manager, he is constantly involved in low-impact and high-impact decision-making processes and thus is a prime candidate to acquire information relating to Best Buy's level of involving participation in decision-making.

planitomaha, Inc., the horizontal structured organization represented in this study, consists of a small group of corporate event planners. Katie was specifically chosen as she has held many positions over the years she's been employed at the organization. Starting off as an intern, and having transitioned from positions such as event assistant and event vendor manager, she is now at the senior level position of director of production, settling right under the firm's founders. This small organization is owned and operated by a task force of women who travel to various locations across the United States. Even though there are levels of superiority in the organization, due to the high task level of participation needed for the company to function efficiently, the majority of the decision-making dynamics involve every employee's participation. Due to her experience and growth within the organization, Katie is seen as a prime candidate to acquire information relating to planitomaha's level of involving participation in decision-making.

The interviews conducted were approximately two hours in length. Additional time was spent to observe each participant briefly in their work environment and aided in providing helpful feedback regarding how the structures of these organizations impact the PDM within both organizations. Interview questions regarding organizational structure, power dynamics, organizational culture, and leadership commitment were based on a modified PDM scale (Parnell, 2001). The questions regarding organizational learning were based on Bess et al.'s (2011) research on PDM and its relationship to organizational learning.

(Continued)

Results

The values of Sean's organization regarding employee feedback and involvement in PDM have been undergoing changes for many years. On an organizational level, Sean describes Best Buy as a company that has begun to truly notice that employees from all levels of the organization can provide innovation. Best Buy is currently in the process of developing systems to elicit feedback and incorporating methods for all employees to be able to share their views on items coming down the pipe. On a store level, however, the propensity to involve PDM is a mixed bag. When asked if he believed that effective decisions occurred as a result of everyone participating in the decision-making process, his response was, "Sometimes, it really depends on the employee." He then mentioned how each manager handles employee participation differently, due to the level of trust they individually have with their subordinates, and that there is currently no unified ideology. Sean believed that many organizational problems would "probably" disappear within Best Buy if the company cultivated an organization-wide culture that promoted employee participation in decision-making and followed through with implementation. As it stands currently, however, these ideas are "not promoted officially."

A lot of what Sean and Katie below are describing relate to issues of organizational dissent and workplace freedom of speech.

Katie's organization has some level of superiority due to experience, but is a team-oriented task force. However, the level of involvement that is needed from group members or who has the final say in the matter depends on the complexity of the task at hand. For example, if a team member needed an increase budget for an event, then the organization's top executives would decide, not the team. PDM is used as an effective tool in Katie's organization to encourage group participation resulting in successful decisions. Katie believed that problems tend to disappear through PDM, because by allowing everyone to take part in making the outcome new ideas or solutions manifest that can improve the organization.

(Continued)

Sean's organization, while undergoing many organizational changes in how the company as a whole values PDM, has varying levels of employee buy-in. At the store level, Sean mentioned that there is a diverse range of age levels that could affect an employee's willingness or desire to participate in decision-making processes. Currently, the two methods are in place that involve employees in PDM. The first method is through informal communication by supervisors or managers and Sean mentioned this is "infrequent" and "extremely situational." The second method involves weekly reviews between a manager and each of their subordinates. Through this, managers are able to provide subordinates with organizational information coming down the pipe and give the employee an official avenue to provide feedback on these items.

The core make-up of Katie's organization heavily relies on PDM. Depending on the subject matter Katie and her counterpart are often sought out for advice or to act as a sounding board by the owners. When asked how she felt concerning her subordinates or co-workers being properly informed with the level of experience she answered,

This can be a struggle at times from information they want and what they are given. Small businesses don't always have the same processes and procedures as large companies and as we grow we are trying to put those policies in place.

As mentioned earlier, Sean related Best Buy's commitment to PDM practices as currently being developed but as not officially in place. On a personal level, Sean felt that there were many potential benefits of PDM but had mixed feelings on his, as well as his organization's, "execution" in involving PDM. As it stands, Sean was much more comfortable making the final say on a decision due to his level of expertise but did mention that it is very dependent on the situation. Specifically, Sean stated, "I tend to want to involve employees when a decision directly affects their job."

(Continued)

Through the adoption of PDM as an organizational philosophy in Katie's organization, she mentioned that employees feel as though they are part of the process instead of being told what is happening. PDM is a proven factor of how reliant each team member is and how valued they are within the organization. In this small organization, members closely work side by side and depend on one another to get the tasks completed. "You need to know you're supported," said Katie. They take time and interest to invest in team members. Sometimes they take part in activities as a team outside of the workplace, to promote instillation and unity.

Sean firmly agreed with the importance that participating in decision making has on an employee's organizational learning despite being "hesitant to give [employees] responsibility for making decisions relating to work." Hesitation does not warrant resistance, however, as Sean felt that his leadership style promoted inquiry and dialogue, more so than many of his fellow managers. Sean mentioned that on an organizational level, the idea of on-the-spot coaching and encouraging employee participation in the final decision was already in practice by many managers within the company and used in interactions with customers. As demonstrated by Sean, it allows employees to provide their feedback on the interaction regarding their perceptions on client's willingness to return to Best Buy and their opinions on "what is the best thing to do for the client and the business."

There were often multiple projects and events taking place at planitomaha, which required everyone to assist in collaborative processes with different team members. This was done by staying in constant communication throughout the organization. Subordinates were encouraged to take responsibility and feel comfortable knowing they could always ask a superior to guide them in making the best decision for the situation. Katie stimulated inquiry, critical reflection and open-communication to subordinates as a way to empower other members of her team by helping them to grow within the organization.

We can see more elements of dissent and workplace freedom of speech in these previous paragraphs. Moreover, both Sean and Katie describe different organizational cultures at Best Buy and planitomaha.

(Continued)

Best Buy is structured in a way where employees are constantly evaluated, including supervisors and managers. Regarding everyday work activities, employees are not only guided by their supervisors/managers, but Sean also stated fellow employees police each other to ensure that everyone is on task. This however, is not always the case regarding decision making. Social loafing is a genuine concern of Sean's in his attempts to engage his subordinates in PDM at Best Buy. His concern stemmed from many occasions where an attempt to foster employee participation in making a decision responded from one idea being generated and the tendency for everyone else involved to "just agree."

In Katie's organization, proving herself to the group to impact PDM varied on the topic and how passionate she felt toward the subject matter. When company decisions needed to be made, she would reflect a great deal before voicing her opinion. She felt this aided in expanding her management skills by looking at all parts. Everyone has a set list of duties and are evaluated on them bi-annually. If problems arise, or production does not seem to be equally distributed, then supervisors would settle the issue. Subordinate are not officially evaluated by peers, but possession of who-did-what on group work or 'bean counting" did take place.

Analysis

With the interviews complete, and a theoretical framework outlined for guidance, critical analysis can be conducted. While these results are preliminary at best, and more sophisticated research can be conducted to root these claims in empirical data, our data does show a sharp disparity between a vertical organization's level of involvement in PDM and horizontal organization. planitomaha, Inc. has worked hard to cultivate and maintain an organizational culture where PDM flourishes, whereas Best Buy, while making attempts at PDM involvement, tends to infrequently involve PDM when most convenient to the task at hand.

(Continued)

Through observing our interview data, PDM did not appear to be directly correlated to social loafing as both organizations mentioned some form of policing employees, either by direct supervisor evaluation or by peer evaluation. Regarding groupthink, Best Buy did identify a previous history where this concept was noticeable but our participant would challenge these ideas to help foster critical thinking. The horizontal organization in this study did not appear to have much of an issue with groupthink as our participant mentioned that inquiry and critical reflection are promoted when sharing ideas to help combat this.

It was also observed that both organizations have a slightly different focus on organizational learning through PDM. While both organizations' participants agree that organizational learning can be greatly enhanced by involvement in PDM, Best Buy appears to be in its infancy in implementing this, as a very minimal amount of systems are in place to cultivate this, whereas planitomaha, Inc. has built their organization around a PDM culture. As there are many more decisions being made participatively at planitomaha, organizational learning through these decisions has been much more observable.

Strengths/Limitations

This study comparing vertical and horizontal organizations provided useful research that could be applied by other groups who want to expand on this model. PDM has an extensive amount of empirical research to back up its claims. The questions used in recording data were powerful and vibrant. They were simple and to the point, while allowing room for participants to expand on the subject. The questions were sequenced in a way to make sure each subject area would not be repeated and created a nice flow. The data offered both positive and negative portions, thereby enriching the study and adding to the research already conducted.

The main limitations pertaining to the outcome of this study lay with the horizontal organization. The

An important area of analysis in this paper really could relate to the different cultures in these organizations. Both organizations have very different cultures that promote dissent and workplace freedom rather differently. This could be really interesting to expand on in the analysis and in the Further Research area that follows below.

(Continued)

organizational culture, in which Katie is a part of, consists of all women that inhabit the same demographics, educational backgrounds, and regional upbringing. These factors affected the diversity aspects of the research conducted, thereby limiting the outcome of producing an accurate consensus of their organizational culture. This then leaves the question, had the organization been more cross-gendered and diversified, how could the PDM dynamic have been affected?

Another limitation to this study can be examined by the vertical representation of Sean's organization. Best Buy, in general, is mainly seen as a cross-gendered organization. There are many leadership roles, like that of Sean, where men outnumber women in managerial positions, which could lead to the organization being considered a "boys' club."

The disparity of age groups within these organizations can also be considered a limiting factor. Both our sample organizations were quite different in this demographic. Best Buy has a wide age range for employees: 16–40. planitomaha, Inc. has a much more narrow age range: early 20s–early 30's. The differences in the age range of employees between these two organizations could definitely affect results relating to PDM involvement.

Further Research

Advancement for further research on this topic would involve observing PDM involvement of many different vertical and horizontal organizations, with a wide range of different demographics. Having a much larger sample size could result in finding much stronger correlations between PDM and the various concepts mentioned in this study.

Additionally, the theoretical framework utilized in this study may need to be re-evaluated. This model was a preliminary amalgam of concepts all backed by empirical research directly correlated with PDM. Further research utilizing this framework may not provide fruitful results, concluding that some of

(Continued)

these concepts may not be necessarily prevalent to observe together.

References

Bess, K. D., Perkins, D. D., Cooper, D. G., & Jones, D. L. (2011). A heuristic framework for understanding the role of participatory decision making in community-based non-profits. *American Journal of Community Psychology*, 47, 236–252.

Driscoll, J. W. (1978). Trust and participation in organizational decision making as predictors of satisfaction. *Academy of Management Journal*, 21, 44–56.

Erez, A., Lepine, J. A., Elms, H. (2002). Effects of rotated leadership and peer evaluations on the functioning and effectiveness of self-managed teams: a quasi-experiment. *Personnel Psychology*, 55, 929–948.

Erhardt, N. (2011). Is it all about teamwork? Understanding processes in team-based knowledge work. *Management Learning*, 42, 87–112.

Jackson, S. E. (1983). Participation in decision-making as a strategy for reducing job-related strain. *Journal of Applied Psychology*, 68, 3.

Moorhead, G, Neck, C. P., & West, M. S. (1998). The tendency toward defective decision making within self-managing teams: The relevance of groupthink for the 21st century. *Organizational Behavior and Human Decision Processes*, 73, 327–351.

Parnell, J. A. (2001). Rethinking participative decision making: A refinement of the propensity for participative decision making scale. *Personnel Review*, 30, 523–535.

Parnell, J. A. (2010). Propensity for participative decision making in Latin America: Mexico and Peru. *The International Journal of Human Resource Management*, 21, 2323–2338.

Sagie, A. & Zeynep, A. (2003) A cross-cultural analysis of participative decision-making in organizations. *Human Relations*, 56, 453–473.

Singh, S. K. G. (2009). A study on employee participation in decision-making. *Unitar E-Journal*, 5, 20–38.

Stark, E. M., Shaw, J. D., Duffy, M. K. (2007). Preference for group work, winning orientation, and social loafing behavior in groups. *Group & Organization Management*, 32, 699–723.

7 INTERCULTURAL COMMUNICATION

Stephen M. Croucher,
Diyako Rahmani, & Mélodine Sommier

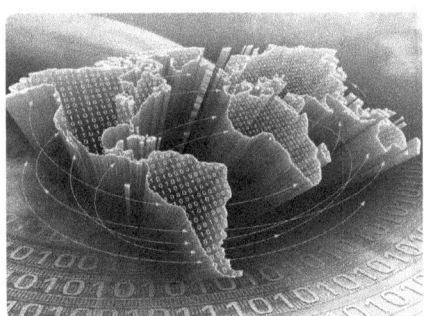

We live in an increasingly interconnected world where international travel, international communication, multiculturalism, and other forms of international mobility are easier than ever before. I have been studying intercultural communication for more than a decade, since I started my master's degree program. I have traveled the world and experienced many intercultural interactions in my life, but it was not until my spouse and I moved to Finland in 2012 from the United States that I truly began to experience "intercultural" communication. Moving to Finland, integrating (slowly) into Finnish culture, and working in a Finnish university has practically opened my eyes to the joys and difficulties of living in an intercultural world. I am an American by birth, and I was raised in the US, and every day, as part of my job and personal life, I communicate with people who are from many nations. My ability, and lack thereof sometimes, to effectively negotiate cultural differences profoundly affects my day-to-day intercultural communication.

Intercultural communication is the study of communication that takes place between unlike individuals (people from different cultures). This chapter explores intercultural communication and its communicative aspects.

The theories and concepts in this chapter, like those in the other chapters, differ considerably. In the first section we will define intercultural communication, briefly discuss its development, and then describe some sub-fields in intercultural communication. In the second section we will discuss dimensions of cultural variability, which have been regularly used to compare national cultures. In the third through fifth sections we will examine three key theoretical areas in intercultural communication. These theories have been chosen because they represent historical and developing theories in intercultural communication. In section three we will examine anxiety uncertainty management theory. In the fourth section we will analyze identity theories, focusing on face negotiation and ethnolinguistic identity theories. In the fifth section we will evaluate the process of cultural adaptation by analyzing cultural adaptation theory. Within this discussion of cultural adaptation a case study about the "dreamers" is provided to illustrate the applicability of intercultural theory. In the sixth and final section you will find a student paper. This paper is an intercultural communication student paper by Lacey McKivison reviewing anxiety uncertainty management theory, which is included to serve as an example of the kind of writing assignment you *could* do for an intercultural communication theory assignment.

What is Intercultural Communication?

When considering the term "intercultural," it is impossible to deny its complexity. Intercultural communication has typically been defined as communication between unlike individuals, typically from different national cultures. However, the field of intercultural communication has grown considerably since its early beginnings. In the first systematic review of intercultural communication theories the *International and Intercultural Communication Annual* (Gudykunst, 1983), a group of researchers theorized about the interpersonal communication between people from different cultures. These initial theories were followed up five years later in a later publication (Kim & Gudykunst, 1988) by empirical support and research on communication between people from different cultures. This early intercultural communication theory building, supported by previous work by the likes of Hall, Trager, and many others, laid the groundwork for the discipline today. However, the discipline has drastically changed since then.

Global communication, diplomacy, and business after World War II created a need for practical frameworks of communication not solely based on linguistics (Leeds-Hurwitz, 1990). The first steps in came from Whorf (1940) and Freudian psycho-analytical theory. Then the work of Edward T. Hall revolutionized the field with the publication of *The Silent Language* (1959). After this book, it took ten years for the field to find its way into communication departments. The first official university class and workshop was offered at Pittsburgh University in the late 1960s (Gudykunst & Nishida, 1978). In 1970, the International Communication Association (ICA) founded an intercultural communication division, and the Speech Communication Association (name changed later to the National Communication Association (NCA)) did the same in 1975. These were key steps in developing the field, as they helped to produce texts books, journals, and other academic items that developed the discipline (Rogers, Hart, & Miike, 2002). After the 1980s, intercultural communication became more developed as researchers defined and developed theories and measurement scales to investigate cross-cultural characteristics of different nations and cultures.

Sub-disciplines of intercultural discipline have developed in recent years: cross-cultural, inter-ethnic, interracial, and international communication. Each of these sub-disciplines has been shaped by intercultural communication, other communication fields, and other academic disciplines. We will talk about each of these sub-disciplines in the various sections of this chapter. **Cross-cultural communication** is studying (comparing) the same phenomena in different cultures. **Interethnic communication** is the study of communication among and between ethnic groups. **Interracial communication** is the study of race, and communication between racial groups. **International communication** is the study of mass-mediated communication that takes place between individuals from two or more countries that are unlike.

Intercultural communication, and the different sub-disciplines, evolved in different ways in different countries. This evolution has been dependent on social and political mainstreams of different countries and societies where intercultural programs have been institutionalized. Due to the multicultural nature of the US society, integration and intercultural understanding was a great motivation for universities to develop intercultural communication programs. However in Japan, the need for communicative skills in English language and business provided a necessity to offer intercultural communication in these departments (Rogers et al., 2002). Recently, more programs have been established in China, Taiwan, and Singapore. This new tradition of intercultural communication tries to differentiate cultural characteristics of Asian countries and redefine Western-based paradigms of intercultural communication, mainly influenced by US scholars (Min-Sun, 2010).

KEY TERM 7.1

Intercultural communication – the study of communication that takes place between unlike individuals (people from different cultures).

WHAT DO YOU THINK 7.1

Think about your future professional plans (jobs for example). In what ways do you think you will need to communicate interculturally?

Cultural Variability

In an attempt to understand and explain differences between national cultures, Hall (1959, 1966, 1976) and Hofstede (1980, 2001) asserted that national cultures have distinctly different cultural elements that make them unique. Both researchers offered starting points for cultural comparison. A couple of important facts to keep in mind when reading these dimensions/ elements: 1) these are continuums; and 2) cultures have both elements working at the same time according to Hall and Hofstede. Essentially, you will see that a culture can be both high and low context, or individualistic and collectivistic. It also depends on how strongly the culture swings toward either side.

Hall: Context, Time, and Space

In Hall's work he delineated three distinct cultural factors: context, time, and space. Hall divided culture into high- and low-context cultures. In **high-context** cultures there are multiple contextual elements/aspects that help individuals to understand the rules and norms of society. As a result of this, much communication is taken for granted and much communication is implied. It is more typical to find such communication in Asian nations, Brazil, and France to name a few. In a **low-context** culture, very little is taken for granted, as most communication is explicit, open, and little is left for miscommunication/ misinterpretation. Such communication is more typical in "Western" cultures like the United States and most European nations.

EXAMPLE 7.1

Low-context people are more direct with communication in the workplace. High-context people will often think there is knowledge of a problem without communicating the problem. So, high-context people will expect others to understand the problem without communicating it, while low-context people will directly communicate it.

KEY TERM 7.2

High and low context – the extent to which contextual elements that help people to understand the rules and norms of a society are explicitly or implicitly communicated.

Hall (1976) also discussed how national cultures differ in terms of how they use time. He defined two types of time that are typical: monochronic and polychronic. In a **monochronic** time culture, individuals tend to do one thing at a time, and careful planning is essential. This type of time management is most common in low-context cultures. In a **polychronic** time culture, individuals multitask more, value human interaction more than time, have less concern for getting things done than on how they get them done. This type of time management is most common in high-context cultures.

EXAMPLE 7.2

Business people high on the monochronic side often get frustrated at how many high on the polychronic side will multitask "too much" during the day. People high on the polychronic side do not understand why many monochronics focus on getting a job done and do not often talk about the human aspect of jobs.

KEY TERM 7.3

Monochronic and polychronic time – cultural ways in which time is managed.

Hall (1966) described individuals' relationships within space. He defined this area of research as **proxemics**, or the study of space. Hall explained how each of us needs a different amount of personal space to be comfortable. When people violate our personal space, or territory, we see this violation as a threat because it violates our **territoriality**. Hall divided cultures into high and low territoriality. Cultures with high territoriality have a high concern for ownership, clearly mark their territory, and often use words like "mine." This concern for space is common in low-context cultures. Low-territoriality cultures have less concern for ownership, boundaries are less important to them, they typically share territory and ownership, and they have less concern for ownership. This concern for space is common in high-context cultures.

EXAMPLE 7.3

US-Americans and Northern Europeans generally have a larger personal space bubble than many individuals from Asia. US-Americans or Northern Europeans riding on a crowded bus are more likely to feel uncomfortable when a person touches them, while a person from Asia will more likely be accustomed to this.

KEY TERM 7.4

Territoriality – our concern for space, which is culturally specific.

WHAT DO YOU THINK 7.2

Based on Hall's three cultural elements, how do you place your cultural group? Is your group high/low context, poly/monochronic in time use, and is your group high or low in territoriality? What brings you to these conclusions?

Hofstede's Cultural Dimensions

In a further analysis of cultural similarities and differences, Hofstede (1980) explored how national cultures differ in his landmark exploration of how IBM employees differed globally. Based on his study he identified four dimensions of cultural variability (individualism and collectivism, masculinity and femininity, power distance, and uncertainty avoidance); a fifth was later added (Hofstede, 2001). What follows are brief explanations of these dimensions, as they are regularly used by researchers for cultural comparison. The first dimension, and most studied, is individualism/collectivism. The basic element of this dimension is the extent to which individuals see themselves in terms of "we" or "I." A key aspect of this dimension is the extent to which "we" or "I" impact your decision making. Individuals high on **individualism** tend to focus more on themselves and their immediate families, prefer a loosely knit societal framework, and are more "me" focused. Individuals high in **collectivism** tend to focus more on others and not themselves, prefer a tightly knit societal framework, and are more "we" focused. Hofstede's research showed East Asian nations (Japan, China, and Korea for example) tended to be higher in collectivism, while Western European nations (Germany, the United Kingdom, and the US) tended to be higher in individualism.

EXAMPLE 7.4

I work with many Chinese students and it is common for them to say that when choosing where to go to school and work, they consult and get permission from their family. This is because such choices are family choices ("we" choices); unlike in the US where such choices are often individual choices, with maybe some consultation.

KEY TERM 7.5

Individualism and collectivism – a dimension of cultural difference that considers the extent to which "we" or "I" impact our decision making.

A second dimension offered by Hofstede (1980, 2001) is that of masculinity/femininity. This dimension represents the extent to which nations/cultures prefer gender role equality. Nations that tend toward **masculinity** are more assertive, competitive, strive more for achievement and heroism, and more highly value success. Nations that tend toward **femininity** are more cooperative, modest, care more for the weak, and strive for higher quality of life for all. It is common for initiatives such as maternity and paternity leave to be approved first in more feminine cultures, as such initiatives are seen as more caring. Typically Nordic nations are more feminine and East Asian nations are more masculine.

EXAMPLE 7.5

After being raised in the US and then moving to Finland I now understand this dimension a lot more. The Nordic nations are much more feminine than the US. One example is in health care, which is an example of supporting and caring for people. In Nordic nations it is just accepted that people have health care as a basic right.

KEY TERM 7.6

Masculinity/femininity – a dimension of cultural difference that considers the extent to which nations prefer/represent gender role equality.

A third of Hofstede's dimensions is **power distance,** or the extent to which less powerful members of a society accept and expect power to be distributed unequally. Societies with high power distance show and accept hierarchy, where people have a place in society. It is common in many high power distance (or vertical) cultures for the gap between those who have power and for those who do not to be very large; however, this is often accepted or not challenged, as challenging is often seen as futile. Low power distance cultures have hierarchy, but structures strive to balance the distribution of power within society. It is common in such low power distance (horizontal) cultures for the gap between those who have power and for those who do not to be relatively small, as power inequalities must be justified. Hofstede's (1980, 2001) research, and subsequent research by other researchers has shown Western European, particularly Nordic, nations are low power distance, while Southeast Asian and African nations tend to be high power distance.

EXAMPLE 7.6

In a low power distance culture it is common to call your boss by their first name, and even contradict them, which would not happen in a high power distance culture.

KEY TERM 7.7

Power distance – a dimension of cultural difference that considers the extent to which less powerful members of a society accept/expect power to be distributed unequally.

A fourth cultural dimension is **uncertainty avoidance,** or the degree to which individuals feel uncomfortable with ambiguity and uncertainty. As the future is unknown, how a culture deals with it is of critical importance.

Nations with high uncertainty avoidance have strict codes/rules for behaviors and can be intolerant when the codes/rules are broken. Nations with low uncertainty avoidance generally have a more relaxed attitude, and have fewer codes/rules for behaviors. Many Mediterranean nations, South American nations, and Germany tend to score high on uncertainty avoidance, while Singapore, Jamaica, many Northern European nations, and some Asian nations tend to be low on uncertainty avoidance.

EXAMPLE 7.7

High uncertainty avoidance nations rely on rules and plan everything to avoid the unknown. This can explain why there are numerous steps to doing business in many high uncertainty avoidance nations.

KEY TERM 7.8

Uncertainty avoidance – a dimension of cultural difference that considers the extent to which individuals feel uncomfortable with ambiguity and uncertainty.

The fifth cultural dimension Hofstede defined was the long-short term continuum. Cultures/nations with a **short-term orientation** consider the past or the present more important than the future. These cultures value tradition, the current hierarchies, and prefer immediate gratification. Nations like the US score high on short-term orientation. Cultures/nations with a **long-term orientation** focus on the future. They are willing to go without short-term things (gratifications) to have a better, more successful future. These groups value saving, adaptability, persistence, and perseverance. Nations like China and Japan tend to be long-term oriented.

EXAMPLE 7.8

Nations with a long-term focus, such as China, Singapore, and Japan, have fared well in recent economic downturns, as banks and individuals in such nations tend to invest for the long-haul. On the other hand, more short-term focused nations, like the US, have not fared as well, as banks and individuals do not invest for the long-haul.

KEY TERM 7.9

Long/short-term orientation – A dimension of cultural difference that considers the extent to which a nation values the past, present, and future.

While Hofstede's dimensions have had a profound effect on communication, social sciences, and business research, researchers increasingly criticize these dimensions as being too culturally generic, hegemonic, not applying to culture at all, for having flawed assumptions, for being inconsistent, and for lacking empirical evidence and transparence (Baskerville, 2003; Croucher, 2013; Fougère & Moulettes, 2007; McSweeney, 2002; Signorini, Wiesemes, & Murphy, 2009). Ultimately, these dimensions/classifications are starting points for cultural comparison, and provide a deeper, but not complete picture of national cultures. In the following sections of the chapter we will review some key theories in intercultural communication. Each of these theories has extensive theoretical and practical implications.

Anxiety Uncertainty Management of Meaning Theory

A key line of research for intercultural communication has been how to promote effective and appropriate intercultural communication: intercultural competence. Spitzberg (1988) defined **intercultural competence** as "interaction that is perceived as affective in fulfilling certain rewarding objectives in a way that is also appropriate to the context in which the interaction occurs" (p. 68). According to Spitzberg and Cupach (1984), intercultural competence has four major components: knowledge, affective, psychomotor, and situational. Based on these four components, Shuang (2014) introduced three processes for intercultural competence, which include affective (dealing with the emotions during a communication), behavioral (dealing with proper intercultural behavior), and cognitive processes (dealing with contextual requirements and intercultural awareness).

Intercultural competence is affected by various factors. Cultural sensitivity, defined as the motivation to accept and respect intercultural differences, can positively affect competence (Lakey & Canary, 2002); communication skills, knowledge, behavior (Wiseman, 2002), and gender (Lee, Fredenburg, Belcher, & Cleveland, 1999) are among those factors. Competence is a key element in any communication interaction (Lakey & Canary, 2002) and it has been studied widely in relation to different fields of communication such as business (de Oñate, & Amador, 2013; Matveev, 2004), workplace communication (Keyton et al., 2013), and education (Crook, 2014). Competence is linked to different communication theories, one of which is anxiety uncertainty management of meaning (AUMM).

Anxiety Uncertainty Management of Meaning (AUMM) Theory

Based on Berger and Calabrese's (1975) uncertainty reduction theory (URT), Gudykunst (1993) proposed his **anxiety uncertainty management of meaning (AUMM) theory**. Gudykunst broadened the scope of uncertainty reduction theory in order to explore aspects involved in effective communication between strangers. A central notion in this theory is the "stranger," who is a conceptually unfamiliar individual. That is, somebody about whom you have little or no information, which increases the uncertainty and anxiety of communicating with him/her. AUMM argues that overcoming uncertainty and anxiety are key elements to reach effective intercultural communication. Such communication is characterized as having as few as possible misunderstandings between people from different cultures (Duronto, Nishida, & Nakayama, 2005). **Uncertainty** is a cognitive process referring to an individual's ability to anticipate others' behaviors (Gudykunst & Nishida, 2001). Essentially, how much can we predict or not what others are going to do. **Anxiety** is the emotional counterpart of uncertainty and is the fear that communicating with strangers will have negative outcomes on communication. We all have anxiety when we communicate with someone who is not like us. The key is how much anxiety we have. Like uncertainty, we need some anxiety in all communication activities or we are less likely to want to communicate. However, if we have too much anxiety and uncertainty our communication with people different than ourselves will be more stressful, anxious, and may not be successful. Studies have shown levels of uncertainty and anxiety tend to be higher when interacting with strangers from other groups (e.g. other cultures) than one's own (Gudykunst 1985; Gudykunst & Shapiro, 1997). This is mostly due to the lack of information as regards the interlocutor as well as the overall context and expectations that come with it. During intercultural communication, the individual experiences anxiety along with uncertainty (Neuliep, 2012), which are affected by a variety of factors such as stereotypes, cultural identity, or linguistic competence (Hammer, Wiseman, Rasmussen, & Bruschke, 1998). AUMM argues that strategies to reduce tensions are crucial to reduce anxiety and information seeking is critical to reducing uncertainty (Duronto et al., 2005; Hammer et al., 1998).

KEY TERM 7.10

Anxiety uncertainty management of meaning (AUMM) theory – a social scientific theory proposed by William Gudykunst which argues that to have effective intercultural communication it is critical to overcome and manage uncertainty and anxiety.

Studies of AUMM

AUMM has been studied in relation to different aspects of intercultural communication. In organizational-public relationships (Cai & Ni, 2005), intercultural friendships (Chen, 2006) or educational contexts (Love & Powers, 2002), AUMM is used to study individuals' problems in communicating with people or colleagues from other cultures. It also has been studied in relation to other intercultural communication theories such as theories of planning intercultural communication, which suggest that, within our daily communication, we usually rely on familiar plans and patterns of our long-term memories

(Miller & Samp, 2007). AUMM can be a theoretical frame to study health communication. Previous studies showed that, to have mindful public health communication, it is necessary to have a balanced creation of anxiety and reduction of uncertainty (Johnson Avery & Kim, 2008).

Using AUMM, Hammer and Wiseman (1998) studied the adaptation of the sojourners to foreign cultures. They concluded that an increase in contact with the host would lead to a decrease in anxiety and uncertainty among the sojourners. Hammer and Wiseman also showed that an increased level of interpersonal salience, knowledge of host culture, and, to a lesser extent, cultural similarity will result in reduction of uncertainty, and their study did not show a meaningful relationship between interpersonal salience and reduction of anxiety. The studies about the relationship between anxiety and uncertainty have resulted in different findings. Chen (2010) found that an increase in anxiety is related to higher levels of uncertainty. Studying international students in US-American universities, she showed that students with lower English language proficiency have both higher uncertainty and anxiety in communication. She also showed that more anxious students have less effective intercultural communication, but she found no relationship between uncertainty and the degree of effectiveness of communication.

In recent years, AUMM has been applied to online communication. Based on the idea that the same mechanism persuading individuals to, or preventing them from, engaging in communication can lead to more or less motivation to use technology, Rowe-Whyte, O'Sullivan, and Hunt (2003) used AUMM to investigate the inexperienced users' contact with technology. They showed that while teaching the technology courses, the teachers who take advantage of immediacy in their classroom (in the other words they use a mediated form of immediacy) are more successful in lowering uncertainty and raising motivation and effectiveness of learning.

WHAT DO YOU THINK 7.3

Think about some intercultural interactions you have had. How have you tried to reduce anxiety and uncertainty in these interactions?

Face Negotiation Theory and Ethnolinguistic Identity Theory

There are two ways to approach identity in intercultural communication: the traditional and the modern (Banks & Banks, 1995). The traditional approach posits that communication is an internal source of conflict and identity stress, during which a communicator tries to reduce fear and anxiety (Hall, 1992). Identity is a multidimensional notion consisting of psychological and social factors (Merino & Tileagă, 2011), and negotiated until communicators reach mutual understanding and agreement on identity (Ting-Toomey, 1993). However, the modern approach supposes that identity is an animated and dynamic notion, whose (multi)form is dependent on social context and time (Hoffman, 1989). Under the influence of these two approaches to identity, scholars have proposed different types of identity, such as ethnic (Khakimova, Zhang, &

Hall, 2012; Phinney & Ong, 2007), sexual (Koller, 2012), gender (Wood, 2008), personal (Herat, 2014; Fost, 2013), religious (Koschmann, 2013), and political (Nisbet & Myers, 2010), to mention a few. For space purposes, what follows is a review of two well-cited identity theories: face negotiation theory and ethnolinguistic identity theory.

Face Negotiation Theory

Face is "a claimed sense of favorable social self-worth that a person wants others to have of her or him" (Ting-Toomey & Kurogi, 1998, p. 187). Essentially, face is the positive image we want others to have of ourselves. Face negotiation theory (FNT) focuses on mechanisms associated with losing and saving face. As we lose face, our positive image is affected therefore requiring us to save it and repair damages. It is through social interactions that face can be positively or negatively affected. **Facework** refers to the communicative repertoires that individuals use to build their own face, and challenge or reinforce others' face. Face is composed of three main elements. **Self face** refers to the attention given to one's own image and how one presents him/herself in social contexts. **Other face** refers to the attention given to somebody else's image. Finally, **mutual face** is the attention given by both interlocutors to both of their images (Ting-Toomey, Oetzel, & Yee-Jung, 2001). A central assumption of FNT is the idea that, regardless of culture and type of communication situations, people try to maintain face. However, conflict situations when the individuals need to save lost face because of the factors such as attacking or teasing can be especially challenging. Conflicts bring into question ways of saving one's face and dealing with others' face. Much research has looked into different ways of saving face in conflict situations across cultures. Indeed, according to Ting-Toomey and Kurogi (1998), face and facework are universal aspects; yet they vary according to different cultures. FNT intends to cast light on the "cultural blind spots in facework miscommunication" to provide concrete tools in conflict management (Ting-Toomey & Kurogi, 1998, p. 189). Much attention has been paid to the relation between facework and societies being rather individualistic (focused on the "I"—individual goals and values) or collectivistic (focused on the "we"—group interests and values). FNT argues that individualism/collectivism is one of the elements that significantly influence the facework strategies used by individuals. Other aspects put forth by the theory include power distance (the extent to which less powerful members of a society accept and expect power to be distributed unequally), context, individual characteristics, relationship aspects, and the importance of the conflict (Ting-Toomey & Kurogi, 1998).

KEY TERM 7.11

Facework – communicative repertoires that individuals use to build their own face, and challenge or reinforce others' face. Face is composed of three main elements: self, mutual, and other face.

WHAT DO YOU THINK 7.4

How do you "negotiate" your face on a daily basis?

Research on Face Negotiation Theory

Studies of face negotiation theory have covered different fields of communication. Kirschbaum, (2012) showed that FNT is applicable to health communication and emphasized the role of education and training in building mindful perceptions of face and self-construal in communication between physicians and patients. Zhang, Ting-Toomey, and Oetzel's (2014) study showed that getting more angry is associated with higher independent self-construal and more attention to one's own face, while being more compassionate is related to more attention to other people's face. The relationship between feeling guilty and FNT is contextual. For example, in the US it is related to higher levels of interdependent self-construal and the obliging conflict style, but in China it is related to higher levels of the avoiding conflict style.

FNT has also been studied in relation to conflict management. A study of a supposed conflict with a peer or a person of different status showed more preserving self face was related to more dominating and emotionally expressive styles, while more preserving other people's face or keeping mutual face were related to more integrating, obliging and compromising styles (Oetzel Meares, Myers, & Lara, 2003). Another study showed that an interpersonal conflict is directly and indirectly affected by cultural individualism and collectivism in the culture where the interpersonal conflict happens (Oetzel & Ting-Toomey, 2003). This study also found out that the people with higher independent self-construal had higher concerns about their own faces but the people with higher interdependent self-construal had higher concerns about others' faces. The authors showed the people who care more about their own faces use more of a dominating conflict style while the people who have more considered other people's face use more of avoiding and integrating styles.

Online communication is another field that has been investigated using FNT. One study showed that youths' effort to gain face, give face, and prevent losing face on social networking sites can expose them to the danger of the "context collapse and vulnerability to surveillance by the authorities and rival gangs" (Lim, Vadrevu, Chan, & Basnyat, 2012, p. 346).

Ethnolinguistic Identity Theory

Ethnolinguistic identity theory (ELIT) is based on the idea that language use and style convey information about individuals' statuses, cultural backgrounds, and group memberships. ELIT is used to examine what language strategies are used and for which reasons by individuals who belong to different ethnic groups (Beebe & Giles, 1984). ELIT is informed by aspects of Tajfel and

Turner's (1979) social-identity theory, which argues that we view ourselves and others in terms of group memberships. That is, we perceive individuals through their social identity, which derives from their group memberships. Such group memberships can be based on ethnicity, religion, social class, gender, or subculture. Furthermore, individuals seek positive social identity as they compare the groups to which they belong (**ingroup**) to groups other people belong to (**outgroup**). These aspects, the social identity theory argues, affect ways in which individuals communicate with one another because of (real or perceived) differences in groups' statuses and legitimacy. Building on these tenets, ELIT examines language strategies as members of different linguistic groups interact. **Ethnolinguistic vitality** is used to evaluate such strategy choices looking at three main groups' features: status (low-status or renowned), demographics (number of members, location etc.), and support (in media, by the government etc.) (Giles & Johnson, 1987). ELIT argues that members who perceive their ethnic group as having high ethnolinguistic vitality are more likely to overtly express their group identity and emphasize their ethnic language or speech markers (Giles & Johnson, 1987). That is, high ethnolinguistic vitality is positively perceived by ethnic group members who are thus likely to feel comfortable expressing their group identity and associated linguistic skills or accents when interacting with members from other groups.

KEY TERM 7.12

Ethnolinguistic identity theory – evaluates language strategies as members of different language groups interact. Three main features are often considered: status, demographics, and support.

WHAT DO YOU THINK 7.5

Can you think of any linguistic or ethnic groups in the news or historically who have had to protect their identity from external forces through various strategies? What steps have they taken to protect these ethnic and/or linguistic identities?

Research on Ethnolinguistic Identity Theory

Studies into media studies, nation-building, multilingualism, and language policy have used ethnolinguistic identity theory. Media studies research has shown that minority-language speakers use newspapers to develop a positive sense of uniqueness among speakers of minority languages in bilingual settings (Vincze & Holley, 2013). Another study showed that TV usage patterns among minority language speakers in Finland and Canada are affected by the linguistic identity of TV users (Vincze & Freynet, 2014). Moring Husband,

Lojander-Visapää, Vincze, Fomina, & Mänty (2011) studied how the media help languages with their maintenance and, based on studying the bilingual communities, they concluded that media are important factors in maintaining and supporting ethnolinguistic vitality.

Nation-building and minority integration is another area of study for ethnolinguistic identity theory. One study in this field discussed the role of ethnolinguistic vitality and survival in the process of nationalism in Belarus (Bekus, 2014). The author believed that different political, cultural, and historical factors could affect the important of ethnolinguistic survival and vitality in the process of nationalism in Belarus. Olsen and Olsen (2010) studied the linguistic identity among young female Palestinian students in East Jerusalem to see what factors affected their decision to use one language among English, Hebrew, or Arabic. The authors found out that the students' decision was influenced by hegemonic and social factors. For example, they reported that Arab female students switched their language into Hebrew in the commercial areas of the city or in the checkpoints, while English was used at home or online and in social contexts.

Ethnolinguistic identity studies have also been driven into the field of multilingualism and language policy. One case study dealt with the condition of a local Austronesian language spoken in the islands of Papua New Guinea to investigate the changes in identity and language of these people within the last 80 years (Brownie, 2012). The paper concluded that, due to the introduction of Christianity and educational policies, the three dialects of this local language are approaching leveling. Another study showed the language policy that puts pressure on the minority groups to adapt to the dominant culture will result in resentment and rejection of cultural adaptation by the minority groups. Croucher (2009) studied how the French-Muslim population reacted to the language policies of this country. The investigation revealed that the Muslim population has less motivation for adaptation, and higher resentment toward the dominant culture due to French linguistic policies and pushes to conform to the dominant French culture. Cenoz and Valencia (1993) believed that socio-contextual and social psychological elements affect the language acquisition in the bilingual societies after they studied ethnolinguistic vitality, social networks, motivation, and language proficiency among two samples of Spanish- and Basque-speaking students.

Cultural Adaptation Theory

Cultural Adaptation Theory

Since the Ancient Roman and Greek colonial expansion, and since the times of the Spanish and English colonial powers, how people from various cultures, and from many lands, occupations, religions, and environments, could be melded together into one culture, one nationality, one identity, has been disputed (Sowell, 1994). To attempt to answer these questions surrounding the new colonial identities, politicians, scientists, and scholars have posed various theoretical models and explanations. Models such as social cohesion in political science (Jenson, 2002), immigrant integration from ethnic/international relations (Reinsch, 2001), cultural fusion from philosophy/phenomenology (Gadamer, 2003; Kramer, 2003), and cultural adaptation/assimilation from communication and psychology (Kim, 1976, 1989) have all been proposed and researched.

Intercultural communication researchers, primarily American trained, have taken a keen interest in cultural adaptation/assimilation, particularly using Kim's (1976, 1989, 2001) **cultural adaptation theory**. This theory is a descriptive process of cultural outsiders abandoning their cultural identities to better communicate and culturally "fit" with individuals in a dominant culture, normally researched in the United States (Buenker & Ratner, 1992; Chun & Choi, 2003; Conklin & Lourie, 1983; Croucher, 2009; Gudykunst & Kim, 1997, 2003; Kim, 1976, 1989, 2001; Kramer, 2003; Oh, Koeske & Sales, 2002).

When examining the relationship between communication and cultural adaptation, Kim (1976) asserted:

> Interpersonal communication is one of the key elements of social communication, along with observation of one's environment including mass media content. Interpersonal communication is generally considered more intense, direct, and has a detailed influence on the immigrant's adaptation to the host socio-cultural system. (p. 57)

Gudykunst and Kim (2003) defined **assimilation** as a "convergence of strangers' internal conditions with those of the native and a minimum maintenance of the original cultural habits" (p. 360). The convergence of strangers around an internal condition of the native culture emphasizes the immigrant's responsibility to find a way to function in their new environment. Gudykunst and Kim (1997) defined functional fit as "the operational (or behavioral) capacity that enables a person to carry out behaviors externally in accordance with the host cultural patterns" (p. 342).

Happiness is another logical principle of assimilation advocated by Kim (2002) and Gudykunst and Kim (1997, 2003). They argued that for an individual to effectively overcome differences and be satisfied in their new culture they should abandon their previous cultural identity to facilitate overall cultural happiness and satisfaction (Gudykunst & Kim, 1997, 2003). They further asserted that every "stranger" or newcomer to a culture must find ways to function in a new environment. Complete cultural adaptation is the ultimate, lifetime goal of assimilation (Gudykunst & Kim, 1997, 2003).

According to cultural adaptation theory, individuals go through three stages on their way to assimilation: enculturation, deculturation, and acculturation. At any one time, individuals are in only one of the following three stages, and the individual can go back and forth between stages. All in all, Kim set up a continuum upon which individuals move from one stage to the other, in a linear motion that might not effectively address the complexity of the cultural adaptation process (Kramer, 1998, 2000, 2003; Croucher, 2009).

KEY TERM 7.13

Cultural adaptation theory – a descriptive process of cultural outsiders abandoning their cultural identities to better communicate and culturally "fit" with individuals in a dominant culture. The theory has three stages: enculturation, deculturation, and acculturation.

Enculturation

Kelvin (1970) described the **enculturation** process as the socialization process of children and newcomers to the norms of their cultural milieu. Enculturation stems from sociological and educational research, examining the learning and developmental patterns of children. Gudykunst and Kim (2003) expanded the concept of enculturation to include not only socialization but also communicative response: "socialization provides children with an understanding of their world and culturally patterned modes of responding to it" (p. 359). We are all socialized (enculturated) into our native cultures.

WHAT DO YOU THINK 7.6

Think about when you were growing up and how you learned what it meant to be "American," "Chinese," "Finnish," or "X," if we want to think about nationality as one kind of cultural group. You learned how to be part of this large cultural group (to behave and to think like) from various sources: media, family, friends, and various other sources.

Deculturation

Deculturation is the process that individuals go through when losing their socialized cultural identity. According to Brim and Wheeler (1966), during **deculturation**, individuals learn new cultural habits from the host culture, and in turn as individuals realize that certain behaviors are more acceptable in the host culture, the individuals question/unlearn their native cultural behaviors. Kramer (2003, 2003a) asserted that in order to lose a socialized identity an individual must unlearn the culture they were socialized into, inherently deeming their original culture as less worthy or important than the new surrounding culture. When Stephen (the author of your book) moved to Finland he observed many new cultural things around him. The food, language, work culture, and MANY other elements of life were different. At work Stephen learned that at Finnish universities it is common and acceptable for students to call professors by their first names, which was not the case for him at his previous universities. So, he had to adjust to this cultural element at work.

Acculturation

When individuals abandon their previous cultural habits (deculturation) and adopt the behaviors of the host culture, the individuals are engaged in the final process of cultural adaptation, **acculturation** (Gudykunst & Kim, 1997, 2003; Oh et al., 2002). Kim (2003) defined acculturation as the process when strangers "become acquainted with and adopt some of the norms and values of salient reference groups in the host society" (p. 359). An element of Finnish culture that Stephen and his spouse are acculturating to is language. They have decided that they should learn Finnish to be able to communicate better with people in Finland. Language is a key part of the cultural adaptation process.

WHAT DO YOU THINK 7.7

Do you think it is possible to culturally adapt 100 percent to a new culture? Why or why not?

Cultural Adaptation Studies

Cultural adaptation theory as posited by Kim (1976, 1977, 1988, 1994, 2001), and further expounded upon in her collaborations with Gudykunst (Gudykunst & Kim, 1997; 2003) has been tested (philosophically) with little until recent empirical support of the theory (McKay-Semmler, Semmler, & Kim, 2014; McKay-Semmler & Kim, 2014). Most of these tests have entailed examining newcomer immigrant groups from Southeast Asia, while a few studies have been conducted on African-Americans and Native-Americans. The following list (not an exhaustive list) is an example of such studies, which have focused solely on newcomers to either the US or Canada (Ansari, 1991; Berry & Kim, 1987; Berry & Sam, 1997; Garcia, 1995; Gudykunst & Hammer, 1988; Kim, 1976; Mägiste, 1988; Murphy & Esposito, 2003; Oh et. al, 2002; Szalay & Inn, 1988). Other research into cultural adaptation has focused primarily on the relationship between the cultural adaptation process and social media, and on how the cultural adaptation process is affected by the host culture.

Croucher (2011) proposed a theoretical model to explain the relationship between social networking and cultural adaption. In this model, based on cultivation theory and ethnic group vitality, it was proposed that cultural adaptation would affect immigrants' interactions with the dominant culture, and that social networking use would affect immigrants' in-group communication. These propositions have been forwarded in subsequent research (Croucher &

Rahmani, 2015; Shuter, 2012). Essentially, Croucher (2011) asserted that social media use would influence how immigrants culturally adapt because this form of media would affect how they interact with their own and the dominant cultural groups (Shuter, 2011, 2012).

Research is also increasingly examining the interaction between the host culture and the immigrant group. Kim (1988, 2001) stated that host culture receptivity is a key variable within the cultural adaptation process. Immigrants will have an easier time culturally adapting into cultures with a more receptive host culture. While this assertion was theoretically argued in Kim's (1988, 2001) cultural adaptation research, it has had very little empirical support until recently. McKay-Semmler et al. (2014) found that in the US, more negative media depictions of immigrants were related to reduced host receptivity of immigrants. Croucher (2013) found that when members of the dominant cultures in France, Germany, and the United Kingdom were not receptive to immigrants, the individuals believed that immigrants did not want to adapt to the dominant culture. These studies demonstrated the significant influence of how the dominant culture's perceptions of immigrants influences perceptions of the adaptation process and acceptance of immigrants.

Arizona Dreamers and Driver's Licenses

On December 22, 2014, young immigrants known as "dreamers" began applying for driver's licenses in the United States state of Arizona. Dreamers are young immigrants brought into the US illegally as children. This case was a heated political and judicial issue in Arizona and the US. The then governor of Arizona, Jan Brewer argued the dreamers did not have a right to driver's licenses, as they were not legal citizens of the US. However, the Obama Administration argued they should be allowed the licenses, as they were not the ones who entered the country illegally. Moreover, the Obama Administration argued that giving licenses would afford the dreamers a better chance to adapt into "American culture" because they would have documentation, the ability to drive legally, and more economic chances.

This case is an interesting case into cultural adaptation for many reasons. First, this case shows the cultural split in the US over immigration to the US from Central and South America. During the dreamers debate there was a clear divide over those individuals who wanted to accept dreamers as US citizens and those who did not, and wanted to deport them. Second, many dreamers argued that having a driver's license would be a symbolic sign that they were "American," which is one form of host culture receptivity.

Chapter Summary

In our increasingly interconnected world it is essential to understand the importance of intercultural communication. Through effective intercultural communication we are more able to work through anxieties and uncertainties in interactions, understand our own identities, and better grasp how individuals adapt to new cultural surroundings. The sections of this chapter each provided brief descriptions/summaries of some key areas of research into intercultural communication. The first section defined intercultural communication, discussed its development, and described sub-fields in the discipline. The second section discussed dimensions of cultural variability, which are regularly used to compare national cultures. The third examined AUMM, which helps us to better understand how we manage anxiety and uncertainty when interacting with "strangers." The fourth section described face negotiation theory and ethnolinguistic identity theory. These two theories help us to understand how we frame our identities in a culturally diverse world. The fifth section discussed cultural adaptation theory. An understanding of this theory aids in our knowledge of how newcomers (immigrants) try to adapt to new cultures. As immigration continues to be a hot-button issue, knowledge of this process is integral. The final section of this chapter includes a student paper from the University of Jyväskylä in Finland by Lacey McKivison. This paper focuses on AUMM and is included to show you one way you can write about/ research intercultural communication.

Key Terms

Acculturation

AUMM theory

Cultural adaptation theory

Ethnolinguistic vitality

High context

Intercultural communication

International communication

Low context

Mutual face

Polychronic

Self face

Uncertainty

Anxiety

Collectivism

Deculturation

Facework

Individualism

Intercultural competence

Interracial communication

Masculinity

Other face

Power distance

Short-term orientation

Uncertainty avoidance

Assimilation

Cross-cultural communication

Enculturation

Femininity

Ingroup

Interethnic communication

Long-term orientation

Monochronic

Outgroup

Proxemics

Territoriality

Activities

1. Do some research on the "dreamers." How do you see this case representing cultural adaptation and possibly the divide over host culture receptivity?

2. Looking at your cultural group, where do you place your group on Hofstede's dimensions? If you want to compare your thoughts about your national group or another group try Hofstede's Country Comparison Tool: http://geert-hofstede.com/countries.html.

Student Paper

The following paper is from a Communication Theory Class at the University of Jyväskylä. Stephen Croucher taught the class. This is the assignment for the paper:

Term Paper (200 points) – KVVS 100 – Communication Theory
Your final paper must be:

1) Written in APA Style (6th Edition)
2) It must be 5–10 pages in length not including the references and the title page. The paper does not need an abstract
3) You can work with a partner on this paper if you would like, or you can work alone.
4) You must have your theory approved by the instructor within the first two class sessions.
5) The purpose of this review of literature is to "review" a theory. This means many things. You can review the development of a theory, you can review how scholars have studied a theory, you can topically review a theory, chronologically review a theory, etc. . . . There are many ways to approach a review of literature. Options for this assignment will be discussed on the first day of class.

Literature Review of the Anxiety/Uncertainty Management Theory

Theories and Models of Intercultural Communication

Lacey McKivison
University of Jyväskylä

Introduction

The anxiety/uncertainty management theory is one of the most studied theories in intercultural communication. Developed by William Gudykunst over 30 years, it is a theory of intergroup and interpersonal communication that looks at how people can

(Continued)

communicate effectively by managing uncertainty and anxiety. This literature review presents a chrono-logical review of the development of the theory, followed by examples of how the theory has been used in research, and, finally, offers critiques of the theory.

Literature Review

Early Developments

The anxiety/uncertainty management theory was ini-tially developed as an expansion of the uncertainty reduction theory, which was created by Berger and Calabrese in 1975. Uncertainty reduction theory was developed as a way to look at the initial interac-tions strangers have when meeting one another, based on the claim that when people meet each other for the first time, they often hold uncertainties about the other person and are looking for ways to try to reduce them (Miller, 2002). Uncertainty reduction theory, however, was often thought to be too limited since it just looked at the initial interactions amongst people from the same culture. Due to this, many people tried to expand or enhance the theory in different ways, one being Gudykunst.

After developing an interest in intercultural communication, Gudykunst became interested in developing a theory focused on effective communica-tion in interpersonal and intergroup relationships (Gudykunst, 2005b). He chose to use uncertainty reduction theory as a starting point for his theory because he believed it could easily be extended from interpersonal to intergroup communication, and that the tenets of the theory could be used to improve communication (Gudykunst, 1995). Gudykunst decided to focus on intergroup communication, and not spe-cifically intercultural communication, because he considered intercultural communication to be a sub-category of intergroup communication.

Initially, Gudykunst and Nishida (1984) attempted an expansion of uncertainty reduction theory by

This is a good opening paragraph that provides a nice preview of the paper.

(Continued)

extending it to see if it would cover intercultural encounters. They claimed, "given Uncertainty Reduction Theory's level of generality, its scope should extend to explaining communication across cultures, as well as communication between people from different cultures" (p. 23). In their initial research, they looked at how external variables influenced uncertainty reduction strategies between students from the United States and Japan. Most of their findings supported the axioms of uncertainty reduction theory, indicating that the theory might be extendable to intercultural interactions. Further research conducted by Gudykunst (1985), in which he tested an initial model of uncertainty reduction theory by looking at the relationship between students from the United States and abroad, showed that the model was a good fit in intercultural encounters.

In 1987, Gudykunst and Hammer extended uncertainty reduction theory even further by not only looking at uncertainty reduction in encounters amongst people from different cultures, but also at anxiety management (Hammer & Wiseman, 1998). They were looking to extend the theory to try to explain intercultural adaptation, and they viewed the "reduction of uncertainty and anxiety as necessary" (p. 310) for adaptation. In 1988, Gudykunst made his first reference to the idea of creating a new theory of intergroup communication based on uncertainty and anxiety management (Gudykunst, 1988). He claimed that anxiety was an important factor as well because he believed that everyone has some amount of anxiety when speaking with someone for the first time, especially in intercultural encounters, because they often do not know much about the other culture. His initial proposal included thirteen axioms, which were based around the idea that there are variables that affect how well one manages his or her uncertainty and anxiety when communicating in an intercultural situation and, in return, how well they are able to manage their anxiety and uncertainty will determine whether or not they have effective communication or adaptation.

Lacey has provided a nice overall description of how AUMM was developed from another theory. In this case one theory (AUMM) developed from the tenets of another theory (URT). This is common in social sciences.

(Continued)

Anxiety/Uncertainty Management Theory

In 1993, Gudykunst made his "initial attempt to formally state a general theory of effective interpersonal and intergroup communication" (1993, p. 68).
He developed this theory based on his research and
called the theory the anxiety/uncertainty management theory. This theory was meant to be a practical
theory that people could use to help achieve effective communication by learning to manage anxiety and
uncertainty (Gudykunst, 2003).

Anxiety and uncertainty are, of course, central
to the theory. Anxiety is affective, meaning it is
emotional, and uncertainty is cognitive, meaning it
is a mental process (Berardo & Deardorff, 2012).
Anxiety is "tension, feelings of being uneasy, or
apprehension strangers have about what will happen
when they communicate with hosts" (Gudykunst, 1998,
p. 229). Often anxiety surfaces because people have
negative expectations of what might come from the
situation. Uncertainty, on the other hand, may stem
from being unsure about "hosts' attitudes, feelings,
beliefs, values, and behaviors" (p. 228-229).

The theory that states each person has a "minimum and maximum threshold" (Stephan et al., 1999,
p. 615) for anxiety and uncertainty. When their anxiety and uncertainty go above or below that threshold it often has negative effects on their ability
to communicate effectively, but when they are able
to balance their anxiety and uncertainty they are
often able to make more accurate predictions and
start to feel more comfortable in the situation.
According to Gudykunst (1998), when uncertainty
is above the maximum threshold people are not able
to make accurate predictions about the host and
often they might end the interaction. On the other
hand, if uncertainty is too low they might become
overly confident in their abilities to understand
what the host is trying to say, so they might not
challenge their perceptions, which could lead them
to draw incorrect conclusions. When anxiety is too
high, people often communicate on "automatic pilot"
(p. 229), which means they tend to try to interpret

(Continued)

Look back to the chapter and you will see anxiety and uncertainty were mentioned before. As previously mentioned, it is essential to the theory that we understand and study our threshold of anxiety and uncertainty.

the host's behavior based on their own values and beliefs. When anxiety is too low, often they do not have the motivation to communicate with that person because there is no excitement or curiosity.

The theory states that in most all communication situations people have anxiety and uncertainty, but it is often greater in intergroup situations where they are not as familiar with one another (Stephan et al., 1999). Because of this, it is crucial that they try to reduce and manage their anxiety and uncertainty so they can try to make sense out of the communication. Anxiety and uncertainty are typically reduced over time as people communicate more with someone and start to feel more comfortable with them, but anxiety and uncertainty do not follow a consistent pattern, meaning that the levels can go up and down over time (Gudykunst, 1993).

The theory proposes that the amount of anxiety and uncertainty a person has depends on outside variables known as superficial factors. These superficial factors are described as "surface factors that contribute to the underlying issues of anxiety and uncertainty . . ." (Griffin, 2006, p. 433). What this means is that these factors influence the amount of anxiety and uncertainty strangers will have when communicating with a host, and determine how well they are able to manage that anxiety and uncertainty. How they manage their anxiety and uncertainty will then determine how effective their communication will be.

It is nice to mention that superficial factors impact our anxiety and uncertainty thresholds.

In this initial model of the theory, Gudykunst (1993) divided the superficial factors into three categories; motivation, knowledge, and skill. He explained that the motivational factors represented a person's willingness to want to communicate in an effective manner, and included components such as self-conceptions and social bonds. He explained the knowledge factors as a person's ability to know what they need to do in order to have effective communication, and included such factors as having knowledge of more than one perspective. Finally, he explained the skills factors as a person's ability to understand and use the necessary skills to communicate

(Continued)

effectively, and they included factors such as one's ability to tolerate ambiguity and to empathize.

Up to this point, the structure of the theory was similar to that which was proposed in 1988 except Gudykunst added the idea of mindfulness to the theory. Mindfulness acts as a moderator between anxiety and uncertainty and effective communication. Gudykunst (1993) claimed that it is crucial for one to be mindful to communicate effectively. As previously mentioned, it is important that people are able to manage their anxiety and uncertainty so it does not go above or below the threshold, and they can actively do so by being mindful in their communication (Stephan et al., 1999).

Mindfulness is when one remains aware of their situation and stays open both to learning new information and to the fact that the person they are communicating with might have a different perspective than them (Gudykunst, 1998). Gudykunst (1993) claimed that mindfulness was important because it helps to make sure that when a person is trying to manage their anxiety and uncertainty when communicating with a stranger, they are doing it in the least biased way possible, which will lead to more effective communication. This is why Gudykunst (1993) stressed that it is so important one stays aware of their thought processes and actively tries to understand the other person from their perspective, which will help people to make sure they really do have the most effective communication.

The final stage, and primary goal of the theory, is effective communication. Effective communication is based around the idea that when one communicates with someone, the meaning cannot be exchanged, only the message itself can be (Yoshitake, 2002). Communication is described as being effective only "to the extent that the person who is interpreting the message attaches a meaning to the message that is relatively similar to that which was intended by the person transmitting it" (Stephan et al., 1999, p. 616). In other words, to have effective communication one must be able to view the other person's

(Continued)

The overall
review of
the theory
is really
well done.
In this first
section of
the review
Lacey
outlines
the key
aspects of
the theory,
defines the
key terms
and also
explains
how some of
the terms
were derived
from URT. In
this case,
Lacey did a
chronological
review,
where she
reviewed the
theory's
development.

behaviors from that person's perspective. Gudykunst (1993) believed it was crucial, then, that people try to accurately predict and explain the behavior of the person they are communicating with in order to be effective in their communication. Essentially, effective communication is the "process of minimizing understandings" (Griffin, 2006, p. 427).

Combining all the parts together, the basis of the theory is that when someone is communicating with a stranger, they have some level of anxiety and uncertainty, and there are additional outside factors that influence how well they can manage that uncertainty and anxiety. They, then, must remember to always be mindful in their communication, which, in turn, will determine how effective their communication will be. This is the framework for the initial proposal of the anxiety/uncertainty management theory.

Further Developments

Gudykunst continued working on and developing the theory. In 1995, he proposed revisions. The revised model contained 47 axioms, with ten of those explaining effective communication and the other 37 focusing around how to reduce anxiety and uncertainty (Gudykunst, 1995). He also made some changes to the groupings of the superficial factors, reorganizing and splitting them into six groups: 1) self and self-concept; 2) motivation; 3) reactions to strangers; 4) social categorization; 5) situational processes; and 6) connections with strangers.

Nice
transition
paragraph
into further
theoretical
developments.

Perhaps the biggest addition to his revision, though, was when Gudykunst created an extension that took into account cultural variability (Gudykunst, 1995). He claimed that everyone experiences anxiety and uncertainty, but every culture looks at it differently, indicating that the main theory might not apply to every culture. Using Hofstede's four dimensions of cultural variability as a basis for exploring how different cultures might manage their anxiety and uncertainty, Gudykunst (1995) created

(Continued)

one axiom of cultural variability for each axiom of the main theory.

Over the next few years, research was carried out by Gudykunst and his colleagues in which they tested the validity of the theory, and used it as the foundation for their research. Gudykunst and Shapiro (1996) conducted a study in which they used aspects of the theory to look at everyday interpersonal and intergroup communication. Using a diary method known as RICR, developed using tenets of the anxiety/uncertainty management theory, they compared different aspects of students' interactions with people from the same culture and a different culture. Not only was the study important because it provided insight into what affects everyday communication, but results from the study show that when the students were interacting in intracultural encounters, they typically had less anxiety and uncertainty, which supports the theory.

Hubbert et al. (1999) researched how anxiety and uncertainty decrease over time in intergroup interactions. They studied the interactions of people from different cultural and ethnic groups during four interactions, and results showed that in the majority of interactions there was a significant decrease in the levels of anxiety and uncertainty over time. Again, this supports the theory. They also stressed that understanding how uncertainty and anxiety change over time is crucial because intercultural training programs can be developed using the components of the theory, so better understanding will allow for more effective training to be developed.

Lastly, Gudykunst and Nishida (2001) conducted research to test whether or not the theory could be generalized across cultures. Up to this point, research had only focused on using the theory in the US, so they studied the effect of anxiety and uncertainty on effective communication in students in Japan to test the theory cross-culturally. The results of the study suggested that the theory could be effective across cultures.

(Continued)

In 2005, Gudykunst proposed more revisions to the theory. He considered the anxiety/uncertainty management theory to be composed of two interrelated theories; the main theory—the theory of effective interpersonal and intergroup communication—and the theory of intercultural adjustment (Gudykunst 2005a). Changes to the main theory included the addition of ethical interactions to the superficial factors category. Gudykunst (2005a) stressed that ethics were an important issue in communication because if both parties remain ethical, then there is likely to be less anxiety. He also deleted a few of the axioms from the previous models, including those dealing with shame and adapting behavior (Gudykunst, 2005a). Basically, he took out anything that did not directly relate to managing anxiety and uncertainty.

Another substantial revision to the theory was when he realized he did not need an axiom of cultural variability for each of the axioms of the main theory (Gudykunst, 2005a). He concluded that cultural factors are extremely important in predicting anxiety and uncertainty in different cultures and therefore axioms dealing with cultural variability should be included in the main theory (Gudykunst, 2005a).

The new theory Gudykunst (2005b) proposed—the theory of intercultural adjustment—had a very similar foundation to the main theory but took into consideration factors of cultural adjustment. The structure of the model is the same, in that superficial factors are still seen to influence the amount of uncertainty and anxiety one has, and mindfulness can be used to manage that uncertainty and anxiety. The difference, however, is that the outcome is no longer effective communication but intercultural adjustment (Gudykunst, 2005b). Intercultural adjustment is "a process involving feeling comfortable in the host culture, as well as communicating effectively and engaging in socially appropriate behavior with the host nationals" (Gudykunst, 2005b, p. 425).

Gudykunst (2005b) felt it was important to develop a theory that could specifically help sojourners—people that travel to another country for an extended

(Continued)

period of time but do not plan to stay—because their anxiety and uncertainty are often extremely high as they try to adapt to their new environment. Gudykunst (2005b) again stressed the importance of being mindful, and how, by doing so, sojourners could make choices to help reduce their anxiety and uncertainty. For example, he stressed how studying the language of the host culture and learning more about the host culture in general could be extremely helpful in sojourners' adaptation.

Besides just serving as a practical model sojourners could use to help adjust to their new environment, Gudykunst (2005b) thought this version of the theory could be used to create intercultural adjustment training programs. These programs could be used to meet both sojourners long- and short-term adjustment needs (Gudykunst, 1998). Gudykunst (2005b) stated that these training programs were important because they could show sojourners how anxiety and uncertainty influence adaptation, and then help them learn how to manage anxiety and uncertainty.

> This section offered a nice review of studies that have been conducted in AUMM. The review not only reviews different studies but it also used these different studies to explain the different axioms of the theory.

Recent Research

Sadly, the 2005 revisions to the theory were the last made by Gudykunst as he passed away that year. His theory, however, is still widely studied and has been used by many in their research. The following are some examples of studies conducted since 2005 that test the theory and use it as the foundation for their research.

Duronto et al. (2005) used anxiety/uncertainty management theory as a foundation for their research to test whether anxiety and uncertainty lead to avoidance. They found that anxiety and uncertainty are related when the communication is intercultural, but not when the communication is intracultural. They also found anxiety, uncertainty, and avoidance to possibly be cultural issues. For example, they found the Japanese people in their study tended to have anxiety and avoidance in all communication, but only in intercultural communication did they have uncertainty. They concluded from their findings that

(Continued)

anxiety and uncertainty can be predictors of avoidance, and they stressed that the findings are important because if people use avoidance as a means to
cope when their anxiety and/or uncertainty is high,
then effective communication will not happen.

Samochowiec and Florack (2010) used the principles
of the theory to test whether or not the amount
of anxiety and uncertainty an individual has will
affect their willingness to communicate with people
from different cultures. Their findings showed the
more anxiety and uncertainty a person has, the less
likely they are to participate in intercultural
communication. Neuliep (2012) used the theory as a
guideline to test whether apprehension and ethnocentrism could be included as superficial factors in
the theory. The researcher stated that Gudykunst did
not mention these two things in the theory, but he
believed these factors might have an effect on how
much uncertainty one has. Neuliep was also interested in whether an increase in apprehension and
ethnocentrism led to ineffective communication. The
findings showed that apprehension and ethnocentrism
did indeed have an effect on how much uncertainty
one has, and if a person does not learn to manage
apprehension and ethnocentrism, then ineffective
communication would take place.

Last, Florack et al. (2014) used the theory as
inspiration to test whether cross-cultural friendships are influenced by anxiety and confidence. They
found that amongst the immigrants they studied, the
ones that had host national friends had less anxiety and more confidence, and also had more effective
communication. They stated that their findings show
it could be crucial for immigrants to develop host
national friendships from the very beginning to have
less anxiety and more confidence, thus allowing them
to have effective communication.

Criticism

Like most theories, there has been some criticism
of anxiety/uncertainty management theory. Griffin

> The recent research section is a nice and brief review of other studies. It would be nice and an option for Lacey to do a short thematic review where she could summarize the different thematic areas that have been studied recently.

(Continued)

(2006) criticized the complexity of the theory. He believed the number of axioms and possible theorems that could be derived are overwhelming, and that the theory lacks overall simplicity. He also criticized the fact that there really is no way to successfully test mindfulness, and, because of that, he believed you cannot put much confidence into this aspect of the theory since it cannot be proven. Further criticism comes from another scholar in the field, Ting-Toomey. Ting-Toomey's main critique of the theory is that the process of uncertainty reduction is a Western idea, so she feels that the theory does not accurately reflect how effective communication would be achieved when used in intercultural settings (Griffin, 2006).

Conclusion

In conclusion, the anxiety/uncertainty management theory is a detailed theory that was developed and revised over many years. It remains an important theory in intercultural communication, and continues to be used as the foundation for research. Developed to serve as a practical model that people could follow to achieve effective communication, and to have successful intercultural adjustment, the theory states that people can have effective communication in interpersonal and intergroup communication by learning to manage their anxiety and uncertainty. Gudykunst argued that there are superficial factors that influence how much anxiety and uncertainty a person has when they are communicating with a stranger, but by being mindful, one can manage their uncertainty and anxiety and achieve effective communication and intercultural adjustment.

References

Berardo, K., & Deardorff, D. (Eds.). (2012). *Building cultural competence.* Sterling, VA: Stylus Publishing, LLC.

Duronto, P., Nishida, T., & Nakayama, S. (2005). Uncertainty, anxiety, and avoidance in communication with strangers. *International Journal of Intercultural Relations, 29*, 549–560. doi:10.1016/j.ijintrel.2005.08.003.

These are some nice critiques offered by Griffin and Ting-Toomey. However, it is always good to first of all cite the original author and not a secondary source. In this case Lacey cites Griffin instead of Ting-Toomey. Also, Griffin's text was a theory textbook, like this book. It would be nice to find other peer-reviewed critiques of AUMM.

(Continued)

Florack, A., Rohmann, A., Palcu, J., & Mazziotta, A. (2014). How initial cross-group friendships prepare for intercultural communication: The importance of anxiety reduction and self-confidence in communication. *International Journal of Intercultural Relations, 43*, 278–288. doi:10.1016/j.ijintrel.2014.09.004.

Griffin, E. (2006). Anxiety/uncertainty management theory. *A first look at communication theory* (6th ed.). Boston, MA: McGraw-Hill.

Gudykunst, W.B. (1985). A model of uncertainty reduction in intercultural encounters. *Journal of Language and Social Psychology, 4*, 79–98. doi:10.1177/0261927X8500400201.

Gudykunst, W.B. (1988). Uncertainty and anxiety. In Y.Y. Kim & W.B. Gudykunst (Eds.), *Theory in intercultural communication* (pp. 123–156). Newbury Park, CA: Sage.

Gudykunst, W.B. (1993). Toward a theory of effective interpersonal and intergroup communication: An anxiety/uncertainty management (AUM) perspective. In R.L. Wiseman & J. Koester (Eds.), *Intercultural communication competence* (pp. 33–72). Newbury Park, CA: Sage.

Gudykunst, W.B. (1995). Anxiety/uncertainty management (AUM) theory: Current status. In R.L. Wiseman (Eds.). *Intercultural communication theory* (pp. 8–58). Thousand Oaks, CA: Sage

Gudykunst, W.B. (1998). Applying anxiety/uncertainty management (AUM) theory to intercultural adjustment training. *International Journal of Intercultural Relations, 22*, 227–250.

Gudykunst, W.B. (2003). Understanding must precede criticism: A response to Yoshitake's critique of anxiety/uncertainty management theory. *Intercultural Communication Studies XII, 1*, 28–40.

Gudykunst, W.B. (2005a). An anxiety/uncertainty management (AUM) theory of effective communication: Making the mesh of the net finer. In W.B. Gudykunst (Eds.) *Theorizing about Intercultural Communication* (pp. 281–322). Thousand Oaks, CA: Sage.

Gudykunst, W.B. (2005b). An anxiety/uncertainty management (AUM) theory of strangers' intercultural adjustment. In W.B. Gudykunst (Eds.) *Theorizing about intercultural communication* (pp. 419–450). Thousand Oaks, CA: Sage.

Gudykunst, W.B., & Nishida, T. (1984). Individual and cultural influences on uncertainty reduction. *Communication Monographs, 51*, 23–36.

Gudykunst, W.B., & Nishida, T. (2001). Anxiety, uncertainty, and perceived effectiveness of communication across relationships and cultures. *International Journal of Intercultural Relations, 25*, 55–71.

Hammer, M.R., & Wiseman, R.L. (1998). A test of anxiety/uncertainty management theory: The intercultural adaptation context. *Communication Quarterly, 46*, 309–326.

Hubbert, K., Gudykunst, W.B., & Guerrero, S. (1999). Intergroup communication over time. *International Journal of Intercultural Relations, 23*, 13–46.

Miller, K. (2002). Theories of communication in developing relationships. *Communication theories: Perspectives, processes, and contexts.* Boston, MA: McGraw-Hill.

(Continued)

Neuliep, J. (2012). The Relationship among intercultural communication apprehension, ethnocentrism, uncertainty reduction, and communication satisfaction during initial intercultural interaction: An extension of anxiety and
uncertainty management (AUM) theory. *Journal of Intercultural Communication Research*, *41*, 1–16. doi:10.1080/17475759.2011.623239.

Samochowiec, J., & Florack, A. (2010). Intercultural contact under uncertainty:
The impact of predictability and anxiety on the willingness to interact with
a member from an unknown cultural group. *International Journal of Intercultural Relations*, *34*, 507–515. doi:10.1016/j.ijintrel.2010.05.003.

Stephan, W., Stephan, C., & Gudykunst, W. B. (1999). Anxiety in intergroup
relations: a comparison of anxiety/uncertainty management theory and
integrated threat theory. *International Journal of Intercultural Relations*,
23, 613–628.

Yoshitake, M. (2002). Anxiety/uncertainty management (AUM) theory: A critical examination of an intercultural communication theory. *Intercultural
Communication Studies*, *11*, 177–193.

8 SMALL GROUP COMMUNICATION

Chapter Outline

- What is Small Group Communication?
- Structuration Theory
- Functional Approach
- Groupthink
- Symbolic Convergence Theory
- Student Paper

All of us are part of small groups. Many of these groups we belong to are personally focused (e.g., family, friends, religious, other social groups), while some are more task focused (e.g., work, other professional), and many of these groups emphasize both personal and task focuses. Some of us gravitate toward small groups and some of us dislike small groups. Communication within small groups can be rewarding and complicated for a variety of reasons. Just think about any group you are a part of and you can most certainly remember a time when there have been communication breakdowns, miscommunication, and/or innovations and supportive communication. *Small group communication* is the study of how these groups function and the various kinds of communication and roles people play in groups.

In this chapter we will explore small group communication—or the study of how groups function—and the various kinds of communication and roles/tasks people have in groups. The theories and concepts, like those in many other chapters, vary considerably. Many of the issues discussed in this chapter come from a more theoretical perspective, while others come from a practical perspective. Moreover, the issues range from the social scientific to the critical/cultural approach. In the first section we will define small group communication and discuss the different components of groups and the various kinds of small groups. In the second section we will describe structuration theory, which views groups as systems that produce structures and are produced by structures. In the third section we will explain the functional approach to small groups, which is concerned with the outcomes or results of communication in groups. In the fourth section we will outline groupthink, a functional approach theory detailing the process of, and result of, conformity in groups. Within this discussion of groupthink a case study about the Penn State University sex-abuse scandal is provided to further illustrate the applicability of small group theory. In the fifth section of this chapter we will discuss symbolic convergence theory, which is the study of the sensemaking function of communication. In the sixth and final section you will find a student paper. This paper is a small group communication student paper by Emmi Jelekäinen focusing on groupthink, which is included to serve as an example of the kind of writing assignment you *could* do for a small group communication theory assignment.

What is Small Group Communication?

Research on how groups communicate has been conducted for decades, since the 1920s, in fact, beginning with the work of Sigmund Freud. Group research has explored various aspects of how groups develop, function, handle conflict, how members construct identity within groups, the links between groups, decision-making within groups, the temporal aspect of groups, how groups evolve, and how groups terminate (Arrow, McGrath, & Berdahl, 2000; Bennis & Shepard, 1975; Boehm, 2000; Bormann, 1996; Putnam & Stohl, 1996; Thibaut & Kelly, 1959). This line of research has shown that we are all part of small groups. Think about what you did in the past week. How many of you spent time with two other people trying to accomplish a "task"? This "task" may have ranged from working on a project with colleagues at school or work (three or more people), playing a sport with three or more people, eating dinner with a family and discussing the events of the day (three or more people at dinner), or countless other activities that involve three or more people who share a common goal/purpose. **Small group communication** is the study of when three or more people come together to work interdependently to complete a task. This task can be a relational or personal task, such as uniting a family, planning a wedding, cooking a meal, etc. The task can also be a professional task, such as studying for an exam, completing a blueprint for work, writing a budget, etc.

KEY TERM 8.1

Small group communication – study of when three or more people come together to work interdependently to complete a task.

Being a part of a small group has advantages and disadvantages. There are two major advantages of being in a small group: access to resources and diversity of opinions. When more people are involved in working together on a task, more resources come together, such as time, expertise, information, money, etc. Moreover, when a group works on a task you are more likely to have diverse opinions on the task, which could lead to more creative solutions. Along with the advantages of working in a group there are disadvantages. There are three major disadvantages: poor coordination, too much socializing, and conflict. As the size of a group increases there is a higher likelihood that communication and coordination between the members will break down.

Second, when people get together in a group there is a chance that they will focus more on socializing than the task in front of them. This can lead to group task-stagnation, and inevitably cause the group not to complete a task efficiently. Finally, conflict is inevitable in groups. Whenever people get together relationally or professionally, conflict is likely to develop. Often members of groups may feel as though their contributions are not valued, or interpersonal problems will develop in groups. However, as long as conflict is properly managed, conflict will not damage a group's progress.

There are a few components that make up a small group. First, small groups have between three and fifteen people; the ideal number is between five and seven (Cragan & Wright, 1999). When a group is too big it is hard to have effective communication among the members; when a group is just two people we have dyadic or interpersonal communication. Second, in order for a group to be a group, the members must be united by a common goal/purpose. The members of the group come together to do something as a group; this is the common goal/purpose: the task. The **task** is an activity whose completion depends on the activity of the group. Steiner (1972) identified two kinds of tasks: additive and conjunctive. An **additive task** is where group members work individually on parts of a task and when they have completed their individual tasks they join their individual work together to complete the joint task. A **conjunctive task** is when group members coordinate their efforts. So instead of working individually on individual tasks, members work together on all tasks to complete the overall task. Third, members of a group need to recognize that they are part of the group and feel as though they belong. The notion of inclusion is important because a small group needs its members to have a level of inclusion for the group to function more efficiently. Fourth, groups have **interdependence**, meaning that the actions of one member affect the other. A group is a system of interconnected members, ideas, and processes.

Consider the following example to explain interdependence. Your boss has asked your Public Relations team to prepare a campaign for a new client. One of your associates gets sick the night before the presentation and this associate is the one most familiar with the client's history of crisis management. As the rest of the team relied on this associate's knowledge about the client's crisis management the whole team will be in a lot of trouble during the meeting, and will probably lose the account because they relied too much on this now ill associate. Interdependence reveals how the actions of one member affect the whole group.

KEY TERM 8.2

Task – an activity whose completion depends on the activity of the group.

WHAT DO YOU THINK 8.1 AND 8.2

What is small group communication?

How do additive and conjunctive tasks differ? Which do you prefer?

There are various types/kinds of small groups. Eisenberg and Wynn (2003) identified seven kinds of small groups. Figure 8.1 lists the groups and the key characteristics of each group. An eighth kind of group is added to this list—a virtual team. With the rapid growth of the Internet, social networking, virtual offices, and online communities, this group was included. When considering these groups please keep in mind that some groups overlap and these categories are not mutually exclusive.

KIND OF SMALL GROUP	GROUP CHARACTERISTICS
1. Primary Group	Members in an intimate relationship. Membership based on sentiment. Ex: family or close friends.
2. Social Group	Members share a common interest or participate in activities that bring them together. Ex: fraternities/sororities, sports teams, debate teams.
3. Self-help Group	Members all have a common "problem" or life "issue." Once the "problem" or "issue" is believed to be resolved many members will leave the group. Ex: Alcoholics Anonymous.
4. Learning Group	The goal of this type of group is to improve members' cognitive abilities, skills, or other processes. Ex: Study groups, language training groups, yoga classes.
5. Service Group	Volunteers who give their time and energy to help others. Ex: Big Brothers Big Sisters, United Way, other smaller volunteer groups on campus or in communities.
6. Public Group	A group where the members interact with one another to benefit an audience. Ex: panel discussion, symposium, forum.
7. Work Group	A group that exists in a work or organizational context to fulfill a work-related task. Ex, advisory, budget, negotiation, military, etc.
8. Virtual Team/Group	A team/group that does not exist in a physical space but exists only online. This kind of group develops online. While many of the same processes of the other groups may exist, interdependence among members will differ because of the medium of communication. Ex: World of Warcraft, an online class, a chat forum.

Figure 8.1 Kinds of Small Groups

WHAT DO YOU THINK 8.3

What kinds of small groups do you belong to?

Structuration Theory

All in all, there are various kinds of small groups and, while they share many similar traits, they differ in many ways as well. What all of the groups have in common is that each of them is a system. Each of these unique systems produces structures and is produced by structures. Essentially, members of these groups follow group norms/rules and patterns in the group interactions that create outcomes, which affect the group's future internal and external interaction (communication). This is the essence of **structuration theory**. This theory has been widely used in various fields of study, including communication, accounting (Englund, Gerdin, & Burns, 2011), information technology (Jones & Karsten, 2008), organizational studies/discourse, and management.

Giddens, the father of structuration theory (1984) defined structures as guidelines for acting that have a set of rules and norms that members recall to generate action. Poole, Siebold, and McPhee (1996) similarly defined structures in small groups as the rules (statements about how things are done) and resources (knowledge, materials, and skills) that members generate or take from other group members/processes to create and keep the group system functioning. A system in a group is a set of practices comprised by the structuring behaviors of members.

The concept of structuration rests on two key arguments. First, structures are **dualities**; this means that structures are both the medium and the outcome of action. They are the medium of action in that members of groups draw on structures to interact in the group. They are also outcomes in that rules and resources exist only because they are used in practice. For example, when a board votes on a budget, the board is following protocols for voting on a budget, which entails reminding members that protocols/rules exist. In such a structure it is typical for a majority of members to review a budget or any kind of initiative before it can be approved; the idea of majority rule is a typical structure in many societies, organizations, and groups.

KEY TERM 8.3

Dualities – structures are both the medium and the outcome of action.

The second key argument for structuration is that various factors influence structuration (Arrow, Henry, Poole, Wheelan, & Moreland, 2005). Group characteristics such as the members in the group, the group history, etc. will influence how the group functions. The situation, or the reason for the group/its task also influences the group's structure.

Structuration Theory Research

Structuration theory has been studied in a variety of theoretical contexts/settings. A great deal of research has examined the relationship between structuration and working life situations/issues (e.g., Golden, 2013; Hoffman & Cowan, 2010; Kirby & Krone, 2002). Hoffman and Cowan (2010) for example explored the rules and resources that employees employ while trying to balance work and life. Group discourse has also been extensively studied in relation to structuration theory (e.g., Heracleous, 2013; Kirby & Krone, 2002; Poole, 2013). Kirby and Krone (2002) studied the discursive responses that individuals have in the workplace to individuals using work-family benefits, such as time-off to raise or tend to a family. In the study, the structure of the discourses about these practices and people's responses to the practices were analyzed to show the various perspectives on the issue.

Structuration theory has shown great promise in its ability to explain action in organizations, to describe how structures and discourses emerge in groups, and to explain group/institutional practices, norms, and procedures (Giddens, 1984; McPhee, 2004). In the next section we will discuss the outcome/result of communication in groups, which is the functional approach to small groups.

WHAT DO YOU THINK 8.4

Think about a group you are a part of. How does that group create structures (what are they?) and at the same time how is that group created by those same or similar structures?

Functional Approach

The **functional approach** to small groups emphasizes outcomes or results of group behaviors and/or structures (Hirokawa, 1982, 1985). Groups use communication to make decisions and achieve their objectives. From this perspective, researchers focus on identifying and describing effective communication within groups that help them to achieve the best outcomes or results. Four arguments make up the functional approach to groups: 1) groups have a goal orientation; 2) the behavior and performance of groups varies and can be measured; 3) communicative interactions have utility and can be controlled; and 4) various factors (internal and external) affect group performance.

All groups have goals or tasks to complete. These goals can be relationally/personally or professionally oriented. From the functional approach, researchers explore the effective completion of these goals/tasks. This line of research asks questions, such as how able is the group to effectively complete its goals/tasks? (e.g., Hirokawa & Rost, 1992; Orlitzky & Hirokawa, 2001).

Each group behaves and performs differently and the behaviors and performance of these tasks can be measured. Essentially, group behavior and performance is measured via some criterion. The criterion can be many things; such as how well a group achieves a goal, or how effectively its members perform a task. When a group performs adequately its members (internal and external) generally remain pleased with the group. However, when the group does not meet the established criterion the group members may become disenfranchised and intervene in group decision-making processes.

Communicative interactions and processes have usefulness and can be controlled within groups during decision-making processes. Some of these interactions/processes are more useful than others though to help groups reach their goals. When a task is more relational, many of the interactions/processes will involve relational development and maintenance, which facilitates better group performance. When a task is more professionally oriented, many of the interactions/processes will be task oriented; such as trying to make rational decisions. From the functionalist approach, researchers suggest a variety of steps to help to make sure that the communication in groups helps them to achieve their goals: procedures and rules, norms, and/or communication technologies.

Internal factors (members of the group, its size, its location, and other factors within the group), as well as external factors (external actors, pressure from the outside, time to complete task, other external forces) all influence how a group performs. The various factors interact with one another. When more time or performance pressure is put on a group to complete a professional task (a paper for school for example) by a deadline, the group members may get anxious or nervous about their performance. In such a situation some members may not perform to their best ability, while others may rise to the occasion. Think about some of the small groups you have been a part of and you will surely know how some members rise to pressure and others crumble under pressure to complete a job. The pressure can come from within or from outside the group and is an example of one kind of pressure affecting group performance.

WHAT DO YOU THINK 8.5

Have you ever thought you were part of a group that did not function well? Why do you think it did not function well? What about a group that did function well? What made that group function well compared to a group that did not?

Functional Approach Research

The goal of research within the functional approach is to understand how groups best "function." A variety of different theoretical areas have been proposed to examine functionality in small groups. Three key functional theories/constructs are: effective group decision-making, collective information sharing, and groupthink. The first two are briefly reviewed here while groupthink is discussed at greater length in the fourth section that follows.

Effective group decision-making analyzes the processes that make some groups effective and other groups ineffective in making decisions. Communication patterns within effective versus ineffective groups differ (Hirokawa, 1980; Hirokawa & Rost, 1992; Oetzel, 1998). Hirokawa (1980) asserted that effective groups spend more time interacting and agreeing on procedures. Hirokawa and Pace (1983) explained how effective group decisions are made when small groups: 1) examine multiple opinions; 2) evaluate alternative outcomes; 3) understand the nature of the premises that serve as the basis for group decisions; and 4) understand the influence of influential members in the group. Similarly, Salazar, Hirokawa, Propp, Julian, and Leatham (1994) emphasized the importance of open communication and high-task-oriented discussions focused on the issue at hand to facilitate heightened group performance and potential. This line of research reveals that communication, especially open communication, is essential for groups to effectively make decisions.

One line of research that has grown out of effective group decision-making is the relationship between decision-making and culture. This line of research has collectively shown that cultural differences, particularly individualism/collectivism and self-construal of group members, influences the effectiveness of a group (Oetzel, 1998, 2001; Oetzel & Bolton-Oetzel, 1997). Group members with a more interdependent self-construal (a "we" or group focus) have a higher tendency to participate or cooperate in groups than individuals with a higher independent self-construal (a "me" or individual focus) (Oetzel, 1998, 2001).

Collective information sharing goes back to the work of Stasser and Titus (1985). Members of groups discuss more shared information as opposed to unshared with one another to facilitate decision-making. However, failure to share unshared or private information can lead to poor decision-making because individuals do not have all of the information they need to make an informed decision. Various factors predict whether group members will share private information or not in a group: 1) commitment to the group; 2) thoughts about whether or not the information will lead to organization gain; and 3) perceived value of the information (Kalman, Monge, Fulk, & Heino, 2002). Linking information sharing to technology, research has shown that group behavior and technological competence is positively related to group members using intranets within organizations. These intranets—internal communication networks—provide shared and unshared information about organizational/group issues (Yuan, Fulk, Shumate, Monge, Bryant, & Matsaganis, 2005).

WHAT DO YOU THINK 8.6

In the group decisions you have been a part of why have you decided not to share needed information when making decisions?

Groupthink

A third theory from the function approach is groupthink. **Groupthink,** based on the work of Irving Janis (1972, 1982, 1985) is when a group strives for unanimity, or agreement, over all other things. Janis (1982) defined a group in groupthink as one where "loyalty requires each member to avoid raising controversial issues" (p. 12). This phenomenon has been found to happen in a variety of groups and is largely accepted by researchers (Baron, 2005; Mitchell & Eckstein, 2009). Janis (1982) described antecedent conditions that lead to concurrence seeking or groupthink, which lead to observable consequences. These observable consequences equate to a low probability of a successful group outcome. There are three kinds of antecedent conditions: group cohesion, structural faults in the organization (group insulation, lack of impartial leadership, strong group norms, and group member homogeneity), and situational factors (stress from external threats and low self-esteem from failures, such as difficulties or moral dilemmas).

KEY TERM 8.4

Groupthink – when a group strives for unanimity, or agreement, over all other things.

Janis (1982) identified eight symptoms of groupthink, which are observable consequences. These are outlined in Figure 8.2.

It is often hard for a group suffering from groupthink to realize they are in such a state, as it can be hard for a group and its members to reflect

1) Illusion of invulnerability – Members of the group think they can do no wrong
2) Belief in the group's inherent morality – Members of the group think their decisions are moral
3) Collective rationalization – Members of the group become a "we" and think together
4) Stereotyping of out-groups – Members of the group stereotype people who are not in the group as "outsiders" and possibly less qualified or not as good, since they are not in the group
5) Self-censorship – Members of the group prevent themselves from voicing opinions that may run counter to the group
6) Illusion of unanimity – The group believes that members of the group are in agreement on issues, when they may or may not be
7) Direct pressure on dissenters – Overt pressure is put on members to not voice opposition and to agree with the group
8) Self-appointed mind guards – Members protect the group and the leader from opposing viewpoints

Figure 8.2 Symptoms of Groupthink

1. All members of a group should be critical evaluators of the group's course of action.
2. The leader should encourage an open climate of criticism.
3. Leaders should be impartial and not state personal preferences at the start of group discussion.
4. Set up multiple groups with different leaders to address the issue from various perspectives
5. Divide the groups into subgroups to evaluate effectiveness of proposals.
6. All group members should privately discuss issues and options with trusted peers outside the group and report the reactions.
7. Occasionally, bring in outside experts to challenge the opinions of the members.
8. There should be a devil's advocate during every meeting.
9. In conflicts, time should be spent interpreting the signals from rivals and creating solutions and alternatives.
10. Reconsider decisions in follow-up meetings before going public.

Figure 8.3 Remedies for Groupthink

on themselves (self-reflection is difficult). The identification of groupthink typically only occurs after a problem in the group/organization, in which the group must respond in some way. Along with these symptoms of groupthink, Janis (1982) prescribed various methods a group can take to remedy itself if they are in a state of groupthink. Figure 8.3 shows some remedies for groupthink.

Groupthink Research

While these remedies are straightforward, it is still difficult to solve a groupthink situation once a group falls into one. The severity of group-think can be seen by looking at the different settings in which groupthink has been explored. Numerous researchers have explored groupthink in a variety of small groups and found this phenomenon to have influenced various group decisions. Research exploring NASA (the National Aeronautics and Space Administration) has shown how the agency was in a state of groupthink leading up to and during the Challenger (1986) and the Columbia (2003) space shuttle disasters (Dimitroff, Schmidt, & Bond, 2005; Esser & Lindoedfer, 1989; Maier, 2002; Moorhead, Ference, & Neck, 1991). Groupthink researchers have also explored the phenomenon in historical contexts: the Bay of Pigs and Vietnam (Kramer, 1998), France's 1940 World War II defeat (Ahlstrom & Wang, 2009), and the Iran hostage crisis (Smith, 1984).

Groupthink and the Penn State University Child-Sex Scandal

In November of 2011, Jerry Sandusky, a then assistant football coach at Penn State University, was arrested and charged with multiple counts of sex crimes against young boys. In October 2012 he was sentenced to a minimum of 30 years and a maximum of 60 years in prison. The investigation into the crimes was far reaching, with a report by the former FBI director Louis Freeh detailing an immense cover-up by the university. Reports showed the administration, including former Penn State head football coach, Joe Paterno, were "complicit in concealing Sandusky's activities from the Board of Trustees, the University community and authorities."

There were numerous reactions to these crimes, and the administration's complicit behavior. When head coach Joe Paterno was ousted (forced to retire), an estimated 10,000-plus students and non-students protested in support of Paterno. Many members of the university community did not respond favorably to the Freeh report, as they saw it as biased against Penn State. Many members of the university administration and the Board of Trustees resigned. The National Collegiate Athletic Association (NCAA) also levied numerous sanctions against the university's athletic program in response to reports of the program lacking a healthy culture. Finally, numerous lawsuits have been filed by Sandusky's victims, which may cost the university more than $60 million.

After these abuses became public, a major question was on many people's minds: how could this have happened? Six of the symptoms of groupthink were clearly present in this scandal. Self-censorship, direct pressure on dissenters, and self-appointed mindguards were all factors related to a key incident that happened in 2002. In 2002 Sandusky was caught by one of the team's graduate assistants (Mike McQueary), in a shower room on the Penn State campus, while he was in the act of molesting a young boy. McQueary did not stop or report the incident to police. McQueary did however report the incident to the head coach, Paterno, who also did not call the police. Paterno did notify the Athletic Director (Tim Curley), who also did not call the police, but did notify the university President (Graham Spanier). The university President notified no one. The mother of the boy did report the incident to the police. However, the police later stated no report had ever been filed, an example of mindguarding.

Beliefs in the group's inherent morality, collective rationalization, and illusion of unanimity were factors related to the negotiation of Sandusky's retirement package in 2009. Many of the same individuals who knew about the 2002 incident in the shower (Paterno, Curley, and Spanier) helped to negotiate Sandusky's retirement package. As part of his retirement package, Sandusky requested full access to the

Penn State locker rooms and showers. Knowing what happened in 2002, the group knowingly put more young boys in danger, as many used the locker rooms and showers for athletic camps. This group consciously put people in harm's way. Collectively, the athletic program and the university showed with the Sandusky case that they were a dysfunctional group and in a state of groupthink.

WHAT DO YOU THINK 8.7

Many small group case studies have been conducted on NASA and the groupthink phenomenon within the organization, and this state attributed to the Challenger and Columbia disasters. Get into small groups and think about other historical examples where groups and leaders may have been in groupthink? What are those possible examples? Why do you think groupthink was involved? What were the symptoms? What were the effects? How could you remedy the group if you could talk to them now?

Symbolic Convergence Theory

Groups consist of verbal and nonverbal messages that members try to make sense of, or understand. These messages are symbols, and the coming together to understand the symbols is when members converge toward a common understanding/meaning. Hence, **symbolic convergence theory** (SCT) is the study of how groups come together to achieve a common understanding of shared communication (verbal and nonverbal) within groups.

KEY TERM 8.5

Symbolic convergence theory – the study of how groups come together to achieve a common understanding of shared communication (verbal and nonverbal) within groups.

An important part of SCT is that groups form and share fantasies, which act as integral parts in forming the group's collective identity. **Fantasies** are stories that help group members to interpret past events, norms, or rules in the group. Fantasy themes (Bormann, 1996) develop when members dramatize or embellish on the fantasies. These fantasies and fantasy themes are important to the development of a group's culture. Such fantasies and themes often help to unify the group around norms and rules of the group. For example, think about a group you may be a part of and how you have more than likely been told a story about a past member who broke from group norms and was punished for it.

> **KEY TERM 8.6**
>
> **Fantasies** – stories that help group members interpret past events, norms, or rules in the group.

When the author of this book was on a speech team he and fellow freshmen were all told about how a former competitor on the team forgot their speech in the middle of a competition. The person walked out of the room and went to another room and picked up a desk and threw it against the wall. She then returned to the original room and asked to start over. The judge let her and she delivered a flawless speech, and won the round. Every time they heard this story the act of throwing the desk got more violent, from throwing it against the wall to against the window, to out of the window, etc. The moral of the story was to never give up; look what happened to Student X . . . she messed up, let off some steam, and won. Whenever the story was told the older members all embellished the story as they passed it on to the younger members. As Stephen and his peers became veterans on the team, they passed on this story. In Stephen's senior year this competitor became a national champion; the fantasy grew to help newer members learn about and become part of the team.

There are various strengths and weaknesses to SCT as a theory. As for strengths: 1) SCT offers a productive way to describe how group and organizational members interact because through the telling of fantasies we can explore cultures within groups and organizations (Keyton, 1999); 2) SCT explains how groups develop a common identity or consciousness, which further elaborates on group/organizational identity and culture; and 3) SCT can help to explain how social movements endure because this theory describes how members take ownership of different aspects of a movement through actions and fantasies (stories) (Underation, 2012). Regarding potential weaknesses (Frey & Sunwolf, 2005): 1) some scholars criticize SCT for being too descriptive and not predictive enough; 2) while fantasies may take on a collective meaning, we cannot assume all members of a group understand these fantasies in the same way; 3) we should not assume that all group members have equality in influencing the fantasy themes, and 4) some researchers see SCT focusing too much on a fully conscious, autonomous subject or population, and not an unconscious, imaginary, collective (Gunn, 2003).

Symbolic Convergence Theory Research

Researchers of SCT have covered diverse areas of study, from academia, the media, prison culture, and corporate culture (Cragan & Shields, 1992). In academia, researchers have used SCT to examine the reasons why individuals choose a master's degree program (Stone, 2002), and to understand collective bargaining among teachers (Putnam, Van Hoeven, & Bullis, 1991). In SCT studies of the media, researchers have for example noted that media depictions of politicians have a significant rhetorical impact on how the public perceive politicians. For example, Benoit, Klyukovski, McHale, and Airne (2001) showed how the coverage of the scandals surrounding former US President Bill Clinton (Monica Lewinski and the Kenneth Starr investigation) led to the creation of various metaphors and interpretations of the fantasies about Clinton and these scandals. In her analysis of a prison newspaper, Novek (2005) showed how prisoners create collective visions (fantasy themes) of spirituality, compassion, and humor to endure their time while incarcerated.

All in all, the shared fantasies among group members help members form a group identity and become a part of the collective group. The themes are typically congruent or representative of the established visions and histories of the groups (Bormann, 1982). While some have challenged SCT, it has been applied by many researchers in different practical and theoretical settings.

WHAT DO YOU THINK 8.8

Can you think of any fantasies you have been told in the groups you are a part of? How have these fantasies helped you to identify with the group?

Chapter Summary

We are all part of numerous small groups. Countless processes interact when three or more people come together to complete a task in these groups. These interactions are fundamental to what we call small group communication. The five sections of this chapter offer a glimpse into "small group communication." The first section defined small group communication and outlined the different components of groups and the kinds of small groups. The second section described structuration theory. The third section explained the functional approach to small groups. The fourth section outlined groupthink, a functional approach theory detailing conformity in groups. The fifth section discussed symbolic convergence theory (SCT). The concepts in this chapter provide a variety of opportunities for further inquiry. Moreover, these concepts also explain group practices, which is helpful in understanding and improving how groups function. The final section of this chapter includes a student paper from the University of Jyväskylä in Finland by Emmi Jelekäinen. This paper focuses on groupthink and is included to show you one way you can write about/research small group communication.

Key Terms

Additive task

Conjunctive task

Effective group decision-making

Functional approach

Collective information sharing

Dualities

Fantasies

Groupthink

Interdependence
Structuration theory
Task

Small group communication
Symbolic convergence theory

Activities

1. Thinking back to the Penn State sexual abuse scandal case study in this chapter, brainstorm ways in which the university could have groupthink.
2. In a group, write down any fantasies you know about your university. Choose one of those fantasies that is important to your university and try to research how the fantasy started, and research the facts behind the fantasy.

Student Paper

The following paper is from a Communication Theory Class at the University of Jyväskylä. Stephen Croucher taught the class. This is the assignment for the paper:

Term Paper (200 points) – KVVS 100 – Communication Theory
Your final paper must be:

1) Written in APA Style (6th Edition)
2) It must be 5–10 pages in length not including the references and the title page. The paper does not need an abstract.
3) You can work with a partner on this paper if you would like, or you can work alone.
4) You must have your theory approved by the instructor within the first two class sessions.
5) The purpose of this review of literature is to "review" a theory. This means many things. You can review the development of a theory, you can review how scholars have studied a theory, you can topically review a theory, chronologically review a theory, etc. . . . There are many ways to approach a review of literature. Options for this assignment will be discussed on the first day of class.

```
Groupthink

Emmi Jelekäinen
University of Jyväslylä

People have worked in different kinds of groups
throughout history, and still nowadays the impor-
tance of group-working skills is highlighted in
many fields of life. In many ways this world is run
by groups. Small-group communication is one of the
```

(Continued)

central themes in the field of communication, and in this field many researchers are interested in group decision-making (Littlejohn, 2002). When groups work well, they may create a pleasant group environment for every member to bring in their own ideas and for the group to come up with creative solutions. However, the decision-making process in groups is not always easy and there are several matters that could impact the results. As Janis stated "[g]roups bring out the worst as well as the best in terms of decision-making" (as cited in Paultz & Forrer, 2013, p. 1). Some groups have a tendency to seek painless unanimity to smooth the decision-making process and this can easily destroy the creativity of the group and lead to bad decisions (Hart, 1991). In this literature review I will summarize groupthink, look at the fields it is applied to, and also explore the different views about its validity.

The "groupthink" theory was coined by Janis in 1972 (Paultz & Forrer, 2013). According to Janis, groupthink means an excessive form of concurrence-seeking among the members of the group (as cited in Hart, 1991). Janis describes the term groupthink as "a mode of thinking that people engage in when they are deeply involved in a cohesive in-group, when the members' strivings for unanimity override their motivation to realistically appraise alternative courses of action" (as cited in Hartley, 1997, p. 148). So, normally groupthink occurs when the cohesiveness of the group is high and the membership of the group is even more important than the individual values. In this case people may easily agree with matters they usually would not endorse (Johnson & Weaver, 1992).

Janis identified eight symptoms of groupthink: invulnerability, rationalization, morality, stereotyping, pressure, self-censorship, unanimity, and mindguards. When these symptoms, or some of them, occur in a group, the group may be more prone to negative forms of groupthink. For instance, when the group has an invulnerable and powerful image of themselves, they may become overly confident and optimistic, and thus are prone to making risky decisions (Lunenburg, 2010).

The author does a nice job here of defining what the paper is going to be about in the introduction. The introduction also offers a nice preview statement for the paper.

The author has provided a nice definition of groupthink very early on in the paper, which is good as it makes it easy for the reader to know how the author perceives groupthink.

In the above paragraph the author said: "Janis identified" but does not provide a reference. It would be helpful to know what Janis reference the author is referring to. Aside from this, it is nice to see the symptoms referenced again, as they are in the chapter you just read.

(Continued)

Hartley (1997) mentioned in his book, *Group communication*, some common features of groups with groupthink tendencies. First, when the information does not move well enough between the leader and the members, the group has a potential for groupthink. Second, if the leader is too strict and not open to other perspectives, the performance of the group cannot be very good. Last, very formal communication within the group and the lack of open disagreements can make the group prone to groupthink. According to these features, it would be extremely important for the group leader to make sure that information flow between the participants is kept open and debate is encouraged (Hartley, 1997).

Janis based a lot of his theory on many decision-making "fiascoes," primarily in the fields of politics and military situations on occasions such as the Bay of Pigs and the Pearl Harbor attack, but the theory has also been applied to group communication in many other situations as well, for example, classroom communication. Johnson and Weaver (1992) considered the classroom a potential contributor to the groupthink phenomenon. This is why they encouraged teachers to expand their teaching methods to stay fresh and to avoid groupthink in their classroom. They presented four suggestions for teachers to encourage independent thought and to avoid groupthink. These four suggestions recommend adding conflict management skills, decision-making skills, small group communication skills, and critical-thinking skills to the curriculum.

According to Johnson and Weaver (1992) many of the conditions that predispose groupthink are often commonplace in classrooms and most importantly most of them are seen as positive elements of a successful class, which means that classrooms may have a high tendency for the unwanted form of groupthink. For instance, for many teachers a high level of cohesiveness in the classroom is an important goal and this cohesion is of course valuable for educators, but it can also predispose the class to groupthink. Also, the directive role of the teacher may interfere with the decision-making process in the class.

Once again, in the above paragraph the author said: "Janis identified" but does not provide a reference. It would be helpful to know what Janis reference the author is referring to. Not referring to an exact year when referencing can lead to confusion.

(Continued)

Teachers often have a strong influence on the children's lives and opinions because in many situations they are the most powerful adults in children's lives after their parents. The stressful conditions can lead the group to groupthink as well. The groupthink groups and classrooms both often work under a high level of stress, which again implies another connection between these two groups.

Groupthink can also be found in business and other organizations. Fitzsimmons, Miska and Stahl (2011) argued that multicultural employees can have a positive influence on teams' effectiveness, for example, by acting as bridges across cultural fault lines and safeguarding groups against groupthink. This approach introduces an idea of bringing in "a fresh mind" to a group prone to groupthink. In this case the "fresh mind" are the multicultural employees. Fitzsimmons et al. (2011) claimed that because of their multiple cultural perspectives, multicultural groups have more new ideas and unconventional solutions. So, by using multicultural groups instead of monocultural ones, we could get more creative and active solutions.

Although some research has supported Janis' theory about groupthink, it is still not well known why some groups create this behavior and other groups do not (Johnson & Weaver, 1992). There is also some research that criticizes Janis' theory. One example of this is Whyte (2001) who reconsidered Janis' groupthink theory. He argued whether is it possible or not to recognize any patterns like this in decisions, such as the decision to invade Cuba at the Bay of Pigs or the Watergate cover-up, or whether they are simply difficult decisions that went wrong. He found some gaps in the groupthink theory and thus he argued that we cannot explain bad and risky decisions by groupthink. According to Janis one of the main topics of groupthink is concurrence-seeking (as cited in Hart, 1991) but Whyte (2001) claimed that it occurs generally in group decision-making, not only in poorly performing groups. Another gap Whyte (2001) pointed out is that groupthink theory does not take into account some of the current research

This is a nice review of the Johnson and Weaver (1992) study and how groupthink was applied to this setting.

(Continued)

If you look back at the chapter you just read you will also find a discussion of the strengths and weaknesses/critiques of groupthink. Do you see any similarities with what the author here (Emmi) says and the chapter?

about group dynamics, such as group polarization. Groupthink may be a relevant but also an incomplete pattern for explaining these decision fiascoes, and thus is in need of testing and further research (Whyte, 2001). Also, Rose (2011) showed that there is plenty of research for but also against this theory by combining a great number of studies and their results.

Although the groupthink model divides people's opinions and its empirical support is quite limited, it is still used in an even broader variety of applications, such as hockey teams, juries, and cultural groups (Rose, 2011). Several researchers have proposed different variants of the groupthink model to understand group problem solving better. One of these proposals is "the general group problem-solving model" (GGPS), by Aldag and Fuller (1993), in which they argued for a more modern and broader framework for group problem solving. It has used Janis' model as a base but has recast it (Aldag & Fuller, 1993).

However, groupthink is not always bad and it does not always happen. It does not necessarily lead to bad decisions and it is true that not all bad decisions are a result of groupthink (Griffin, 2009). Some "fiascoes" can simply be due to human errors. Some researchers have found some positive attributes of groupthink, which include properties such as improved reasoning and the ability to correct errors, uncover presuppositions, and recognize new ideas (Paultz & Forrer, 2013). In particular, the group cohesiveness is often seen more as a positive than negative attribute. Meyers (2010) found in her study that a cohesive group motivated the students to work together in a positive manner, so groupthink showed some signs of improving the groups' performances. There has even been some research that has found more positive groupthink examples that negative ones (Rose, 2011).

There have been several suggestions on how to avoid negative groupthink. Research has suggested actions such as nondirective group leaders, diversity of group members, encouragement of criticism,

The previous two paragraphs nicely show the author's grasp of groupthink. In these paragraphs the author shows she knows the debate about the theory and how researchers have debated various sides of this group state of mind.

(Continued)

and using several groups working on the same problem (Solomon, 2006). In addition to these actions, assigning the roles for group members can be helpful in preventing groupthink (Meyers, 2010).

In conclusion, there have been several suggestions as to what causes groupthink and how it could be avoided. The groupthink model has been applied to a large variety of research involving group work and decision-making. However, it has faced some critique, and the advantages and disadvantages of it need some further research and clarification (Paultz & Forrer, 2013). Still, in spite of the critique, groupthink seems to be widely used in research on group decision-making and problem solving.

References

Fitzsimmons, S. R., Miska, C., & Stahl, G. K. (2011). Multicultural employees: Global business' untapped resource. *Organizational Dynamics, 40*, 199–206. http://dx.doi.org/10.1016/j.orgdyn.2011.04.007.

Griffin, E. (2009). *A first look at communication theory*. Boston: McGraw-Hill.

Hart, P. (1991). Irving L. Janis' victims of groupthink. *Political Psychology, 12*, 247–278. Retrieved from http://www.jstor.org/stable/3791464.

Hartley, P. (1997). *Group communication*. London: Routledge.

Johnson, S. D., & Weaver, R. L. (1992). Groupthink and the classroom: Changing familiar patterns to encourage critical thought. *Journal of Instructional Psychology, 19*, 99–106. Retrieved from http://connection.ebscohost.com/c/articles/9607180018/groupthink-classroom-changing-familiar-patterns-encourage-critical-thought.

Littlejohn, S. W. (2002). *Theories of human communication*. Albuquerque, NM: Wadsworth Group.

Lunenburg, F. C. (2010). Group decision making: The potential for groupthink. *International Journal of Management, Business and Administration, 13*, 1–6. Retrieved from www.nationalforum.com/Electronic%20Journal%20Volumes/Lunenburg,%20Fred%20C.%20Group%20Decision%20Making%20IJMBA%20V13%20N1%202010.pdf.

Meyers, E. M. (2010). Mediating group search: Lessons from a middle school study. *Teacher Librarian, 38*, 24–26, 28–29. Retrieved from http://search.proquest.com/docview/846786573?accountid=11774.

Paultz, J. A., & Forrer, D. A. (2013). The dynamics of groupthink: The Cape Coral experience. *Journal of International Energy Policy, 2*, 1–14. Retrieved from www.professorforrer.com/Research_Data/Papers/%282013%29-TheDynamicsofGroupthink-TheCapeCoralExperience.pdf.

Rose, J. D. (2011). Diverse perspectives on the groupthink theory. *Emerging leadership Journeys, 4*, 37–57. Retrieved from www.regent.edu/acad/global/publications/elj/vol4iss1/Rose_V4I1_pp37-57.pdf.

(Continued)

Solomon, M. (2006). Groupthink versus the wisdom of crowds: The social epistemology of deliberation and dissent. *The Southern Journal of Philosophy*, 44, 28–42. Retrieved from http://onlinelibrary.wiley.com/doi/10.1111/j.2041–6962.2006.tb00028.x/abstract.

Whyte, G. (2001). Groupthink reconsidered. *Academy of Management Review*, 14, 40–56. Retrieved from www.owlnet.rice.edu/~ajv2/courses/12c_psyc438001/Whyte%20%281989%29.pdf.

9   HEALTH COMMUNICATION

Every day millions of people around the world go to their medical provider (e.g., doctor, dentist, etc.) and many of them feel stressed, not from their physical or mental pain but from the frustration they have from communicating with their providers. How many of you have ever not understood what was happening around you, not had your questions answered, felt ignored, etc. Communication in healthcare is of paramount importance. Increasingly, communication researchers, and medical practitioners too, are recognizing this and taking steps to understand and also improve the communication that takes place in health contexts. This is one of the many facets of what makes up *health communication*. This chapter addresses not only this part of health communication, but also other parts of this field of communication.

In this chapter we will explore health communication, or the influence of communication on our health. The theories and concepts in this chapter vary a great deal in terms of their theoretical approaches and outcomes. This is a result of the theoretical and practical nature of health communication as a field of study and practice. Each of the concepts/theories discussed however, focuses on ways to better understand the influence of health on communication, and on ways to promote health. In the first section we will define health communication and discuss the place of theory within health communication. In the second section we will examine research on patient–provider interactions. In the third section we will discuss research on how we will seek out information about our health, with a focus on the comprehensive model of information seeking (CMIS). Within this discussion of CMIS a case study about the Ebola outbreak of 2014 is provided to further illustrate the applicability of the CMIS. In the fourth section we will explore the relationship between our understanding of health-related issues and how we will behave regarding these issues. In this section we will introduce the theory of planned behavior and the health belief model. In the fifth and final section you will find a student paper. This paper is an undergraduate health communication student paper by Pierre Noble about race and organ donation, which is included to serve as an example of the kind of writing assignment you *could* do for health communication theories/models.

What is Health Communication and Where Does Theory Fit?

One thing you have probably noticed after reading through the first eight chapters of this book is that communication is a multidisciplinary field. **Health communication** as a field of inquiry draws on various communication and non-communication disciplines to study the influence of communication on health and also on healthcare delivery. Health communication as a field is a vibrant and growing field of communication; this has not always been the case. Before 1980, little research on what is considered health communication was published by communication researchers (Cassata, 1977; Costello, 1977). However, in the late 1970s and the early 1980s, communication researchers began to study health-related issues more, and by 1984, 105 of the 325 health and social service related articles were from communication journals or conferences (Thompson, 1984). What happened? Research funds were increasingly available for research on health-related issues and there were publication outlets for health communication pieces, like *Health Communication* in 1989 and the *Journal of Health Communication* in 1996. Health communication as a field has grown rapidly within communication, and in other fields.

KEY TERM 9.1

Health communication – a field of inquiry drawing on various communication and non-communication disciplines to study the influence of communication on health and also on healthcare delivery.

If you think back to Chapters 2–4 on the different approaches to theory, you should remember that researchers approach theory from a wide array of paradigms/approaches. Health communication researchers are no different. In addition to the varied paradigms influencing how researchers approach research, four others issues are of particular importance to health communication researchers. The first is that health communication theory and research is useless unless it has a practical influence on promoting healthy practices and preventing illness (Babrow & Mattson, 2003; Craig, 1989). For many health communication researchers, theory should not only be scholarly, but also practical. The second is that researchers should carefully consider the relationship between their theoretical postulations or arguments and reality. While a study may argue one thing in theory, theorizing that people should do something in practice could lead to poor health decisions. Thus, researchers should be careful, as theories are not always used for good health behaviors. The third is axiology, or the study of values, which is important when evaluating the usefulness of health communication theories. When a researcher deems a theory "useful" or "practical," they have made a value statement, and this value statement must be acknowledged (Babrow & Mattson, 2003). The fourth is that theories should be approachable for health practitioners. This is why many theories are broken down and simplified into what are called models. Theories and models are both helpful for health practitioners to plan, implement, and evaluate health messages, strategies, and interventions (Trifiletti, Gielen, Sleet, & Hopkins, 2005). However, a **model** is a simplified version of a theory, which includes key elements of a theory that helps explain health behaviors, which in turn further helps practitioners to shape the health decision-making process and puts theoretical ideas/explanations into practice. You will often find in the health communication literature numerous references to models and theories working hand-in-hand to guide discussions, research, and policy about health.

The following three sections of the chapter review some of the research that has/is taking place in health communication. Each of these sections is merely a snapshot of the depth of health communication research. If you are interested in knowing more about any of these areas of study, look to some of the provided references, the online references, or talk to your instructor for more details.

WHAT DO YOU THINK 9.1

Why would someone use a model over a theory?

Patient–Provider Interactions

Research into the interactions and relationships between providers and patients has focused on various aspects of these intricate interactions and relationships. A shared theme of studies over the past three decades is that interpersonal communication has a profound effect on the patient–provider interaction, as effective interpersonal communication is essential for "satisfactory" health care delivery (Bohnert, Zivin, Welsh, & Kilbourne, 2011; Cegala & Lenzmeier Broz, 2003; Scholl & Ragan, 2003). Three areas that have received a particularly high amount of attention are: patient and provider skills/competence; interaction outcomes; and disclosure in the interactions.

The current healthcare environment emphasizes patient-centered care (Bergman & Connaughton, 2013). In this environment increasing attention is being devoted to training health providers to better communicate with patients. Effective communication between patients and providers is essential to meeting the needs of patients in healthcare settings and providing quality healthcare (Lipkin, 2010). Without effective communication between all parties involved, the outcomes can be very bad. When patients and providers do not communicate, patients are less likely to trust providers, listen to the provider, and a provider is less likely to listen to a patient. In turn, patients' health will not improve because patients are less likely to follow the providers' advice, which leads to higher healthcare costs, among other things. Considering the significance of communication in patient–provider interactions, more and more medical/health programs are offering communication-related courses to teach health providers to better "communicate" with patients. Aside from these kinds of standardized programs, similar to the communication courses you may have taken, other instructional strategies are often used.

WHAT DO YOU THINK 9.2

Have you ever had a difficult communication interaction with a healthcare provider? If so think about what happened, what was the effect(s), and what could the provider(s) or you have done to have improved it?

Cegala and Lenzmeier Broz (2003), in their review of provider skills training research from 1990 to 2003, found various kinds of skills training were used for providers. In their work they asserted that training ranges from instructional videos, readings, work-rotations, lectures, and other hands-on approaches to "teaching" providers effective communication. All in all, the authors argued that effective communication skills could be taught to health care providers. Recently, researchers have used different methods to teach communication competence, empathy, and other skills to providers, including the use of theater and social media/email (Koponen, Pyörälä, & Isotalus, 2010; Nijland, van Gemert-Pijnen, Boer, Steehouder, & Seydel, 2008).

WHAT DO YOU THINK 9.3

Why is communication training needed for health care providers?

Information Seeking and Health

The patient–provider interaction is not, *or* it should not, be a one-way interaction. Thus, along with teaching providers how to communicate effectively, attention is being given to educating the public (patients) on how to be more active, informed, and/or communicative patients. The focus of health communication researchers has been primarily on information seeking. With the growth of the Internet and prescription advertising, information seeking about medical conditions has exponentially increased. Patients seek out numerous kinds of information: information about illnesses, prescriptions, or about providers, for example (Deshpande, Menon, Perri, & Zinkhan, 2003; Dutta-Bergman, 2005; Guo, 2001). Information can decrease and increase illness anxiety. Numerous models have been proposed to explain how people seek out health-related information. A variety of health-information-seeking models have been proposed, each with its own subtle differences from the other. For example, the health information acquisition model describes the process people go through when they access, use, and evaluate health-related information (Freimuth, Stein, & Kean, 1989). A model that introduces our perception of risk(s) and how these perceptions influence information use and cognitive processing is the risk information seeking and processing model (Griffin, Dunwoody, & Neuwirth, 1999). Other models include the model of patient information seeking (Czaja, Manfredi, & Price, 2003), information adequacy and uncertainty reduction (Sheer & Cline, 1995), and the theory of motivated information management (Afifi & Weiner, 2004), to name a few. A model that has received considerable attention in relation to patient-information seeking about prescription drugs is the comprehensive model of information seeking (CMIS).

Comprehensive Model of Information Seeking (CMIS)

The **CMIS** explains antecedents that affect information seeking and explores how information source characteristics may affect seeking behaviors (Johnson, 1997; Johnson & Meischke, 1993). This model combines three other theoretical perspectives: the model of media exposure and appraisal (Johnson, 1983), uses and gratifications (discussed in Chapter 8) (Blumer & Katz, 1974), and the health belief model (Rosenstock, 1974) (discussed later in this chapter). The basic assumptions of CMIS are based in those of uses and gratifications, in that: 1) people are active information seekers and initiate source choice; 2) information source use is purpose directed; 3) people select a variety of sources to satisfy a variety of needs; and 4) sources satisfy informational needs while other sources compete against those sources to satisfy this need for people (Rubin, 1986).

KEY TERM 9.2

Comprehensive model of information seeking (CMIS) – a model that explains antecedents that affect information seeking and explores how information source characteristics may affect seeking behaviors.

The CMIS also emphasizes four health-related factors and two information-carrier-related factors. The health-related factors focus on the individual and their perception and use of health information sources, which in turn determine the effectiveness of a source at providing health information: demographics, direct exposure to the health situation, salience, and beliefs to manage the health situation. The information-carrier factors include the characteristics and utility of the information. Combined, health-related and information-carrier factors predict information-seeking behaviors of individuals in health-care situations (DeLorme, Huh, & Reid, 2011; Johnson & Meischke, 1993). All in all, the CMIS states that a person's health-information-seeking behaviors are guided largely by the perceived usefulness of sources, which is determined by things like demographics, exposure to the illness, etc. (Johnson & Meischke, 1993).

The CMIS has been tested in numerous contexts. First, it was tested among cancer patients and their use of magazines (Johnson & Meischke, 1993). In this preliminary work it was found that source factors like the characteristics of the source and the usefulness of the source explained more exposure to information from the sources than the health-oriented variables (demographics, exposure, salience, and beliefs). For most cancer patients, CMIS studies have shown that sources with authority, like physicians, are typically the most respected and sought after (Johnson, 2003). DeLorme et al. (2011) found that, when it comes to prescription drug information, individuals are more likely to seek out information about prescriptions from the Internet, pharmacists, and doctors. The diversity of information-seeking sources shows how consumers, regardless of demographics, seek out information from a variety of sources that they find "useful." The CMIS has numerous theoretical and practical applications. This model is used to gain a theoretical understanding of how people seek out information about different kinds of health-related issues. Such information could help medical providers and advertisers to better reach individuals about health-related issues. Explaining health issues is not always an easy task. DeLorme, Huh, and Reid (2007), in their analysis of seniors' perceptions of prescription drugs, discussed the imperative of providing accurate information about medical issues to seniors. One important aspect of this process is to first understand how seniors access information. In their study they found many seniors are more likely to trust medical professionals (doctors and pharmacists) or friends when it comes to health issues. Such research shows the practical applications of the CMIS and other similar models that help to explain how patients seek out information about their health care. This growing body of research is significant in understanding how information is shared and how patients and providers interact.

Ebola Outbreak of 2014

In March 2014 an epidemic of the Ebola virus was detected in Guinea, Liberia, Nigeria, and Sierra Leone. As of August 6, 2014 the World Health Organization had reported 961 confirmed deaths from the illness. Numerous international aid workers were working in the region to contain the virus and treat those either infected or suspected of being infected with the deadly virus. Dr. Mohammed Ag Ayoy, a UNICEF representative in Guinea said:

> There is no specific treatment for Ebola, which is spread by contact with the bodily fluids of infected people or animals. Therefore, prevention is one of the best ways to contain the virus. Access to timely and accurate life-saving information is hence absolutely crucial. This is where UNICEF is focusing its efforts moving forward (UNICEF, Communication for Development, 2014).

However, UNICEF and other aid workers recognize that, for many in Africa, the information on their website will not reach those who need it on the ground. While many young Africans have access to the Internet, they are not accustomed to using it to seek out health-related information (Dionne, 2014). In most cases, it is still common to trust local traditions, customs, family members, and in some situations political figures for health/medical information. Thus, understanding who many West Africans trust or who they get their health/medical information from is a key factor for international health organizations in containing and responding to the Ebola outbreak.

WHAT DO YOU THINK 9.4 AND 9.5

Have you ever sought out information on your own about your health care? Has a family member or friend of yours done this? If so, how have they done it? Why did you or they choose this particular medium?

What do you think is the most "credible" medium for getting medical information?

Cognition, Behavior, and Health

A considerable body of research in health communication has been devoted to studying how people perceive their health, how their behavior affects their health, and what people believe regarding their health. This literature focuses largely on how to create health messages to stimulate or motivate change in an individual's perceptions, behaviors, or beliefs (Ajzen, 1991; Janz & Becker, 1984; Rosenstock, 1974; Witte, 1992). The notion that health-related messages can be designed to stimulate changes in an individual's behavior guides both the theory of reasoned action (revised to the theory of planned behavior) and the health belief model.

Theory of Planned Behavior

The **theory of planned behavior** (TPB) is a modified version of the theory of reasoned action (TRA) (Ajzen & Fishbein, 1980). The TRA proposed that any persuasive intervention, like a health message, attempting to alter behaviors must focus on an individual's beliefs. Beliefs directly affect our attitudes and expectations. When we believe something to be true we have an attitude about that thing/issue and those beliefs affect our expectations of our behaviors, or of what has or what will happen. Moreover, these attitudes and expectations influence our intentions and behaviors. If we do not think we are susceptible (attitude) to HIV/AIDS, and we do not expect to ever get the disease (expectation), we do not intend (intention) to use protection during sex (behavior).

KEY TERM 9.3

Theory of planned behavior – a theory proposing that any persuasive intervention attempting to alter behaviors must focus on an individual's beliefs.

In a revision to TRA, to create TPB, Ajzen (1991) added the element of perceived behavioral control. Intent to act/perform is based on three factors in TPB:

1) Attitude toward the behavior – a cost–benefit analysis is done regarding the behavioral choice
2) Subjective (societal) norms – pressure is felt regarding the behavior, for example from family, peers, media, etc.
3) Perceived behavioral control – the perception the person has about their ability to do the behavior and his/her control over the behavior

In explaining these elements of perceived behavioral control, consider this: the more positive a person is toward the behavior, the more socially acceptable the behavior is, and the more ability or control over the behavior the person has . . . the more likely that person will perform the behavior. Figure 9.1 shows the theory of planned behavior.

TPB research has been conducted in a variety of contexts, and not all health-communication related. An examination of recently published literature outside of health communication shows that TPB has been applied to the study of risky credit behaviors among college students (Xiao, Tang, Serido, & Shim, 2011), to understand preferences for "animal-friendly" foods (Nocella, Boecker, Hubbard, & Scarpa, 2012), and to understand why people choose one web browser over the other (Rivera-Sánchez, & Lin, 2012). When it comes to research on TPB and health behaviors, research is plentiful. There are far too many areas of research to review in a chapter of this length and for

Attitude Toward
The Behavior
+
Subjective/Societal Norms + Behavioral Intentions + More Likely to
+ Perform the Behavior
Perceived Behavioral Control

Figure 9.1 The Theory of Planned Behavior

a chapter in this level of textbook. To show the depth of TPB and health communication research, three contexts will be detailed: organ donation, obesity, and smoking cessation.

In a study among American, Korean, and Japanese college students, Bresnahan et al. (2007) found perceived behavioral control significantly predicted Japanese willingness and intent to register as organ donors, but not Korean. In all three nations spirituality was found to be a significant factor in whether or not a person registered to be an organ donor. One interesting finding was that most Koreans declined to be organ donors. Thus, the authors recommended more research to address this lack of registration. In another study on organ donation, focusing specifically on cornea donation, Bae and Kang (2008) found that issue involvement, or relevance of the issue to potential donors, is a key factor that needs to be included. One way to increase issue involvement is through educational entertainment programs. Thus, when trying to persuade people to donate corneas or other organs, the issue must be made relevant to the potential donors.

As obesity, particularly childhood obesity, has become an international health crisis, more and more research has begun to explore ways in which to combat this growing crisis (Kitzmann & Beech, 2006). Andrews, Silk, and Eneli (2010) addressed this issue as they focused on how parents can better promote healthy eating habits among children. In their study they asked parents to respond to questions related to how they encourage or limit healthy and unhealthy eating habits of their children. Ultimately, the authors argued that healthy food and diet campaigns should target parents as they are the first ones who can help fight the growing obesity pandemic. Parents do respond to appeals for better eating, but the appeals need to be well-crafted, especially since parents' BMI predicted children's BMI.

Another major global health concern is cigarette smoking. In 2000, more than 60 percent of college students in the US admitted to smoking at least once (Rigotti, Lee, & Wechsler, 2000). While one cigarette is not a major health risk (although I am not encouraging you to smoke here), the cumulative effects of cigarette smoking and second-hand smoking are in the billions each year (Centers for Disease Control and Prevention, 2008). Thus, health practitioners and governments are regularly reaching out to try to prevent people from starting to smoke, and to try to get smokers to stop smoking. Brann and Sutton (2009), in a study of college student smoking behavior found two interesting results. First, peer pressure to smoke or not did not have a major effect on behavioral intentions. The students expressed a belief that they made their own decisions about smoking, irrelevant of peers. Second, smoking is perceived as a different kind of health risk than another relevant risk to college students—drinking. Drinking is seen as a much more pressing risk because the chances of getting hurt or dying from say drunk driving or alcohol poisoning are in the present (could more likely happen in the near future), unlike a smoking-related illness, which students perceive as being more long-term illnesses. In another study of TPB and smoking behavior, Lee, Ebesu Hubbard, Kulp O'Riordan, and Kim (2006) linked the TPB to self-construal; see the chapter on intercultural communication for a reminder of self-construal. In this study they found perceived behavioral control and subjective (societal) norms were related to an individual's intent to quit smoking, which supports the TPB model. Furthermore, the study showed that interdependent self-construals positively predicted socially expected ways of behaving; basically more interdependent people behaved in socially acceptable ways regarding smoking. Independent self-construal positively predicted self-efficacy in relation to behavior; in essence more independent people thought they had more control over their behaviors (Lee et al., 2006).

WHAT DO YOU THINK 9.6

Matthew has been approached by a fellow student at a party. The other student has offered him ecstasy. The other student says the ecstasy will make him feel great and forget about the fact that Matthew's girlfriend just broke up with him. Matthew has been brought up being told that drugs are bad and he should not use them. He also comes from a religious family and is close to graduating from his university with a perfect grade point average. Using the TPB, do you think Matthew will take the ecstasy? Why or why not?

Knowing how people process information can help health organizations, companies, and governments to better tailor health-oriented messages with the aim of changing/affecting health behaviors. This line of research has immense practical implications. Without knowing how to properly stimulate change and motivate individuals, it is extremely difficult to change their behaviors. In a similar vein, research into health beliefs has shown that messages must be carefully designed to effectively address various aspects of beliefs. If health messages are not carefully designed, the messages may likely fail. A model that has been proposed to study how to affect health beliefs, which in turn could lead to behavioral change, is the health belief model.

Health Belief Model

The **health belief model** (HMB) is a way to describe and prescribe how preventative health behaviors are a function of both efficacy of the recommended response (perceived benefits and barriers) and readiness to act (perceived seriousness and susceptibility) (Janz & Becker, 1984; Rosenstock, 1974a). Depending on the disease, health situation, services being offered, and the person, a variety of factors (demographic, psychological, communicative, etc.) have been shown to affect preventative health behavior step taking. The HBM contains five factors that affect preventative behaviors (Janz & Becker, 1984; Rosenstock, 1974a):

1) Perceived susceptibility – the belief a person has about whether it is possible or not for them to be affected by the health issue (disease, illness, etc.).
2) Perceived seriousness – this is the belief about how serious the health issue could be.
3) Perceived benefits – what are the possible benefits or not of doing the recommended behavior(s) (feeling/getting better, living longer, a healthier life, etc.).
4) Perceived barriers – what are the possible barriers preventing the person from doing the recommended behavior(s) (time, cost, pain, inconvenience, etc.).
5) Cues to action – what triggered the person to think about the behavior (physician, dentist, advertisement, other media, etc.).

KEY TERM 9.4

Health belief model – a model that describes and prescribes how preventative health behaviors are a function of both efficacy of the recommended response and readiness to act.

The HBM, and its factors, has been applied in numerous health contexts. It has been shown to be helpful in explaining exercise behavior (Sorenson, 1997; Taggart & Connor, 1995). Its use is to enable an increase in understanding dietary behaviors (Chew, Palmer, & Kim, 1998; Schafer, Keith, & Schafer, 1995). It is being used regularly to understand smoking, alcohol, drug, and steroid use (Beisecker, 1991; Minugh, Rice, & Young, 1998; Quick, 2010). A considerable amount of HMB work has focused on cues to action and disease prevention (cancer and HIV/AIDS). For example, in an analysis of the influence of communication on colorectal cancer (CRC) screening, Yoo, Kwon, and Pfeiffer (2013) found that the factors of the HBM are consistent, which means that perceived CRC threat is positively related to going in for a stool blood test, and having positive expectations for a CRC screening were positively related to going in for a stool blood test. However, the study showed that the communication channel through which people learn about and testing did not affect an individual's willingness to go for a CRC screening. There are numerous practical implications of this study: future communication messages about CRC and screening need to better outline the risks of CRC and the benefits of screening; health providers need to be more educated about which communication channels will best reach people; and more work should be done to promote CRC and screening.

Researchers have also applied the HBM to a controversial issue for many: the human papillomavirus (HPV) vaccine (Briones, Nan, Madden, & Waks, 2012; Staggers, Brann, & Maki, 2012). Briones et al. (2012) explored 172 YouTube videos related to the HPV vaccine to better understand media coverage of the vaccine. Their content analysis revealed that most of the videos discussed how the vaccine was ineffective, even though medically the vaccine has been shown to be effective. Moreover, more than 50 percent of the videos indicated serious health risks associated with the vaccine, even though this has been shown to be false as well. The videos increased individuals' perceptions of the seriousness of HPV, even if doing so with misinformation (Briones et al., 2012). On the same token, the clips provided cues to action: do not get the vaccine or allow the women in your lives to get the vaccine. On a practical level, this study offers a glimpse into the rhetoric doctors and medical providers must face when encouraging patients to get the vaccine.

 WHAT DO YOU THINK 9.7

Dorothy has been smoking for 35 years. Six months ago her sister Lucy died from lung cancer. Lucy smoked three packs of cigarettes a day. Dorothy smokes three packs of cigarettes a day as well and just saw a poster with a smoking cigarette in it and an X through it. She also regularly sees the warnings on her cigarette packages about how smoking kills. Using the HBM, do you think she will quit smoking? What factors will influence this behavioral choice?

Chapter Summary

Ultimately, the study of how people behave, understand, and perceive their health behaviors has theoretical and practical implications. The four sections of this chapter merely scratched the surface of the myriad ways in which health communication is studied and used today. The first section provided a working definition of health communication as a concept and as a field of study. The second section explored theoretical and practical areas of study on patient–provider interactions. The relationship between patient and provider is an important relationship, and one that health communication researchers and practitioners continue to seek to break down barriers and improve. The third section described the relationship between information seeking and health. People are constantly seeking out information about their health. One model offered in this chapter to explain this process was the comprehensive model of information seeking (CMIS) (Johnson, 1997; Johnson & Meischke, 1993). The fourth section discussed how cognition, behavior, and health relate one another. Specifically, the theory of planned behavior (TPB) (Ajzen, 1991) and the health belief model (Janz & Becker, 1984; Rosenstock, 1974a) were offered as ways to understand how people understand and behave regarding their health.

For communication researchers these theories and models open up many avenues of study into health, interpersonal, organizational, intercultural, and other communication-related fields. On a practical level, this understanding offers health providers a wealth of information and ways to promote healthy behaviors/actions. The final section of this chapter includes an undergraduate student paper from the University of Georgia by Pierre Noebes. In this paper, Pierre reviews literature related to organ donation. This paper, like with the other chapters, is included to show you one way you can write about/research health communication.

Key Terms

Comprehensive model of information seeking	Health belief model
Health communication	Model
Theory of planned behavior	

Activities

1. Conduct a self-analysis of where and how you receive information about health-related information/issues? What outlets do you use the most and why?
2. Choose a preventative health campaign and analyze the factors that affect the likelihood of enacting the preventative behaviors.

Student Paper

The following paper is from a Health Communication Class at the University of Georgia. Tina Harris taught the class.

Term Paper (XXX points) – XXX Health Communication

Race and Organ Donation: A Literature Review

Pierre Noebes
University of Georgia

Abstract

Currently there is an incredible gap between the number of patients waiting for life saving organ transplants and the number of registered organ donors. Promoting the practice of organ donation is a crucial step in ensuring there will always be newly registered donors. Unfortunately, though, even with promotional strategies already in place, the demand for organs still far exceeds the supply and thousands of Americans die every year while waiting for an organ that will never come. This is due at least in part by the fact that very few members of communities of color ever register to be organ donors. With such a large part of the population either fearful or mistrusting of the medical community, or simply lacking the knowledge to understand what organ donation is, steps need to be taken to properly inform every individual about the practice of organ donation. Ignoring this section of the population will not make the problem we are currently facing any better, and unless something is done about the way organ donation is promoted in communities of color the number of minority donors may continue to fall. While this may seem like an almost impossible task, I am hopeful that through continued research a solution to this problem can and will be found.

An all too common trend found in the literature that focuses specifically on organ donation is that, to put it quite simply, there are not enough transplantable organs to go around. With our current life expectancy higher than it has ever been before, and projected to only move higher, more and more individuals are left to face illnesses and organ failures woefully unprepared. We must not blame modern medicine for their advancements in medical technology, though, for medical professionals have been working to solve this problem since the dawn of

While this is a well-written abstract in many ways, Pierre could have done more to explain what he is going to do in the paper. The abstract reads a little bit more like an introduction and a bit less like an abstract. However, it does introduce the topic, which is a requirement of a "good" abstract.

(Continued)

organ transplantation. Instead one must focus their attention to the underlying problem, the incredibly underwhelming number of registered organ donors around the world. Unlocking, or at least understanding, the reason why so few individuals decide to become organ donors would provide academics and medical professionals alike the opportunity to create a communication strategy that would hopefully close the gap between the nearly 111,000 patients awaiting a transplant and the fewer than 15,000 living and deceased donors (Klein et al., 2010). Even more troubling than these numbers is the discrepancy between the supply and demand of transplantable organs in communities of color. It is within these communities that the demand for organs is even higher than the national average, and the supply is proportionally much lower.

For many, tackling this problem first will not only provide communities of color with much needed relief, but will also provide valuable insight into how to best approach this global epidemic. It is for this reason that continued research must be done to discover a better way to promote the practice of organ donation, especially in communities of color. However, before one can approach this problem one must first understand the practice of organ donation as a whole and how it is currently promoted to the general population. Then one must understand the current techniques being used to promote organ donation in communities of color and why they are not working, along with the research currently being done in this area of study. From here one will then be prepared to understand the need for continued research into race and organ donation.

With the first successful organ transplant in 1954, the practice of organ transplantation and donation has made incredible strides in its 60 years of existence. For nearly ten years donors were only available in the form of direct relatives, as the practice had not matured enough to expand outside of familial ties. However, the early 1960s saw the first successful deceased donor transplantation, helping to deepen the pool of potential organ donors (Organ

The introduction is really well written. In the introduction Pierre clearly states the purpose of his paper, which is to explore organ donation, specifically in the context of communities of color. He also outlines some of the concerns/ problems currently regarding organ donation; this gives his topic significance. Finally, the introduction previews the paper for the reader. Preview statements are a really nice way to frame the paper and tell the reader what to expect in the paper.

(Continued)

Transplant History, 2013). With these steps forward, medical professionals were now able to provide patients with at least the potential of renewed life after suffering a life-threatening illnesses. As time went on, greater advancements in organ transplantation continued to be made as living donors from outside of one's family became available to patients suffering from organ failure. Along with medical advancements, legislative progress was being made as well. From the early 1980s until today laws have been passed that provide greater protection to both donor and recipient, as well as allowing surgeons greater access to organs and drugs that help to ensure successful transplants. However, a successful transplant is only one half of the equation.

Playing just as large of a role in the whole process is the organ donor, the person who makes the conscious choice to become either a living or deceased donor. A living donor is someone who is alive and healthy enough to donate an organ to someone in need, while a deceased donor is anyone who agrees to have all of his or her vital organs donated and used for transplantation. Living donors are most commonly related to or have a close relationship with the person in need of a transplant, for organs such as a kidney, or a small piece of lung or liver. These transplants, however, only make up a small portion of all the organ transplant operations done, as there are a much larger number of patients who lack direct access to transplantable organs from family or friends. In addition to this, there are also a number of hurdles that both donors and doctors must clear before the actual donation of organs takes place. A process that becomes even more complex and sensitive when the donor has recently been declared deceased, in which case a medical professional must gain consent from an immediate family member before any of the organs can be harvested for transplant use. Before any of this can take place, though, is the most crucial step in the entire process, actually getting people to register as organ donors. Without any new donors the disparity between the supply and demand of organs would grow to no

(Continued)

end, leaving even more patients with no hope of ever receiving their lifesaving organ. Currently, though, there are a number of steps being taken to ensure that this does not happen.

Convincing individuals to consciously and willingly accept that they may be called upon to donate a piece of their body is one of the most difficult tasks faced by the medical community. Promoting organ donation and registering new donors is an extremely difficult, but necessary, challenge that must be completed in order to ensure the wellbeing of generations to come. Currently, the medical community is experimenting with several different ways to promote organ donation and register new donors. Of all the techniques being used to promote this practice and attract new donors some of the most common are educational campaigns, opt-out systems, and incentive programs (Kline, 2010). Some of these techniques have been met with great success, for example in Spain the use of an opt-out system, in which consent is presumed, has helped to meet the needs of nearly 85 percent of all patients awaiting a transplant. Incentive programs have also been found to be a great success in that they reward those who register and donate with money, or with privileges such as being able to receive organ transplants themselves, as is the case in Austria. However, while these programs and techniques may have found success around the world their implementation into the United States would probably end in failure as individuals would more than likely feel as if their personal rights were being infringed upon. This has forced medical professionals in the US to focus on the promotion of registering to become an organ donor through different mass media outlets. Traditionally, the medical community would create campaigns tailored for traditional mass media, such as television, or rely on interpersonal communication efforts in order to promote registration and donation drives. The growth of the Internet within the last ten to fifteen years, though, has provided an additional avenue to be explored as a promotional tool, especially with the incredible popularity of social media websites

This is a nice historical review of the development of organ donations. As Pierre is focusing on organ donations it is necessary for him to provide some kind of historical review.

(Continued)

that allow organizations to reach millions of people for a fraction of the traditional cost. With nearly 80 percent of all adults using the Internet, a number that jumps to 95 percent when looking at 18–29 year olds, it has quickly become one of the most important communication tools ever created (Stefanone et al., 2012). For organizations and causes that need extremely large numbers of people in order to reach their goals, the Internet has proven to be an almost perfect way of raising awareness and getting individuals interested in some of the issues we are facing. Stefanone et al. (2012) explored the use of the Internet as a campaign tool, with a specific focus on how social media can and is being used as a way to promote organ donation to college-aged individuals. Through the use of three different campaign forms—traditional, student seeder, and challenge campaigns—Stefanone and his team were able to explore and evaluate the effectiveness of promoting organ donation through online social media outlets. By measuring the number of unique users accessing their online content and which users later requested a donor registration card, the team was able to calculate which method was the most effective. This three-year study left over 30 million impressions and lead to nearly 9,000 clicks on the different ads used throughout the project, resulting in 671 requests for organ donor cards and 196 completed/ returned. Unfortunately, while the ads used were able to reach an incredibly large number of people, this study found that online media campaigns did little in terms of effectiveness and impact on the audience. This result means that, for the purposes of encouraging and actually getting individuals to register as organ donors, the use of an online media campaign may not be the way to go. However, one must not be quick to rule out all contemporary media outlets as they provide new avenues of exploration and possible success in promoting the practice of organ donation.

   As the popularity and accessibility of devices like the iPod, iPhone, and others continues to grow so too does the opportunity to use them as tools for

Do you think Pierre will integrate research from a theoretical model like the CMIS, TPB, or HBM to help explain the "influence" of media on an individual's willingness to donate an organ in the United States?

(Continued)

promoting organ donation. For example, a study by Thornton et al. (2012) explored just how effective the use of iPods could be in promoting the practice of organ donation. By conducting their experiment throughout twelve branches of the Ohio Bureau of Motor Vehicles (BMV) Thornton and his team were able to randomly assign nearly 1,000 individuals, ranging in age from 15 to 66 years old, to either watch a five minute video addressing organ donation or proceed through the BMV as normal. This study was focused specifically on understanding the impact and effectiveness of showing a brief video about organ donation to individuals just before they received their driver's license or identification card. The research team hypothesized that an individual is more like to register as an organ donor if they are exposed to information addressing potential barriers to registering just before they receive a license or identification card. By immediately following up with the participants of this study the researchers were able to determine if their video had had any impact at all on the attitudes of individuals toward registering as an organ donor. What they found was that of the 443 participants who watched the video 84 percent of them registered to be organ donors, compared to the 72 percent of those in the control group who registered as organ donors. This study shows that by providing individuals with information that addresses their potential concerns and educates them about organ donation they feel better prepared and are more willing to register as organ donors. While a 12 percent increase in registration may not seem like much, it means that many more people have taken the all-important step toward helping reduce the gap between the number of transplant patients and the number of transplantable organs available. Thornton et al.'s study did not stop here, though; included in the investigation were questions to ascertain whether or not people would be willing to become a living donor for a close friend or family member. Here again those individuals who were a part of the experimental group were more willing to act as a living donor for a loved one than those who were a

(Continued)

part of the control group. Of the reasons given as to why individuals decided they would act as living donor, those in the experimental group cited the knowledge they gained about organ donation from the video. From here the researchers were able to find that by showing a video, which provided individuals with information relevant to their concerns about organ donation, they were able to increase the number of people willing to register as organ donors. Informational and educational efforts such as this have been found to create an increase in the number of those registering to be organ donors around the world. However, promoting organ donation through educational means it not a cure all and is not without its pitfalls.

In a 2010 study, Coppen et al. studied the impact of educational campaigns on the Dutch attitudes toward organ donation. Having recognized that nearly every nation in the world is facing a large shortage of transplantable organs, Coppen et al. wanted to not only understand traditional campaigns, but also what impact, if any, new strategies or campaigns had on the promotion of organ donation. With the Dutch system of organ donation, much like the one use here in the US, requiring explicit consent, maintaining positive attitudes towards organ donation is crucial. In order to conduct this study Coppen et al. first reviewed the contents of the national policy on donor education; it was through this that they were able to distinguish between the direct and indirect effects of the education campaigns. The direct effects were those directly attributed to policy measures, such as the size and scope of the educational campaign. The indirect effects, on the other hand, were those that measured the success of the campaign like the number of newly registered donors, and the final procurement of organs. This study's importance cannot be understated, in that after only a year of enacting the Organ Donation Act the Dutch medical community saw a dramatic decrease in the number of registered organ donors. Knowing that attitude plays an incredibly important role in determining whether or not an individual is

There are lots of ways to apply the models from this chapter to what Pierre discussed above.

(Continued)

likely to register as an organ donor, Coppen et al. began investigating what the Dutch government was doing to promote and educate individuals about organ donation and what impact these promotional strategies had had.

Initially, the government used more traditional means of advertising the need for transplantable organs, such as print and television ads, but these were met with limited success. The Dutch government decided to take a dramatic and controversial step forward, and created a reality-donation show called "The Big Donor Show" in which several patients in need of a kidney were interviewed by a terminal patient who then selected one person to give their kidney to. Almost immediately the show was an incredible success, and while it did draw in a significant amount of criticism it was able to get the public actively engaging in a discussion about organ donation. Beyond this, the show was also able to show just how much of a lottery it is to get an organ transplant, making many individuals rethink their apathy towards organ donor registration. By sending out donor registration cards through the mail, Coppen et al. were able to determine what impact the promotional and educational campaigns had had on the Dutch citizenry. The study concluded that while the television show did raise awareness about the organ donation issue, it was not the driving factor for most people to actually become donors. Instead it was the government's explicit support of organ donation and the educational campaigns that convinced a significantly larger proportion of people to become organ donors. Here, again, we see that education plays a crucial role in promoting organ donation. However, while the previously mentioned strategies have worked for most people generally, they have had little success in promoting organ donation among communities of color, an issue that more and more researchers are facing when studying promotional strategies for organ donation.

This paragraph discussed some great examples of cues to action, from the HBM.

As the number of patients on organ transplant waiting lists continues to rise every year, and with minority individuals making up an ever-larger

(Continued)

portion of the patients on these lists, the need for organ donors is at an all-time high. However, this demand will never be met without the removal of the fears and hesitations that currently plague communities of color. In the hopes of better understanding what exactly is causing these roadblocks to donation, Brown (2012), in her pilot study, looked to better understand this very phenomenon and hopefully create an avenue for a future solution to be found. To conduct this study Brown conducted an online survey of 70 African-Americans that enabled them to express their thoughts, feelings, and hesitations about organ donation. With a 78.6 percent return rate for the survey, Brown was able to find that there are at least five areas of reluctance associated with organ donation among African-Americans. These areas are: a lack of awareness; lack of trust in the medical profession; fear of premature death; fear of discrimination; and misconceptions caused by religious beliefs. From here Brown was able to create possible ways to dispel these common misconceptions about organ donation among African-Americans. Taking first lack of awareness, Brown believed that through a targeted educational program communities of color will become more aware of the problem faced by their community and what they can do to help. An educational program tailored specifically to a community of color will also provide an excellent inlet for information concerning some of the other areas of reluctance, such as fear of premature death, for example. With a targeted educational campaign information could be distributed and explained to people in a non-threatening way that simply heightens their awareness of the issue and remedies any internal struggles an individual might face when deciding to become an organ donor. Possibly the two hardest reluctances to address are the lack of trust in the medical profession and fear of discrimination. With communities of color and the medical profession having an extremely troubled past, due to the medical communities history of discriminating against and taking advantage of minority patients, it may be next to impossible to dispel these reluctances.

(Continued)

However, there is still hope that the medical community will continue to try to break down racial boundaries and work towards mending its relationship with minority individuals. Finally, what may possibly be one of the biggest hurdles in minority organ donation may also be one of the best opportunities for increasing minority participation. While many people in communities of color cite religion as one of the reasons as to why they are not an organ donor, most major religions do not actually condemn organ donation at all. This means that, for example, by holding town-hall-style discussions or private meetings a religious leader within a community could share the church's views on organ donation with the congregation and provide answers to individuals who are skeptical of the practice. This finding is echoed in Uskun and Ozturk's study (2013). Brown's work may have only been a pilot study, but it does expose a number of serious problems currently facing the medical community when it comes to addressing organ donation in communities of color.

Once again, how could Pierre apply the HBM, TMIS, or TPB to this discussion of organ donation?

This challenge is extremely important for the medical community to not only face, but to overcome as well. As life expectances continue to rise around the world, especially in developed nations such as the US, having a donor pool comparable to the demand is crucial. Beyond this the medical community is also in constant need of organ donors willing to provide organ, tissue, and brain samples to be used for medical research. This area of the medical field goes largely without an adequate number of samples, especially from donors belonging to minority groups. A further explanation of this can be found in Danner, Darnell, and McGuire's study (2011). In this study Danner et al. worked to better understand and explain why there is such limited participation of African-Americans in medical research such as Alzheimer's research, which includes brain donation. Similarly to the pilot study conducted by Brown, Danner et al. discovered that there are several misconceptions keeping the majority of African-Americans away from organ donation. In the case of organ donation for medical research, one of the

(Continued)

biggest barriers to increased minority participation
was found to be mistrust of the predominately white
research establishments. This coupled with a general
lack of knowledge about medical research not only
creates an unwillingness to participate, but actually intimidates many individuals from ever exploring the subject. In order to better understand why
these barriers exist and how the medical community
can best remove them, Danner et al. contacted 46
African American individuals, all of whom were 65
and older and recruited through the registered voters database in Kentucky, who were willing to participate in the study, which consisted of different
interviews either over the phone or in the participant's home. This interviewing technique was used
because from previous research it was determined
that having a face-to-face interaction and conversation with an individual about organ donation led to
better understanding and greater acceptance of the
practice. With organ donation being such a sensitive
subject, the researchers used these interviews as
a way of gaining general knowledge on the thoughts
and feelings of an older generation towards this
practice. However, the researchers had to also be
sure not to intimidate the participants and decided
to include questions about other, more routine
medical procedures such as getting an MRI. Participants were also asked to describe their knowledge
about several different medical procedures, before
finally discussing donating one's brain to be used
for medical research. This discussion happened only
if the researcher believed that the participant was
comfortable with conversation, as again this is an
extremely sensitive issue for many people. What this
study found was that a lack of knowledge deters most
individuals away from receiving different lifesaving medical treatments and procedures. However,
once given a clear definition and explanation about
what the treatment or procedure is almost all of the
participants in the study said they would definitely
choose the lifesaving option. The same can be said
for brain donation. Initially, a majority of the
study participants stated that they would not like

(Continued)

to donate their brain to be used in Alzheimer's research, despite not really knowing what exactly takes place during the research process. However, once they were told what the process was and why it was so important, nearly 70 percent of the study's participants said they would in fact donate their brains to be used in medical research.

This research conducted by Danner et al. is extremely important because it continues to support the findings of many medical researchers before them. Most notably, this research helps support the practice of communicating with patients face-to-face, especially when discussing something as serious as organ donation after death. Through their efforts, Danner et al. were also able to find evidence that supports strategies such as meeting individuals in their homes, churches, community centers, and other familiar locations in order to provide potential donors with as much comfort as possible when discussing a somewhat unnerving topic. Taking these steps, in addition to having calm and light, yet informative conversations about organ donation helps to build rapport and trust between a potential donor and medical professional/researcher. It is this trust and rapport that most significantly helps to reduce the fears of potential donors and potentially lead to higher than expected organ donor registration rates. However, it is important to remember that the fear of being abused by the medical system is still extremely prevalent in communities of color. This means that a promotional strategy similar to this must be carefully implemented so as to not come off as a way to trick or deceive individuals into becoming organ donors.

While increasing the number of registered organ donors in African-American communities is incredibly important, one must not overlook the other racial and ethnic minorities found within the US. There is a whole host of reasons why members of different racial and ethnic backgrounds chose to forgo registering as organ donors, and studying these in order to better understand how to address them is incredibly important. One such study conducted by Padela,

(Continued)

Rasheed, Warren, Choi, and Mathur (2011) looked to understand the attitudes of Arab-Americans towards organ donation. Specifically, Padela et al. focused their study on the factors associated with positive attitudes towards organ donation, and hypothesized socioeconomics along with health status and health awareness influence the potential for a minority individual to register as an organ donor. With many racial minorities already citing religion and lack of public awareness as barriers to organ donation, understanding what is preventing Arab-Americans, a rapidly growing population, from registering as organ donors is important.

Interestingly enough, Padela et al. again found religion and religious beliefs to be a considerable barrier to registering as an organ donor, mainly because of the ambiguous nature of the language used in religious texts about what is acceptable to do with one's body after death. However, while conducting their study, Padela et al. also uncovered what they believed to be three factors that greatly impact an Arab-American's decision on whether or not to register as an organ donor. These three factors are: health status; socioeconomic status; and acculturation. From their nearly 1020 respondents Padela et al. were able to determine that, for Arab-Americans, religion plays an extremely important role in their life, and is used as a way to inform any number of life choices. Second, the research team was able to conclude that those Arab-Americans with higher incomes and higher levels of education were more likely than others to either already be registered as organ donors or be willing to register as organ donors. Here, again, education and awareness of the issues play a vital role in determining the likelihood of an individual registering as an organ donor. However, Arab-Americans also cited other factors that would greatly increase their likelihood of registering, including cultural and religious sensitivity exhibited by the medical community, and a stronger relationship between them and the medical professionals that serve their community.

(Continued)

Working towards an increased understanding of how to best promote organ donation in communities of color is an extremely important area of study. Currently, there is extremely limited research on the topic, yet every year more and more members of racial minorities find themselves on organ transplant waiting lists with little to no hope in sight. Of the research that is available a large majority of it focuses primarily of the fact that there are so few individuals belonging to a community of color on the registered organ donor list. This calls for a paradigm shift—one that focuses attention away from the problem and moves toward a solution. The current body of research has done an excellent job of establishing the fears and misconceptions that are keeping many individuals within communities of color from registering as organ donors. However, it does not work to establish improved lines of communication between those in the medical community and those in communities of color. By continuing research into this area, academics and medical researchers will be provided with incredibly valuable insights into a very complex and important issue, and gain an even greater understanding of interracial communication. As individuals become more sensitive to those in communities of color through continued research, race relations and interracial communication will be positively impacted by the richer understanding of one another that will result from working towards a solution to this problem for all of us—regardless of our racial backgrounds.

One of the things you will notice from this paper is that there are a lot of places where Pierre could have incorporated elements from the HBM or TPB. Throughout the paper Pierre discusses a great deal of information that relates to elements that would relate to factors from the HBM or the TBP in particular. In papers like this, one can focus more on the contextual, the historical, or the theoretical. The key is for you to address your main focus, which Pierre did in this paper.

References

Brown, E. R. (2012). African American present perceptions of organ donation: A pilot study. *The Association of Black Nursing Faculty, 23(2)*, 29–33.

Coppen, R., Friele, R. D., Gevers, S. K., & van der Zee, J. (2010). Donor education campaigns since the introduction of the Dutch Organ Donation Act: Increased cohesion between campaigns has paid off. *Transplant International, 23*, 1239–1246.

Danner, D. D., Darnell, K. R., McGuire, C. (2011). African American participation in Alzheimer's Disease research that includes brain donation. *American Journal of Alzheimer's Disease & Other Dementias 26*, 469–76.

(Continued)

Klein, A. S., Messersmith, E. E., Ratner, L. E., Kochik, R., Baliga, P. K., & Ojo, A. O. (2010). Organ donation and utilization in the United States, 1999–2008. *American Journal of Transplantation, 10,* 973–986.

Organ Transplant History. (Dec. 9, 2013). *History of Organ Donation & Transplants.* Donate Life NY.

Padela, A. I., Rasheed, S., Warren, G. J., Choi, H., & Mathur. A. K. (2011). Factors associated with positive attitudes toward organ Donation in Arab Americans. *Clinical Transplantation, 25,* 800–808.

Stefanone, M., Anker, A. E., Evans, M., & Feeley, T. H. (2012). Click to "like" organ donation: The use of online media to promote organ donor registration. *Progress in Transplantation, 22,* 168–174.

Thornton, J. D., Alejandro-Rodriguez, M., León, J. B., Albert, J. M., Baldeon, E. L., De Jesus, L. M. . . . Sehgal, A. R. (2012). Effect of an iPod video intervention on consent to donate organs. *American College of Physicians: Annals of Internal Medicine, 156,* 484–490.

Uskun, E., & Ozturk, M. (2013). Attitudes of Islamic religious officials toward organ transplant and donation. *Clinical Transplantation, 27,* 37–41.

10 MASS COMMUNICATION

Chapter Outline

- What is Mass Communication?
- Media Effects Theories
- Media and Public Opinion
- Agenda Setting Theory
- Spiral of Silence Theory
- Student Paper

Mass communication is all around us. We turn on the television and have a world of options at one click of a remote control button. On the Internet, millions of websites and countless social networking sites (Facebook, Linkedin, Instagram, Twitter, etc.) vie for our attention. Now with smart phones we are able to make telephone calls, watch television, listen to music, surf the Internet, play games, and countless other things (all on a handheld device). The following statistics help explain American media: 90 percent of Americans have a cell phone and 58 percent have a smart phone, significant increases since 2008; 96.1 percent of American households have a television, a high number, but lower than in 2000; 92 percent of Americans listen to AM/FM radio at least once a week, a relatively high and stable percentage; and less than 30 percent read a paper daily newspaper, a number which has been steadily declining (Pew Research Center, 2010, 2014; Nielsen, 2014; State of the Media, 2013).

These statistics show the changing nature of mass communication in the United States. Mass communication technology continues to evolve. Individuals can now access thousands of television channels, networks such as Netflix are challenging traditional television programming, Internet bandwidth continues to increase making the Internet faster and easier to access, and newspapers are moving towards a majority online readership. While mass communication may be evolving, the key aspects and questions surrounding mass communication and media messages remain relatively stable.

In this chapter we will explore the study of **mass communication** or the delivery of messages to the general public through media messages, with a particular emphasis on how those media messages affect the opinion and/ or behavior of the public receiving the media message(s). There are various theories, approaches, and ways to study mass communication. The concepts in this chapter cover a broad range of theoretical approaches. More specifically, the theories in this chapter focus on two distinct aspects of mass communication: media effects on society, and how media influence public opinion. In the first section we will define mass communication. In the second section we will examine different theories related to media effects: social cognitive theory and uses and gratifications theory. In the third section we will review key theories related to how media influence public opinion: agenda setting theory and spiral of silence theory. This section also includes a case study about the Obama elections in 2008 and 2012, which shows the practical aspects of spiral of silence theory. In the fourth and final section you will find a student paper. This paper is a mass communication student paper that is included to serve as an example of one of the many kinds of writing assignments you *could* do for a mass communication theory assignment.

KEY TERM 10.1

Mass communication – delivery of messages to the general public through media messages, with a particular emphasis on how those media messages affect the opinion and/or behavior of the public receiving the media message(s).

What is Mass Communication?

Mass communication, or the delivery of messages to the general public through media messages, with a particular emphasis on how those media messages affect the opinion and/or behavior of the public receiving the media message(s), has a long history. To understand how mass communication works, we must first define the term media. **Media** is a means of communication. Communication media are technological processes that aid in communication between the senders of a message and the receivers. For example, people receive (watch) a television news show, which is sent (broadcast) to them from a news network (e.g., CNN, Fox, MSNBC). Not only do people receive media, they also use it. With the increased use of and production of social media, which we will talk more about shortly, people are able to update their Facebook status, tweet, post videos on YouTube, etc. This active use of media has altered the media landscape from just a receiver model to also a user model.

Media can be divided into three kinds: print, broadcast, and social. Print media, the oldest form of media, includes newspapers, books, magazines, and other print materials. This form of media has evolved over thousands of years. In 100 CE papermaking developed in China and by 700 CE it had spread through Asia to the Arab lands and to the West. The proliferation of papermaking promoted the spread of printed ideas and messages (media). By 1450 Gutenberg developed his hand-press in Germany, which allowed for mass production of printed materials, such as the Bible. Shortly after in the 1600s the first newspapers appeared in Belgium, France, and Germany. In 1702 the first daily newspaper began, London's *Daily Courant*. In 1833, the *New York Sun* began printing the first mass-circulated penny press newspaper. From this moment on print media continued to grow, as more and more newspapers, magazines, books, and other print material around the world were developed and spread to mass consumers.

At the time when print media was being mass circulated (1830s), broadcast media began. Broadcast media includes: radio, television, and other media broadcast via a satellite. In 1837 the first telegraph message was sent. This marked a breakthrough in media, as a message could now be sent over a wire. Nearly 40 years later, in 1876, Alexander Graham Bell made the first telephone call, further showing the power of sending messages over wires. Over the next two centuries broadcast media continued to develop. In 1884, film was developed, which led to motion pictures in 1894, and later television in 1933. Marconi transmitted the first radio messages in 1895. Radio, motion pictures, and television were and remain a key form of broadcast media, as they are multifaceted. All have the ability to share information and entertain. In the twentieth century, broadcast media has dramatically evolved into more advanced formats: cassette tapes to CDs, VHS to DVD, network TV to cable to digital television, etc.

More recently a new version of media has emerged, that of social media, which includes: Friendster, Myspace, Facebook, Twitter, Instagram, YouTube, etc. These forms of **social media**, or electronic communication where users can create online communities to share content (ideas, information, messages, etc.) would not have been possible without the wide distribution of the Internet. In 2002 the first social networking site Friendster was developed. Shortly after that in 2003 Myspace, and then in 2004 Facebook were developed. YouTube was started in 2005, with Twitter starting shortly after in 2006. Each of these sites affords users a chance to share content with one another, which is more of a user approach to media than a receiver approach.

KEY TERM 10.2

Social media – electronic communication where users can create online communities to share content.

Think about each of these kinds of media and how each of them is received and/or used by the public. Technology has had a significant effect on how media is produced and consumed. Look to the Internet as one example of the influence of technology on media. As the Internet has become more commonplace, and in many ways an essential part of our everyday lives, many media have adapted to, or even been developed for the Internet. Many television and stations now stream content online. Many newspapers now emphasize online advertising, particularly as they see print sales and advertising profits dwindling. The key is that media have developed and tried to adapt to changing environments. What has remained consistent is that media affect us emotionally and cognitively, and often can be developed to swing our public opinion. In the next section we describe the various effects of media through the lenses of social cognitive theory and uses and gratifications theory.

WHAT DO YOU THINK 10.1

Think about your media use. How is your media use affected by technology?

Media Effects Theories

From the 1920s to the 1940s motion pictures increased in popularity, newspaper circulations increased, and radio program listenership was high. Each of these forms of media was also used extensively for social and national propaganda in the United States. How individuals process media and the effects of media became a significant issue of study not just for the government, but also for researchers (McQuail, 2010). Researchers at the time proposed hypotheses for media's effects on society. Hypotheses such as the hypodermic and the magic bullet effects emerged. These theories proposed that media were able to shape how the public thought about issues (public opinion). Essentially, the media were the hypodermic needle or magic bullet, and shot the wishes/thoughts of the sender directly into the receiver(s)/the audience. These theories assumed the following: the audience is psychologically isolated; the audience is impersonal; and the audience is free of social obligations (DeFleur & Ball-Rokeach, 1989). Both theories were eventually replaced as researchers realized that, among other factors: the models did not consider external factors; they did not consider the limitations of the media; and they did not consider the ability of the audience to learn. Eventually, researchers looked to the relationships between how we learn and see the world with how we receive and use media. The foundation of this thinking is social cognitive theory.

Social Cognitive Theory

Social cognitive theory was developed from Miller and Dollard's (1941) theory of social learning. Bandura and Walters (1963) expanded social learning theory to include vicarious reinforcement and observational learning, with Bandura (1977) later adding self-efficacy to the theory. **Social cognitive theory** describes how individuals obtain and keep behavioral patterns, while at the same time the theory offers behavioral intervention strategies—ways to design, implement, and evaluate behavioral change initiatives. Behavior, environmental factors, and personal factors all influence one another in this theory (Bandura, 1997). Unlike the magic bullet and hypodermic needle theories, which gave all the credit to the message, this approach strongly considers the role of the individual and environmental factors in behavior.

KEY TERM 10.3

Social cognitive theory – a theory that describes how individuals obtain and keep behavioral patterns. The theory is based on a social learning approach.

In this theory, behavior is the way in which an individual (an audience member for example) conducts themselves. Environment refers to social and physical factors that can potentially influence our behavior. Social factors include factors such as our family, friends, work colleagues, and other elements of our social circle. Physical factors of the environment focus on the surroundings: the room we are in when we receive a message; the size of the message (is it on a big or small screen?); the volume of the message (loud or soft), and so forth. The individual refers to affective (emotional), cognitive, and biological aspects of the person receiving the message(s). Various factors influence how we interpret messages. For example, if we were been bitten by a dog in the past we may be afraid of dogs. This past experience will affect us cognitively and affectively. Demographic factors, such as our sex, religion, ethnicity or racial background, political affiliation, and other demographics will affect how we interpret messages. We will naturally have more interest in something that relates to who we are in some way.

Additional key elements of social cognitive theory illustrate how this theory applies to mass communication and media. **Observational learning** is when individuals learn through observing models in their lives. These models are often members of their inner social circle, such as family or friends. However, these models can also be mass media models: celebrities, politicians, sports figures, and other media figures. When someone watches the Rachael Ray show and then follows a recipe to make a new pasta dish, that person has modeled their cooking behavior after a celebrity chef. When someone cuts their hair like a celebrity, that person has modeled themselves after that celebrity. However, why do we model ourselves after these celebrities, or anyone for that matter? We do so because we have expectations and expectancies (Bandura, 1986). Outcome expectations are when we see our celebrity chef (our model) be rewarded or punished—we expect the same outcomes for the same behavior. We attach value to our expectations—outcome expectancies—which consider the extent to which an action is rewarded or punished. If we see people enjoy the cook's food we have the expectation that the food is good, because the cook was rewarded. The extent to which they are rewarded affects how much we expect to be rewarded or not.

KEY TERM 10.4

Observational learning – when individuals learn through observing models in their lives.

Social cognitive theory also takes into consideration **self-efficacy**, or an individual's ability to do a behavior and the confidence the individual has in doing that particular behavior (Bandura, 1977). Think back to the Rachael Ray show and the new pasta dish. I am not a seasoned chef; in fact I am lucky I can boil water. More than likely I do not have the self-efficacy to adequately learn how to make the pasta dish that Rachael Ray shows people how to make on her show. Social cognitive theory clearly has application for mass communication and media. In the next section we will go through some social cognitive research in mass communication and media contexts.

WHAT DO YOU THINK 10.2

Think about your media observations. Have you ever modeled your behavior(s) after something or someone in the media? Why or why not?

KEY TERM 10.5

Self-efficacy – an individual's ability to do a behavior and the confidence the individual has in doing that particular behavior.

Research Linking Social Cognitive Theory to Mass Communication and Media

Researchers have studied social cognitive theory in conjunction with mass communication and media in a variety of ways. The research has shown individuals have some amount of self-regulatory mechanisms to observe their own behaviors, judge and compare these behaviors in relation to societal norms, and adjust their behaviors if need be (Bandura, 1986; Lee & LaRose, 2007). Various lines of research exist, but for space purposes three will be briefly reviewed: social cognition and television depictions; social cognition and video games; and social cognition and children's media use.

Individuals observe media behaviors and the rewards and punishments associated with those behaviors (on television, on the Internet, etc.). For example, when we see positive intergroup interactions among media characters we are more likely to have positive intergroup attitudes and want future contact with other groups (Mazziotta, Mummendey, & Wright, 2011). Joyce and Harwood (2014) argued that "exposure to a positive intergroup narrative should result in the audience perceiving intergroup contact as more rewarding and desirable, and as a result lead to the modeling of the attitudes and behaviors observed in the intergroup narrative" (p. 629). This argument was supported in their study of portrayals of interactions of border patrol agents and illegal immigrants in the United States. Research on media depictions related to sex and social cognition have also shown that to encourage positive sexual behaviors among viewers, media characters should enact positive sexual behaviors (e.g., practice safe sex) (Bandura, 2002; Nabi & Clark, 2008).

A growing form of mass media is video games. As video games increase in popularity, so does our need to understand why people play them, how they play them, and the effects of these games on society (Williams, 2002). The excitement of a new video game release may often overwhelm an individual's rational consideration of other aspects of the game, Internet usage, or their playing habits (LaRose, Lin, & Eastin, 2003; Lee & LaRose, 2007). Essentially, media hype around a game can cloud our cognitive abilities. Lin (2013) expanded our understanding of how social cognition relates to video games, and argued that learning from playing games (experience) elicits higher aggression than observational learning, when violence in the game is present. In this case, when a game has violence in it, playing the game (participation) is more correlated with aggression (modeling) than simply observing the behavior in the game.

Briefly, research into media consumption, children, and social cognition has shown numerous results. Adolescents' self-concept has been found to be directly influenced by the models (e.g., television, film, music) they see and hear (Arnett, 2002; Kistler, Boyce Rodgers, Power, Weintraub Austin, & Griner Hill, 2010). In research focusing on preschoolers, Zimmerman, Oritz, Christakis, and Elkun (2012) explained how limiting and targeted TV viewing could promote healthier behavior. The next theory furthers our appreciation of how individuals process and understand media: uses and gratifications.

Uses and Gratifications

Uses and gratifications (U&G) is a valuable approach to investigating the powerful effects of media usage and consumption. This theoretical framework helps scholars and practitioners to understand the ways in which changes in mass communication have impacted media (Appadurai, 1990). This media effects approach originated in the 1940s as researchers (notably Herza Herzog) began to question the reasons audience members might have for consuming (Wimmer & Dominick, 1994). Since its beginning, the theory has been applied to numerous media studies, including what some consider the first official use of U&G by Katz, Blumler, and Gurevitch in the early 1970s. In this work, the theorists outlined the **uses and gratifications** (U&G) framework as:

(1) the social and psychological origins of (2) needs which generate (3) expectations of (4) the mass media or other sources, which lead to (5) differential patterns of media exposure (or engagement in other activities), resulting in (6) need gratifications and (7) other consequences, perhaps mostly unintended ones. (1974, p. 20)

KEY TERM 10.6

Uses and gratifications – a theory that describes the needs that generate expectations of media, which lead to differential exposure resulting in need gratifications and other consequences.

In other words, media consumption is based on the social and psychological needs of the audience/consumer and if such needs are met, or gratified. Herzog (1940) proposed that individuals seek three different types of gratification from media: compensation; emotional release; and/or advice. Lazarsfeld and Merton (1948) further suggested three additional gratifications found through media consumption: enforcement of social norms; status conferral; and narcotizing dysfunction. Other distinctions among gratifications have included "content versus process gratifications, cognitive versus affective/imaginative gratifications, and instrumental versus ritual gratifications" (Miller, 2005, p. 257). As U&G utilization has continued, multiple typologies of gratifications have emerged. Katz, Blumler, and Gurevitch (1974) explained that "each major piece of uses and gratifications research has yielded its own classification scheme of audience functions. When placed side by side, they reveal a mixture of shared gratification categories and notions peculiar to individual research teams" (p. 512). All in all, this approach highlights the existence of an active audience who choose media (uses) to serve their interests (gratifications). This is a slight step away from the social cognitive approach, which explains how audience behaviors are affected through observing models in media.

A significant development to the U&G framework was the distinction between gratifications sought and gratifications obtained (Miller, 2005). What we seek from media usage (**gratifications sought**) may not always be what we get (**gratifications obtained**). Palmgreen and Rayburn (1979) sought to understand this distinction in a study regarding gratifications sought and obtained from public TV viewing. Their findings revealed a need to "integrate the roles played by gratifications and other factors into a general theory of media consumption" (p. 177). Another progression regards active audiences, as research shows media usage is generally purposeful and intentional (Rosengren, 1974; Ruggiero, 2000).

WHAT DO YOU THINK 10.3

When was the last time your media usage gratifications sought did not match with your gratifications obtained? Why do you think this was the case?

Uses and Gratifications Research

Traditional U&G research has focused on TV, radio, and print audiences. This research has overwhelmingly shown individuals' gratifications sought do not always match the gratifications obtained (Ruggiero, 2000; Shyman Sundar & Limperos, 2013). Ruggiero (2000) stated that at the beginning of U&G studies involving the Internet, "U&G research may well play a major role in answering initial Web-use questions of prurience, curiosity, profit seeking, and sociability. U&G also holds the prospect for understanding the Internet's mutability, or its broad range of communication opportunities" (p. 23–24). Recently, U&G researchers have expanded U&G into studies of web-based media. Raacke and Bonds-Raacke (2008) demonstrated how people use social networking sites as a means to make new friends and reconnect with old friends. Also using U&G, Song, LaRose, Eastin, and Lin (2004) found a connection between gratifications (sought and obtained) and Internet addiction, and Diddi and LaRose (2006) discovered that surveillance and escapism gratifications were predictors of Internet news consumption. Chen (2011) applied U&G to Twitter usage to analyze the connection between time spent on Twitter and the need to connect to others. She found the more time an individual spent on Twitter the more the person felt camaraderie (gratification sought). Wei and Lu (2014) explored why people play mobile social games (e.g., Draw Something). The researchers found that gratifications such as personal enjoyment and interaction with others predicted intent to play mobile social games.

While U&G research has extended past traditional forms of media (print and broadcast) into social media, there are critiques of the U&G approach. Most researchers do not explore the origins of media needs and/or the consequences of gratifications. Thus, we do not yet have a full understanding of how U&G works (Miller, 2005; Palmgreen, 1984). The lack of studies considering media needs and/or consequences of gratifications shows how researchers have not taken into consideration the whole U&G model in their studies, which can "hold back the pace of theoretical development" (DeFleur, 1998, p. 92). The theory has also been criticized for being too individualistic a theory. This means the theory might give too much credit to an active audience who believe they can control the effects of the media on their lives, a departure from the social cognitive approach. A final critique relates to how individuals interpret the messages they receive. The U&G approach never explicitly explains the processes through which the audience decodes messages to determine the difference between gratifications obtained and sought. Even with these critiques, researchers continually use this theory to better understand media's effects on audiences.

Media and Public Opinion

Another way to understand how the media affects and/or relates to its audience (us) is to look at how the media influences public opinion. As I write this book a popular show on Netflix is *House of Cards*. The political drama follows the Underwood couple and their political rise to power. A key part of this rise to power is their ability to manipulate public opinion, often through manipulating the media. While part of me hopes that politicians do not manipulate the media like the Underwoods do, another part of me thinks it probably does happen. In numerous episodes the power couple and their inner circle leak stories to the media to get their (very skewed) version of the "truth" out to the American people. The media then spins the stories and the American public responds. The following section of the chapter examines the process of how media can determine key issues, sway public opinion, and how, in some cases, opinions will be silenced in public debate. Two theories of keen interest are agenda setting theory and spiral of silence theory.

Agenda Setting Theory

For centuries researchers, politicians, media practitioners, laymen, etc. have recognized the power of the media to shape public opinion. In Lippmann's (1922) seminal work, *Public Opinion,* Lippmann described how the media generate thoughts and images of events in the minds of the audience. These thoughts and images influence how the audience thinks about issues. Research previously discussed in this chapter—the hypodermic and the magic bullet theory, as well as socio cognitive theory—have been influenced by these assertions. While researchers have generally abandoned the assertion that media has such strong and direct effects on the audience (as those asserted in the magic bullet or hypodermic needle theories), researchers have and continue to explore the more subtle influence that media has in swaying public opinion. In reviewing the history of public opinion and propaganda, Cohen (1963) stated that the media "may not be successful much of the time in telling people what to think, but it is stunningly successful in telling its readers what to think about" (p. 13). A key theory in this line of inquiry, and one of the most studied in communication, is agenda setting theory.

In 1972 Max McCombs and Donald Shaw published a study analyzing the influence of the media in the 1968 presidential election. They proposed and supported in this study the argument that the salience of issues reported by the media were reflected in people's minds. Essentially, the media effectively told the audience what issues to think about in the election. McCombs and Shaw named this process **agenda setting**. Since then hundreds of published studies have shown the theory's predictive power in various contexts (McCombs, 2004).

KEY TERM 10.7

Agenda setting theory – a theory that explores how the media influence the public's thinking on issues.

Agenda setting theory focuses on three related agendas: the media, public, and policy agendas. The **media agenda** are the topics that the media addresses. The **public agenda** are the topics that the public (audience) believes are important. The **policy agenda** are the set of issues that decision makers (government officials and other officials) believe are important. Within the agenda setting theory, each of these three agendas can be thought of as a dependent variable in a cause–effect argument. For example, the media agenda can be seen as affecting the policy and public agendas, while the policy agenda can be seen as affecting the public and media agenda, and so forth. For mass communication researchers the key relationship, and thus the bulk of research, has been how the media agenda influences the public agenda.

KEY TERMS 10.8, 10.9 AND 10.10

Media agenda – the topics on which the media focuses.

Public agenda – the topics that the public (audience) believes are important.

Policy agenda – the issues or topics that decision makers (government) believe are important.

WHAT DO YOU THINK 10.4

Can you think of any examples in the news recently where the media agenda is affecting the public and/or the policy agenda? How is this the case?

In exploring the relationship between the media and the public agenda, it is important to note the following. Generally, the media does not directly tell the public that an issue is important. Instead the media sets the agenda by giving an issue more time and space, by focusing on it more than other issues. These tactics have been very successful in making the media agenda the public agenda. In the original McCombs and Shaw (1972) study, the researchers found that the media agenda was directly reflected in the public responses to the 1968 Presidential candidates (public agenda). Unlike other communication theories, which tend to stray away from arguing causality (cause and effect), agenda setting research has been quite successful in showing how the media agenda causes a change in the public agenda (Iyengar & Kinder, 1987; Scheufele & Tewksbury, 2007; Shaw & McCombs, 1977; Tan & Weaver, 2010; Tien Vu, Guo, & McCombs, 2014; Zhu, Watt, Snyder, Yan, & Jiang, 1993).

A few additional elements of agenda setting are necessary to explain, before we move on to a brief review of some of this *large* body of research. Research has shown that while the media can influence the public, the effect(s) is not always the same. The variations in the effect(s) depend on the issue, and on the audience. Some issues are more relevant or salient to the audience, or the public, than other issues. If an issue is not seen as important to the audience, the media's influence might be less (Kim, Han, Choi, & Kim, 2012; Sheafer, 2007). Second, the extent to which an issue is obtrusive or not will influence the extent of the media's effect(s). Obtrusive issues are ones where the audience has more direct contact with the issue, such as national/domestic or social issues. Unobtrusive issues are ones where the audience has less direct contact with the issue, such as foreign policy issues. The agenda setting effect tends to be higher for unobtrusive issues because the audience relies more on the media for information (Zhu & Blood, 1997).

The audience's need for orientation also impacts the media's influence on the public agenda. Need for orientation includes the audience's interest in the issue and uncertainty about an issue. Individuals who may care deeply about an issue (high interest) but know little about that issue (high uncertainty) are more likely to be swayed by the media because they turn to the media for their information.

The final issue to consider is the difference between first and second-level agenda setting. **First-level agenda setting** is the media affecting, or setting, what issues are part of the public agenda, a traditional approach to agenda setting. **Second-level agenda setting** takes things a step further and here the media influences *how* the audience thinks about those issues (McCombs, Shaw, & Weaver, 1997; Moon, 2011). Consider this: an agenda setting analysis may reveal that the media has set police abuse of power as a public topic (first-level). If the media presents the topic in a way that is pro-police, or anti-police, to influence public opinion, this is second-level agenda setting. Critical to second-level agenda setting is the notion of framing. **Framing** is when the media focus on specific parts or aspects of an issue and not others. Whenever individuals accuse media of having a liberal or conservative bias, they are in essence accusing the media of framing stories and issues to serve a particular political agenda, which in turn influences the public agenda.

KEY TERMS 10.11 AND 10.12

First-level agenda setting – where the media sets or establishes what are important topics or issues for the public.

Second-level agenda setting – the media influences how the audience (public) thinks about topics or issues.

WHAT DO YOU THINK 10.5

How does framing differ from reporting the news?

Agenda Setting Research

As previously mentioned, there have been hundreds of studies conducted examining agenda setting. Thus, it is impossible to offer a full review of this rich line of inquiry. For space purposes, let's review some agenda setting studies on political and social issues. The bulk of agenda setting research has emphasized how media report and frame political issues and ideologies.

Collectively, this research has supported both first- and second-level agenda setting. In their analysis of the *New York Times* from 1956 to 2004, Tan and Weaver (2010) supported the causality of agenda setting, and found a positive relationship between media bias and Congressional policy, and between public mood and policy liberalism. Specifically, Tan and Weaver noted that:

> The more liberal the national media's citation bias is, the more liberal the Congress's policies are. Therefore, second-level agenda-setting, between the media's attribute agenda and the policy's attribute agenda, and between the public's attribute agenda and the policy's attribute agenda, is supported. (p. 429)

In a similar study by Tan and Weaver (2007), this time on the *New York Times* and *Gallup*, the authors also found that media framing of issues directly affects the public agenda. All in all, the research showed that media framing of issues (bias in this case) has a direct effect on the public mood (agenda) and the Congress (policy agenda). In additional research on agenda setting on political campaigning in non-US contexts, research has consistently shown significant agenda setting effects (Weaver, 1996; Weaver, McCombs, & Shaw, 2004). Research in the United Kingdom, Sweden, Germany, Spain, Italy, Denmark, the Netherlands, and Latin America has shown relationships between the media's and the public's agenda (Brandenburg, 2006; Djerf-Pierre & Wiebull, 2005; Hopmann, Elmelund-Praestekaer, Albaek, Vliegenthart, & de Vreese, 2012; Stein & Kellam, 2014; van Praag & van der Eijk, 1998).

Agenda setting research has also examined how the media's agenda influences the public's agenda regarding social issues, such as obesity, abortion, and same-sex marriage, for example. Lee and Len-Ríos (2014), in a second-level agenda setting analysis, identified how general audience newspapers and black newspapers ascribe causes for obesity. The data showed how both kinds of newspapers ascribe individual causes for obesity, which means that the newspapers blame individuals for obesity. This research showed how the negative portrayal of obesity by media negatively affects how the audience perceives obesity. Oakley (2009) explored state policies on abortion (called fetal killing policies) and how these policies (or shifts in policies) are linked to media attention. The results showed that many states between 1970 and 2002 changed their policies partially due to media attention on the issue, which supports the agenda setting theory. On the issue of same-sex marriage, Hester and Gibson (2007) compared the impacts of national and local news coverage on the public salience of the issue. Their study showed that media coverage of same-sex marriage, an unobtrusive issue for many people, directly affected public perception of the issue. However, the authors pointed out that the salience of the issue differed locally, and thus the impact of local media coverage varied in the two cities under analysis: Chicago and Atlanta. All in all, agenda setting effects were shown to differ significantly at the local versus national media levels, and based on the salience of the issue, which further supported the agenda setting theory. The next, and final theory in this chapter extends our understanding of the relationship between media and public opinion: spiral of silence theory.

Spiral of Silence Theory

Spiral of silence theory explains how an individual's willingness to voice their opinion on an issue (generally controversial) depends on if they feel they are in the minority or majority viewpoint on the issue. This determination is made by evaluating the climate of opinion on an issue (Noelle-Neumann, 1974, 1977, 1984, 1985). Four arguments are key to an individual's ability to detect a spiral of silence effect in a population (Noelle-Neumann, 1974, 1984). First, most are afraid of being isolated for their views. Second, people observe the attitudes of others around them and express their views accordingly. Third, people will attempt to discover which viewpoints can be expressed without creating feelings of isolation. Fourth, people are more likely to express a viewpoint if the viewpoint is similar to the majority's opinion and less likely to express that opinion if it is inconsistent with the climate of opinion. To understand these arguments, we need to dig deeper into both climate of opinion and fear of isolation and how both help us understand public opinion.

KEY TERM 10.13

Spiral of silence theory – a theory that explains how an individual's willingness to voice their opinion on an issue (generally controversial) depends on if they feel they are in the minority or majority viewpoint on the issue.

Climate of Opinion

Climate of opinion relates to who speaks up and who remains silent on an issue (Noelle-Neumann, 1984). This is a cognitive decision-making process, often made through observing media (Noelle-Neumann, 2004). Often we think that the minority viewpoint will not go against the majority. Thus, we often fall into a "spiral of silence," refusing to be a part of a vocal minority (Noelle-Neumann, 1974, 1984). The amount of public support for an opinion influences how the public perceives an opinion. Individuals evaluate the level of public support through evaluating media messages. If a person thinks their opinion is unpopular, they will be less likely to voice it, thus a group that perceives they are in the minority will fall into a spiral of silence on a particular issue. The opposite is also true, if a group thinks its view to be the truth, or dominant viewpoint, the group members are more likely to speak out. However, we are not always able to properly evaluate which groups we are in, meaning we often lack the ability to accurately gauge the climate of opinion (Noelle-Neumann, 2004; Prentice & Miller, 1996; Taylor, 1982).

Fear of Isolation

Noelle-Neumann (1977) defined public opinion as the judgment of citizens made in a rational manner and as the pressure to conform. It is from the concept of conforming that she devised **fear of isolation**. Noelle-Neumann (1984) stated that "[o]ur social nature causes us to fear separation and isolation from our fellows and to want to be respected and liked by them" (p. 41). However, Salmon and Kline (1985) argued that reference groups might play more of an important role in reinforcing a person's minority opinion and their willingness to speak out on an issue. The classis test to examine fear of isolation for Noelle-Neumann was the train test. In this test individuals are asked to imagine they are on a long train ride with an individual who expresses an opinion about a controversial topic (e.g., death penalty, or abortion). The person is then asked to express a contrary opinion on the issue. Spiral of silence theory asserts that the individual would be less likely to express an opinion out of fear that their opinion may be the minority opinion, thus isolating them. Other similar tests have included having individuals wear controversial buttons or attend protests, where their wearing of the material or attendance could lead to isolation. In any case, their participation or speaking out involves them assessing the climate of opinion and measuring the potential fear of isolation.

Noelle-Neumann has pointed out three issues to consider when studying spiral of silence. First, the theory only works when the issue at hand is a moral one, not a factual issue. Individuals are not likely to fall into a spiral of silence on gasoline prices or interest rates, but many will on issues such as same-sex marriage, abortion, and/or the death penalty. Second, more educated individuals are less likely to experience spiral of silence than less educated individuals. Third, for some issues, staunch supporters or opponents will always be willing to voice their opinions.

WHAT DO YOU THINK 10.6

Is there an issue you have ever been fearful to speak out about because you thought you were in the minority? What was the issue and how did you evaluate the climate of opinion?

Spiral of Silence Research

Spiral of silence research has been conducted on a variety of social and political issues and in a variety of contexts. While the bulk of the research has focused on political issues, such as willingness to voice opinions about political issues, spiral of silence research has been extended into analyses of moral issues, and the theory has been studied increasingly in non-US settings. Noelle-Neumann (1979) argued that public opinion "confers legitimation" in the political arena. Research has affirmed the spiral of silence effect in voting behavior and outcomes. Studies show that voters can be afraid to say they will vote for a controversial candidate; will vote or will not for a candidate based on ethnicity; and that people are often afraid to state that the media influences their opinions on a candidate (Carroll & McKleod, 1984; Croucher, Spencer, & McKee, 2014; Matthes, Morrison, & Schemer, 2010; McDonald, Glynn, Kim, & Ostman, 2001).

Turning away from fear of isolation or willingness to voice opinion on political issues, research has also looked at the spiral of silence effect in regards to various social issues (e.g., affirmative action, homosexuals in the military, and sexual freedom). Moy, Domke, and Stamm (2001) for example extended spiral of silence and showed how individuals often experience unwillingness to voice their opinions about affirmative action. Mosher (1989) explored perceptions that individuals have toward sexual freedom and asserted that individuals are often afraid to voice opinions about sexual liberation. In their analysis of the influence of media in the representation of gays in the military Gozenbach, King, and Jablonski (1999) found people that who think their position is starting to lose public support might actually feel compelled to voice opinions, which runs counter to spiral of silence theory. This counter result was attributed to the significant influence of media messages and framing of media.

Spiral of silence researchers are also starting to explore this effect in non US-settings. A study conducted in the US and Singapore asked respondents to speak out against the perceived climate of opinion regarding interracial marriages and equal rights for homosexuals (Waipeng, Detenber, Willnat, Aday, & Graf, 2004). This project concluded a spiral of silence effect was found in Singapore but not in the US. Kim, Kim, and Oh (2014), analyzed how South Koreans feel about GM foods (genetically modified) and found the Internet significantly influences willingness to voice an opinion. Dailsay (2012) also explored the influence of media on a key issue, in this case in Guam, that of troop relocation. Dailsay found perceived support from local media was related to public support, and that many individuals also experienced an unwillingness to voice opinions on the issue of troop relocation.

Barack Obama, Race, and the Presidential Elections

In 2008 and 2012 Barack Obama won Presidential Elections in the United States. Obama was the first African-American candidate in American history to win the US Presidency. In both elections the political discourse shifted to issues of ethnicity, particularly in 2008. For many voters, Obama's ethnicity was a key issue in determining whether or not they would vote for him. However, this issue was kept private for many voters (Henninger, 2008; Miah, 2009). Many issues and policies proposed in the 2008 campaign and again in 2012 were overshadowed by issues of race and ethnicity (Croucher et al., 2014). In fact, Croucher et al. (2014), in examining people's likelihood of expressing an opinion about Obama's ethnicity in the 2008 election found that: Democrats were more likely to discuss Obama's ethnicity; Asian-Americans were more likely to discuss ethnicity compared to Caucasians; highly religious individuals were more likely to express their opinions; and Catholics were less likely to express an opinion. These results reveal that some groups fell into a spiral of silence and did not feel comfortable discussing aspects of race/ethnicity in relation to Obama, for one reason or another: Republicans, Caucasians, less religious individuals, etc. In these cases, political and social reasons silenced some groups and bolstered other groups into speaking.

Henninger, D. (2008, June 5). Obama's "identity" beat Hillary's "identity." *Wall Street Journal*, A19.

Miah, M. (2009). What Obama's victory means about race and class: A landmark election result. *Against the Current*, 23, 2–8.

Chapter Summary

Mass communication impacts our lives on a daily basis. The three sections of this chapter describe the various ways in which mass communication and media relate to our lives. The first section defined mass communication as a field of study, and defined media in many forms (print, broadcast, and social). The second section discussed how media affects our lives. Within this section social cognitive theory (Bandura, 1977) and uses and gratifications theory (Katz et al., 1974) were offered as examples to better understand how media affects society. In the third section we reviewed key theories related to how media influences public opinion: agenda setting theory (McCombs & Shaw, 1972) and spiral of silence theory (Noelle-Neumann, 1977) were provided.

The concepts and theories outlined in this chapter offer ways to understand the influences of media in our everyday lives. The final section of this chapter is a student paper from the University of Jyväskylä in Finland by Maziar Attarieh. This paper is a literature review on uses and gratifications theory. This paper, like the other papers in this book, is included to show you one of the many ways you can write about/research mass communication.

Key Terms

Agenda setting	Climate of opinion	Fear of isolation
First-level agenda setting	Framing	Gratifications obtained
Gratifications sought	Mass communication	Media
Media agenda	Observational learning	Policy agenda

Public agenda	Second-level agenda setting	Self-efficacy
Social cognitive theory	Social media	Spiral of silence theory
Uses and gratifications		

Activities

1. Look to news coverage of the most recent election. Is there an issue that you think people fell into a spiral of silence on? Why do you think it happened? How do you think groups differed in the levels of their spiral of silence?
2. Conduct a self-analysis of your social media uses and gratifications. Write down three uses you have for social media. Then write down three gratifications you seek from social media. Are these gratifications met/obtained?

Student Paper

The following paper is from a Communication Theory Class at the University of Jyväskylä. Stephen Croucher taught the class. This is the assignment for the paper:

Term Paper (200 points) – KVVS 100 – Communication Theory
Your final paper must be:

1) Written in APA Style (6th Edition)
2) It must be 5–10 pages in length not including the references and the title page. The paper does not need an abstract
3) You can work with a partner on this paper if you would like, or you can work alone.
4) You must have your theory approved by the instructor within the first two class sessions.
5) The purpose of this review of literature is to "review" a theory. This means many things. You can review the development of a theory, you can review how scholars have studied a theory, you can topically review a theory, chronologically review a theory, etc. . . . There are many ways to approach a review of literature. Options for this assignment will be discussed on the first day of class.

A Review of the Literature: Uses and Gratifications Theory

Uses and Gratification Theory

Maziar Attarieh
University of Jyväskylä

There have been many theories and models introduced by communication scholars in different time

---

(Continued)

periods to explain the relationship between media and its audience. Many of these efforts were trying to understand the effect of media messages on the people who use those media, especially after the emergence of radio and subsequently television in the twentieth century. The "hypothermic needle model," also known as the magic bullet theory, was one of the earliest of such models based on which media messages are deliberately sent with homogenized and standardized content, with the audience entirely accepting them (Hartley, Saunders, Montgomery, & Fiske, 1994). Another approach contradicted the magic bullet theory and was based on the idea that the audience is able to select which messages they prefer. This approach gave life to the uses and gratifications (U&G) model.

The uses and gratifications model tries to look into the motivations behind people's decision to consume a specific type of media and also the gratifications they may gain from it. This model bases its efforts on the social and psychological background of the audience (Katz, Blumler, & Gurevitch, 1974). According to this theory, users are capable of explaining why they use media and also stating the fact that media is one of the sources for obtaining the gratifications they seek (Palmgreen, 1984).

One of the first examples of applying the U&G model was the work done by Herzog to find why people watch soap operas (Herzog, 1940). Katz et al. (1974) mentioned five assumptions that could be considered as founding elements of U&G:

1) the audience decides what media to consume based on their goals and they are considered an active element in the whole process;
2) the choice of media lies within the audience and this issue limits the possibility of theorization of direct media effects on behavior or attitudes of the audience;
3) there are different sources of gratification for the users and these sources compete with each other;

(Continued)

4) the audience are capable of self-reporting not only the amount of the media they use, but also the reason(s) behind their media consumption; and

5) the researchers who use U&G should avoid value judgments about cultural differences and such judgments should be left to the user himself/herself.

They also suggested that U&G researchers should consider:

(1) the social and psychological origins of (2) needs, which generate (3) expectations of (4) the mass media or other sources, which lead to (5) differential patterns of media exposure (or engagement in other activities), resulting in (6) need gratifications and (7) other consequences, perhaps mostly unintended ones. (Katz et al., 1974, p. 20)

The notion of an active audience made researchers try to categorize different needs that form media users' behaviors in their media use. One of these categorizations was put forward by Blumler (1979) who suggested that there are four basic types of activities media users perform in relation to their use:

1) Utility (using the media to perform tasks);
2) Intentionality (using media based on previous motivations);
3) Selectivity (uses that reflects the users' interests; and
4) Imperviousness to influence (the meaning that the audience give to the content presented by the media which is not capable of influencing the users all the time).

Another model for categorizing media users' needs was proposed by McQuail, Blumler, and Brown (1972). This model suggested four main categories for the gratifications that users seek:

(Continued)

1) Diversion: escaping from everyday routines and problems;
2) Personal relationships: utilizing media for companionship;
3) Personal identity: exploring reality and rein-forcing one's values; and
4) Surveillance: information seeking in order to accomplish goals.

Katz, Gurevitch, and Haas (1973) also distin-guished five basic categories of needs that different media users may have:

1) Cognitive needs that are related to gaining more information and knowledge;
2) Affective needs that are related to emotions and aesthetic issues;
3) Personal integrative needs that are related gaining credibility and confidence and status;
4) Social integrative needs that are related to maintaining interaction with family and friends; and
5) Tension release needs that are related to escaping from social roles to an extent.

Moreover, Palmgreen (1984) made a more clear dis-tinction between gratification sought and gratifica-tions obtained, which are not always the same. The former builds the way the audience behaves while using the media and the latter is what the audience gains based on those sets of behaviors.

U&G and New Media

Ruggerio (2000) claimed that uses and gratifications theory "has always provided a cutting edge theoreti-cal approach in the initial stages of each new mass communications medium: newspapers, radio, televi-sion, and now the Internet" (p. 27). New technolo-gies, social media, and the Internet provide users with new sources, so they can satisfy their needs and also act as a means of interpersonal communi-cation as well as mass communication. According

This is a really good introduction to the basic topic of uses and gratifica-tions. Maziar does a really good job of defining the topic in the first two pages of the paper. What he could do is provide a stronger preview to the paper though . . . to frame the paper better for the reader.

(Continued)

to Angleman (2000), throughout history new media caused the audience to develop new gratifications and motivations, turning U&G into a logical option for studying these new media.

Marghalani, Palmgreen, and Boyd (1998) applied a need-based uses and gratifications perspective to study how consumers of direct satellite broadcasting (DBS) gratify their needs using this media as a somehow new form of technology. Examining the use of pagers among students, Leung and Wei (2000) confirmed the claim made by Rogers (1995) that higher-status individuals are more likely to start using new media as a way of social distinction.

One of the areas in which U&G has been applied for understanding the use of new media is interactive mobile services, which includes various activities including surfing the web, playing games, payments etc. (Jih & Lee, 2004; Varshney, 2003). To improve the application of U&G model to new media, some other aspects have been added to this model, including "learning" and "socialization" (James, Wotring, & Forrest, 1995), "personal involvement" and "continuing relationships" (Eighmey & McCord, 1998).

One of the most important aspects of applying the uses and gratifications model to understand the relationship between the Internet and its users is the fact that the Internet is an interactive media and, since U&G deals with active audience, this theoretical approach could be regarded as highly suitable for studying the Internet (Hanjun, 2000). The fact that the Internet is an interactive media also makes its users more actively involved in using the Internet (Kaye & Johnson, 2004). Weiser (2001) suggested two main categories for reasons to use the Internet, namely "social orientation" and "practical orientation". Moreover, Stafford, Stafford, and Schkade (2004) added social gratification as a unique characteristic of the Internet to pre-existing process gratification and content gratification.

One of the most notable differences between social gratifications of the Internet (the ability to start conversations with other people at any time) and such gratifications from other social networks is

(Continued)

that the Internet provides the chance to extend these networks, unlike media such as telephones that provide gratifications only based on existing social networks (Krishnatray, Singh, Raghavan, & Varma, 2009). Papacharissi and Rubin (2000) developed an Internet usage scale and stated motivations for using the Internet, which can be categorized into five main types, including interpersonal útility, pass time, information seeking, convenience, and entertainment.

The U&G approach has been used frequently to understand the behaviors of Internet users in America and Europe (Roy, 2008). There have also been efforts to apply it to other contexts like India (Roy, 2008, 2009) and Romania (Balaban & Bǎltǎaretu, 2010). Besides, Internet use has been compared in different parts of the world (Spencer, Croucher, & Hoelscher, 2012).

Applying the uses and gratifications approach to Facebook users who are in Facebook groups has shown that their uses are based on four types of needs, including socializing, entertainment, self-seeking, and information (Park, Kee, & Valenzuela, 2009).

Studying young users' motivations for using YouTube to watch traditional and comedy-related news videos showed that these motivations are similar to those already recognized in research on news-visiting in the past (Hanson & Haridakis, 2008). Mosemghvdlishvili and Jansz (2013) studied different attitudes towards Islam among users who used YouTube to video-blog on this issue and suggested that "one could generalize and state that in terms of the under-representation of Muslim sources in the Western mainstream media (Richardson, 2006), YouTube offers them a revitalized 'public sphere' in which to present their own perspective and interpretation of events" (p. 495).

A study of Twitter users based on the U&G approach showed that creating content and mentioning other users, i.e interacting with them rather than with the content, is the most important activity on this micro-blogging site (Ballard, 2011). Lim and Ting (2012) also applied a U&G approach to investigate

There is a lot of great information being provided in this section on how U&G research has been expanded into new media, such as the Internet. However, Maziar could do a bit more to transition between the paragraphs, or could have done a bit more at the start of the section to preview it to shape the section even more.

(Continued)

how Malaysian consumers develop their attitude and online shopping intentions.

U&G in an Intercultural Context

The uses and gratifications model provides strong enough tools for researchers to compare users from different cultures based on their media activities and motivations. Blumler, Gurevitch, & Katz (1985) encouraged researchers to examine the question of if the gratifications mentioned by this model apply to individuals from various cultures.

U&G has been applied in a number of studies to see if there is a difference in how people from different cultures use media. Albarran and Umphrey (1993) used this model to compare television motivation and program preferences between three ethnic groups in the United States, namely whites, blacks, and Hispanics. Grace-Farfaglia et al. (2006) tried to measure the social impact of online community participation in American, Korean, and Dutch users and found that these communities have different motives for their web usage, which are unique to their national culture and subculture.

Researchers have used U&G to understand the reason individuals consume media while being in the process of acculturation, including research on Chinese (Hwang & He, 1999; Huang, 1993), Korean (Moon & Ha, 2005), East Asian (Ye, 2005; Reece & Palmgreen, 2000), and African-American (Abrams & Giles, 2007) immigrants in the US.

Another instance of applying U&G in intercultural contexts is the study by Kamm (2011) that tried to understand why the practice of live action role-playing is not common in Japan, despite the fact that masquerading as media characters exists.

Applying U&G to the Context of Television and Cinema Viewing

Relations between the audience and television programs, including soap operas and series, have been one of interesting issues for researchers who use

This is a nice short review of U&G in an international context. As you can see from the structure of the review, Maziar has chosen to do a topical or thematic review of literature. It would be nice though to link the sections together a bit more clearly.

(Continued)

U&G, i.e Carveth and Alexander (1985), Rubin (1983), Rubin and Perse (1987), and Nabi, Stitt, Halford, and Finnerty (2006). As Rubin (1983) stated, there are two types of television audiences—those who consume it as an instrument and those who use it in a ritualized way.

Although television viewing used to be considered as a more ritualized and passive activity with a low level of involvement (Ehrenberg & Wakshlag, 1987), emergence of the Internet and web 2.0 has turned this activity to a more instrumental and active way through which fans perform activities, which can be divided into two main categories. First, they use the Internet to gain information about their favorite shows, and second, they create their own content regarding their loved shows in fan websites and forums (Andrejevic, 2008). The latter has been the subject of some U&G studies. Moreover, Godlewski and Perse (2010) suggested that related online activity after watching reality TV, including searching more content related to the program or show, can happen when the audience is not satisfied with the program.

The audience activity takes an even more interactive form when it comes to voting for the content of reality TV shows that may affect the output of the show; the audience who has voted has actively participated in the process of creating the program (Liu & Shrum, 2002).

According to Papacharissi and Mendelson (2007), individuals watch television reality shows mainly with the purpose of passing time in an almost ritual way; however these programs can potentially be used for the purpose of entertaining as well. Adriaens, Van Demme, and Courtois (2011) examined TV-viewing based on the spatial and social context. Moreover, viewing *Telenovela*—soap operas from Latin America—has been the subject of U&G studies (Mayer, 2003; Rios, 2003).

Television consumption by children from different cultures has been one of the issues tackled by researchers using the U&G approach (Rubin, 1977; Zohoori, 1988). There have also been a significant number of studies that used the uses and gratifications

(Continued)

model to analyze the watching of religious TV programs (Petterson, 1986; Abelman, 1987). The U&G approach has also been used to study the viewing of violent television programs and crime dramas (Brown, Lauricella, Douai, and Ziadi, 2012) and the relationship between exposure to violent television programs and behaviors such as sensation seeking and verbal aggressiveness (Greene & Krcmar, 2005).

Examining how viewers from different cultures try to gratify their needs by watching television shows has been one of the areas of study which have applied U&G in an intercultural context. Zhou (2011) used U&G as well as perceived impact to find out how American television programs may affect Chinese college students.

Some studies have examined the way in which audiences and fans from different cultures perceive specific TV drama shows, e.g. the cases of Chinese viewers of *Friends* (Xiaying, 2012) and *Prison Break* (Li, Chen, & Nakazawa, 2013). In the case of *Prison Break*, it was uncovered that the viewers who watched this TV series via the web, had nicknames for the characters of the show and even identified with one of the characters whose activities were considered inhuman, mostly because of his rare merciful acts.

Abdulrahim, Al-Kandari, and Hasanen (2009) suggested that viewers from cultures different from that which a television program is attributed to are likely to accept concepts from the other culture, e.g. gender equality:

> In this study, heavy viewers endorsed equal gender roles and liberal outlooks in society to a greater extent than did light viewers. Such heavy viewers perhaps see the world through American eyes. Even if it has been suggested hypothetically that the American media industry limits the presentation of equal gender roles or liberal outlooks, they are, at least, not very conservative in comparison with the presentation of these ideas in the Arab media. (p. 69–70)

According to some researchers, the media, including television shows, can have positive effects

(Continued)

on the acculturation process of immigrants (John-son, 1996; Somani, 2010). Moreover, Abrams (2010) found that there is a positive relationship between selecting television for entertainment by Asian-American audiences and their perception of Caucasian vitality as the dominant cultural group.

There have been a number of studies that tackled the media consumption of film audiences using the U&G approach (Austin, 1986; Tesser, Millar, & Wu, 1988; Young, 2000). Young (2000) suggests that U&G stud-ies of films should take cultural backgrounds into account, since consumption of this form of media does not "take place in a cultural vacuum" (p. 463).

Movie fans probably use the Internet and web to view films, seek information, and even create related content just as fans of TV shows do. It is safe to assume these new opportunities have helped movie fans to become an active audience, which is an impor-tant concept to the uses and gratifications model, therefore U&G can provide new directions for study-ing how the audience perceives films. Moreover, there is room for conducting such studies in intercultural contexts as well.

The section on U&G and cinema or film viewing offered a different area of review on this theory than what is discussed in the text. As you can see from this paper and the chapter, many of the theories you will read have been studied in many different contexts.

Criticism

Although uses and gratifications model has been a useful tool in media studies, it has been the tar-get of some criticism. Katz (1987) stated one of the early criticisms of this approach:

> Early gratifications researches had leaned too heavily on self-reports, was unsophisticated about the social origin of the needs that audi-ences bring to the media, too uncritical of the possible dysfunctions both for self and society of certain kinds of audience satisfaction, and too captivated by the inventive diversity of audience uses to pay much attention to the con-straints of the text. (p. 9)

According to Ball-Rokeach (1998) the inability of U&G to address the outcome of the use of media

(Continued)

by the audience is one of the limitations of this model. Moreover, LaRose, Mastro, & Eastin (2001) stated that "[a]ttempts by uses and gratifications researchers (Babrow & Swanson, 1988) to distinguish gratifications from formulations involving outcome expectations were of no avail and failed to produce more robust explanations of media exposure, suggesting that they may be related constructs" (p. 399).

One of the attempts to make the U&G model more productive was made by Swanson (1987) who suggested that research based on this model should focus on the role of gratification seeking in using mass media; the relation between gratifications and mental frames used by the audience in order to understand media content; and the link between gratifications and media content. Also Rubin (1994) stated that using the U&G model and media effects research combined could be highly productive.

References

Abdulrahim, M. A., Al-Kandari, A. A., & Hasanen, M. (2009). The influence of American television programs on university students in Kuwait: A synthesis. *European Journal of American Culture, 28,* 57–74.

Abelman, R. (1987). Why do people watch religious TV? A uses and gratifications approach. *Review of Religious Research, 29,* 199–210.

Abrams, J. R. (2010). Asian American television activity: Is it related to outgroup vitality? *International Journal of Intercultural Relations, 34,* 541–550.

Abrams, J. R., & Giles, H. (2007). Ethnic identity gratifications selection and avoidance by African Americans: A group vitality and social identity gratifications perspective. *Media Psychology, 9,* 115–134.

Adriaens, F., Van Damme, E., & Courtois, C. (2011). The spatial and social contexts of television-viewing adolescents. *Poetics, 39,* 205–227.

Albarran, A. B., & Umphrey, D. (1993). Profile: An examination of television motivations and program preferences by Hispanics, blacks, and whites. *Journal of Broadcasting & Electronic Media, 37,* 95–103.

Andrejevic, M. (2008). Watching television without pity the productivity of online fans. *Television & New Media, 9,* 24–46.

Angleman, S. (December, 2000). *Uses and gratifications and Internet profiles: A factor analysis. Is internet use and travel to Cyberspace reinforced by unrealized gratifications?* Paper presented at the Western Science Social Association 2001 Conference held in Reno, NV. <www.jrily.com/LiteraryIllusions/InternetGratificationStudyIndex.html> (01.12.2013).

Austin, B. A. (1986). Motivations for movie attendance. *Communication Quarterly, 34,* 115–126.

(Continued)

Babrow, A. S., & Swanson, D. L. (1988). Disentangling antecedents of audience exposure levels: Extending expectancy-value analyses of gratifications sought from television news. *Communications Monographs*, *55*, 1–21.

Balaban, D. C., & Bălăreţu, C. M. (2010). Motivation in using social network sites by Romanian students. A qualitative approach. *Journal of Media Research-Revista de Studii Media*, 1, 67–74.

Ball-Rokeach, S. J. (1998). A theory of media power and a theory of media use: Different stories, questions, and ways of thinking. *Mass Communication and Society*, *1*(1–2), 5–40.

Ballard, C. L. (2011). *"What's happening" @Twitter: A uses and gratifications approach*. Unpublished Master's Theses. University of Kentucky, Lexington, Kentucky. Retrieved from http://uknowledge.uky.edu/cgi/viewcontent.cgi?article=1150&context=gradschool_theses.

Blumler, J. G. (1979). The role of theory in uses and gratifications studies. *Communication Research*, *6*, 9–36.

Blumler, J. G., Gurevitch, M., & Katz, E. (1985). Reaching out: A future for gratifications research. *Media gratifications research: Current perspectives*, 255–273.

Brown, D., Lauricella, S., Douai, A., & Zaidi, A. (2012). Consuming television crime drama: A uses and gratifications approach. *American Communication Journal*, *14*, 47–61.

Carveth, R. & Alexander, A. (1985). Soap opera viewing motivations and the cultivation process. *Journal of Broadcasting & Electronic Media*, *29*, 259–273.

Ehrenberg, A. S., & Wakshlag, J. (1987). Repeat-viewing with people-meters. *Journal of Advertising Research*, *27*, 9–13.

Eighmey, J., & McCord, L. (1998). Adding value in the information age: Uses and gratifications of sites on the World Wide Web. *Journal of Business Research*, *41*, 187–194.

Godlewski, L. R., & Perse, E. M. (2010). Audience activity and reality television: Identification, online activity, and satisfaction. *Communication Quarterly*, *58*, 148–169.

Grace-Farfaglia, P., Dekkers, A., Sundararajan, B., Peters, L., & Park, S. H. (2006). Multinational web uses and gratifications: Measuring the social impact of online community participation across national boundaries. *Electronic Commerce Research*, *6*, 75–101.

Greene, K., & Krcmar, M. (2005). Predicting exposure to and liking of media violence: A uses and gratifications approach. *Communications Studies*, *56*, 71–93.

Hanjun, K. (2000). *Internet uses and gratifications: Understanding motivations for using the Internet*, Paper Presented at the Annual Meeting of the Association for Education in Journalism and Mass Communication.

Hanson, G., & Haridakis, P. (2008). YouTube users watching and sharing the news: A uses and gratifications approach. *Journal of Electronic Publishing*, *11*(3).

Hartley, J., Saunders, D., Montgomery, M., & Fiske, J. (1994). *Key concepts in communication and cultural studies* (p. 267). London: Routledge.

(Continued)

Herzog, H. (1940). Professor quiz: A gratification study. In P. F Lazarfeld (Ed.), *Radio and the printed page* (pp. 64–93). New York, NY: Duell, Sloan, & Pearce.

Huang, B. (1993). *Media use in the acculturation process of Chinese immigrants in Silicon Valley*. Unpublished master's thesis, San Jose State University, California.

Hwang, B. H., & He, Z. (1999). Media uses and acculturation among Chinese immigrants in the USA: A uses and gratifications approach. *International Communication Gazette, 61*, 5–22.

James, M. L., Wotring, C. E., & Forrest, E. J. (1995). An exploratory study of the perceived benefits of electronic bulletin board use and their impact on other communication activities. *Journal of Broadcasting & Electronic Media, 39*, 30–50.

Jih, W. J. K., & Lee, S. F. (2003). An exploratory analysis of relationships between cellular phone uses shopping motivators and lifestyle indicators. *Journal of Computer Information Systems, 44*, 65–73.

Johnson, T. J., & Kaye, B. K. (2004). For whom the web toils: How Internet experience predicts web reliance and credibility. *Atlantic Journal of Communication, 12*, 19–45.

Kamm, B. O. (2011). Why Japan does not Larp. In T. D. Henriksen, C. Bierlich, K. F. Hansen, & V. Kelle (Eds.), *Think Larp: Academic Writing from KP2011* (pp. 52–69). Copenhagen: Rollespilsakademiet.

Katz, E. (1987). Communication research since Lazarsfeld. *Public Opinion Quarterly, 51*, 525–545.

Katz, E., Blumler, J., & Gurevitch, M. (1974). Utilization of mass communication by the individual. In J. Blumler & E. Katz (Eds.), *The uses of mass communication: Current perspectives on gratifications research* (pp. 19–34). Beverly Hills, CA: Sage.

Katz, E., Gurevitch, M., & Haas, H. (1973). On the use of mass media for important things. *American Sociological Review, 38*, 164–181.

Kaye, B. K., & Johnson, T. J. (2004). A web for all reasons: Uses and gratifications of Internet components for political information. *Telematics and Informatics, 21*, 197–223.

Krishnatray, P., Singh, P. P., Raghavan, S., & Varma, V. (2009). Gratifications from new media: Gender differences in Internet use in Cybercafes. *Journal of Creative Communications, 4*, 19–31.

LaRose, R., Mastro, D., & Eastin, M. S. (2001). Understanding internet usage: A social-cognitive approach to uses and gratifications. *Social Science Computer Review, 19*, 395–413.

Leung, L., & Wei, R. (2000). The gratifications of pager use: sociability, information-seeking, entertainment, utility, and fashion and status. *Telematics and Informatics, 15*, 253–264.

Li, L., Chen, Y., & Nakazawa, M. (2013). Voices of Chinese Web-TV audiences: A case of applying uses and gratifications theory to examine popularity of Prison Break in China. *China Media Research, 9*, 63.

Lim, W. M., & Ting, D. H. (2012). E-shopping: An analysis of the Uses and Gratifications Theory. *Modern Applied Science, 6*, 48.

(Continued)

Liu, Y., & Shrum, L. J. (2002). What is interactivity and is it always such a good thing? Implications of definition, person, and situation for the influence of interactivity on advertising effectiveness. *Journal of advertising, 31*, 53–64.

Marghalani, K., Palmgreen, P., & Boyd, D. A. (1998). The utilization of direct satellite broadcasting (DBS) in Saudi Arabia. *Journal of Broadcasting & Electronic Media, 42*, 297–314.

Mayer, V. (2003). Living telenovelas/telenovelizing life: Mexican American girls' identities and transnational telenovelas. *Journal of Communication, 53*, 479–495.

McQuail, D., Blumler, J., & Brown, J. (1972). The television audience: A revised perspective. In D. McQuail (Ed.), *Sociology of mass communications* (pp. 135–165). Middlesex, England: Penguin.

Moon, S. J., & Ha, J. Y. (2005). Korean immigrants' media uses and gratifications in Los Angeles' Koreatown. *MEDIA ASIA-SINGAPORE-, 32*, 211.

Mosemghvdlishvili, L., & Jansz, J. (2013). Framing and praising Allah on YouTube: Exploring user-created videos about Islam and the motivations for producing them. *New Media & Society, 15*, 482–500.

Nabi, R. L., Stitt, C. R., Halford, J., & Finnerty, K. L. (2006). Emotional and cognitive predictors of the enjoyment of reality-based and fictional television programming: An elaboration of the uses and gratifications perspective. *Media Psychology, 8*, 421–447.

Palmgreen, P. (1984). Uses and gratifications: a theoretical perspective. In R. N. Bostrom (Ed.), *Communication yearbook, 8* (pp. 20–55). Beverly Hills, CA: Sage.

Papacharissi, Z., & Mendelson, A. L. (2007). An exploratory study of reality appeal: Uses and gratifications of reality TV shows. *Journal of Broadcasting & Electronic Media, 51*, 355–370.

Papacharissi, Z., & Rubin, A. M. (2000). Predictors of Internet use. *Journal of Broadcasting & Electronic Media, 44*, 175–196.

Park, N., Kee, K., & Valenzuela, S. (2009). Being immersed in social networking environment: Facebook groups, uses and gratifications, and social outcomes. *Cyber Psychology & Behavior, 12*, 729–733.

Petterson, T. (1986). The audiences' uses and gratifications of TV worship services. *Journal for the Scientific Study of Religion, 25*, 391–409.

Reece, D., & Palmgreen, P. (2000). Coming to America: Need for acculturation and media use motives among Indian sojourners in the US. *International Journal of Intercultural Relations, 24*, 807–824.

Rios, D. I. (2003). US Latino audiences of "telenovelas". *Journal of Latinos and Education, 2*, 59–65.

Roy, S. K. (2008). Determining uses & gratifications for Indian Internet users. *Case Studies in Business, Industry & Government Statistics, 2*, 78–91.

Roy, S. K. (2009). Internet uses and gratifications: A survey in the Indian context. *Computers in Human Behavior, 29*, 878–886.

Rubin, A. M. (1977). Television usage, attitudes and viewing behaviors of children and adolescents. *Journal of Broadcasting & Electronic Media, 21*, 355–369.

(Continued)

Rubin, A. M. (1983). Television uses and gratifications: The interactions of viewing patterns and motivations. *Journal of Broadcasting & Electronic Media*, 27, 37–51.

Rubin, A. M. (1994). Media uses and effects: A uses and gratifications perspective. In J. Bryant & D. Zillmann (Eds.), *Media effects: Advances in theory and research* (pp. 417–436). Hillsdale, NJ: Lawrence Erlbaum Associates, Inc.

Rubin, A. M., & Perse, E. M. (1987). Audience activity and soap opera involvement a uses and effects investigation. *Human Communication Research*, 14, 246–268.

Ruggiero, T. (2000). Uses and gratifications theory in the 21st century. *Mass Communication & Society*, 3, 3–37.

Somani, I. S. (2010). Becoming American. *Journal of International and Intercultural Communication*, 3, 59–81.

Spencer, A. T., Croucher, S. M., & Hoelscher, C. S. (2012). Uses and gratifications meets the Internet: A cross-cultural comparison of U.S. and Nicaraguan new media usage. *Human Communication*, 15, 228–239.

Stafford, T. F., Stafford, M. R., & Schkade, L. L. (2004). Determining uses and gratifications for the Internet. *Decision Sciences*, 35, 259–288.

Swanson, D. L. (1987). Gratification seeking, media exposure, and audience interpretations. *Journal of Broadcasting & Electronic Media*, 31, 237–254.

Tesser, A., Millar, K., & Wu, C. H. (1988). On the perceived functions of movies. *The Journal of psychology*, 122, 441–449.

Varshney, U. (2003). Wireless I: mobile and wireless information systems: applications, networks, and research problems. *Communications of the Association for Information Systems*, 12, 155–166.

Weiser, E. B. (2001). The functions of Internet use and their social and psychological consequences. *Cyberpsychology*, 4, 723–741.

Xiaying, X. U. (2012). Chinese Audiences and U.S. Sitcoms: The Case of Friends. *Projections*, 1, 1–30.

Ye, J. (2005). Acculturative stress and use of the Internet among East Asian international students in the United States. *CyberPsychology & Behavior*, 8, 154–161.

Young, S. D. (2000). Movies as equipment for living: A developmental analysis of the importance of film in everyday life. *Critical Studies in Media Communication*, 17, 447–468.

Zhou, Z. (2011). *The impact of American television on Chinese college students.* (Unpublished doctoral dissertation). Wake Forest University, Winston-Salem, North Carolina, United States. Retrieved from http://wakespace.lib.wfu.edu/bitstream/handle/10339/33450/Zhou_wfu_0248M_10147.pdf.

Zohoori, A. (1988). A cross-cultural analysis of children's television use. *Journal of Broadcasting & Electronic Media*, 32, 105–113.

11 PERSUASION

Chapter Outline

- What is Persuasion?
- Cognitive Dissonance
- Elaboration Likelihood Model
- Inoculation
- Student Paper

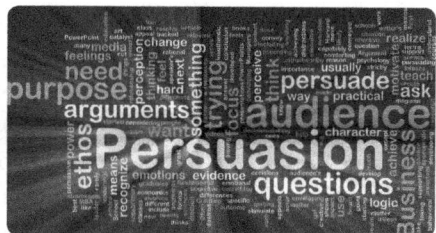

We have all been persuaded to or have persuaded someone to do something (or at least tried). You may have been persuaded to buy something recently by a salesperson, or you might have tried to persuade someone to loan you some money or their car, you may have also tried to persuade an instructor to give you an extension on an assignment. In some cases we are able to persuade or influence people to do what we would like them to do, and in other cases we are not successful. How we persuade someone, the types of appeals we use when trying to influence a person to do what we would like them to do, and the appropriate ways to persuade have been studied for centuries. In Ancient Greece philosophers like Gorgias, Plato, Corax, and Tisias wrote some of the first known works exploring the art of persuasive communication. **Persuasive communication** or **persuasion** is the study of "any message that is intended to shape, reinforce, or change the responses of another, or others" (Miller, 1980, p. 11). This chapter addresses the communicative aspects of persuasion and different models of persuasion.

In this chapter we will explore persuasive communication or the study of messages that shape, reinforce, or elicit a change response in another or others. The theories and concepts, like those in many other chapters, vary considerably. In the first section we will define persuasion and discuss the essential elements and outcomes of persuasion. In the second through fourth sections we will examine three key theoretical areas and/or models in persuasive communication. There are a variety of persuasive communication theories and models that could be included in this chapter. These have been chosen because they represent key historical and developing theories/models with both theoretical and practical applications. Therefore, in the second section we will examine cognitive dissonance theory. In the third section we will explore the elaboration likelihood model. In the fourth section we will describe inoculation theory. Within this discussion of inoculation, a case study about extremist propaganda is provided to further illustrate the applicability of inoculation. In the fifth and final section you will find a student paper. This paper is an undergraduate persuasive communication student paper by Jennifer Wagner on inoculation, which is included to serve as an example of the kind of writing assignment you *could* do for a persuasive communication theory assignment.

What is Persuasion?

Persuasion is "any message that is intended to shape, reinforce, or change the responses of another, or others" (Miller, 1980, p. 11). It is key to start this discussion about persuasion by describing the fine line between persuasion, coercion, and manipulation. **Coercion** is the act of using political or economic sanctions, or guns to force change in someone or an organization. **Manipulation** is the act of influencing or managing someone deviously or shrewdly. There are elements of coercion and manipulation in persuasion, but with differences. All three (persuasion, coercion, and manipulation) rely heavily on verbal and nonverbal symbols to get their messages across. However, coercion includes the use of force or threats to accomplish an agenda. The verbal and nonverbal symbols in manipulation are devious, and can verge on dishonest to help a person to "manipulate" another. Coercion and persuasion are often linked together, though, as coercive tactics are often preceded by persuasive messages. For example, seldom is a war started between nations without a series of messages being exchanged. These messages are aimed at persuading one of the nations in the dispute to give up some territory, to pay a fine, or to pay some other economic/political penalty. If the persuasive tactics do not work, then political/economic sanctions or military force could be used to achieve the desired outcome. Thus, while persuasion is not directly coercion, it is indirectly coercive in that the effectiveness of many messages is determined by the credibility of messages that may be deemed threatening. If a rival nation does not perceive their opposing nation's threats of economic penalties as real or a threat to their economic livelihood, they will be less likely to take persuasive appeals seriously, and thus not be persuaded (Miller, 1980, 2002).

While these three communication strategies may share elements, they differ as well. First, the motives of the persuader determine if a persuasive attempt will go from persuasion to manipulation to coercion. Second, persuasion can serve as defense against manipulation. Third, persuasion is generally perceived as a more ethical form of communication than manipulation and/or coercion (Dillard & Pfau, 2002).

KEY TERM 11.1

Persuasion/persuasive communication – the study of any message that is intended to shape, reinforce, or change the responses of another, or others.

WHAT DO YOU THINK 11.1

Think about coercion, manipulation, and persuasion. Can you think of a time when you were persuaded, manipulated, and coerced? How were these three situations different? How were the situations similar?

The theories and models in this chapter focus on messages and how those messages relate to shifts in an individual's responses. Before we move onto these theories and models, we should look at what is often "shifted." The purpose of persuasion is to influence people's attitudes, behaviors, beliefs, motives, and values. **Beliefs** are things that people believe to be true or false—facts. For example, people say, "I believe in God." They are stating a fact to them. A **value** is something we think to be good/bad, right/wrong, etc. For example, a person may say, "I value universal health care." To that person universal health care is a good thing that should be available. A **motive** is a self-interest or desire we have for others or ourselves. When a person says, "I want to live a healthy life" they are describing a motive. An **attitude** is "a relatively enduring predisposition to respond favorably or unfavorably" toward something or someone (Simons, 1976, p. 80). Since attitudes are enduring they are hard to change. However, attitudes are learned, and are thus changeable. Attitudes also influence behaviors. A **behavior** is an intentional action (physical or verbal). The goal of most persuasive messages is to affect behavior in some way: to shape, to reinforce, or to change it. To do so, the sender(s) of the persuasive message(s) must understand the receiver's beliefs, values, motives, and attitudes, as all influence behavior. Consider the following example:

EXAMPLE 11.1

If a person believes (belief) prison sentences for drug offenders deters drug use, and this person values a drug free community, it is likely that person will have a positive attitude toward long prison sentences for drug offenders. If such a person is motivated (persuaded), he/she may vote (behavior) to pass stronger laws against drug users.

WHAT DO YOU THINK 11.2

Using the example above about prison sentences for drug offenders, create your own example of how beliefs, values, attitudes, and behaviors are related.

With this basic discussion of the persuasive model behind us, let's discuss three possible outcomes of persuasion that apply to various theories/models: shaping, reinforcing, and changing. One desired outcome of persuasion is to shape or condition an individual's responses, particularly when they have limited experience with a message or concept. Similar to "learning" and "socialization," persuasion to shape or condition is when people are taught abstract values and attitudes valued by society, and taught new societal concepts (Rokeach, 1968, 1973). Such values and attitudes include: what is a good person and how to be independent. New societal concepts include concepts like "the Internet." Society has had to learn this concept and be persuaded to use it. A second desired outcome of persuasion is to reinforce existing beliefs. Miller and Burgoon (1973) said that much persuasive communication aims to reinforce "currently held convictions and to make them more resistant to change" (p. 5). Most religious messages (a sermon on Sunday), a political speech at a rally, or other speeches given to audiences typically reinforce current beliefs, values, and attitudes. The third desired outcome is the one most of us are probably most familiar with: persuasion as a process of change. Many classic and current definitions of persuasion emphasize how being persuaded is being changed, modified, influenced, or affected (Brembeck & Howell, 1952; Miller, 1980, 2002). While so many definitions of persuasion focus on changing behaviors and attitudes, researchers note how difficult it can be to change, or at least measure the change in behaviors and attitudes (Fishbein & Ajzen, 1975; Miller, 1980, 2002).

The following three sections of the chapter address different ways in which messages shift individuals' responses and focus on different persuasive communication outcomes. Within each section you will find different ways to persuade or to protect oneself from persuasion. Each section is just a glimpse into the depth of persuasion theory. If you want to know more about any of these areas of study, look to some of the provided references, the online references, or talk to your instructor for more details.

Cognitive Dissonance

Probably one of the most well-known and researched theories in persuasion is Festinger's (1957; Festinger & Carlsmith, 1959) cognitive dissonance theory. **Cognitive dissonance theory** explains the relationship between attitude and behavior. Specifically, this theory describes our need for consistency between attitudes and behaviors, and how we feel when attitudes and behaviors do not match up (dissonance). When developing cognitive dissonance theory, Festinger was interested in how people seek consistency with their behaviors and attitudes. What happens when behaviors and attitudes are inconsistent, when there is a discrepancy? When there is a discrepancy people generally take steps to reduce it because inconsistent or contradictory beliefs lead to mental and emotional disharmony (dissonance), which most of us try to avoid. The amount of dissonance we feel about particular issues will depend on a variety of variables, such as how much we value a belief, and the extent to which our beliefs, behaviors, and attitudes are inconsistent. When trying to reduce dissonance, there are three key strategies. First, we can try to focus on more supportive beliefs that outweigh the dissonant behavior(s) and/or belief(s). Second, we can attempt to reduce the significance of the conflicting behavior(s) and/or belief(s). Third, we can try to change the conflicting behavior(s) and/or belief(s) so they are more consistent with other behavior(s) and/or belief(s). Consider the following examples of cognitive dissonance.

A man who considers himself to be an eco-friendly person just purchased a new car. Unfortunately, he did not do a good job at the dealership when it comes to looking into the gas mileage the car gets. His new car is a "gas guzzler." The conflict for him is that he is an environmentally conscious person who just bought a car that is not environmentally friendly. To reduce this internal conflict he has two options: 1) get rid of the car somehow (sell it or trade it in) and get another one that is environmentally friendly like he is, or 2) be less environmentally conscious. With the second option he could drive the car very little to try to minimize the effects of using so much gas. The key is he needs to find some way to resolve this dissonance or internal conflict between his attitude toward the environment and his behavior (buying a gas guzzler).

Festinger (1957) provided an example of a smoker who knows smoking is bad for his health. In the case of smoking, people know it is bad for their health, that is a given. However, people continue to smoke cigarettes because: 1) they enjoy it; 2) they think the chances of getting really sick are not all that high; 3) people think they can't avoid everything that will get them sick; and 4) some people say if they quit smoking they gain weight, and gaining weight is a worse fate than what smoking can bring.

KEY TERM 11.2

Cognitive dissonance theory – a theory that explains the relationship between attitude and behavior. Specifically, the theory describes our need for consistency between attitudes and behaviors, and how we feel when attitudes and behaviors do not match up (dissonance).

Smoking (behavior) conflicts with beliefs we are taught about health, for example, don't do things that will cause you harm. Yet, people still do it because their health attitudes and behavior (smoking) are not that inconsistent with one another (Festinger, 1957). While the Festinger reference may be from 1957, the arguments still hold true today. Since Festinger's 1957 and 1959 experiments, researchers have been exploring dissonance, particularly from the 1960s to the 1980s. During this time research showed overall support for the theory (Cooper & Fazio, 1984; Oshikawa, 1969). However, the theory has also been criticized over the decades, with two main critiques lodged against it. First, researchers have argued that the theory is not falsifiable, in that if a person's attitude does not change a researcher can argue there may not have been any dissonance present to begin. This is where researchers such as Oliver

(1997) have argued that a person must be committed to a behavior in order for dissonance to exist. If your belief in behavior X contradicts your attitudes about it, but you really do not care about the behavior, you are not likely to have dissonance, unlike if you are emotionally or logically vested in the behavior. Second, some researchers have argued that people do not change their behavior to reduce emotional or psychological disharmony from dissonance, but instead alter behaviors because our self-perception requires us to act a certain way (Bem, 1967). In this line of thinking we do not juggle attitudinal discrepancies and try to reduce them, but we see ourselves act a certain way and then assume our attitude must match the behavior(s).

WHAT DO YOU THINK 11.3

Think about any recent purchases you have made. Did you experience any dissonance afterward? It is common for people to feel regret for a purchase, which is a kind of dissonance. How have you dealt with this if you have had it?

Cognitive Dissonance Theory Research

Since Festinger's (1957) early work, cognitive dissonance research has explored dissonance (emotional and psychological) in various settings. Three settings that have received considerable, and/or growing attentions are: smoking cessation, consumer purchases, and fundraising. Dissonance research on smokers has found that when first exposed to information showing a relationship between smoking and health risks (like cancer), regular smokers are likely to be in a state of dissonance. The knowledge that an individual (regardless of age) is a regular smoker who wants to continue smoking is dissonant with the knowledge that heavy smoking is harmful to his or her health (Feather, 1962; Gibbons, Eggleston, & Benthin, 1997; Johnson, 1968; Simmons, Webb, & Brandon, 2004). Regular smokers, even healthcare practitioners who smoke (nurses and doctors), lower this dissonance by avoiding information that causes the dissonance (i.e., information about cancer caused by smoking) (Clark, McCann, Rowe, & Lazenbatt, 2004; Gibbons et al., 1997). Thus for medical practitioners and personnel interested in smoking cessation, a concern is how to get past this dissonance. How anti-smoking campaigns or therapies that affect attitudes about smoking could be enhancing dangerous health dissonance has become a public health concern (Simmons et al., 2004).

In addition to studying smoking, researchers have focused extensively on dissonance in relation to consumer behaviors, particularly consumer purchasing. Oliver (1997) described how the act of purchasing an important product or service leads to apprehension and anxiety (discomfort) before and after the act or purchase. These feelings of apprehension and anxiety increase as an individual contemplates the purchase and then mutate into dissonance once a decision is made to purchase. The dissonance happens because people begin to evaluate all of the other options they had and did not choose immediately following the purchase, but normally before the experience or use of the purchase. Oliver (1997) noted three conditions which must be present for dissonance over a purchase to arise: 1) the decision must be important to the buyer; 2) the buyer must be free to make it; and 3) the decision must be irreversible. Subsequent research has shown this dissonance to exist in the purchasing process (Powers & Jack, 2013; Sweeney, Hausknecht, & Soutar, 2000).

A growing area of cognitive dissonance research is that of the relationship between dissonance and fundraising. Research demonstrates that individuals who donate after a crisis are more likely to express dissonance than non-donors. However, the act of donating has been found to reduce the dissonance (Therkelsen, 2011; Waters, 2009; Waters & Tindall, 2011). In essence, giving money in the wake of a crisis restores mental and emotional balance to individuals who see images of pain and suffering on television. Donating money helps them to feel better (Waters, 2009). This knowledge can help non-profits, as they should know that the public needs to see some level of pain and suffering after a crisis in order to be encouraged to donate.

Cognitive dissonance theory has theoretical and practical applications, as demonstrated by the different ways in which researchers have explored and developed this persuasive theory. In the next section we explore a persuasion model that also has theoretical and practical applications: the elaboration likelihood model.

WHAT DO YOU THINK 11.4

Of the three different settings in which dissonance was discussed, which do you find to be the most interesting and why?

Elaboration Likelihood Model

People are motivated to have the "right" attitudes on issues for a variety of social reasons. However, for a multitude of reasons we may not be able to or willing to process messages in a way that is suitable to achieve the "right" attitude. Petty and Cacioppo (1981, 1984, 1986) developed a model to help explain the process individuals go through when processing persuasive messages. Their model, known as the **elaboration likelihood model (ELM)** describes the ways individuals process messages; identifies and explains the different modes of processing; and discusses the results of these different processes on attitudinal change. The ELM posits that there are two routes to persuasion: a central route and a peripheral route.

The **central route** to persuasion involves thoughtful processing of information, relevant to attitudes, to determine the merits of a persuasive message. Individuals who process a persuasive message through the central route think critically and evaluate the arguments in a persuasive message. Elaboration in this case means that an individual will create their own thoughts in response to the persuasive message, thoughts that develop from and go beyond those provided in the message itself (Petty & Wegener, 1999). Central route processing is a process of evaluation and scrutiny of the logic of a message. However, attitude change through this route is not always based on objective reasoning/thought. Petty and Wegener (1998) stated that bias could affect elaborative processing. Overall, though, central route processing generally results in attitudes that are more resistant to change, longer lasting, and more predictive of future behavior than those formed through peripheral route processing (Petty & Cacioppo, 1986). Let's imagine you receive a brochure about binge drinking. If you process the message through the central route you will critically read the message and evaluate its persuasive arguments. If you find these arguments logically appealing, you will likely not binge drink.

The **peripheral route** to persuasion involves: 1) less quantitative consideration of the argumentation or logic within messages; and 2) attitude change that is focused more based on "rules of thumb" or affect (emotion). First, individuals who process persuasive messages through this route are more likely to thoughtfully consider less of the arguments in a message. If there are four messages, individuals who process through this route will process one or two, and may only do so briefly (Petty & Wegener, 1999). Along with this quantitative difference, the peripheral route differs qualitatively in how individuals process messages. Messages processed through the peripheral route will often be evaluated based on "rules of thumb" or based on affect. An individual may read a message that essentially says "bigger is better." Instead of evaluating this message critically, they may assume, "well, bigger is normally better, so this message is right." This logically may not make sense to many people, but if you are processing via the peripheral route, it may make sense indeed. Moreover, messages processed through this route can be influenced by emotional appeals (Cacioppo, Priester, & Bernston, 1993). Seeing a sad, happy, or other emotional image can often be more persuasive than a logical argument, which is the case if a message is processed through the peripheral route. Peripheral route processing generally results in attitudes that are more open to change, shorter lived, and less predictive of future behavior than those formed through peripheral route processing (Petty & Cacioppo, 1986).

KEY TERM 11.3

Elaboration likelihood model – a persuasive model that describes how individuals process messages, explains the different modes of processing, and discusses the results of these different processes on attitudinal change. The ELM posits that there are two routes to persuasion: a central route and a peripheral route.

Several factors determine the route an individual will take in processing a persuasive message. The two most studied factors are motivation and ability. Some messages are just more important to us than other messages, and thus we are more motivated to pay closer attention to them. When we are more motivated to process a message, or need to understand a message, we are more likely to process that message through the central route (Cacioppo & Petty, 1984). For example, you receive a persuasive message about how you should start saving for your child's college education (the chances are you are in college yourself). You probably do not have a child. Even if you are planning on having children, not having a child at this time means this message will not be as relevant to you as it will likely be to someone who has a young child. Yet, if you receive a message that promotes safe alcohol use on college campuses, you may more thoughtfully and critically consider this message, as it may be more relevant to your age group and current situation.

Along with motivation, an individual's ability to process a message determines which route they take in processing a persuasive message. Individuals may lack the basic intellect, knowledge about a subject, the message could be too complex, and/or the environment in which the message is received could be cluttered with noise. In such situations where an individual lacks the ability to critically process a message (central route), they will turn to peripheral processing. You may for example have the ability to process a message about the evils of drinking and driving. However, a message that incorporates chemical descriptions about the effects of alcohol on the blood stream and nervous system may confuse some, as they may lack the ability to understand the terms, and thus individuals will process it through the peripheral route.

In short, persuasive messages can form and/or change attitudes in a variety of ways. The ELM explains how different routes to persuasion influence our attitudes and predict other judgments and behaviors. While research has generally supported the ELM, and shown that central route processing leads to attitudes that are more resistant to change, longer lasting, and more predictive of future behavior than those formed through peripheral route processing, the ELM has also been criticized. The primary critique against the ELM is the notion that individuals process through the central *or* the peripheral route. Researchers have argued it is not only possible, but also very likely that messages are processed through both routes simultaneously (Stiff, 1986, 1994; Stiff & Boster, 1987). Stiff (1986), referencing *The Wizard of Oz*, quoted the Scarecrow and described how, "of course, some people go both ways." Based on an individual's level of motivation and ability, theorists have posited that it is possible for us to process messages through both routes at the same time.

WHAT DO YOU THINK 11.5

Think about a recent persuasive message you received (read, heard, or watched). How do you think you processed it? Why did you process it through the central or peripheral route, or did you process it through both routes at the same time?

ELM Research

Research exploring the theoretical and practical applicability of the ELM has been conducted in many contexts. Three contexts are discussed below: advertising, healthcare, and information technology. The significance of various aspects of an advertisement influencing an individual, such as the verbal elements in an ad (if applicable), and background elements (such as models in the ad, music, source expertise, etc.) differ depending on the receiver's level of involvement or interest in the product (Miniard, Bhatla, Lord, Dickson, & Unnava, 1991; Oh & Jasper, 2006; Petty, Cacioppo, & Schuman, 1983). Individuals who have higher involvement (motivation) to buy a product are more likely to cognitively process an advertisement, while those who have less motivation to purchase a product are more likely to process an ad through the peripheral route of persuasion.

Billions of dollars are spent each year to develop effective public service announcements (PSAs) that deter unhealthy behaviors. PSAs (radio, television, print, online) inform individuals about the potential dangers of numerous behaviors such as unprotected sex, of various substances like alcohol and tobacco, and of ways to promote healthy behaviors like dieting and healthier talk about weight (Garnett, Buelow, Franko, Becker, Rodgers, & Austin, 2014). Regarding tobacco and alcohol, sophisticated steps have been taken to develop warning labels to notify individuals of the potential risks of using such products. While countless financial resources have been spent developing ways to persuade people not to engage in dangerous behaviors, or not to use harmful substances, the effectiveness of such campaigns has been modest (Garnett et al., 2014; Penchmann & Reibling, 2000). A key issue determining the effectiveness of such persuasive campaigns is the relevance of a message to the receiver. If the message is relevant to an individual, they are more likely to be motivated to interpret the message via the central route (Petty & Cacioppo, 1986). When it comes to health issues, a mixture of central and peripheral cues are essential in messages, particularly when dealing with sensitive issues as such issues can be difficult for people to process through one route (Rucker & Petty, 2006).

ELM is also increasingly being applied to information technology (IT). Specifically, researchers have explored web personalization as a persuasive strategy. Web personalization is when a company automatically customizes its web content for a user. For example, a website may place content specifically relevant to you on the top of its webpage, such as advertisements geared toward your demographic and based on your previous web searches. Ho and Bodoff (2014) explored the relationship between these specialized ads and individuals' attitudes towards the ads. The researchers found an individual's attitude (positive or negative) toward having ads targeted to them influenced whether or not they bought the products advertised. Tam and Ho (2005) found similar results in that the relevance of the ads motivated individuals to click on the specifically targeted ads.

WHAT DO YOU THINK 11.6

Considering how the ELM has been applied in advertising, health campaigns, and in the IT realms, can you think of any other ways we can apply/use the ELM?

Inoculation

While the ELM outlines how people process persuasive messages, the following section describes a theory of persuasion that explains how people can resist persuasion. **Inoculation theory** examines the processes through which individuals resist attempts at attitude change brought forth through mass communication and/or other communicative means (interpersonal, group, organizational, etc.). There are attempts to change our attitudes on a daily basis. Sometimes we do change our attitudes, and sometimes we don't. Here are a few examples of attempts to change our attitudes that we may run into on a daily basis:

1) A group of teenagers is planning a party for the weekend and has an older friend who will buy them liquor. They are encouraging you to come to the party and drink with them because everyone does it, but drinking is something you have never done before.
2) During an election primary you turn on the television and see an advertisement for a candidate challenging the incumbent. The challenger calls the incumbent a Washington loyalist who has lost touch with the people and says you should vote for "new blood."
3) At work you are interviewing candidates for a new position and you and another colleague think you have your favorite candidate chosen. A third colleague meets you privately over lunch and speaks praises about another job candidate.

In each scenario someone or something is trying to get you to change an attitude. Persuasion theorists have been interested in how people respond to such pressures to change attitudes for a long time. McGuire (1964, 1966), drawing on the work of selective exposure and relative comparativeness explained how people are resistant to persuasion and asserted that people could be trained to be more resistant to persuasion. The key is that people can be stimulated to build up a resistance to attacks against their attitudes from threatening messages by being exposed to a weakened version of the threatening message(s) (Pfau, 1992; Szabo & Pfau, 2002).

The process of inoculation against persuasion works very much like the process of a medical inoculation. Papageorgis and McGuire (1961) defined **refutational pretreatments** as counterarguments that threaten a person's attitudes and responses to those counterarguments. Arguments that threaten an individual's attitudes motivate individuals to reinforce their attitudes, which is resistance to persuasion (Pfau, 1997). Refutational pretreatments have two components, which are critical components to inoculation: threat and refutational preemption.

Threat is a warning that an attack on an attitude is likely to take place. Pfau (1997) stated that "the threat component is the most distinguishing feature of inoculation" (p. 137). Threat motivates individuals to acknowledge that their attitudes are vulnerable to change, and thus their attitudes must be protected. The threat message needs to be balanced, which means it cannot be too threatening as it could then backfire. On the other hand if the message is not threatening at all it will not motivate individuals to think their attitudes are under attack (McGuire, 1964). Some examples of threat messages, based on our previous examples above are:

1) Some of your friends may try to get you to do things that you do not agree with now that you are old enough to drive and go to parties.
2) There are a lot of new political challengers out there this election season questioning incumbents and calling them "Washington loyalists."
3) You know that the other guy in our office is going to try to persuade you to support the other candidate and not support the one we both have liked from the start.

The second essential part of an inoculatory message is the **refutational preemption**, which is replying to counterarguments before they occur. This process gives receivers of the message arguments that they can use when they receive persuasive arguments in the future that are truly meant to challenge their attitudes. Some examples of refutational preemption messages, based on our previous examples above are:

1) Your friends will tell you that it's perfectly safe to have a couple of beers while at a party and to then drive home. However, states have cracked down on drunk driving and an arrest for drunk driving is a serious offense.
2) The challenger has said that (X incumbent) is a "Washington loyalist" and out of touch with his/her constituents. However, in the past two years (X incumbent) has done the following (list of accomplishments) to improve the Congressional district.
3) The other guy in our office will try to push the other candidate on us. However, we have to consider the work experience and how our preferred candidate also is not related to the boss.

Pfau (1997) explained how "the two components, threat and the refutational preemption, work in tandem: first threat and then refutational preemption" (p. 137). The threat message(s) provides motivation for individuals to care about their attitudes, and then the refutational preemption provides a script for individuals to respond when their attitudes are challenged. Think of the whole process as like receiving an inoculation against a virus. Many people receive a flu shot every year. The purpose behind the inoculation is to give the body a small dose of the flu to make the immune system immune to the virus when it encounters the full virus. In the case of a persuasive message, an inoculatory message gives an individual a small dose of a message meant to change their attitude to prepare them to resist future attitude changing messages. A healthy dose of threat and well-designed refutational preemption in the message can confer resistance to future persuasive messages.

KEY TERM 11.4

Inoculation theory – a theory that examines the processes through which individuals resist attempts at attitude change brought forth through different means of communication. Essential to inoculation are refutational pretreatments messages, which include threat and refutational preemption.

Originally, research on inoculation focused on non-controversial issues, specifically "cultural truisms," or a belief that most members of a culture accept without much question, such as people should brush their teeth two or three times a day. However, further developments in the theory since McGuire have found the theory to be more robust and to apply to numerous controversial topics such as smoking, advertising, drinking prevention, and political campaigning.

WHAT DO YOU THINK 11.7

It's time for you to think about and develop an inoculatory message. Your goal is to change people's attitudes about wearing seatbelts. Even though research shows you are more likely to survive an auto accident if you wear a seatbelt, many people still do not wear them. Design a threat and refutational preemption message to encourage people to wear seatbelts when they are faced with messages or examples from others to not wear a seatbelt.

Inoculation Research

There are numerous subtle nuances to inoculation theory, far too many to discuss in this short introduction to the theory. Sufficed to say, since McGuire's early work on the theory, researchers have been working to better understand how individuals resist, and how to better condition individuals to resist attempts to change attitudes. For example, researchers have shown that central and peripheral route inoculatory messages are equally effective, depending on the receiver's level of issue involvement, or how much they care about the attitude (Pfau et al., 1997). In other research, Pfau, Holbert, Zubric, Pasha, and Lin (2000) explored whether the communication medium of the message (print, or video) was more superior at eliciting resistance. The results showed no difference in the ability of the two sources to confer resistance, but the two mediums produced resistance in different ways. The theoretical and practical applications of inoculation are vast, with interest in a variety of contexts. Two contexts are reviewed below, which have received a great deal of attention in recent years: smoking prevention among adolescents and political campaigns.

Inoculation has been found to be useful in contexts where attitudes are regularly exposed to challenges. In this case, smoking prevention has received a great deal of attention as non-smokers and smokers alike receive numerous persuasive messages to not start or to quit smoking. Adolescents in particular are a key demographic that public health officials want to reach. Research has shown that younger adolescents are more likely to express negative attitudes toward smoking (Pfau, 1995). However, during the transition from younger to older adolescents, the negativity toward cigarettes decreases and many adolescents become indifferent and think they are invulnerable to the dangers of cigarettes (Gilpin & Pierce, 1998). To prevent teens from picking up smoking, various inoculatory message strategies have been employed (games, advertisements, role-playing, etc.). These strategies have been successful when the subjects (teens for example) have moderate to high self-esteem (Pfau, Van Bockern, & Kang, 1992) and when the media messages are hands-on or approachable (Banerjee & Greene, 2006, 2007). In essence, an adolescent's emotional state and cognitive ability both affect his or her ability to be inoculated against smoking. Research continues to explore countless other variables that impact smoking prevention and adolescents, as smoking is "the leading cause of preventable morbidity and mortality in the United States" (Banerjee & Greene, 2006, p. 773).

Anyone who has watched television, listened to the radio, opened a newspaper, or consumed any media during an election has seen a growing trend in recent years—the increase in attack ads. Increasingly, advertisements in local, state, and national elections are seen as more negative than positive, while some argue that the messages really are not all that negative, but just portrayed that way (Benoit, 1999, 2007). Whether political ads are becoming more negative or not, a key issue for political candidates and parties is how can they protect themselves from the attacks of their opponents? This is where inoculation has become a political advertising strategy. Pfau and his colleagues (Pfau & Burgoon, 1988; Pfau, Haigh, Sims, & Wigley, 2007; Pfau, Kenski, Nitz, & Sorenson, 1990) explored the effectiveness of inoculatory messages in countering messages of political opponents. Results showed that well-designed inoculatory messages made potential voters more resistant to attacks against their candidate(s). These findings have immense practical and theoretical implications. If political parties and politicians can design effective inoculatory messages they can better protect their base audience against attitudinal attacks.

WHAT DO YOU THINK 11.8

Can you think of any other areas where you can apply inoculation?

ISIS, Inoculation, and Adolescents: Is There an Antidote for Protecting Teens from Extremist Propaganda?

– Jeanetta D. Sims and Hung-Lin Lai,
University of Central Oklahoma

It happened again for the third time. First, three Denver girls under the age of eighteen fled their homes to join the Islamic State of Iraq and Syria (ISIS). Next, a US nineteen-year-old female and certified nurse's aide left to be with her jihadist suitor and to assist an Islamic camp in Syria. This time, three Chicago siblings (ages sixteen, seventeen, and nineteen) abandoned their family to join the Islamic Nation in Syria, with each leaving letters of their intentions for their parents. The three girls travelled from Colorado, to Chicago, and then to Frankfurt where authorities stopped them in Germany. The nurse's aide was stopped at the Denver International Airport. The three siblings were detained at O'Haire International Airport as they were trying to go to Turkey. In each instance, the final travel destination was intended to be Syria to join the extremist group, ISIS, which traces its history to the Sunni terrorist organization of al-Qaeda in Iraq.

All teens were influenced by ISIS persuasive media campaigns full of propaganda messages offering the adolescents a chance to take part in a sort of holy war in Syria, and to go overseas to wage jihad. The messages offered a promise for spiritual purpose, relevant mission, and personal meaning amid routine activity in the lives of adolescents. The ISIS propaganda calls for the teens to reject America, argues that Muslims have been crushed for far too long, and supports the establishment of an Islamic homeland. Peace, according to ISIS, can only be achieved if adolescents take part in the holy war. The teens' unified response to the messages appears to be a new US trend—join or attempt to join the Islamic State by travelling to Syria.

In 2014, US officials detained at least fifteen US citizens—nine of them female—who had intentions of traveling to Syria to join extremist militants. Nearly all of them were adolescents, and almost all were arrested at airports waiting to board flights. Through Twitter, Facebook, Skype, and other social media platforms, the Islamic State aggressively targets youths as young as fourteen in more than 20 languages, according to a senior US official. "They are broadcasting their poison, and their propaganda is unusually slick," FBI Director James B. Comey said. He added that the terrorist group is trying to attract "both fighters and people who would be the spouses . . . to their warped world."

In a September 2014 United Nations speech, US President Barack Obama said, "[Islamic State's] propaganda has coerced young people to travel abroad to fight their wars and turned . . . young people full of potential into suicide bombers. We must offer an alternative vision."

Indeed an alternative strategy is needed to combat the sophistication of ISIS propaganda in the United States. However, the US is not alone. Two Austrian teenage girls were labeled, "poster girls," because they left their homes in Vienna to fight for ISIS and have been used by ISIS to attract other young girls to Syria. According to Austrian police, the girls left behind a note that read, "Don't look for us. We will serve Allah—and we will die for him." Officials believe that upon arrival in Syria, the girls were given to local fighters for marriage and became pregnant soon thereafter. The teens' social media accounts are being used to broadcast deceptive messages about their new lives in Syria in an effort to entice others. Austrian officials say the teens have contacted their families and have asked to come home.

Yet, returning to their homes with the same life experiences they once knew can be impossible. Once young people have succumbed to ISIS ideals, conceived elaborate plans, and implemented their intentions, governments get involved and prosecutions typically follow. Rather than being viewed as law-abiding citizens, the ISIS-supporting adolescents are regarded by their governments as potential threats capable of willingly aiding a foreign terrorist organization.

"We have to find a solution," said the lawyer who represented the three siblings in court against the Assistant US Attorney. "They are not barbarians. They are our children."

Ferran, L., & Momtaz, R. (2015). ISIS trail of terror. Retrieved from: http://abcnews.go.com/WN/fullpage/isis-trail-terror-isis-threat-us-25053190.

Sandell, C., & James, M. S. (2014, July 2). US teen allegedly falls in love online, tries to join ISIS fighters in Syria. Retrieved from: http://abcnews.go.com/US/us-teen-allegedly-falls-love-online-join-isis/story?id=24407029.

Siemaszko, D. (2014, June 26). ISIS plans to make suicide bombers out of kidnapped teens, escaped boy says. Retrieved from: www.nydailynews.com/news/world/isis-allegedly-plans-turn-teens-suicide-bombers-article-1.1845000.

Sullivan, K. (2014, December 9). Three American teens, recruited online, are caught trying to join the Islamic state. Retrieved from: www.msn.com/en-us/news/us/three-american-teens-recruited-online-are-caught-trying-to-join-the-islamic-state/ar-BBgwJus?ocid=iehp.

Vienna Jihad girls want to come home. (2014, October 10). Retrieved from: www.viennatimes.at/news/General_News/2014-1010/30128/Vienna_Jihad_Girls_Want_To_Come_Home

Chapter Summary

The study of messages intended to shape, reinforce, or change the responses of another, or others has vast theoretical and practical implications. The four sections of this chapter provide a glimpse into the different ways in which persuasion is used and studied today. The first section defined persuasion and discussed essential elements and outcomes of persuasion. The second section examined cognitive dissonance theory. The relationship between our attitudes and behaviors is not always clear, which can sometimes lead to dissonance. Understanding this relationship is critical to decision-making. The third section explored the elaboration likelihood model, which describes the different routes to understanding persuasive messages. The fourth section described inoculation theory. The ability to confer resistance to persuasion has vast practical utility. The ability to persuade or to resist persuasion is a powerful tool. The theories and models in this chapter give you the building blocks to understand both processes. The final section of this chapter is an undergraduate paper from Oklahoma Christian University by Jennifer (Gill) Wagner. In this paper, Jennifer discusses how inoculation can be used as a rhetorical tool to establish a plan of action to strengthen Christians when facing persecution.

Key Terms

Attitude	Behavior	Belief
Central route	Coercion	Cognitive dissonance
Elaboration likelihood	Inoculation theory	theory
model	Peripheral route	Manipulation
Motive	Refutational	Persuasion
Persuasive communication	preemption	Refutational
Threat	Value	pretreatments

Activities

1. How might the ISIS propaganda be similar to the Korean propaganda that was effective with US POWs during the Korean War? Can you think of other situations or contexts where inoculation might be an effective strategy for combating or protecting against outside influences?
2. Develop persuasive messages that appeal to the central and peripheral routes of persuasion.

Student Paper

The following paper by Jennifer Wagner is from a Persuasion Class at the University of Central Oklahoma. Jeanetta D. Sims taught the class.

Theory Paper Project

Guidesheet

Course: COMM4113: Persuasion
Instructor: Dr. Jeanetta D. Sims

Course Description:

Persuasion is an upper-level course designed to provide students with a solid grounding in theories, principles, and strategies of social influence as they apply in everyday contexts in which influence attempts take place and as they are discussed in the extant literatures related to persuasion (social psychology, communication, etc.). During this course, you will familiarize yourself not only with theories, but also with scholars whose works have formed the trajectory of current thinking in persuasion and social influence.

Summary of Assignment and Associated Deadlines:

Assignments	Total Points	% of Total
Term Paper Project		
Term Paper Proposal – due at end of the 4th week	20	2%
Term Paper Rough Daft – due at end of the 10th week	0	0%
Term Paper Presentation – due last week of class	30	3%
Term Paper – due during final exam week after presentation	150	15%
Total	200	20%

Assignment Instructions:

Each student will submit a proposal outline (see the attached sample proposal), a rough draft, and a term paper that applies a particular theory to an issue of interest concerning an aspect of social influence. You may choose the topic for this assignment from the textbook or readings and it may be related to any communication context (e.g., interpersonal, organizational, mass, public, health, political, and/or public relations). The paper must (a) summarize current literature relevant to the issue; (b) feature and explicate a theory or paradigmatic model applicable to the topic; (c) examine the range of strategies and tactics used by those seeking to influence and/or those seeking to resist influence attempts; and finally, (d) form a conclusion.

This paper should include a separate title page, a separate page containing a 100-word abstract, and include a *minimum of 8–10 double-spaced pages of text* (not counting title page, abstract, and references). All work must be solely your own and must be properly referenced using APA format. Papers not in

APA format will not be accepted. Together, the proposal, paper, and paper presentation will account for 20 percent of the final grade.

Note:

Your writing should display your thinking ability; the ability to understand theories; grasp complex concepts; discover interrelationships; and generate your own insights. Naturally, you should proof-read your paper for grammatical and syntactical errors. You should pay proper homage to published authors by citing their works whenever you refer to their words, ideas, or data. All papers should conform to APA guidelines.

YOUR NAME (Sample Paper)

Proposal for Semester Term Paper
Jeanetta D. Sims, COMM4113-01
University of Central Oklahoma

Working Title

Redirecting Diversity Research from the Minority to the Majority: Using Psychological Reactance to Explain the Impact of Value-in-Diversity Campaigns

Thesis

Research (Martins, Milliken, Wisenfeld, & Salgado, 2003; Mollica, 2003) has proven individuals view an organization's value-in-diversity efforts from competing perspectives. While these studies have focused on the experiences, group processes, and perceptions of minority members in an organization, none have primarily focused on majority members, and none have used psychological reactance as an explanatory vehicle for the impact of value-in-diversity campaigns or interventions.

Rough Abstract

Diversity has become a "buzzword" in academic organizational literature (Allen, 1995). Unlike some organizational diversity research which focuses upon the experiences and perceptions of minorities, this study investigates the motivational arousal of majority members of an organization. Using Brehm's (1966) psychological reactance theory, this study explores the impact of value-in-diversity campaign messages upon majority members of an organization. With reactance as a theoretical framework, it is predicted value-in-diversity campaign messages provoke reactance among majority members of an organization. The magnitude of reactance, the impact of reactance upon attitudes, and the impact of reactance upon attraction of the restricted freedoms is explored as well as implicit message strategies. The aim of this research is to investigate strategies by which value-in-diversity campaign messages can be rendered more persuasive and less reactant among majority organizational members.

References Drawn from the Following

Allen, B. J. (1995). "Diversity" and organizational communication. *Journal of Applied Communication Research, 23,* 143–155.

Brehm, J.W. (1966). *A theory of psychological reactance.* New York, NY: Academic Press.

Martins, L. L., Milliken, F. J., Wisenfeld, B. M., & Salgado, S. R. (2003). Racioethnic diversity and group members' experiences: The role of the racioethnic diversity of the organizational context. *Group & Organizational Management, 28,* 75–106.

Miller, G. R. (1967). [Review of the book *The theory of psychological reactance*]. *Quarterly Journal of Speech, 53*(3), 293.

Mollica, K. (2003). The influence of diversity context on white men's and racial minorities' reactions to disproportionate group harm. *The Journal of Social Psychology, 143,* 415–431.

With Additional Books and Articles by

Alderfer, Brewer, Cox, Jackson, and Kossek.

Jennifer Gill (Jennifer Wagner)

Senior Capstone

Abstract

This paper attempts to show the influence of rhetoric in Christian history and offer a postmodern version to help Christians better prepare for opposition based on McGuire's inoculation theory. His theory, starting from 1961, will be reviewed as well as later research done by Michael Pfau to better understand inoculation and the persuasive mechanisms that affect its usefulness. Finally a discussion including suggestions on how inoculation can be used as a rhetorical tool to establish a plan of action to strengthen Christians when facing persecution is offered.

Jennifer provides a nice preview for the reader of what the paper will cover.

(Continued)

Inoculation as a Rhetorical Tool to Mirror Sophists of the Nineteenth Century

While persuasion has been a part of human interaction far before any means of recording it was established, the nineteenth-century scholars transformed this oratory into an art form that was perfected and used as a way to educate and enlighten; this practice was deemed rhetoric (Bizzell & Herzberg, 1990). Classical rhetoric was associated primarily with persuasive discourse, and its original purpose was to persuade an audience to act or think a certain way. This changed however as "[t]he principles of rhetoric were extended to apply to informative or expository modes of discourse, but in the beginning, they were applied almost exclusively to the persuasive modes of discourse" (Corbett & Connors, p. 16). What started as an informative public tool soon developed into a societal form of art. "Public speaking was inseparable from the business of government and civil affairs, and early on some enterprising orators turned to teaching the art of persuasive speech as well as practicing it" (Bizzell & Herzberg, 1990, p. 2). This social outlet gained popularity and developed into a powerful social manifestation well into the Medieval period; it became much more than just a social gathering, but "[r]hetoric thus came to designate both the practice of persuasive oratory and the description of ways to construct a successful speech—a complex art of great power" (Bizzell & Herzberg, 1990, p. 2). Not only did persuasion, through rhetoric, influence government structure, but it also brought about heavy controversy into the religious realms as Christianity was on the rise.

A common conviction held among Christian believers suggested the idea that knowledge came from revelation and not from commonplace, making rhetoric an inhibitor of a full faith (Bizzell & Herzberg, 1990). A Christian's faith was to be a matter of the heart and should not rely on persuasive appeals to logos for understanding (Bizzell & Herzberg, 1990) However, this all changed when Augustine of Hippo,

> While this is an interesting quotation, the reference is not in the reference list. This happens a lot . . . just double check the reference list.

(Continued)

stepped into power in AD 386 and contradicted this common outlook on the view of rhetoric.

> Augustine in his role as bishop instructs Christian pastors not only in biblical hermeneutics but also in a homiletics that makes significant use of classical rhetoric. Augustine argues that it would be foolish for Christians to neglect this powerful means of teaching. (Bizzell & Herzberg, 1990, p. 369)

He saw the great potential for rhetoric, and viewed it not as an immobilizer of a Christian faith, but instead as a catalyst tool that could be used to add an intellectual case to Christian faith (Bizzell & Herzberg, 1990). Augustine encouraged the use of rhetoric, saying, "Christianity cannot afford to eschew a powerful tool for defending and expounding principles and beliefs" (Bizzell & Herzberg, 1990, p. 8). With this authoritative public acceptance of rhetoric, the Christian public used language, written and spoken, as effective oratory, and developed it into an idealized art form. These classic philosophers, known as sophists, used rhetoric to proclaim their informed faiths to the masses (Bizzell & Herzberg, 1990).

However a new buzzword, "modern," was introduced, and the public practice of rhetoric was pushed to the back burner. Sophists lost their appeal to the masses as the word modern began to describe a time period that claimed to have moved from a pagan past into an officially Christian culture in the fifth century. This societal transition dated rhetoric as a pre-modern word that was posed as a counterpoint to the modern. "The progressive birth of the modern entailed the decline and ossification of rhetoric" (Hobbs 2). As rhetoric was slowly pushed into its grave, it was seen by modernists as outdated, a contradiction to the new ways of life. "[T]he very term modern rhetoric could seem an oxymoron—for was not rhetoric itself what modernity made obsolete and irrelevant?" (Hobbs 2). In light of its rejection in the social world, the positive ramifications of

This has been a very nice, succinct discussion of the development of rhetoric in Christian faith.

This quotation is a great transition and very descriptive. However, Jennifer needs to make sure the reference is in the list.

(Continued)

rhetoric can still be seen as a valuable in solidifying Christian beliefs with solid informative views and dismissing doubts that Christians are faced with. Even Augustine, a man with great theories of knowledge, still dealt with uncertainties about his faith: "At one stage in his development, St. Augustine had a scarifying experience of doubt, not as a philosophical premise or intellectual pose, much less an emancipation from some sort of intellectual slavery, but as a frightening state of confusion and insecurity" (Keyes, 1966, p. 26). Despite his own education of persuasive techniques as a sophist, Augustine still went through periods of doubt, as is common with Christians. He, however, was able to fight off these uncertainties with his extensive knowledge as a Christian rhetoric. Social gatherings during this time period provided an atmosphere that dismissed doubts and supplied Christians with intelligent defense mechanisms to protect themselves from doubt. However, without such a strong public venue today, it causes one to question what would happen if certain social groups were not prepared to defend themselves against resistance.

During the Korean War in the 1950s, United States soldiers were put into a situation where their American values and ideals were questioned. While being held as prisoners of war, they were not tortured; instead, Americans were faced with questions about beliefs concerning freedom, democracy, and equality in America (Booth, 1996). Many found themselves unable to provide sufficient answers, let alone stand up for their country. Troops started to question the political and social beliefs that had been instilled in them since birth (Booth, 1996). Their inability to defend their country and the values originally instilled in them caused them to be inundated with doubt, in turn causing many troops to actually change sides and willingly cooperate with the enemy. Bombarded with American pride while on the home front, soldiers were not confronted with possible attacks about their country, its government, or its values. If soldiers had been pre-exposed to rhetorical strategies for defending American beliefs

You can see from this review of literature that it is a clearly chronological review of literature up to this point. The paragraphs are detailing the development of rhetoric, which is discussed in the next chapter (Chapter 12).

(Continued)

prior to embarking into Korean territories, the soldiers would have been more likely to withstand oral attacks on their nation.

> [W]e would develop the resistance to persuasion of a person raised in an ideologically aseptic environment by pre-exposing him to weakened forms of the counterarguments, or to some other belief threatening material strong enough to stimulate, but not so strong as to overcome, his belief defense. (McGuire, 25)

It is not clear from the referencing which McGuire reference this comes from.

Spurred on by these treasonous acts of the American soldiers, Dr. William McGuire proposed the idea of inoculation theory. McGuire defined inoculations as a process in which individuals receive "weakened, defense stimulation forms of the counterarguments" (McGuire 327). Often explained best using medical analogies, inoculation is represented in the form of a shot. Patients are exposed to a small dose of a deadened virus, which in turn causes their bodies to build up antibodies and over time defend themselves against that virus. Much like the immunization, inoculation is used by providing a receiver with small doses of information from the opposing side, which causes a reaction, which forms counterarguments, and allows the receiver to defend their truisms in the future. This clearly correlates to the social practices of Christian sophists in the nineteenth century, when rhetorical debates provided a safe haven for Christians to inundate themselves with small doses of the opposing side's argument.

I think this reference has been left out of the paper, while many other really good McGuire ones have been included.

This description of McGuire's work is really well done and links it well to the history of American acts in the wars.

While rhetoric ceased to be a vital discipline in the nineteenth century, the principles of rhetoric and the works of sophists of the classical period are still held in high regard today. With books filled with the antidotal means for creating well-developed Christian ideologies, it is impossible to overlook the influence and enlightenment rhetoric brought. While the nineteenth century focused on rhetoric in education, today it seems that Christians have lost the means for positive social discourse as a way to fortify beliefs. It is undeniable, however, that

(Continued)

in this fast-paced world where knowledge is only a mouse click away, an informed faith is absolutely essential. In seeing the positive effects of the rhetoric used in the Classical era, one cannot help but wonder why a re-structured version of rhetoric is not used to reinforce a faith in Christ today. However since social gatherings in the city square have become a thing of the past, the question is then posed: how can Christians fortify their faith? A possible solution is found when looking at inoculation as a modern-day model for rhetoric.

> This is a good transition paragraph to the theory of inoculation.

McGuire's Theory of Inoculation

For many years, the spotlight of social persuasion was strictly focused on how to persuade others. However, as William J. McGuire studied social influence, he realized that there was an entire side of persuasion that researchers had failed to recognize. While many had theorized for decades over how to manipulate, using persuasion in various situations and cultures, the idea of how to *avoid* persuasion was an idea that other communication theorists had sidestepped. In 1964, McGuire decided to shift his focus from persuasion to inducing resistance, stating, "[w]hen I realized social scientists had neglected the ways to immunize people against persuasion, I redirected my research . . ." (McGuire, 1970, p. 36). Thus McGuire wanted to offer a way to defend one's beliefs instead of accepting the persuasive views of others:

> The question has often been raised as to whether a persuasive communication is more effective when it concentrates exclusively on the arguments supporting the communicator's position or when it includes some discussion (and/or refutation) of the opposing arguments. (Lumsdaine & Janis, 1953, p. 2)

With all of this in mind, one cannot help but pose the question: can Christians be armed with the tools necessary to defend Christianity while creating

(Continued)

This is the key point of Jennifer's paper. She is interested in using McGuire's theory of inoculation, later expanded on by Pfau to see if this theory can be used to persuasively protect Christians against attacks on their beliefs.

self-instilled beliefs allowing them to hold fast to their own values? The answer may come from a theory McGuire introduced known as inoculation theory. Inoculation is a method used to arm individuals with the knowledge to prevent persuasive attempts as well as provide tactics to fight off an attack (McGuire, 1961, p. 197). While McGuire's studies did not specifically evaluate religious beliefs, the principals behind the inoculation theory prove beneficial when brought into a Christian light. His studies on inoculation, first introduced in 1964, provide Christians with a rhetorical solution; providing the means for premeditated thoughts to produce an effect on the listener. However, for inoculation to work, a threat is necessary.

Introduction to the Inoculation Theory

Based on McGuire's theory of inoculation (1962), a threat will create stimulation for a reaction, and in turn generate a need to initiate defenses against the threat. When put in the Christian realm, inoculation would put an attack upon ones belief system, or on a cultural truism that will "elicit a response and cause a Christian to create 'supportive defense(s)'" (McGuire, 1964, p. 194). Cultural truisms are certain undeniable beliefs that are taken for granted. McGuire acknowledged these truisms as, "[b]eliefs so widely held within the person's social milieu that he would not have heard them attacked, and indeed, would doubt that an attack was possible" (McGuire, 1964, p. 201). McGuire found that a strong attack on an undefended truism could result in the severe decline of belief in the truism. In lieu of this, people tend to avoid situations that oppose their own truisms. This idea is known as selective exposure. It suggests that people seek out information affirming their existing beliefs and actively avoid information contrary to their beliefs. With the confirmed idea that people are not likely to place themselves in situations where their beliefs will be subject to inquiry, inoculation is a viable option to arm receivers with tactics that fend off persuasion.

This is a nice overall description of McGuire's inoculation theory.

(Continued)

Inoculation Mechanisms

Without any threatening stimulation an initial step to defend truisms will never occur. McGuire said that threat is a "precursor to resistance in that an individual must be made aware of the vulnerability of his truism" (Sims, 2005, p. 6). Threat is an important factor in the inoculation process, without it, an individual isn't aware his truisms are under attack. One way to create a threatening stimulation is through extrinsic means.

Forewarning is a mechanism used to make an individual aware of possible counter attitudinal attack. According to Papageorgis and McGuire (1961) there are two possible ways to forewarn; by simply informing that a persuasive attack is coming, or by informing them about the topic and position taken. Both tactics are moderately helpful at provoking resistance to persuasion as it makes the receiver aware of a possible counter attitudinal attack (Papageorgis & McGuire, 1961).While forewarning is effective in informing the receiver of an attack, it does not arm the individual with the information necessary to resist the persuasion.

Refutational preemption is a mechanism that takes forewarning to the next level. McGuire defined refutational preemption as "[d]efenses which involve pre-exposing the person to the mention of counterarguments against his beliefs together with a detailed refutation of these counterarguments" (McGuire, 1964, p. 194). Here, receivers are provided with knowledge of opposing sides, as well as tactics to help them defend their original truisms. Not only does refutational preemption pre-expose to a coming threat, but it also offers repudiation to these opposing threats.

While these two mechanisms are helpful in starting the inoculation process, there are also factors that are involved in how well inoculation is received. Michael Pfau and many other researchers have spent a majority of the past fifteen years trying to better understand how different factors play a role in inoculation, two of them being involvement and emotion.

Inoculation theory assumes that an individual will be involved in the topic, and thus sustain a truism

(Continued)

or belief that is personally relevant. Therefore, only already existing values and beliefs are in need of protection from susceptibility; a person's involvement in those values are key to inoculation (Sims, 2005). Involvement has been attributed to the amount by which individuals are motivated to process information (Burnkrant & Sawyer, 1983). Therefore, the more involved an individual is in a topic, the more likely they will be motivated to muster arguments that would strengthen their attitudes. Involvement is an important factor for inoculation to occur; another mechanism that plays a part in the process of inoculation is emotion.

While most research over inoculation through the 1990s focused on cognitive processes, Lee and Pfau's (1997) research instead "compared the effectiveness of cognitive and affective inoculation treatments in promoting resistance to cognitive and affective attacks" (Sims, 2005, p. 11). Lee and Pfau theorized that cognitive treatments would prove to be much more effective because they included a high quality of refutational materials, as well as a threat factor. They also hypothesized that affective treatments would be less effective because they lacked quality of refutation materials (Lee & Pfau, 1997). What they found was that affective positive and affective negative treatments brought about resistance. It is important to realize that not all decisions are based exclusively on cognitive processing, but affective reasoning as well.

Inoculation in Christianity

Inoculation is the process through which individuals are equipped with the information and tools necessary to prepare and fight off persuasive attacks. By bringing this theory into a Christian light, tactics to defend religious truisms can be positively reinforced and strengthened. Imagine members of a church dressed in military gear bearing full arms and looking as if they are ready to go to war. These families pull into the church parking lot, climb out of their Honda vans, and crawl, army style, to the doors of

This section offered a nice brief summary of how other researchers, aside from McGuire, have expanded the inoculation theory.

(Continued)

the building for Sunday service. It is not until they reach the safety of the church auditorium that they put the safety on their rifles. Service is a time of strategic planning, a time where these soldiers re-load their ammunition. In-between communion, members are informed of the enemy's tactics and given instructions on how to avoid certain death. These devices are taught to build up the defenses of the troops. After an hour of tactical planning and an invitation, the congregation is ready to leave the sacred walls, their weapons loaded, a plan of action in hand, prepared for battle. They have armed themselves accordingly for the war waging outside of the baptized walls.

While a bit overemphasized, this illustration relays a message, of the often-negligent mindset that Christians have. While there is a time for fellowship, it is important to recognize that the Christian walk is full of spiritual turmoil. Church should be a place of instruction where Christians learn how to fend off attacks of conflicting views. This spiritual battle has been ongoing for decades, and generations of believers have flocked to the sacred church grounds to load up on ammunition to ward off the enemy. The problem is, sometimes the stock room has run dry and the church has not always provided the ammo necessary to fight back. This was not the case in the nineteenth century church when an informed faith was an emphasized criterion, and rhetorical resources were used to educate. "In a broader view, he was preparing young gentlemen to practice all the arts of discourse, which, accord-ing to Isocrates, teach how to think well . . ." (Clark, 1957, p. 64). Christians fall away, loose their faith, and families crumble. Church has become a place of positive affirmation when what is really needed is the means for refutational reinforcement. The ideals of the sophists in Augustinian times should be mirrored, inoculating Christians with the opposing arguments, and providing them with an opportunity to build up defenses. Christians need to be equipped with the knowledge to stand firm against pressures of resistance. A problem then arises, since

(Continued)

Jennifer has
taken a
persuasive
stand here
and argued
that a
group, in
this case
Christians,
need to
persuasively
protect
themselves.
Is this a
subjective
or objective
argument?

the church has operated under this system of affirmative instilment for so long, a method for improving
refutational ability seems far off. Inoculation, a
modern form of rhetoric, offers a practical solution
to this generation.

Applying Inoculation Theory

Two mechanisms discussed earlier that affect the
process of inoculation are involvement and emotion.
The inoculation theory assumes an individual will
be involved in the topic, and thus sustain a truism
or belief that is personally relevant. Knowing that
the ultimate goal of Christianity is eternal life,
a substantial involvement is the topic implied.
Individuals, then, are more likely to be motivated
to muster up arguments that would strengthen their
beliefs in Christ. Rhetors of the classical era
knew the importance of being sentimentally engaged
in the topic they were disputing: "Occasional oratory of itself invites ranging in both emotion
and thought . . ." (Baldwin, 1959, p. 230). Being
a Christian involves a heartfelt commitment that
engages emotion; whether those feelings are guilt,
love or conviction, Christianity is as much cognitive as it is affective. A threat presented to any
of these truisms will cause a reaction.

McGuire's inoculation theory states that for individuals to begin the refutational process to build
up self-instilled beliefs, a threat must first be
presented. One way to pose an attack on Christians'
religious truisms is through forewarning. Inoculation works by pre-exposing individuals to weakened
forms of counterarguments strong enough to stimulate, but not strong enough to overcome our belief
defenses. Christians therefore must be exposed to
weakened arguments of the conflicting side. Nineteenth-century rhetoricians accomplished this by
unearthing contrasting arguments: "he concentrated
on the rhetorical virtues . . . pointing out how
the orators had gone about finding arguments, ordering them for presentation to a given audience, and
clothing them with proper language" (Clark, 1957,

(Continued)

p. 65). This can be done today by introducing Christians to possible counterarguments they may encounter from different religious views. For example one specific issue to start with would be discussing discrepancies with the Christian faith held by many worldviews. While it may seem a difficult task, by pre-exposing Christians to these arguments, they are able to prepare themselves to have intelligent discourse about opposing worldviews.

Refutational preemption is an even more advanced step to solidifying an individual's ability to defend religious truisms. First they must discuss inconsistencies other religions have with Christianity and then find the counterarguments of their own side by study not only of their own bible and commentaries, but also the texts of other religions. These studies will provide them with the ability to counteract the threats posed to them. Rhetoricians required this during the intense schooling of all their students. "[T]he boys had a thorough workout in applying logical proof in confirmation and rebuttal and in detecting fallacies" (Clark, 1957, p. 64). By providing opposing worldviews to Christianity and then going a step further to supply specific tactics to counter oppose, Christians can be fully prepared to protect themselves. Christians can build up their rhetorical defenses through forewarning and refutational preemption.

During the process of inoculation, it is important for Christians to establish strong religious truisms. Advanced school of rhetoric enforced this through a variety of ways. "The professor of rhetoric led his pupils to apply the precepts and imitate the models in their own themes . . . The controversial argued pro or con on the issues of a fictitious or hypothetical case" (Clark, 1957, p. 65). While we do not have the luxury of Christian rhetoric schooling anymore, truisms can still be enforced through a less direct approach. Sharing the gospel to unbelievers, for example, provides situations for Christians to apply rational evidence to substantiate their beliefs to non-believers. Active participation is key to instilling these truisms (McGuire, 1964, p. 195).

(Continued)

While it is necessary for Christians to have the motivation to defend their religious beliefs, it is also important to be armed with the suitable defenses to fight off attacks. One way to do this is to memorize important scripture for use when truisms are under attack. Primary schools in Augustinian days knew the importance of memorization when it came to learning the art of rhetoric: "he grounded his pupils in the complicated theory of rhetoric by making them memorize the precise definitions and the elaborate classifications and sub-classifications formulated in the precepts of rhetoric and embodied in textbooks . . ." (Clark, 1957, p. 65). Isocrates and rhetors alike, knew the importance of committing the knowledge to memory. By mirroring the memorization practices that sophistic professors enforced, Christians can attain the best resistance possible to fight of persuasive attacks.

The benefits of rhetoric have been undeniable, even in the Christian realm. "Training in rhetoric also helped a boy to participate in the debates of a legislative assembly and make appropriate speeches . . . for hundreds of years training in rhetoric prepared boys for future careers as Christian preachers" (Clark, 1957, p. 64). A rhetorical approach may prove the most beneficial in an effort to inundate Christians with the tools necessary to fend off persuasion.

Conclusion

While it started as a powerful social manifestation in the medieval period, rhetoric can be modified and tailored to Christians as a means of discourse today. It is clear that Christians during the Augustinian rule were given the means to defend their faith with informed tactics through pre-meditated oratory. Similar principles can be put into use by means of the inoculation theory as guidelines to re-enforce a knowledgeable faith. For Christians, the enemy is everywhere; they are on public transportation, at fast food restaurants, and work at bank counters. Sometimes the temptation is too strong, and defenses

---

Jennifer has nicely applied the main arguments of inoculation theory to how she believes Christians can be inoculated to help protect and reinforce their views. She addressed issues like motivation, preemption, refutation, etc.

(Continued)

lacking. Comparable to the sophists teaching in the nineteenth century, McGuire's theory of inoculation offers a postmodern solution to a generation in need of spiritual defense mechanisms. By utilizing the principles of inoculation as a way to withstand conflicting discourse, such as forewarning and refutational preemption, self-imposed beliefs of Christians can be fortified and strengthened to fight off attacks from an unbelieving world.

References

Baldwin, C. (1959). *Ancient rhetoric and poetic: Interpreted from representative works.* Gloucester, MA: Peter Smith.

Bizzell, P., & Herzberg, B. (Eds.). (1990). *The rhetorical tradition: Readings from classical times to the present.* Boston, MA: St. Martin's Press.

Booth, S. (1996). Inoculation: Ouch! But it's good for you. Retrieved from: www.as.wvu.edu/~sbb/comm221/chapters/inocul.htm.

Burnkrant, R. E., & Sawyer, A. G. (1983). Effects of involvement and message content on information-processing intensity. In R. J. Harris (Ed.), *Information processing research in advertising* (pp. 43–64). Hillsdale, NJ: Lawrence Erlbaum Associates, Inc.

Clark, D. (1957). *Rhetoric in Greco-Roman education.* Morningside Heights, NY: Columbia University Press.

Keyes, G. L. (1966). *Christian faith and the interpretation of history: A study of St. Augustine's philosophy of history.* Lincoln, NE: University House of Nebraska Press.

Lumsdaine, A. A., & Janis, I. L. (1953). Resistance to "counterpropaganda" produced by one-sided and two-sided "propaganda" presentations. *Public Opinion Quarterly, 17,* 311–318

McGuire, W. J. (1961). The effectiveness of supportive and refutational defenses in immunizing and restoring beliefs against persuasion. *Sociometry, 24,* 194–197.

McGuire, W. J. (1964). Inducing resistance to persuasion: Some contemporary approaches. In L. Berkowitz (Ed.), *Advances in experimental social psychology* (Vol. 1, pp. 191–229). New York, NY: Academic Press.

McGuire, W. J. (1970, February). A vaccine for brainwash. *Psychology Today,* pp. 36–39, 63–64.

Papageorgis, D. & McGuire, W. J. (1961). The generality of immunity to persuasion produced by pre-exposure to weakened counterarguments. *Journal of Abnormal and Social Psychology, 62,* 475–481.

Sims, J. (2005). *The most-traveled road to resistance: Exploring inoculation theory's past, present, and future.* Norman, OK: University of Oklahoma.

12 RHETORICAL THEORY

Jansen B. Werner & Daniel Cronn-Mills

Chapter Outline

- Three Characteristics of Rhetoric
- Aristotle's Influence
- The Rhetorical Situation
- The Classical View
- The Imagined Audience
- Genres in Rhetorical Theory
- Metaphors in Rhetorical Theory
- Kenneth Burke
- Student Paper

Introduction

Rhetoric is an ancient term broadly referring to the art of public communication. The ancient philosophers typically understood rhetoric as a form of discourse intended to influence or persuade. Historically, rhetoric has been primarily associated with oratory (public speaking). The picture you see above is an ancient theatre on the island of Rhodes used for public presentations (and possibly for instruction in rhetoric). In fact, many ancient scholars are known to have studied rhetoric at Rhodes (and possibly at this theater). However, in our contemporary world, rhetoric surrounds us in many forms: political speeches, advertisements, social media posts, television shows, music, and even architecture. In this chapter, we will focus mainly on rhetoric as oral or written communication intended for a public audience. Since rhetoric has been around for thousands of years, we cannot hope to cover everything about this powerful area of communication studies, but the chapter will provide a good overview. If you find the concepts of rhetoric exciting you may be compelled to take up the study of rhetoric.

In the first section of this chapter we will discuss the three primary characteristics for defining the parameters of rhetoric. The second section covers one of the most significant individuals in the long history of rhetoric—Aristotle. You will read about how Aristotle defined rhetoric, the types of proofs he identified, and the argument structures known as the enthymeme. The third section moves into the contemporary time period with an exploration of the rhetorical situation. The fourth section demonstrates how the classical view connects the past and the present. The fifth section is an explanation of the imagined audience and how it changed our understanding of rhetoric. The sixth section is about genres in rhetoric and how they can influence our understanding of symbols. The seventh section considers the role that metaphors play in rhetorical theory. We will provide a brief metaphor case study in this section focusing on "King Obama." The eighth section concludes with one of the most influential contemporary scholars in rhetoric—Kenneth Burke. Burke's ideas about rhetoric have dramatically changed how scholars understand communication. The final section is an undergraduate student paper by Jessica L. Benham, which shows the connections between rhetoric and the popular culture figure of Captain America. Let's start by briefly discussing the three basic characteristics of rhetoric.

Three Characteristics of Rhetoric

First, rhetoric is **discursive**. Rhetoric consists of the purposeful arrangement and usage of words and symbols. The **rhetor** (e.g., speaker, writer, symbol user) uses language to convey a message to an audience. Although we sometimes take it for granted, language is crucial to our everyday lives. Without language (the common words and symbols we use to communicate), even a seemingly simple task, such as ordering a cup of coffee, becomes impossible. If we did not have symbols (e.g., words, gestures, images) for "cup" or "coffee," how could we communicate our desire for a few ounces of that delicious hot liquid in our favorite red mug? Now, imagine if your task was more complex, such as delivering a persuasive speech about climate change to an audience of your peers. How could such a task be accomplished without the use symbols? Discourse—the use of symbols to communicate—is essential to the creation and exchange of meaning.

KEY TERMS 12.1 AND 12.2

Rhetor – a user of language to convey a message to an audience.

Discourse – the use of symbols to communicate.

Second, rhetoric refers to **public communication**. Communication happens in various different settings, but not all of them are public. For example, even the above scenario, in which you're attempting to order a cup of coffee, may not be *public* communication. You may order a cup of coffee *in* public, but the message might not be addressed to a public audience. We must think carefully about the association of rhetoric and persuasion. Not all forms of persuasion will be rhetorical. For example, if you had an extra ticket to a concert and you were trying to convince your roommate to skip her night class to join you, that is persuasive, but since it isn't *public* communication, it may not be considered by some to be rhetorical. Now, if you tried to convince all the people in your residence hall to skip class for the concert and you communicated with them by sending a mass message on social media, then the message becomes an instance of *public* communication. Although persuasion can occur in various communication settings, rhetoric is primarily concerned with *public* communication.

Third, rhetoric is **functional**. Rhetoric performs a function for both the rhetor who delivers the message and the audience members who interpret the message. Rhetoric responds to social, political, and cultural problems. In communicating a message, the rhetor proposes a solution to a problem. For example, when the President of the United States delivers the annual State of the Union address, he or she responds to the various issues presently facing the country (we will talk more later in the chapter about how the State of the Union is a form of genre rhetoric). The speech serves a function for the President in the sense it allows him or her to convey to the American people what issues he or she deems significant, and how he or she expects common citizens to respond to those issues. Rhetoric also serves a function for the audience by providing an opportunity to exercise their rights of citizenship. If a citizen agrees with the President's message, then a sense of belonging and involvement may encourage one to act in conformity with the President's message. But if a citizen disagrees with the President's message, the speech still serves a function by providing an opportunity to unite with other like-minded individuals who disagree with the President. Such individuals may then exercise their citizenship in ways that run explicitly counter to the President's message. Rhetoric is functional, whether seeking to persuade a collection of individuals to adopt one's position or encouraging a collection of individuals to band together as a community who share a common cause or concern.

WHAT DO YOU THINK 12.1 AND 12.2

How do you understand rhetoric?

How does your understanding of rhetoric match with the three characteristics of rhetoric we have provided?

Aristotle's Influence

One of the most influential thinkers to the study of rhetoric was the Greek philosopher Aristotle. **Aristotle** defined rhetoric as "an ability, in each particular case, to see the available means of persuasion" (1355b). This definition was important because it influenced the way in which people understood the scope and function of rhetoric. Once thought to be simply a practice or performance used in special circumstances, Aristotle directed people to recognize how rhetoric is an ever-present social force, which constantly influences the environment. Aristotle's view carried an important insight for individuals. If people were constantly surrounded by rhetorical possibilities, an individual could, in any circumstance, use rhetoric to influence her or his social setting.

WHAT DO YOU THINK 12.3

What do you know about Aristotle (before reading the rest of the chapter)?

One of Aristotle's greatest contributions to the study of rhetoric was his challenge to the belief that rhetoric is just a kind of cheap trick that only works in certain occasions. Although Aristotle rejected this view, he did not reject the relationship between rhetoric and occasions altogether. After all, his definition of rhetoric suggested that the "available means of persuasion" would vary according to one's situation. Along these lines, Aristotle identified three different **genres** of rhetoric: **deliberative, epideictic,** and **forensic.** We go into detail on Aristotle's three types in the section on genres in rhetorical theory later in this chapter.

Aristotle and Proofs

Aristotle argued that a rhetor could employ three kinds of persuasive "proof" or evidence when making persuasive claims. These three types of rhetorical proof include: **pathos, ethos,** and **logos.** Pathos refers to a rhetor's ability to invoke emotion; ethos refers to a rhetor's capacity to display a sense of good character; and logos refers to a rhetor's effort to demonstrate logical reasoning to an audience. Although tempting to think about pathos, ethos, and logos simply as resources available to a rhetor, we need to remember that rhetoric is transactional—rhetoric always consists of a rhetor *and* an audience. The audience must be considered in the process. Think of the rhetorical proofs as an audience's rhetorical "needs" or "demands." In other words, a speaker must satisfy an audience's various desires for pathos, ethos, and logos. In this sense, a speaker does not *use* the proofs, so much as she or he appeals to them. Let's consider an example appealing to ethos. One of your classmates delivers a speech without any conscious consideration of ethos. Yet even without a conscious effort to "use" ethos, the rest of the class will still make judgments about your classmate's personal qualities (character).

KEY TERMS 12.3, 12.4, AND 12.5

Pathos – a rhetor's ability to invoke emotion.

Ethos – a rhetor's capacity to display a sense of good character.

Logos – a rhetor's effort to demonstrate logical reasoning.

WHAT DO YOU THINK 12.4

What role does ethos, pathos, and logos play in your everyday interactions?

Aristotle and the Enthymeme

This audience-centered focus is captured in one of Aristotle's most noteworthy rhetorical concepts: the **enthymeme**. Enthymemes are three-part deductive arguments, which consist of a major premise, a minor premise, and a conclusion. However, unlike standard modes of argumentation, where all premises are made explicit, in the enthymeme the major premise remains unstated. In order to illustrate how this works, let's look at the standard example of the enthymeme.

> **Major premise** (assumed): All humans are mortal.
> **Minor premise** (stated): Socrates is human.
> **Conclusion** (stated): Therefore, Socrates is mortal.

Since rhetoric naturally assumes "all humans are mortal," a rhetor can leave the major premise unstated and the audience can still arrive at the same conclusion. In fact, all the rhetor needs to say is "Socrates is human. Therefore, Socrates is mortal." Enthymemes work by letting the audience fill in the unstated assumption. The rhetor did not persuade the audience, but, rather, the audience arrived at the conclusion on their own. An important take-away about the enthymeme, and Aristotle's view of rhetoric in general, is the strong emphasis on the audience. Aristotle's notion of the enthymeme operates from what we might consider a "demographic" view of the audience. So long as a rhetor sufficiently understands the demographics of her or his audience, she or he will craft a message that implicitly appeals to the audience's values.

Overall, Aristotle's theory of rhetoric responds to three main concerns. First, as his definition of rhetoric suggests, rhetoric is concerned with **discovery**. Before a rhetor can craft a message, she or he must first discover what persuasive possibilities are available. That notion of availability leads to the second concern: **situations**. Aristotle's theory of rhetoric portrays rhetoric as situational. The available means of persuasion are not the same for every situation. Just because something is persuasive in one situation does not mean the same appeals will work in other situations. Finally, the **audience** is of primary concern. While some of the theories we discuss later will consider the possibilities of an "imagined audience," Aristotle's notion of audience is fairly literal. From this standpoint, the more a rhetor understands about the demographics of her or his audience, the more persuasive she or he is likely to be.

WHAT DO YOU THINK 12.5

Watch (or read) a news story. Can you identify any enthymemes in the story? How do those enthymemes influence your understanding?

The Rhetorical Situation

Aristotle's imprint can be detected in several modern theories of rhetoric. One theory that especially reflects Aristotle's notion of rhetoric is Lloyd F. Bitzer's (1968) **rhetorical situation**. According to Bitzer, "[t]he presence of rhetorical discourse obviously indicates the presence of a rhetorical situation" (p. 2). Bitzer maintains that any expression of rhetoric comes in response to some particular situation. Bitzer's situational framework suggests that rhetoric always responds to something that occurs prior to it. From this angle, rhetoric is **reactive** rather than **active**.

Bitzer (1968) believed all rhetorical situations are composed of three parts: exigence, audience, and constraints. We'll begin by discussing "exigence." An **exigence**, according to Bitzer, "is an imperfection marked by urgency; it is a defect, an obstacle, something waiting to be done, a thing which is other than it should be" (p. 6). We must remember that Bitzer is discussing *rhetorical* situations and, therefore, an "exigence" cannot be just *any* "imperfection," "defect," or "obstacle." As Bitzer argued, some exigencies, such as "death, winter, and some natural disasters" (p. 6) are simply outside of our control. In contrast to these types of exigencies, a *rhetorical exigence* refers to things that can be modified by rhetorical action, which means that in order for an exigence to be rhetorical it must be possible to 1) identify it with rhetoric and 2) resolve it through human action. A brief example may help to illustrate the difference between an exigence and a rhetorical exigence. A hurricane is an example of a *non-rhetorical* exigence. Regardless of how hard we try, no amount of rhetoric or human effort can prevent or alter the path of a hurricane (at least with today's technology). However, the aftermath of a hurricane pushes us in the direction of a rhetorical exigence. We would be dealing with a rhetorical exigence if we were trying to determine how best to respond to people who had lost their homes in a hurricane. The situation can be addressed with rhetoric and can be resolved through human action.

KEY TERM 12.6

Exigence – an imperfection marked by urgency; a defect.

The second part of Bitzer's (1968) rhetorical situation is the **audience**. According to Bitzer, rhetoric "produces change by influencing the decision and action of persons" who can create change (p. 8). Like Aristotle, Bitzer suggested rhetorical situations consist of **literal audiences**. A rhetor, in response to a rhetorical situation, targets her or his discourse at a specific group of real people. However, the audience is not defined by simply a "body of mere hearers," but, rather, "persons who are capable of being influenced by discourse and of being mediators of change" (p. 8). For example, imagine the exigence of our situation is a local initiative to remove candy machines from schools. Thirteen-year-old Wanda accompanies her parents to a local meeting where people are debating about the initiative. On the one hand, Wanda might be considered just a "mere hearer" because, at only thirteen years old, she's not old enough to vote on the initiative. On the other hand, while attending the meeting, Wanda uses her unique perspective as a student to influence the opinions of some of the adults. In that case, even though she did not impact the situation directly through voting, she impacted it indirectly by changing the way another person voted. Bitzer encouraged us to re-think notions of audience in terms of possible outcomes. If a person cannot impact a given situation, do they actually count as part of the rhetor's audience?

The final aspect of a rhetorical situation is constraints. Bitzer (1968) maintained, "every rhetorical situation contains a set of constraints." **Constraints** refer to things such "beliefs, attitudes, documents, facts, traditions, images, interests, [and] motives" (p. 8). Borrowing from Aristotle's terminology, we can think of constraints as factors limiting a person's "available means of persuasion." Let's return to the above example about the initiative to remove all candy machines from schools. Suppose a rhetor who is advocating for the removal of the candy machines is addressing an audience of teachers who work in the schools. The teachers appreciate the concerns for children's health, but some of them enjoy the occasional candy bar in the teacher's lounge. The teachers are worried that the initiative might remove their candy machines. In this case, the teachers' motivations to keep their candy machines are a constraint. To gain the teachers' support, the rhetor must strategically respond to the constraint. In short, constraints affect rhetorical situations by limiting a rhetor's range of persuasive possibilities.

Ultimately, Bitzer suggested that the rhetor has no choice but to respond to the rhetorical situation. As he states, "the situation controls the rhetorical response in the same sense that the question controls the answer and the problem controls the solution" (p. 6). Richard E. Vatz (1973) took an opposing view and argued that rhetors do not respond to situations, but, rather, they *create* them. Vatz encouraged us to recognize how a rhetor's description of a situation is itself a rhetorical act and, in describing a situation, a rhetor has a hand in shaping the way an audience will understand a situation. Other scholars challenged the assumption of a literal audience. As we will see, this move away from relying upon a literal audience would revolutionize the shape and scope of rhetorical theory.

WHAT DO YOU THINK 12.6

Go back and review the news story from 12.5. What rhetorical situation(s) are evident in the story? Can you identify the exigence, audience(s) and constraints?

The Classical View

Though separated by more than two millennia, Aristotle and Bitzer held a similar view of rhetoric. We might call this a **classical view** of rhetoric. One of the hallmarks of the classical view is the assumption of a stable and identifiable audience. From the classical perspective, rhetorical transactions typically consist of an orator who conveys a message to a physically present audience. The classical view considers an orator's rhetoric successful if an audience agrees with his position and disagreement as evidence of an orator's failure. In short, the classical perspective focuses mainly on questions related to "effectiveness." The classical view seeks primarily to identify and explain the reasons why particular discourses succeed or fail. The classical view is complicated by contemporary communication technology and social media.

The Imagined Audience

Beginning in the mid-twentieth century, rhetorical theorists began responding to social and technological changes by proposing innovative extensions and re-imagining rhetorical theories. One such innovation was the conceptualization of the **imagined audience**. The literal interpretation of audience is the actual people who consume a rhetor's message. Supporters of the imagined audience see radical possibilities in viewing an audience as something a rhetor can symbolically *create* through their discourse.

KEY TERM 12.7

Imagined Audience – something a rhetor can symbolically create through their discourse.

The Second Persona

Edwin Black (1970) was one of the first to support the imagined audience with his idea of the **second persona**. "Persona," in the theatrical sense, refers to a role or character played by an actor. In Black's framework, the "first persona" is the rhetorical performance that a rhetor presents to an audience. We can identify the "first persona" with familiar social roles such as "leader," "teacher," "parent," or "friend." In contrast to the first persona, Black proposed the notion of a "second persona," which consists of the author's verbal "tokens" (p. 110). The first persona identifies the implied author, while the second persona represents the author's implied *audience*. By tracing the verbal tokens in the discourse, we can come to identify the rhetor's *intended* audience. The concept encourages us to consider how rhetoric can reach out to an audience without being explicitly addressed to that audience. Scholars have profitably extended Black's persona framework to examine phenomena ranging from marginalized audiences (Wander, 1984), performances of identity (Morris, 2002), and strategic rhetorical silences (Cloud, 1999). All of these extensions mirror Black's (1970) move away from the idea of a preexisting audience in favor of the position that an audience is rhetorically constructed.

"The People"

Another significant contribution to the imagined audience perspective was Michael Calvin McGee's (1975) reformulation of **"the people."** McGee noted that in Western societies such as the United States, we often appeal to notions of collectivity in the discursive form of "the people." Consider, for instance, the prominence of "We *the people*" in the opening line of the US Constitution, or Abraham Lincoln's iconic "of the people, by the people, for the people" phrase in the *Gettysburg Address*. McGee urged us to recognize the rhetorical dynamics at play in appeals to "the people." He explained,

> "[t]he people" . . . are not objectively real in the sense that they exist as a collective entity in nature; rather, they are a fiction dreamed by an advocate and infused with an artificial, rhetorical reality by the agreement of an audience to participate in a collective fantasy. (p. 240)

McGee's point is that any notion of a collective "people" must be viewed as a rhetorical product because collective entities (e.g., groups, movements, societies) do not occur independently from rhetoric. This idea begins to make more sense if we think carefully about some of the historic *social movements* in the United States. The modern Civil Rights Movement provides a fitting example. Although African-Americans shared a common experience of institutional racism during the momentous struggles of the 1950s and 1960s, civil rights organizations did not just occur naturally. Such organizations were formed through rhetoric—the oratory of leaders like Martin Luther King, Jr., and everyday rhetorical appeals to some notion of "the people." This raises a point that McGee makes: "the people" are always temporary. As McGee demonstrated, at any point, "the people" can revert back to being "merely a collection of *individuals*" (p. 242). Again, the modern Civil Rights Movement provides an example. Following the pinnacle of the movement in the mid-1960s, many of the leading civil rights organizations either radically transformed or disbanded. The rhetoric had changed.

WHAT DO YOU THINK 12.7

Let's go back to the 12.5 news story one more time. Can you identify any imagined audience(s) for the story? How does second persona and "the people" alter your understanding of the story?

Genres in Rhetorical Theory

Genres in rhetorical theory are one of the oldest established practices in the communication discipline. The practice identifying genres dates back to the classical period of ancient Greece. But before we get into the details of genres in rhetorical theory, we need to take a few minutes to set a definition for the concept of "genre."

Harrell and Linkugel (1978) offered a definition of genre. They contend that a **genre** is a "set of *organizing principles* found in *recurring situations* that generate discourse characterized by a family of *common factors*" (pp. 263–264; emphasis in original). Therefore, genre rhetorical theory is the practice of classifying communication into different groups and categories. Each category is a type a communication bound together by a distinctive structure, argument, or situation. Most genre scholars agree that the categories are not mutually exclusive. In other words, a speech may belong to more than one genre. A researcher can explore the nature of a speech through a study focusing on one (or multiple) genres. The scholar works to identify the unique components and constraints, which characterize the genre and then analyze how the genre influenced both the communication and the audience.

KEY TERM 12.8

Genre – a set of organizing principles found in recurring situations that generate discourse characterized by a family of common factors.

Let's pause for a moment and consider all the genres we find around us every day. Your daily paper is divided into front-page news, local news, national news, international news, editorial, entertainment, and sports. We divide our sports into amateur, collegiate, professional, and Olympics. Our music is divided into classical, rock 'n' roll, folk, and country-western (or in famous line from *The Blues Brothers* (1980), "We have both kinds, country and western").

Let's review for a moment Bitzer's idea of the rhetorical situation we covered earlier in the chapter. The generation of different genres can emerge from different rhetorical situations. Bitzer believed the **rhetorical situation** is "a natural context of persons, events, objects, relations, and an exigence which strongly invites utterance" (p. 5). A rhetorical situation invites a response from a speaker. How the speaker defines the response is through a genre. Similar rhetorical situations invite use of the same genre.

Certain genres are fairly flexible and can adapt or morph under different circumstances and speakers. Other genres are fairly rigid and not "sticking to the script" for the genre can result in displeasure by the audience. The mass within the Roman Catholic Church, for example, is a highly predictable form within the genre of preaching. You can enter almost any Catholic church on Sunday morning and know, with a certain degree of comfort, the order of the mass. In fact, when Dan was a young boy on vacation with his family, they attended a mass in New Mexico. Little did they know the mass was in Spanish. Yet the familiar pattern held. The sequence of prayers, first reading, responsorial psalm, second reading; the sequence of standing, kneeling, sitting all were the same as his hometown church.

Much has been written on the various types and genres. We provide a quick overview of a number of genres from classical to contemporary. Please note we are not covering all the possible genres—if we did this, your textbook would be very thick and cost much more! Your instructor may have ideas for other genres you should explore. When a particular genre rings true with you, then a closer examination of the genre in the scholarly journals is the appropriate next step.

WHAT DO YOU THINK 12.8

What additional genres can you identify in your life? Think about news, games, social media, and technology.

Aristotle's Three Categories

One of the earliest genre forms was established by Aristotle during the period of the ancient Greeks. Aristotle had three primary classifications for a speech. The three groups are identified by both time and purpose.

1) **Forensic** oratory focuses on the post and in the classical sense was primary involved in the judicial process. The purpose of a forensic presentation was either to accuse or to defend an individual. Forensic addresses the past, since the purpose of the judiciary is to determine what happened yesterday/last week/last year and what guilt or innocence should be ascribed to the persons involved. Your school may have a forensics team. However, you will soon find the term *forensics* for the team has little resemblance to Aristotle's classification. Forensic teams "back in the day" were debate teams that had a judiciary focus, but as time passed the debate teams shifted from judiciary to deliberative (our next category) and the introduction of individual events tournaments soon included competition in some forms of epideictic speaking (our last category).

2) **Deliberative** oratory focuses on the future and is frequently associated with legislative speeches. The purpose of legislators is to persuade one's colleagues (and citizens) toward (or away) from a particular course of action. For example, a US senator who pushes for passage of a new law is engaging in deliberative oratory because the new law will affect how the country operates in the future.

3) **Epideictic** is the final Aristotelean category and focuses on the present with the main purpose being to praise or blame. Epideictic is most commonly understood as ceremonial speech. For example, a eulogy is a common ceremonial speech to praise the life of the recently deceased.

WHAT DO YOU THINK 12.9

What speeches can you think of which meet with Aristotle's three categories (forensic, deliberative, epideictic)?

Cicero's Three Categories

Cicero lived during the declining years of the Roman Republic. He believed that an orator had three primary aims toward which a speech should be targeted. Cicero believed an everyday orator may use any one of his categories, but a true master of the craft will weave all three categories together into a powerful presentation.

1) **Docere** is a Latin term, which roughly translates as "to teach." Cicero included docere since he argued the first premise for an orator is to establish the foundations for your thesis. In other words, to instruct your audience on the subject.
2) **Movere** means "to move" your audience toward a particular thought, belief, or action. Movere is the basis for the word motivation.
3) **Delectare** is the process of entertaining or pleasing your audience. An effective story, a clever phrase, or compelling humor are tools an orator may call on to please the audience.

WHAT DO YOU THINK 12.10

Can you identify a television show with a focus for each of Cicero's categories (docere, movere, delectare)?

Fisher's Categories

Fisher's (1970) categories are based on the motives of the speaker. What drives the individual to respond to a particular situation? The motive combined with the situation compels the speaker toward a particular choice of words, phases, and structure. Fisher identified four categories:

1) **Affirmation** focuses on the creation of a particular mental image for the audience.
2) **Reaffirmation** works to revitalize an image for the audience.

3) **Purification** is the process of modifying or refining a previously established image for the audience.

4) **Subversion** is an attempt to undermine or attack an image.

 **WHAT DO YOU THINK 12.11**

Go back to the television shows from 12.9. Do the shows focus on affirmation, reaffirmation, or purification?

Presidential Address

The president of the United States wields significant power. A speech by the president can frequently interrupt our regular TV shows. *Where* the president speaks from can tell us much about the content. A speech delivered directly from the main hall of the White House, the Rose Garden, the pressroom in the West Wing, or before a joint session of the US Congress are all indicators of the style and content of the speech. Let's pause for a quick fun fact. Did you know that when the president delivers the State of the Union before the House of Representatives, the US Senate, the Cabinet, and the Justices of the Supreme Court, the president orders one member of the Cabinet *not* to attend? If some calamity occurs and everyone in the chamber is incapacitated, the one member of the Cabinet is in the line of succession and has the Constitutional authority to become president. Along with the State of the Union, other presidential speeches include the inaugural address and declarations of war.

Apologia

One of the most common genres within rhetoric is **apologia**. Apologia is the art of expressing remorse for some type of wrong-doing. In other words, the speaker is apologizing for doing something bad. Apologia is most common in politics and public relations. Famous political apologia have been delivered by President Nixon, President Clinton, Governor Eliot Spitzer, and Representative Anthony Weiner. A slightly more intricate form of apologia is the art of the non-apology apology. This happens when a speech has the characteristics of an apology but on close examination lacks actual remorse for committing the deed.

The realm of genres is an ever-evolving area of study. The growth of interactive social media has disrupted many of the traditional genre parameters. While for some the disruption is an area of concern, for others the disturbance has opened up new avenues of scholarship. In reality, this is one of the beauties of studying communication. Communication practices are an ever-changing, adapting, growing, and fluctuating area of research. Communication scholars will never run out of opportunities for new areas of exploration.

Metaphors in Rhetorical Theory

Metaphors are an exciting and interesting part of rhetorical theory and rhetorical criticism. Using metaphors from a rhetorical perspective can provide many unique and compelling insights into the communication happening all around us.

First, we need to distinguish between **metaphors** and **similes**. The two concepts are frequently confused with each other and while they look and sound similar, they are very different in terms of how we frame and understand the world. A simile makes a comparison between two dissimilar items. Similes are fairly easy to identify since the words "like" and "as" usually accompany a simile. A metaphor implies certain qualities are identical from one item to another. In philosophical terms, the metaphor imparts the ontological essence of the item(s). A few examples might help to play out the distinction.

KEY TERMS 12.9 AND 12.10

Metaphor – implies certain qualities are identical to one another.

Simile – makes a comparison between two dissimilar items.

Similes

- The wicked queen has a heart <u>as</u> black as night.
- The bumbling prince was <u>like</u> a newborn kitten.
- Competitive kite combat is <u>like</u> a WWII aerial dogfight.
- The coach treated her players <u>as</u> part of her own family.

Each simile compares the qualities between the two terms. We know the queen's heart is not really black, but the quality implies her wickedness is core to her being (imbedded in her heart). We know the prince is not really a kitten (unless, of course, you're watching the *Lion King*). Similes allow us to envision the queen, the prince, the kites, and the coach because we are already familiar with the concepts of a black heart, a newborn kitten, an aerial dogfight, and a family.

Metaphors

- The queen's black heart is evident in her evil plans.
- The prince has the personality of a newborn kitten.
- Competitive kite fighting is an all-out war.
- The coach knew her players were family.

Each metaphor claims certain properties are part of the character of the item. Metaphors are stronger than similes since the qualities are an inherent part of the item, not just a comparison of qualities.

Two of the metaphors in the above examples are among the most common—war and family. The US currently has a war on drugs, a war on poverty, a war on crime, a war on cancer. Fox News even declared a war on Christmas (just type Fox News war Christmas into a search engine). Certain terms are linked to the war metaphor, including ceasefire, battleground, attack, frontlines, retreat, charge, truce, troops, blockade, neutral zone, bomb, grenade ("he tossed a grenade into that conversation"). Any of these war-related terms draw on the war metaphor without even using the word "war". Listeners/readers can get caught up in the "heat of battle" by a speaker/writer calling on the war metaphor. You will want to become familiar with the most common metaphors, which makes identifying metaphors in communication much easier. Check out www.metaphors.com for "A Big List of Metaphors" and even Wikipedia may helpful in this instance at http://en.wikipedia.org/wiki/List_of_English_language_metaphors.

An extended pop culture example may help play out the power and limitations of metaphors. "Darmok" is an episode of the popular television show *Star Trek: The Next Generation*. The episode revolves around an encounter by the crew of the Enterprise with the Tamarian race. The Tamarians speak entirely in metaphor. While Federation technology could translate the Tamarian's language into contemporary twenty-fourth century words and phrases, the meanings imbedded in the metaphors require understanding of the culture and history of the Tamarians. Councelor Deanna Troi provides an example from the English language—the metaphor "Juliet on her balcony" could be used as a metaphor for a romantic encounter. But if the listener does not understand the history and culture, the phrase is meaningless. Part of the lure of the episode is grasping the metaphors to comprehend the meaning. Here is a brief list of various metaphors Captain Picard and his crew had to "decipher" to hold a conversation (the episode includes more than a dozen Tamarian metaphors):

- "Shaka when the walls fell" = a failed attempt at a task
- "Darmok and Jalad on the ocean" = working together against a common threat or enemy
- "The beast at Tanagra" = a difficult problem to solve
- "The river Temarc in winter" = be still or quiet
- "Darmok and Jalad at Tanagra" = working as a team (this phrase has become fairly popular in certain tech-geek-nerd communities; many online stores carry T-shirts with the phrase)

So, next time you need help with an assignment in your communication theory course, just say to your professor "Darmok and Jalad on the ocean" and when assigned to a group project you can declare "Darmok and Jalad at Tanagra."

The key with metaphors in rhetorical theory and rhetorical criticism, as noted by Croucher and Cronn-Mills (2015), is to: 1) identify the particular metaphor(s) at play in the communication; 2) classify the various qualities the metaphor implies; 3) ascertain how those qualities attempt to influence our understanding, our beliefs, our values, and our actions; 4) decide, in your scholarly opinion, if the metaphor—and the qualities—is appropriate or justified for framing the items or issues.

President Barack Obama and Metaphors

Let's take a moment to examine a specific metaphor at play during President Barack Obama's second term in office. President Obama and the Republicans were constantly at odds on most issues facing the country. In 2014, President Obama started signing a series of executive orders taking action on a variety of issues including immigration, tax policy, gay rights, and Cuba. The president believed this was within his constitutional authority; adversaries were less than impressed. Many legislators and news groups started referring to the president as King Obama. They tagged Obama with the royal moniker to stress how the president was taking unilateral action without the involvement or consent from Congress. Just do a web search for "King Obama" and you can read tens of thousands of articles on the topic. Let's play the metaphor out through the four steps listed by Croucher and Cronn-Mills (2015):

1) Identify the particular metaphor(s) at play in the communication. We already accomplished the first step by identifying the "king" metaphor attached to President Obama.

2) Classify the various qualities the metaphor implies. A king has absolute authority, his word is unchallenged, and all power of government is concentrated in one person.

3) How do these qualities attempt to influence our understanding, our beliefs, our values, and our actions? The king metaphor has potential to catch on with the public. The United States deliberately chose not to have an imperial form of government, opting instead for a balance of powers between the executive, the legislative, and the judicial branches of government. The US did not want their country run by a king or anything that looks too much like a king. However, on the other hand, the United States has a fascination with kings including Lebron "King" James, the Los Angeles Kings, the Sacramento Kings, Burger King, Kings County (CA), Kings Mountain (NC), and the US naval submarine base at Kings Bay (GA).

4) Is the metaphor—and the qualities—appropriate or justified for framing the items or issues? Presidential executive orders are king-like since the president has unilateral authority to issue the orders. However, Congress can always pass bills, which limit or reverse the executive orders. Labeling President Obama a king may have legal limitations, but the metaphor does have the potential to sway the public against the president's actions.

WHAT DO YOU THINK 12.12

Take a few minutes and scroll through your favorite social media (e.g., Facebook, Twitter, Instagram, Pinterest, Tumblr, LinkedIn, Reddit, Vine). What metaphors can you identify on these social media sites?

Kenneth Burke

Of all contemporary rhetorical theorists, few have impacted the study of rhetoric as significantly as **Kenneth Burke**. A prolific and wide-ranging scholar, Burke's work spanned nearly half a century and encompassed issues related to literary studies, religious studies, political science, sociology, and several other fields. However, Burke embraced the title of rhetorician and was chiefly interested in the study of rhetoric, particularly as it pertained to the relationship between symbol use and human motivation. In the interest of space, we limit our discussion here to a few of Burke's main contributions to rhetorical theory. If you find Burke's ideas interesting, you may want to join the Kenneth Burke Society (yes, an entire professional organization of scholars is dedicated solely to the study of Burke's work).

The Pentad

Burke used the term dramatism to describe the combination of his method and field of study. To put it simply, **dramatism** centers human action in language use. Burke suggested that language use is a symbolic act. In contrast to those who view language as something that merely describes action, Burke (1966) argued that language actually *is* action.

One of Burke's key contributions to the study of rhetoric is the **dramatistic pentad**. The pentad is Burke's (1969a) critical instrument for examining how humans use language to assign motives. As suggested by its name, the pentad consists of five key terms: act, scene, agent, agency, and purpose. Burke described the function of the pentad as:

> In a rounded statement about motives, you must have some word that names the *act* (names what took place, in thought or deed), and another that names the *scene* (the background of the act, the situation in which it occurred); also you must indicate what person or kind of person (*agent*) performed the act, what means or instruments he used (*agency*), and the *purpose*. (p. xv)

In any given statement about motives, one of the pentad terms will emerge as dominant. According to which term is given the most intensity, we can better understand the way in which a rhetor is trying to get her or his audience to interpret the given situation. The pentad provides us with opportunities for charting the relationships between terms. Sometimes the relationship between terms plays a crucial role in shaping the meaning of the situation. For instance, let's assume we have a particularly scandalous act: MURDER. Isolated from any of the other terms, murder carries a negative meaning, and, given such an act, we begin to question the character of the "agent." But the act of murder within a "scene" of WAR may alter our interpretation of the "act" and lessen our concerns about the agent. In context of war, "murder" becomes a natural part of the scene. As this example illustrates, the pentad enables us to better critically assess the ways in which a rhetor articulates motives in a given discourse.

WHAT DO YOU THINK 12.13

How might a speaker's motivation alter our perceptions of the content of a speech?

Identification

Among Burke's significant contributions to rhetorical theory is his notion of identification. Burke (1969b) challenged classical views of rhetoric by suggesting that **identification** is the precondition to persuasion. Explaining his concept of identification, Burke argued that through rhetoric two individuals can become **consubstantial** (share a common substance):

> A is not identical with his colleague, B. But insofar as their interests are joined, A is *identified* with B. Or he may *identify himself* with B even when their interests are not joined, if he assumes that they are, or is persuaded to believe so. (p. 20)

If we imagine "A" as an audience member and "B" as a rhetor, to the extent A sees his interests represented in B's discourse, A will identify with B. According to Burke, identification lays the groundwork for persuasion. That is, if B can convince A to identify with him, B will have rendered himself more persuasive to A. At a broader level, Burke asserted that any act of identification implies a corresponding state of division. As he stated, "If men were not apart from one another, there would be no need for the rhetorician to proclaim their unity" (p. 22). As we saw with McGee's (1975) notion of "the people," Burke draws our attention to the idea that people do not unite with one another naturally—any sense of unity is the result of rhetorical action. At a fundamental level, Burke complicates the nature of rhetoric. Rather than viewing rhetoric from the competitive lens of "persuasion," Burke argued that rhetoric is a cooperative gesture of identification.

Chapter Summary

From its ancient origins to contemporary practice and critique, the power and influence of rhetoric is with us every day. We are compelled and repelled by rhetoric; we are influenced by rhetoric; we use the power of rhetoric.

Rhetoric frames and filters how we see the world, understand the world, and experience the world. If you pause and think about it, every chapter in this book, in many ways, draws on the functions of rhetoric to explain how the symbols of all those other theories work. The sections of this chapter provide a foundation for understanding rhetorical theory, the original study of communication. In the first section we addressed the three characteristics of rhetoric. The second section focused on the contributions of Aristotle. The third section provided an explanation of the rhetorical situation. The fourth section demonstrated how the classical view is connected to the past and the present. The fifth section explained the imagined audience and how it changed rhetoric. The sixth section illustrated genres in rhetoric and how they can influence our understanding of symbols. The seventh section explored the link between metaphors and rhetorical theory. The eighth section concluded with Kenneth Burke and his ideas about rhetoric. The final section is an undergraduate student paper from Bethel University (MN) by Jessica L. Benham. The paper illustrates the connections between rhetoric and the popular culture.

Key Terms

"The people"	Active	Affirmation	Apologia
Aristotle	Audience	Classical view	Constraints
Consubstantial	Delectare	Deliberative	Discourse
Discovery	Discursive	Docere	Dramatism
Dramatistic pentad	Enthymeme	Epideictic	Ethos
Exigence	Forensics	Functional	Genres
Identification	Imagined audience	Kenneth Burke	Literal audience
Logos	Metaphors	Movere	Pathos
Public	Purification	Reactive vs. active	Reaffirmation
Rhetor	Rhetorical situation	Second persona	Similes
Situations	Subversion		

Activities

1. Think about your everyday activities. How many different genres and genre sets can you identify in your average day? Think about your schedule, food, and entertainment. How do the different genres constrain the language we use?
2. Pick your favorite television series. Using Burke's pentad, can you identify the act, scene, agent, agency, and purpose? Can you chart any of the connections between the different terms?

Student Paper

The following paper is from COM 463: Topics in Communication Analysis—Mythic and Value Approaches to Rhetorical Criticism taught by Dr. Michael Dreher, Bethel University (MN). The course was divided into five components:

1) Introduction to Rhetorical Criticism. Course serves as a basic introduction to the field of rhetorical criticism. The introduction demonstrates where mythic and value analysis fit within rhetorical theory.
2) Introduction to Value Analysis. Examine theory as applied in a variety of rhetorical contexts.
3) Introduction to Mythic Analysis. Examine theory as applied in a variety of rhetorical contexts.
4) Application. Specific artifacts will be examined through a close textual analysis of an artifact of the students' and/or instructor's choosing. Students will do mini rhetorical criticisms with the goal to extend readings to particular types of rhetorical artifacts.
5) Preparation and completion of a significant rhetorical project.

A Captain for Today's America: The Relevance of the American Dream

Jessica L. Benham
Bethel University (MN)

[Authors' Note: This is an abbreviated version of a longer paper.]

Introduction

Captain America has been a comic-book icon since his creation in 1941, an expression of American dreams, hopes, and ideals during World War II. He has been re-incarnated several times in comic books, television, and movies, always a leader in the fight against American enemies. Roger A. Lee (2011) writes that, "[a]s a living emblem of American pride, the American sense of justice and a true believer in American freedom and liberty, Captain America often, and naturally, finds his duty as defeating the enemies of justice, freedom, and liberty."

Jessica has a strong opening for her paper and "sets the stage" for the rhetorical symbols she is exploring in her paper. However, the quotation she uses in her introduction should have a page number for the citation.

(Continued)

Rationale

The Captain America story was taken up again by Hollywood, when *Captain America: The First Avenger* was released in July 2011. However, unlike previous re-incarnations in comic book form, where Captain America is re-contextualized in a setting current to his audience, *Captain America: The First Avenger* is interesting because of its historic setting and traditional storyline, heroes, and enemies; all major plot points and characters from *Captain American Comics* #1, published in March 1941, appear in the 2011 film.

The 2011 film is set during World War II, as American agents attempt to battle both Hitler and HYDRA, an anti-American, but also anti-Hitler, agency. Not only is Captain America the original Steve Rogers, the enemy he faces, the Red Skull, also appeared in the original series. Adolf Hitler, another traditional enemy of the captain, gets his own reference when Rogers punches a Hitler look-a-like during his shows as he tours the US; this echoes the cover of the first issue of the original series. The Red Skull retains his traditional source of power as well, though the "cosmic cube" of the comic books is referenced as a "tesseract" (*Captain America: The First Avenger*).

The movie also follows the traditional creation story of Captain America as a government project geared toward creating super-soldiers. Dr. Abraham Erskine (Professor Reinstein in the comics) is tasked with Rogers' transformation, but is shot by an enemy agent, which is exactly what occurs in the comic books. Sidekicks Bucky Barnes and Sharon Carter, who appear extensively in the comics, also feature prominently in the movie, though Sharon is renamed "Peggy."

Research Question

The 70-year-old plot and character elements of the film lead to questions about its relevance for a modern audience and its reflection of current American

Jessica provides context for understanding the Captain America movie she is using rhetorical theory to critique. The information is essential to help frame the historical background for establishing the societal importance of Captain America.

(Continued)

ideals. Is the traditional Captain America myth, as communicated through *Captain America: The First Avenger*, compatible with the modern American Dream?

Method

This paper will utilize narrative analysis, focusing on the rags-to-riches narrative of the 2011 movie, to examine the compatibility of the Captain America story with the ideological system of the American Dream myth. Mishler (1995) emphasizes the importance of examining how a narrative functions within society and culture. Riessman (2004) notes that there is no standard method for narrative analysis, but that "narrative analysis can forge connections between personal biography and social structure—the personal and the political" (p. 6). A narrative is not a perfect reproduction of the past, but rather an interpretation by the storyteller (Riessman, 2004, p. 6). This paper will analyze the narrative of the 2011 Captain America movie and look at the connections between the themes of the movie and the modern American Dream.

Literature Review

An examination of the nature of the American Dream myth is necessary in order to understand the research question. Rowland and Jones (2011) write that "[f]unctioning as the narrative embodiment of classical liberalism, the American Dream works as a mythic, ideological system" (p. 132). At the heart of the Dream myth is the idea that "land was plentiful and resources were abundant in America" (Pileggi et al., 2000, p. 209).

Variants of the American Dream Myth

The Dream myth is not uniform; rather, there are two distinct narratives that fit under its umbrella. Pileggi et al. (2000) note that "[t]wo seemingly contradictory narratives, rags-to-riches and money-can't-buy-happiness, articulate different dimensions

Jessica is using a rhetorical set of theories called narrative analysis. The narrative approach is closely related to the dramatistic perspective of Kenneth Burke we discussed in the chapter. Notice how she is drawing on specific rhetorical *functions* for her analysis. She connects the rhetorical functions with the broader metaphor of the American Dream. She could strengthen her theory section by explicitly tying in the American Dream metaphor to her analysis. Right now, the metaphor dimensions are only implied.

(Continued)

of the American dream" (p. 210). Fisher (1973) notes that the myth of the American Dream contains two narratives that appear to be at odds with each other: the "rags to riches, materialistic myth of individual success and the egalitarian moralistic myth of brotherhood" (p. 161).

To provide a framework for the analysis of Captain America's rise from scrawny boy to super soldier, this paper will focus on the rags-to-riches aspect of the American Dream myth, which is characterized by its unique narrative, characters, and themes.

A Narrative of Hope

The myth is based on a narrative of hope, the idea that anyone can succeed in America. The American Dream myth posits the claim that success is not dependent on situation, but rather on the actions of the individual. This is accomplished, as Burns (2009) notes, by starting these narratives with "an individual who had very little and worked to gain social and economic status" (p. 25). Anyone can succeed in the rags-to-riches myth, regardless of origin. Smith (2009) furthers this idea by claiming, "The American Dream, by example, exemplifies the most valued of cultural beliefs—that in America, the 'land of opportunity,' anyone, regardless of background, can achieve his or her goals" (p. 224). The myth communicates a sense of opportunity that exists for everyone.

Characters Reflect American Values

The myth contains characters that reflect American values and, as a result, provoke empathetic reactions from the audience. These characters achieve these results by creating a larger-than-life persona, but also by appearing ordinary.

Smith (2009) notes that "[p]ersona, as defined by Ware and Linkugel (1982) is the mythical mask worn by an individual who assumes a character that exists separately from his or her 'real' self" (p. 226). Characters in the dream myth are literally or

(Continued)

figuratively masked to hide their true identities from the audience. Smith (2009) goes on to claim that the construction of a persona allows the character to so reflect societal values that "it may be impossible to separate the two" (p. 226). As a result, the audience is sympathetic to the struggles of the character (Smith, 2009, p. 227).

Additionally, characters reflect the ordinary nature of American citizens, while being capable of extraordinary actions. Rowland and Jones (2011) write that "[t]he individualistic variant emphasizes the extraordinary heroism of ordinary individuals" (p. 133). They go on to say:

> One possible explanation is that the heroes of the American Dream are both ordinary people and the personification of something larger. It is the very fact that they are ordinary that makes their actions so extraordinary. In the progressive vision of the American Dream, it is not the larger-than-life hero who achieves the "more perfect union" but the ordinary citizen. It is precisely the fact that the American Dream is open to ordinary citizens that makes it such an extraordinary story in human history. (pp. 147–148)

The ordinariness of the hero functions to balance the concept of the persona, allowing the audience to empathize with the hero while also admiring his extraordinary accomplishments and abilities. This aspect of the hero's character promotes the idea that even the ordinary citizen is capable of greatness.

Themes of the Myth

Hard work

The idea that individual hard work is key to overcoming obstacles is central to the myth's thesis. Burns (2009) writes that "overcoming extreme obstacles is a common theme that is heard in stories of

(Continued)

the American Dream" (p. 24). In order to achieve success, characters in rags-to-riches narratives must persevere.

Pileggi et al. (2000) continues this idea, stating that "this dimension of the American dream myth posits hard work and personal integrity as the key ingredients for unlimited spiritual, social, and financial growth" (p. 211). Interesting, here, is the concept of "unlimited" growth; the American Dream myth communicates the idea that, once obstacles are overcome, there is nothing the heroes can't accomplish.

Personal Sacrifice

Burns (2009) states that "sacrifice is a common term heard or seen when studying American Dream stories" (p. 26). The myth may claim that heroes, through hard work, can overcome obstacles and achieve great things, but it does not argue that doing so will be easy. The characters within a rags-to-riches narrative will be forced to make sacrifices in order to continue to pursue their goals.

Societal Good

The rags-to-riches narrative promotes the idea that individual success contributes to the good of society. Rowland and Jones (2011) state that "[t]he American Dream places the idea of progress toward a better society as the ultimate societal goal . . . variants of the story emphasize the heroism of the individual in moving the nation forward" (p. 132). The hero's hard work and sacrifices not only have personal ramifications, but also have a beneficial impact on the hero's surroundings. Pileggi et al. (2000) note that this narrative, "also applauds ambition, which is often characterized as a hunger or desire for self-improvement that ultimately benefits the larger society" (p. 211).

Jessica has a strong literature review exploring many of the themes connected to Captain America, the American Dream and narrative analysis. For an undergraduate paper, this is, in our opinion, very good work.

(Continued)

Conclusion

The myth of Captain America, despite its historical origins, is still closely tied to the ideals of the American Dream. The tension between perseverance and quick fixes in the narrative reflects a shift in values from hard work to easy solutions. Sadly, *Captain America: The First Avenger* draws attention to negative aspects of the American Dream, revealing a culture that desires an easy rise to success, no matter what the cost. As it is so entrenched in American culture, it is unlikely that this myth will become less influential, especially given the increasing popularity of superhero movies.

References

Burns, M. E. (2009). Gold medal storytelling: NBC's hegemonic use of Olympic athlete narratives. *Journal of Communication, Speech, & Theatre Association of North Dakota, 22,* 19–29.

Fisher, W. R. (1973). Reaffirmation and subversion of the American dream. *Quarterly Journal of Speech, 59*(2), 160–167.

Johnston, J. (Director), Markus, C. (Writer), & McFeely, S. (Writer) (2011). *Captain America: The First Avenger* [DVD].

Lee, R. A. (2011). *Captain America villains and enemies.* Retrieved from www.historyguy.com/comicshistory/captain_america_villains.html.

Mishler, E. G. (1995). Models of narrative analysis: A typology. *Journal of Narrative and Life History, 5,* 87–123.

Pileggi, M. S., Grabe, M. E., Holderman, L. D., & de Montigny, M. (2000). Business as usual: The American dream in Hollywood business films. *Mass Communication and Society, 3*(2), 207–228.

Riessman, C. K. (2004). Narrative analysis. In M.S. Lewis Beck, A. Bryman, & T. F. Liao (Eds.), *The Sage encyclopedia of social science research methods.* Retrieved from http://srmo.sagepub.com/view/the-sage-encyclopedia-of-social-science-research-methods/n611.xml.

Smith, G. D. (2009). Love as redemption: The American dream myth and the celebrity biopic. *Journal of Communication Inquiry, 33*(3), 222–238.

Whedon, J. (Director & Screenplay) & Penn, Z. (Writer). (2012). *The Avengers* [DVD].

13 CRITICAL CULTURAL THEORY

James P. Dimock & Kirsti K. Cole

Chapter Outline

- The Marxist Critique
- Critical Theory
- Critical Race Theory
- Critical Gender Theory
- Student Paper

Movies, television, music, and literature all shape our perceptions of the world by influencing our sense of what is, of what is good, and of what is possible. Cultural, religious, and educational institutions, communication networks such as newspapers, radios, television, and the Internet, all of these institutions—high or low, sophisticated or popular—function to shape our ideas, our understandings, and the assumptions on which our society is founded. Critical cultural theory is a way to begin unpacking and grappling with assumptions, with the beliefs, with the **ideology** that we make based on our participation in such institutions.

At the time we are writing this chapter, riots are taking place all over the United States in outrage that a grand jury in Missouri failed to hand down an indictment in the shooting death of Michael Brown. Brown was an unarmed, black teenager. The man who shot him, Darren Wilson, was a white police officer. The sense of outrage and injustice felt by many African-Americans was not understood by white Americans (see Eric Michael Dyson's [2014] editorial in the *New York Times* as a particularly well-written reflection on this topic). Since at least the early 1970s, films like *Dirty Harry* have reinforced the image of the heroic police officer, his hands tied by regulations and technicalities, who goes beyond the law to mete out justice. Not surprisingly, the criminals in such films are often people of color. This is not one film or even a couple. It is an entire genre of films. In the rare instances when police officers are depicted as corrupt, it is an aberration—a bad apple not a rotten barrel. In the climax of the film the corruption is rooted out by the story's hero, who is usually a good cop, and order and justice are restored to the police. Such stories are told over and over to the point where they become what the Italian Marxist Gramsci called **hegemonic**. An idea is hegemonic when it can simply be taken for granted. It becomes part of the body of common sense suppositions. So a person can say, for example, that "police officers are heroes" or that "we would have less crime if the police's hands weren't tied by excessive regulations" and you would (typically) not be expected to back up or defend the claims. They can be expressed without evidence whereas to express their opposites—"the police are corrupt" or "police routinely violate people's civil rights with impunity"—then you have attacked popular wisdom and must be prepared to defend your utterances.

In this chapter we will explore critical cultural theory or the study of how social, cultural, and political believes effect the various kinds of communication and roles/tasks people have. The theories and concepts, like those in many other chapters, vary considerably. Many of the issues discussed in this chapter come from a more theoretical perspective, while others come from a practical perspective. Moreover, the issues range from the social scientific to the critical/cultural approach. In the first section we will define critical theory and discuss the different components of class by discussing the philosophy of Karl Marx. In the second section we will describe ideology and discuss the ways in which ideological apparatuses can impact our understanding of ourselves, and others in the world. In the third section we will explore critical race theory, which emphasizes race instead of class. In the fourth section we will outline critical gender theory, with a focus on feminism and queer theory. Within this discussion of gender theory, and in the final section of this chapter you will find a student paper to further illustrate the applicability of critical cultural theory.

The Marxist Critique

Not all critical theorists are Marxists, but the ideas of the German historian and social critic underscore much of critical and radical thought not only in the United States but also around the world. Few thinkers have had so great an impact. Karl Marx was born in 1818, in the town of Trier in the German Rhineland. He would go on to become one of the most insightful critics of the emerging socio-political order in Europe, which we today call **capitalism**. Capitalism is an economic and political system in which a country's trade and industry are controlled by private owners for profit, rather than by the state. How does Marxist critique work? An example:

A Marxist View of the State

In the 1999 film *The Matrix*, filmmakers Andy and Lana Wachowski introduced audiences to Thomas A. Anderson, an anonymous everyman who by day works in a sterile office building but at night becomes Neo, a rebellious computer hacker. Anderson cannot escape the feeling that something is wrong, that the reality in which he is living is somehow . . . off. Neo eventually meets a mysterious figure called Morpheus, another computer hacker who promises to show Neo the truth about something called the Matrix, which will answer all of his questions.

Morpheus: You have the look of a man who accepts what he sees because he is expecting to wake up. Ironically, this is not far from the truth . . . Do you believe in fate, Neo?

Neo: No.

Morpheus: Why not?

Neo: Because I don't like the idea that I'm not in control of my life.

Morpheus: I know exactly what you mean. Let me tell you why you're here. You're here because you know something. What you know you can't explain but you feel it. You've felt it your entire life—that there is something wrong with the world. You don't know what it is but it's there, like a splinter in your mind driving you mad. It is this feeling that has brought you to me. Do you know what I am talking about?

Neo: The Matrix.

Morpheus: Do you want to know what it is?

Neo: [nods]

Morpheus: The Matrix is everywhere. It is all around us even now in this very room. You can see it when you look out your window or when you turn on your television. You can feel it when you go to work, when you go to church, when you pay your taxes. It is the world that has been pulled over your eyes to blind you from the truth.

Neo: What truth?

Morpheus: That you are a slave, Neo. Like everyone else you were born into bondage, born into a prison that you cannot smell or taste or touch. A prison for your mind. Unfortunately, no one can be told what the Matrix is. You have to see it for yourself. This is your last chance. After this, there is no turning back.

[Morpheus removes two pills, one blue the other red, from a silver case in his pocket]

Take the blue pill. The story ends. You wake up in your bed and believe whatever you want to believe. You take the red pill, you stay in wonderland and I show you how deep the rabbit hole goes.

Remember, all I am offering is the truth. Nothing more.

Of course, Neo takes the red pill and discovers that everything he has ever known was a lie. He isn't him. He has lived his whole life in a vegetative state with a computer connected to his brain projecting into his mind a simulation of lived existence, a fictional reality—the Matrix. The purpose of the Matrix was to make the real world, a nightmarish future ruled by machines and where humans are harvested for the energy their bodies create, invisible. The Matrix is a system of control. Although many people, like Anderson, knew something was wrong, they could never see what it was because the reality of their existence was hidden from them by a false reality.

The Matrix is not the only form of control the machines use. Humans who live outside the mental controls of the Matrix are hunted by Sentinels, squid-like killing machines designed to hunt humans. Within the Matrix there are dangers too. Agents, or sentient programs who inhabit the Matrix in order to prevent malcontents like Morpheus, Trinity, and Neo from disrupting the system. All of this is necessary for the machines to maintain control of humanity who are simultaneously a threat to the machines' domination of the planet and necessary for the machines to survive.

KEY TERM 13.1

Capitalism – an economic and political system in which a country's trade and industry are controlled by private owners for profit, rather than by the state.

The Matrix movie series is a good metaphor for Marxist social thought. Like the Wachowskis' dystopian future, Marx understood society to be a conflict between two classes: the **bourgeoisie**, or the ruling class, and the **proletariat**, or the working class. The conflict between the two classes defines them both. As long as classes exist in *any* form, there will be conflict between them. The class system, moreover, is based on the exploitation of one class—the proletariat—by the other—the bourgeoisie—in the same way that the Wachowski siblings' fictional machine world was based on exploiting human beings for the energy their bodies produced.

At the heart of the class conflict lies the problem of labor and value. The capitalist, or the bourgeoisie as a class, controls the means of production. What makes the bourgeoisie the bourgeoisie is not that they are rich but that they control the means or the resources necessary to keep society functioning: the resources needed (a mine or a forest), the facilities needed to transform those resources into commodities which have value (a factory or a mill), and the technology needed to transport those commodities to markets (trains or ships).

What makes the proletariat the proletariat is they have no control over the means of production and are thus at the mercy of the ruling class. The working class has nothing to sell but its labor. It is this labor, though, that provides value. In transforming an object through the application of labor, the object now contains the labor of the worker.

In a complex industrial society, needs of the system are highly specialized, which creates a need for a large coordinator class or what Marx called the **petite bourgeois**. These are the skilled technicians, researchers and scientists, doctors, lawyers, teachers and other intellectual laborers but also skilled craftspersons and officers in the police and military. These roles are vital to the maintenance of the system.

With control of the means of production, however, it is the bourgeoisie who control the product of the worker's labor. The worker must exchange his or her labor for what is necessary to survive. In a capitalist system, this consists of wages. The capitalist adds no labor to the commodity and thus adds no value to it but when it is sold, keeps the profit. The worker, who creates value, has no control over the exchange. This, Marxists say, results in **alienation**, or the dehumanization of the working class for the benefit of the ruling class.

KEY TERM 13.2

Alienation – the dehumanization of the working class for the benefit of the ruling class.

Fast food workers, for example, have little if any control over the conditions of their labor. They don't get to say when they will and will not work, or what they will and will not do while they are there. Their role in the process is unskilled with few if any opportunities for creative problem solving or innovation. They have no control over who will actually eat the food they make. Their wages are kept as low as possible. These workers have been alienated from their labor. If, according to Marx, it is labor that defines a person then we literally are what we do and so to take that from us is to strip us of our humanity.

The ruling class, however, is also alienated, although this is experienced in a very different way. Because the ruling class does no labor, they are defined by nothing. They have no intrinsic identity and must therefore seek out identities in the form of consumption of commodities. We cannot be what we do because we do nothing. In order to be anything, then, we must consume. Even our relationships are commoditized as we interact with others more exclusively in terms of a relationship of exchange. Most of our encounters with others are mediated by, connected with, or related to some form of commercial transaction. This is what Marx referred to as **commodity fetishism**.

We should not assume, however, that because all persons are dehumanized that all are equal. The system is set up to benefit the ruling class, to protect the privileges and property of the ruling class. The system is built upon the oppression of the proletariat. This is, for Marxists, not only immoral but also unstable, and the question that animates critical theorists concerns how this system of power and exploitation is maintained. How does a relatively small group exert so much power over a much larger class upon whom they are entirely dependent?

Understanding Ideology

Marx's approach to the study of society is both scientific and historical. Throughout his writing, Marx's argument is characterized by the application of scientific methods to the study of history in order to critique the existing socio-political/economic order. History is determined by material forces rather than spiritual or intellectual forces, and thus can be studied and understood. The theory Marx developed is an early form of social theory called **structuralism**. Structuralist theories postulate that, while social phenomena take many forms, the underlying structures are similar. The study of societies, then, is an effort to get at what lies underneath. In the same way an archeologist sifts through the earth, sometimes scraping and other times gently brushing away what is on the surface in order to see what lies beneath, critical theorists try to sift through social, political, and economic systems in order to expose the underlying structure. This process is called "critique."

Marx began by distinguishing between the base, also called the **substructure**, and the **superstructure** of a society. Marx (1978d) argued:

> In the social production of their life, men enter into definite relations that are indispensable and independent of their will, relations of production which correspond to a definite stage of development of their material productive forces. The sum total of these relations of production constitutes the economic structure of society, the real foundation, on which rises a legal and political superstructure and to which correspond definite forms of social consciousness. The mode of production of material life conditions the social, political, and intellectual life process in general. It is not the consciousness of men that determines their being, but, on the contrary, their social being that determines their consciousness. (p. 4)

Social constructionists (see Chapter 3) believe that the world—and the social world in particular—is constructed through discourse and other symbolic interactions. Marxists argue that social realities, including communication practices, are determined by the material conditions of existence. Every social order has resources that determine the order of that society.

Marxists contend that there are two ways to influence a person's behavior—violently or ideologically. The superstructure is made up of mechanisms which do both. Borrowing terminology from the Marxist theorist Althusser, we'll call the former, violent methods of social control **repressive state apparatuses**, and the latter, ideological methods we'll call **ideological state apparatuses**.

As we saw in *The Matrix*, the machines who dominate the Earth use violence in the form of terrifying hunter-killer robots called Sentinels. These squid-like robots kill without hesitation or mercy. It is their purpose. They do what they are designed to do. Marxists point out that, for the working class, life is very much like this. Throughout most of history, the function of the standing military forces was to protect the nobility from both aristocratic rivals and the masses over whom they ruled. Today, in most of the industrialized North, these functions are divided between the military, which addresses external threats, and the police, who are concerned with internal threats. But what really is the function of the police? What purpose do they serve? Marxist historian David White-house (2012) argued in a lecture on behalf of the socialist Center for Economic Research and Social Change that the function of the police is very different from what we may have been taught in school, if we were taught anything at all:

> The police were invented in England and the United States within the space of just a few decades—roughly from 1825 to 1855. The new institution was not a response to an increase in crime and it really didn't lead to any new methods in dealing with crime. The most important way for police to solve crime then and now is for someone to tell them who did it. . . . Crime has to do with the acts of individuals. The ruling elite who invented the police were responding to challenges posed by collective action. The authorities created the police in response to large, defiant crowds: strikes in England, riots in the northern US, and the threat of slave insurrections in the South. The police are a response to crowds not to crimes.

The formation of police departments coincides with the Industrial Revolution, a period of mass dislocation and migration of people. In the United States and England, soon to be followed by Germany and other nations of what is today called the Industrialized North, populations began to shift from rural agricultural communities and small towns to large urban centers. The landless poor, often driven from their land by mechanization, found work in the factories. Millions would migrate from the Old World to the Americas with only their labor to sell. They would often find themselves in cramped, dirty tenements working for starvation wages. In the United States, factory owners encouraged immigration, which led to surplus labor—more people than jobs. The new immigrants were often pitted against one another, divided by ethnicity.

Under such conditions, it should not be surprising that, from time to time, especially during periods of economic slowdown (recessions or depressions), when many workers were unemployed, the working class would turn against the ruling class. Indeed, few things have frightened the bourgeoisie more than the idea of a united and hungry proletariat. Police were introduced to keep tabs on the working class—beat cops who got to know the neighborhoods and the people living there—but primarily to respond to riots, strikes, and other forms of mass discontent by the working class.

Repressive state apparatuses are simply not an effective, long-term strategy of social control. For one thing, as psychologists have long noted, the application of force—called negative reinforcement—has diminishing returns over time. The more repression is used, the less effective it is in controlling behavior. Furthermore, the ruling class must rely on members of the petite bourgeoisie and the proletariat to serve in the ranks of the military and police. When possible, this is done using factions within the working and coordinator classes. So we should not be surprised at all to find white police officers from working-class neighborhoods patrolling black working-class communities. This has divided loyalties of the proletariat, some of whom identify with the police as members of their own communities. Conflicts between police and the communities over whom they exert power are addressed as racial conflict—which exists in the superstructure—rather than as part of an overall system of oppression.

In *The Matrix*, the Matrix is a complex system of control. While there are repressive apparatuses both inside and outside the Matrix—Sentinels and Agents—the Matrix itself is the primary mechanism of control. If the mind is controlled, the body is controlled. This control begins by giving those within it a false view of reality. The actual nature of oppression is hidden and thus even people who understand that something is wrong, who want to resist the oppression they feel, don't know where to begin.

Marx also believed there was a distorted reality that has been drawn over the eyes of the people. He called this false reality **ideology** and the apparatuses with perpetuate this reality and get people to accept it as true, a process Marxists call **interpellation**, are called **ideological apparatuses**. Ideology in a broad sense refers to "that aspect of the human condition under which human beings live their lives as conscious actors in a world that makes sense to them to varying degrees" (Therborn, 1980, p. 2). Try to think of it like this: when you walk around the world you live in, you have a model of the world in your head, a set or matrix of ideas that tells you what things are and how things are related to one another. This model is how you make sense and meaning out of the world you inhabit. It tells you who you are, what your purpose is, and how to relate to and interact with others. According to Therborn (1980), ideology functions on three levels:

1) *What exists*, and its corollary, what does not exist: that is, who we are, what the world is, what nature, society, men and women are like . . .
2) *What is good*, right, just, beautiful, attractive enjoyable, and its opposites . . .
3) *What is possible* and impossible: our sense of mutability, of our being-in-the-world, and the consequences of change are hereby patterned, and our hopes, ambitions, and fears given shape. (p. 18)

KEY TERM 13.3

Ideology – that aspect of the human condition under which human beings live their lives as conscious actors in a world that makes sense to them to varying degrees.

In *The Matrix*, the Matrix is an image, a projection that stands between human beings and the world they inhabit. Because it distorts what exists, what is good, what is possible, it makes it virtually impossible to make meaningful changes in the relations of production (the base). We fight for changes in the superstructure, which are permitted only if they can be safely assimilated into the base without fundamentally altering it.

The Evolution of Marxist Thought into Critical Theory

Marx was driven to understand the events of his time and to base his critique of capitalism on historical events. Other historians, in his view, either based their theories on unrealistic and **idealistic** assumptions about human beings or on **teleological** assumptions about the universe (that there is a destiny or preordained end toward which all of history is directed). The ideas Marx developed, especially his critique of capitalism (*Capital*), would influence leftist and radical thinkers long after his death in 1883. Many of Marx's ideas, especially his historical materialism, would become foundations of leftist thinkers including anarchists, democratic socialists, and communists. While Marx was an important socialist thinker, he wasn't the only influential radical.

Marx had little respect for philosophers and even less for members of the bourgeoisie. Ironically, however, it would be intellectuals funded by the son of a wealthy grain merchant who would play the greatest role in popularizing Marxist thought and applying it to the advanced stages of capitalism, which developed in the twentieth century. Collectively they became known as the Frankfurt School.

The members of the Frankfurt School faced two historical challenges to Marx's theory. First, Marxism did not predict the rise of fascism, which was both a working-class movement and anti-socialist. Second, Marxist thought could not explain how, in societies like the US where radicals were relatively free to speak and organize, these societies had not already been moved to socialist revolution. Their approach to social theory, while Marxist in character, advanced Marx's thought in important ways and has come to be called **critical theory**. Critical theory is a school of thought that relies on reflection, assessment, and critique of the social and cultural. While there are significant differences between different theorists in this tradition, there are some key principles, which unite contemporary critical theory.

KEY TERM 13.4

Critical theory – school of thought that relies on reflection, assessment and critique of the social and cultural.

Critical Theory

Critical Theory is Multidisciplinary

Since the Enlightenment the tendency in education has been toward specialization. This tendency has accelerated since the Industrial Revolution, which treated knowledge as a means to an end. This end has been the development of technology and the amassing of capital. Today, students don't just get an education but they get an education *in* something—accounting or engineering or communication studies.

This division between disciplines has promoted specialization and advanced knowledge in truly amazing ways. For critical theorists, this advancement has come at a price. The separation between disciplines has separated domains of knowledge and experience from one another. Scholars in different fields use different vocabularies and reason in different ways. We both teach argumentation and rhetoric but from different disciplines—Kirsti is from English background and Jim is in Communication Studies. By reuniting disciplines, encouraging collaboration and synthesis between domains of knowledge, critical theorists hope to bridge the gap between theory and practice.

Critical Theory Privileges Praxis

According to the philosopher of science, Karl Popper, "[t]heories are nets cast to catch what we call 'the world': to rationalize, to explain, and to master it" (as cited in Keuth, 2005, p. 51) and it is the function of theories to describe and to explain the world around us. Traditional approaches to theory—including many you will find in this book—make an effort to distinguish between theorizing on one hand and the application of theory to the world on the other. For example, in a debate over the nature of knowledge, Karl Popper and Sir John Eccles (1974) both agreed it was necessary to distinguish between the scientist who "is trying to understand nature" and the technologist who "is interested in using science for some purpose or other that he wants, or society wants" (p. 84).

Critical theorists reject this distinction. Like Marx, critical theorists look for material explanations for social, political, and economic phenomena, but they do so in order to discover the forces of oppression that we might be liberated from them. As Marx said, "philosophers have only interpreted the world, in various ways; the point, however, is to change it." This change, moreover, is about improving the condition of humankind, which brings us to our third principle, that *"critical theories are chiefly concerned with evaluating the freedom, justice, and happiness of societies"* (Ingram & Simon-Ingram, 1992, p. xx).

Critical Theory is Ongoing and Reflexive

As Berlin (1963) noted, the ruling classes have an interest in opposing the spread of criticism. Conservatives, even in our own time, have been quick to oppose "revisionist histories," which challenge traditional interpretations of history. The spread of reason and critical thinking threatens the ideological illusion, which obscures the nature of oppression. Thus Marx (1978b) urged "a ruthless criticism of everything existing, ruthless in two senses: The criticism must not be afraid of its own conclusions, nor of conflict with the powers that be" (p. 13).

This critique, critical theorists contended, should not be limited to the powers that be but must also be **reflexive**, or aimed back at critical theory itself. Unlike traditional approaches to theory, critical theory "must also criticize its own philosophical assumptions . . . by using the method of historical materialism developed by Marx" (Ingram & Simon-Ingram, 1992, p. xxi). Critical theorists are conscious of the fact that their own theories, approaches, and values can become entrenched assumptions, which, although they might have been liberatory at one time, now hold society back.

In this section, we will look at three of the most important extensions of critical theory into what is often today called **postmodernism**: critical race theory, critical feminist theory, and critical queer theory. At the conclusion of this chapter, you will find a sample student paper written by Jordan Christensen. In his work, Christensen applies critical theory to aspects of the conflict between Israelis and Palestinians in an area referred to as the Occupied Territories. As we look at these approaches to communication theory, it is important to keep in mind there is no one approach to critical theory. Critical rhetorical scholar Raymie McKerrow (1989) said that critical theory was more like a perspective or orientation than a prescribed methodology. All critical approaches privilege praxis over abstract theorizing. In communication studies, this **praxis** unfolds along three lines:

1) *Consciousness raising.* One of the most challenging problems facing critical theorists is making people aware of the nature and conditions of oppression. Even those who are exploited do not always understand the forms or roots of their oppression. One of the most important functions of ideological apparatuses is to obscure the nature of oppression. Critical theorists seek to bring about change by unmasking the nature and causes of injustice.

2) *Contemporary orientation.* Marx was very interested in history but not for history's sake. The study of history gives us perspective and understanding on contemporary conditions. Praxis is not about

changing the past but about understanding and impacting the present and the future.

3) *Centering the margins.* Those who have power within a given power structure occupy positions of privilege. They have access to the resources, relationships, knowledge, and capital needed to thrive within a given structure. The oppressed are, in the words of Ford and Airhihenbuwa (2010) "outsiders within." The oppressed assimilate both the ideology of the ruling class through literature, movies, education, and other apparatuses. But the oppressed see these things from a different perspective. In his famous oration "What to the Slave is the Fourth of July?" Frederick Douglass captured this viewpoint, the perspective of one who has lived in slavery joining in the celebration of America's freedom and independence and the establishment of liberty and democracy. To center the margins is to change perspectives, to look at the world from the point of view of the oppressed and to make their voices, their lived experiences, and their values a central aspect of our cultural criticism.

Critical Race Theory

The reggae singer Bob Marley is most famous for his smooth, easy-dancing rhythms. Songs like "Three Little Birds" and "Stir it Up" are just fun to listen to. He is probably most famous, however, for his songs about marijuana use, like "Easy Skanking":

Excuse me while I light my spliff
Good God I gotta take a lift
From reality I just can't drift
That's why I am staying with this riff.
(Marley, 1999)

Songs like this have helped to establish Marley as a fixture in drug culture. In many ways, this affiliation with smoking marijuana—which remains an important part of Rastafarian religious tradition—has been a distraction from the political and revolutionary nature of his music. His "Crazy Baldheads," for example, is about chasing the Baldheads, people of European descent, out of Jamaica. Perhaps one of his most obviously political songs is "War":

Until the philosophy which hold one race superior
And another
Inferior
Is finally
And permanently
Discredited
And abandoned

Everywhere is war
Me say war.
(Marley, 1999)

Such songs rarely appear on the "greatest hits" albums intended for (mostly white) consumers in the United States.

The view of war expressed in Marley's songs is very different from the understanding generally held by persons in wealthy countries like the US. If people are not openly fighting in the streets, we are pretty comfortable calling it peace. Marley said war is present wherever there is racism and oppression even—perhaps especially—when we don't see it.

WHAT DO YOU THINK 13.1

Singer Bob Marley challenged racism in his music while activist Paul Robeson used his status as an actor and performer to promote justice for people of color. Why are they not typically included when we honor those who fought for civil rights?

Why are Some Civil Rights Leaders Remembered While Others are Forgotten?

Paul Robeson was one of the most widely recognized and influential artists of the early twentieth century. An all-American, three-sport athlete in college, Robeson paid his way through law school at Columbia playing professional football. It was on stage, playing roles like Othello and Old Joe in the musical *Old Man River*, that he became internationally famous, perhaps the most famous American in the world during the 1930s and 1940s.

He was, however, an unabashed communist and supporter of the Soviet Union. In a speech delivered in 1949, as the Cold War between the US and the Soviets was taking shape, he said, "[it] is inconceivable that American Negros would fight with those who have oppressed them for generations against the Soviet Union, which, in a generation, has raised them to a position of equality" (as cited in Foner, 1978, p. 4).

Consider the different ideological apparatuses discussed earlier in this chapter. Why are some leaders, like Robeson forgotten in our histories of the Civil Rights Movement while others, like Martin Luther King, Jr., are given places of prominence?

Marley's music is very much a product of his times. In the US, the late 1950s and the 1960s were tumultuous times. The Civil Rights Movement put racial segregation and oppression of people of color on center stage in the US. This movement coincided with liberation movements all over the world. Resistance to **colonialism,** or a political and economic system in which powerful countries, like the US and Great Britain, exploited less powerful nations, like Panama and India, for their own advantage was on the rise all over the world. Since the late fifteenth and early sixteenth centuries, European explorers opened up trade routes between Europe and Africa, the Americas and Asia. The militarily and economically powerful nations used their strength to subjugate the peoples they encountered, establishing a system of **imperialism**. Wealth flowed from the colonies who were often rich in natural resources and labor power, to the mother countries. This wealth was used to develop the infrastructure of the colonial powers. They built roads, dams, factories and universities. This **capital investment** was then used to create even more wealth. In the context of these political, social, and economic changes there emerged a new approach to social and communication theory known as **postcolonialism**. Postcolonialism looks at communication practices from the perspective of colonized and previously colonized peoples.

KEY TERMS 13.5 AND 13.6

Colonialism – a political and economic system in which powerful nations exploit less powerful nations.

Imperialism – wealth flows from the colonies, who are often rich in natural resources and labor power, to the mother countries.

Like Marxist approaches to theory, critical race theories are dialectical but emphasize race over class conflict. To understand critical race theory, it is good idea to revisit some concepts we often use but which are understood differently by critical theorists. The terms racism and prejudice, for example, are typically used interchangeably. In critical theory, however, **prejudice** refers to preconceived ideas about a person or group. A limited number of characteristics, which may be true of individuals, are applied to the group as a whole and to all individuals within that group. Understood thusly, anyone can be racist. A black man who thinks all white men like to golf because he has encountered a few white men who like golf is prejudiced. So is a white man who thinks his black co-worker likes fried chicken because this is how black people are often depicted in movies and literature. Racism, however, is something different.

KEY TERM 13.7

Prejudice – preconceived ideas about a person or group.

Racism can best be understood as prejudice plus power. While all of us probably have some prejudices about other races—some of which may even be positive stereotypes—this is not the same as racism. It becomes racism when it has power behind it. A black person may think that white people are inferior. A white person may think that whites are superior. This is prejudice. A white person holds a black person as a slave. This ownership of one person by another is recognized by statutes and laws, is justified by religious institutions, and is normalized by literature and other art forms. This is racism.

Another concept that needs to be considered is **discrimination**. Some racial prejudices are built into the law. To apply one set of principles or laws to one group of people while applying a different set to another group is to discriminate between them. This was common in the American South during the Jim Crow era and in the country of South Africa under Apartheid. But not all discrimination is built into the law and not all racism manifests as treating one group differently than another. Contemporary critical theorists often prefer the word **privilege** rather than discrimination because it better captures the way in which racism can thrive even within a liberal society where there are no specifically discriminatory laws. If racism is structural then changes to laws, the superstructure, will have little effect on the base or substructure where racism is built.

WHAT DO YOU THINK 13.2

How does the idea of *privilege* differ from the idea of *discrimination*? How does our use of language alter the discussion about race and racism?

Critical Gender Theory

Marxist social-economic-political thought begins with division of labor. Division of labor is what makes specialization and the development of surpluses possible. It is the control of the surplus that makes the bourgeoisie the ruling class. Remember that for Marx, the set of relationships of production make up the base or substructure of society. These relationships are materially and historically determined. The superstructure, which includes institutions like family and government and intellectual developments like science and art are determined by the base. The easiest way to conceptualize poststructuralist thought is to look at this framework without a base. There is only the superstructure, which is determined directly by the material and historical conditions and, for Foucault, the most important of these was discourse.

Michel Foucault is one of the most influential thinkers of the late twentieth century. He described himself as a historian of ideas and the domain of theory that he has most influenced is called **epistemology,** or the study of knowledge. The study of epistemology asks what knowledge is, where it comes from, and wants to understand the relationship between what we (think we) know and the world outside our selves. Foucault was part of a tradition called **poststructuralism** which challenged the assumptions of structuralist thought such as Marxism.

For Foucault, **discourse** was more than just people talking to one another. Discourse—as the totality of language and symbol use in a given time and place—was where power was situated and engaging in discourse was an exercise of power. According to Foucault, "there is no external position of certainty, no universal understanding that is beyond history and society . . . His main tactic is to historicize supposedly universal categories" (Rabinow, 1984, p. 4). Discourse does not reflect reality nor is it produced by reality. It is reality.

Concepts or the expression of ideas, which are not grounded in reason, are, by definition, folly or, to use another concept favored by Foucault, madness. What is mad is irrelevant. It can be safely dismissed as false or as nonsense. But reason is not an objective idea but is itself historically and socially determined. Instead, reason is determined by the *discursive formations*, by the words and language used, who used them, how they were used, and so forth. While we might be inclined to say that surely one of these approaches is the right approach in that it can tell us what is true and what is false, Foucault was more interested in what a discourse does, how it functions, than he was with whether or not a particular claim is true or false. He argued that all knowledge is constructed so all knowledge is historically bound. From this perspective, the history of knowledge is not a slow progression of increasing understanding of the world but a series of radical transformations of knowledge. One way of looking at the world is unseated and replaced by another, which has little, if any, relation to what came before. Foucault applied this approach to knowledge areas of experience such as medicine and hospitals, psychology and madness, and the prison. At the conclusion of his life—he died of AIDS in 1984—he was engaged in a multivolume study of sexuality.

Foucault challenged the discourse of sexuality during the 1970s. At the end of what has been termed the "Sexual Revolution," people often thought of themselves as superior to and much more liberated then their Victorian predecessors and promised a future of unconstrained sexual freedom. While he certainly implies that such a view is simplistic and fallacious, Foucault (1984) was not concerned with the historical accuracy of the characterization. The question that drove him was not: "Why are we repressed? but rather: Why do we say, with so much passion and so much resentment against our recent past, against our present, and against ourselves, that we are repressed?" (p. 297).

In the Victorian period, people were not silent about sex but talked about it all the time. While it seems absurd to us that the table skirt was utilized to hide the table's legs so that men would not become aroused by the sight of a naked leg, it is also indicative of a discourse in which everything is sexualized. Far from being silenced, sex permeates the discourse. In our much more "liberated" sexual culture, highly sexual behavior passes virtually without notice. It must be extreme to violate other social norms (think, for example, about Miley Cyrus's performance at the MTV Video Music Awards in 2014), to attract notice or comment.

Contemporary approaches to gender theory are, most generally speaking, **deconstructionist**, that is to say they attempt to break down the discursive formations which lead to the oppression of people including women, gays, lesbians, bisexuals, and the transgendered. Even such categories, though, are part of the problem. Today, one of the issues which faces gender theory is the tension between those aspects of our sexual identity which are constructed through discourse and those which are essential (e.g. aspects we are born with, part of our genetic make-up). Foucault's approach, as a historian of ideas, is to uncover, like an archaeologist of discourse, how terms like "homosexuality" are used and the effect they have on the discourse.

KEY TERM 13.8

Deconstructionist – contemporary approaches to gender theory that attempt to break down the discursive formations which lead to the oppression of people including women, gays, lesbians, bisexuals, and the transgendered.

Foucault's approach applies to gender theory broadly—to feminist theory and to queer theory. Feminists argue that the first division of labor was along sex, not class, lines. Men and women were understood as essentially separate and power was held by men. Critical feminism is concerned with equity between sexes. Today, feminism is a hotly contested term. The roots of the critical theory are activist: social, political, and economic. An attempt to define feminism leads to a variety of popular culture references. A popular bumper sticker reads "Feminism is the radical notion that women are people" (see Figure 13.1). This has been a slogan of the feminist movement since the Second Wave, a period from the 1960s–1980s of massive mobilization around issues concerning women's rights.

Current feminist activism has been a topic of focus in social and news media and many celebrities are mobilizing around the term and the ideology thereof. At the most basic, however, feminism is pretty simple. Feminists want to expose the substructural relationships which result in a pattern and a history of not taking women seriously. The ideology that doesn't take women seriously is referred to as **misogyny** and misogyny is part of a broader ideological practice, which praises and promotes men while undermining women—this broader ideology is called **patriarchy**. Misogyny and patriarchy would seem to confirm one of the longstanding misrepresentations of feminism: that it is anti-male. In fact, the accusation that feminists hate men is the most common dismissal of feminism.

WHAT DO YOU THINK 13.3

In the previous section, we talked about white privilege. Is there a privilege attached to male-ness? If so what?

Feminism is the radical notion that women are people

Figure 13.1 Syracuse Cultural Workers' bumper sticker

There has been a long tradition of celebrity women rejecting the term. In a recent interview, Shailene Woodley claimed she didn't support the idea of "women over men." Kelly Clarkson, when asked, said she preferred the term "Miss Independent" because the word "feminism" is too strong. Katy Perry and Carrie Underwood both share Clarkson's distaste for the word. Though Lady Gaga later said she was "a little bit of a feminist." As you probably already know, these celebrities are repeating stereotypes about feminists—shying away from the controversy caused by the term while also reinforcing the stereotypes about the movement and the people who participate as feminists.

Recently, however, the nature of comments about feminism has changed with another cadre of celebrities. Spearheaded by Emma Watson, the recently appointed UN Women Goodwill Ambassador, the HeforShe campaign asks men to commit to gender equality. On HeforShe.org, this commitment reads: "Gender equality is not only a women's issue, it is a human rights issue that requires my participation. I commit to take action against all forms of violence and discrimination faced by women and girls." Celebrity men have come out in droves in support of Hefor-She. Initially a Twitter campaign, there has been massive mobilization around the hashtag #heforshe including a number of well-known celebrities including Simon Pegg, Tom Hiddleston, and Harry Styles (see Figure 13.2).

A simple Google image search will display hundreds of pictures of individuals mobilizing around #heforshe. Watson's campaign tactic is brilliant because it undermines all the complaints of individuals like those above who believe that feminism somehow disenfranchises men. Instead, she argues, "I have realized that fighting for women's rights has too often become synonymous with man-hating. If there is one thing I know for certain, it has to stop . . . if you still hate the word, it's not the word that is important. It's the idea and the ambition behind it."

What are the ideas and the ambition behind the term "feminism"? Where does it come from?

Figure 13.2 Simon Pegg, Tom Hiddleston, and Harry Styles, HeforShe Campaign, Twitter

WHAT DO YOU THINK 13.4

One of the central concerns in feminist discourse is the distinction between the essential (what is built into human beings on a genetic level) and the socially constructed. Look at contemporary advertising specifically directed toward men and to advertising specifically directed toward women. How are these advertisements similar? How are they different? Based on these advertisements, what are some of the gendered expectations for men and women in the United States?

A Brief History of Feminism in the United States

Though not entirely accurate, an easy way to think about the feminist movement in the US is that it was divided into three "waves." These waves are meant to indicate an uprising or a surge of activism around issues relevant to women and women's rights. Waves isn't entirely accurate because it's not as though feminists, feminism, and feminist activists disappeared during the time between the waves, but it's a useful way to outline the history of the movement. The information about each of the waves below focuses only on the key issues addressed in each time period. It's important to understand that though the key issues were major motivators for those activists participating, they were not wholly unified or coherent movements, and there was a great deal of disagreement about how to approach the issues, what issues should be included, and who was being represented. This history focuses on US feminism, but be assured there was and is a global feminist movement that mirrors the complications, successes, and configurations of American feminism.

The First Wave: 1848–1928

The Seneca Falls Convention ostensibly marks the beginning of the feminist movement in the US. Taking place in July 1848, Elizabeth Cady Stanton and Lucretia Mott, among others, fought for women's **enfranchisement**. The right to vote was a privilege reserved only for white males at the time. After the convention, joined by such activists as Susan B. Anthony and Lucy Stone, who founded the National Women's Rights Convention in 1849, the right to vote was won in individual states as the movement expanded. Women's enfranchisement and the abolition of slavery were deeply entwined, and supporters of one cause were typically devoted to the other. Many key members of the first wave were not only devoted suffragists, but also abolitionists. The 19th Amendment, prohibiting the government from implementing gender-based voting restrictions, was ratified on August 18, 1920, a full 72 years after the first convention. Elizabeth Cady Stanton did not live to see the amendment pass.

The Second Wave: 1961–1986

If first wave feminism was focused on suffrage and the removal of legal obstacles to gender equality, participants in the second wave were much more broadly focused. A short list of issues tackled by second wave activists includes: **sexuality**, women's role in the family and in the workplace, **reproductive rights**, de facto inequalities, as well as legal inequalities. Feminist advocates also drew international attention to **domestic violence** and **marital rape**, establishing women's shelters and lobbying for changes in divorce and child custody laws. Largely in dispute within the movement during the second wave were issues of sexuality and **pornography**. One of the major legislative issues of the second wave was the attempted passage of the **Equal Rights Amendment (ERA)** to the United States Constitution. The Equal Rights Amendment was written by Alice Paul and Crystal Eastman, and first introduced to Congress in 1923. In 1972, the amendment passed both houses of Congress but failed to be ratified by the states. The ERA is still a point of contention for feminist activists because it states, simply, "Section 1. Equality of rights under the law shall not be denied or abridged by the United States or by any State on account of sex. Section 2. The Congress shall have the power to enforce, by appropriate legislation, the provisions of this article. Section 3. This amendment shall take effect two years after the date of ratification" (Authenticated US Government Information). Though the ERA was a failure, Roe v. Wade was not, and in 1973 abortion became legal and safe for American women. Key activists of the second wave include:

- Betty Friedan, author of *The Feminine Mystique*, which was published in 1963. Friedan objected to the media portrayal of women as happy housewives. She argued that this limited the potential of women. She was named the first president of the National Organization for Women (NOW).
- Gloria Steinem, a freelance journalist who became the most influential figures in the movement. She is still an active speaker and was one of the first editors of *Ms. Magazine*.
- Robin Morgan, editor of *Sisterhood is Powerful*, a collection of feminist writings on key issues such as sisterhood, discrimination, and theory.
- Shulamith (Shulie) Firestone, a radical feminist activist who wrote *The Dialectic of Sex* in which she claims that a culture of sex discrimination can be traced back to the biological structure of life itself. One of the founders of multiple consciousness-raising groups in New York including the Redstockings.

Like the first wave, second wave feminists concentrated on describing or even celebrating the distinctiveness or specialness of women. The celebration of difference is often referred to as **cultural feminism**, which made claims about women being kinder, gentler, more peaceful, and more nurturing than men in dominant culture. **Difference feminism**, however, was less interested in equal rights than in establishing women's difference as superior, in replacing the patriarchy with the matriarchy. Many of the popular negative stereotypes about feminism come from cultural assumptions about difference feminism.

The Third Wave

The Third Wave is a term coined by Rebecca Walker in 1992. Though there is debate over the range of third wave feminism (Is it over? Is it not? What is it?), a few things are clear: the third wave broadened the goals of the movement, focusing on ideas like **queer theory**, abolishing gender role expectations and stereotypes, **anti-racism** and **women-of-color consciousness**, **transgender** politics, and defending sex work, pornography, reproductive rights, and sex-positivity. In the introduction to the idea of third wave feminism in *Manifesta* (2000), authors Jennifer Baumgardner and Amy Richards suggest that feminism can change with every generation and individual:

> The fact that feminism is no longer limited to arenas where we expect to see it—NOW, *Ms.*, women's studies, and redsuited congresswomen—perhaps means that young women today have really reaped what feminism has sown. Raised after Title IX and William Wants a Doll [sic], young women emerged from college or high school or two years of marriage or their first job and began challenging some of the received wisdom of the past ten or twenty years of feminism. We're not doing feminism the same way that the seventies feminists did it; being liberated doesn't mean copying what came before but finding one's own way—a way that is genuine to one's own generation.

An uprising of feminism came about this time not just through political activism and protest, but through music, art, and zine writing (Riot Grrrl, Bikini Kill, Eve Ensler's *The Vagina Monologues*).

The year 1992 was dubbed "The Year of the Woman" because five female Senators were elected to the United States Congress, and with Anita Hill's allegations of sexual harassment against Clarence Thomas, workplace issues such as the glass ceiling, equal pay for equal work, sexual harassment, and maternity-leave policies became key topics around which feminist activists formed coalitions. As Laura Brunell argued in her 2008 "Feminism Reimagined: The Third Wave," "third-wave feminists want to transform the traditional notions of sexuality and embrace an exploration of women's feelings about sexuality that included vagina-centered topics as diverse as orgasm, birth, and rape."

One of the most well-known effects of third wave activism is the reclamation of derogatory terms such as *spinster*, *bitch*, *whore*, and *cunt*, as well as the *transnational* SlutWalks. SlutWalks are protests that take place to raise awareness about rape and rape survivors, and to counter the popular response to rape: that women should dress more modestly. Instead, SlutWalks popularize the idea that men should be taught not to rape.

Feminism in the University

During the second wave, feminist activists began to enter the academy in the US; however, **protofeminist** criticism has been in practice since the early Middle Ages. Pioneers of women's political, social, economic, and literary criticism include Mary Wollstonecraft and Virginia Woolf. Feminist criticism can be broadly understood as using feminist principles and ideological discourses to critique the narrative of dominant oppression in regard to female bodies by exploring economic, social, political, and psychological forces.

Academic feminists introduced a range of theoretical terms based on the identity politics that launched the activist movement. Feminists in the academy have spent a lot of time thinking about identity, discussing **essentialism** and **social construction**. Essentialism is the belief that men and women are just one thing—that they all have set traits that define them. Men are masculine, women are feminine, and when thinking about the sexes they can be essentialized as such. This starts very early—think about the average children's toy aisle at Target. Girls' toys are all bright pink, boys' are camo, black, and blue. While contemporary feminism continues to value the study of patriarchy, it has also gone far beyond the early focus to concentrate on **sex and gender, phallologo-centric language**, and **transnational feminism** and **womanism**. Moving into the twenty-first century, critical feminist theory in the academy has moved to include **critical queer theory** resulting in a larger umbrella of *critical gender studies*. Current trends in queer theory and gender studies reflect the clinical history of sex and sexuality as displayed around the term "queer."

WHAT DO YOU THINK 13.5

What is the role praxis in contemporary critical feminist thought? How should feminist scholarship proceed if it is going to make changes in the world?

What used to be an offensive slang term for a gay man is now a term; the term **queer** in critical studies broadly covers the diversity of human sexuality and gender. Words like *homosexual* as opposed to *heterosexual* are clinical in origin and have historically been used to imply that homosexuality was a divergence from the heterosexual norm. Up until 1974 homosexuality was identified as a mental illness in the *Diagnostic and Statistical Manual of Mental Disorders* (DSM). Less clinical terms like gay, lesbian, and bisexual are difficult to work with on a theoretical level because they are often used in popular discourse and carry with them connotations. Among many peer groups, the use of the word "gay" to mean "lame" or "stupid" is, unfortunately, still common. Moreover, these terms often suggest a degree of fixed-ness and stability.

Since the publication of her groundbreaking work, *Gender Trouble*, in 1990, Judith Butler, a Professor of Comparative Literature and Rhetoric at the University of California, Berkeley, has been one of the most well-known critical theorists and queer theorists in the world. Perhaps one of her most important contributions to queer theory is her re-visitation of conceptual distinction between sex and gender.

Feminist social theory has long distinguished between **sex** and **gender**. Sex, in this view, is biological. It is based on the chromosomes a person received before they are born. A female is born with two Y chromosomes and a male is born with an X and a Y. Gender, on the other hand is something that is performed. So sex refers to the corporeal—the presence of a penis or a vagina for example—while gender refers to the practices and behaviors associated with a particular sex. So a person born with an X and Y chromosome is a male who is more likely to be aggressive and competitive, favor sports, and be logical in his reasoning. A woman, who is a woman because she has two Y chromosomes, is more likely to be maternal, nurturing, and social.

As noted earlier in this chapter, feminism has challenged these sorts of gendered assumptions. Butler, however, challenged the accuracy of the initial distinction between the male on one hand and the female on the other. By embracing that assumption, she argued, feminism reinforced the binary distinction between two mutually exclusive sexes, the male and the female. Reinforcing this binary, she believed, reinforced rather than deconstructed the system of patriarchy.

For Butler, biology is not **binary**. Male and female are not opposites that cover the totality of sex, but broad covering terms, which don't acknowledge but construct an understanding in which there are only two possibilities—male and female—which obscures the diversity of sex among human beings. Butler argued that there is no link between sex and gender nor between sex and sexual desire. Delinked from biology and no longer linked to binary classifications, gender and desire are dynamic and unstable. "There is," Butler (1990) contended, "no gender identity behind the expressions of gender" and "identity is performatively constituted by the very 'expressions' that are said to be its results" (p. 25). Gender is a performance but not "a set of free-floating attributes . . . [but] is performatively produced and compelled by the regulatory practices of gender coherence" (p. 24).

These "regulator practices of gender coherence" are hegemonic (embedded throughout our discourse, often without question). They are also performed, over and over again in our daily lives and tell us what men are supposed to do and what women are supposed to do. Departure from these norms is *queer*. A woman with hair too short or a man who doesn't like sports or an openly gay man who likes to hunt deer presents a challenge to gender normativity.

Each of us is performing gender all of the time. How we talk and move and what we wear all signify gender. Butler's work was about challenging these often invisible, repeated performances which discipline our bodies. According to Catherine Watson (2005), Butler

is often accredited with a call to action through strategies of subversive repetition parodying the heterosexual norm (e.g. in the form of "drag").

Butler maintained that it is possible to challenge the status quo by producing reverse-discourses—using the explanatory modes that produce us as particular subjects in order to resist that categorization; and by producing *competing* discourses (i.e. collections of stories from experience that challenge the "truth" of the discourse), exposing the falsehood of the idea that an original gender (or heterosexuality) exists. (p. 72)

Butler's theory is particularly important in communication studies. Discourse is, after all, communication and the way in which gendered norms are constructed is through our discursive practices. The hegemony of certain forms of gendered performances results from the repetition of some, often with cultural sanctions (leaders, celebrities, academics, and other authority figures) while others are excluded and silenced. Reverse discourses, or **counter-narratives**, challenge the hegemonic norm.

In critical theory, the term queer suggests a greater instability and thinks about identities as being *performative* (what we do) rather than *essential* (who we are). Like other critical approaches, critical feminist and queer theory—and critical gender theory at large—is not a single, unified school of thought but includes a number of different approaches and incorporates any different social and scientific methods of research. While all critical approaches emphasize praxis, critical gender theory has perhaps the deepest roots in political activism.

 WHAT DO YOU THINK 13.6

Judith Butler's work concerns the social performance of gender. How do you perform gender in your life? What are some of the sanctions on performances that violated gender norms?

Chapter Summary

In this chapter, we looked at different forms of oppression. As you think about the relationship between oppression, ideology, the means of production, and the effects of such social and cultural understandings on race, sex, and gender consider: what are some of the other areas that critical theorists might be interested in studying? What are some other forms of (possibly invisible) oppression that exist in our world today? For us, critical theory is a key lens through which to view the world. Instead of accepting the reality constructed by the Matrix, we can start to see the codes through which our realities are constructed. Once the mechanisms of construction become visible, we can affect positive change by dismantling oppressions, by questioning assumptions that allow for state violence, and by pushing back against rules that would continue the disenfranchisement of any individual based on the way they perform their selfhood.

Key Terms

Alienation
Bourgeoisie
Commodity
 fetishism
Critical theory
Difference feminism
Domestic violence
Essentialism
Homosexual
Imperialism
Multidisciplinary
Phallologocentric
 language
Poststructuralism
Proletariat
Racism
Sex
Substructure
Transnational
 feminism
Value

Anti-racism
Capital investment
Counter-narratives
Cultural feminism
Discourse
Enfranchisement
Gender
Idealistic
Interpellation
Performative
Pornography
Praxis
Protofeminism
Reflexive
Social construction
Superstructure
Whore
Binary
Capitalism
Critical gender
 studies

Cunt
Discrimination
Epistemology
Hegemonic
Ideological state
 apparatuses
Marital rape
Patriarchy
Postcolonialism
Prejudice
Queer
Repressive state
 apparatuses
Spinster
Structuralism
Teleological
Womanism
Bitch
Colonialism
Critical queer
 theory

Deconstructionist
Discursive
 formations
Equal Rights
 Amendment
Heterosexual
Ideology
Misogyny
Petite bourgeois
Postmodernism
Privilege
Queer theory
Reproductive
 rights
Transgender
Women-of-color
 consciousness

Activities

1. Pick a film with which you are familiar. How is whiteness portrayed in this film?

Student Paper

The following paper was originally prepared as a speech to be delivered in competitive public speaking (forensics) tournaments throughout the United States including the Minnesota Collegiate Forensic Association State Tournament and the National Forensic Association National Tournament in 2012. The event for which this paper was written is called Rhetorical Criticism which is described by the National Forensic Association thusly:

Rhetorical Criticism

Purpose

A speech designed to describe, analyze, and evaluate the rhetorical dynamics related to a significant rhetorical artifact or event.

Description

Rhetorical Criticisms are characterized by enlightening critical insight, in-depth analysis, description and application of rhetorical principles or a theoretical framework, topic significance, credible sources, and vocal and nonverbal delivery choices that reflect the speech's purpose.

Rules

a. All speeches should be original, constructed, and delivered by the student.

b. Speeches should adhere to the NFA Code of Ethics, Rules, and Procedures.

c. Plagiarism in any form is prohibited.

d. Source citation should be specific, accurate, and honest.

e. Although limited notes are permitted, speeches should be delivered from memory.

f. Audio-visual aids are permitted.

g. Maximum time limit of 10 minutes.*

* Unlike other event rules, minimum and maximum time limits provided for ALL events are enforced at the discretion of the individual judge rather than the association.

A Critical Analysis of Israeli Defense Forces T-Shirts

Jordan Christiansen

The T-shirt, a near ubiquitous clothing item on college campuses, is actually a relatively new fashion item. As Linn (2007) pointed out, it wasn't until the mid-1970s when the T-shirt became a clothing style for all ages. Then, last January, the T-shirt became a central figure in furthering tensions in the Middle East. *The New Zealand Herald* reported that only days after a three-week long conflict between Israeli Defense Forces and Palestinians that left 1,400 Palestinians dead—most of whom were civilians—IDF soldiers began sporting T-shirts with slogans like "One shot, two kills" featuring a pregnant Palestinian woman and "The smaller they are, the harder it is" depicting a child in the crosshairs of a sniper's rifle ("Israeli soldiers," 2009). Uri Blau (2009)

(Continued)

clarified that these shirts were not sanctioned by the Israeli Defense Forces but rather were created in small batches, often at the platoon or even unit level and, as soon as the media began reporting on the offensive T-shirts, they were banned by the IDF.

Although the IDF reacted quickly to silence international criticism before the T-shirts created an international scandal, reactions to the controversy were mixed. The following interview captures one point of view:

> This past January, the "Night Predators" demolitions platoon from Golani's Battalion 13 ordered a T-shirt showing a Golani devil detonating a charge that destroys a mosque. An inscription above it says, "Only God forgives."
>
> One of the soldiers in the platoon downplays it: "It doesn't mean much, it's just a T-shirt from our platoon. It's not a big deal. A friend of mine drew a picture and we made it into a shirt."
>
> What's the idea behind "Only God forgives"?
>
> The soldier: "It's just a saying."
>
> No one had a problem with the fact that a mosque gets blown up in the picture?
>
> "I don't see what you're getting at. I don't like the way you're going with this. Don't take this somewhere you're not supposed to, as though we hate Arabs" (Blau, 2009, p. 39–44).

Other observers, however, did think these shirts were a big deal. A commenter using the screen name Ummah Protector (2009), lashed out on the blog Mujahideen Ryder: "You are stupid and weak . . . You will wear this t-shirt in the grave."

Now if the IDF T-shirts are just what some say they are, a tasteless joke, then the IDF policy of banning such materials is likely to be effective. However, if the IDF T-shirts indicate the formation of a violent subculture, rather than just a few tasteless jokes, then this is a serious issue. In order to address this question, I propose the following research question:

(Continued)

> *RQ: Does the IDF T-shirt scandal indicate the presence of a defined subculture within the Israeli Defense Forces?*
>
> ## Method
>
> In order to answer the question, we must develop a set of criteria by which we can define subculture and on that basis determine whether or not the IDF T-shirt scandal of 2009 indicates the presence of a subculture. The connection between T-shirts and subcultures has previously been explored by Sylvia Jean Miller (2002). Miller looked at the connection between T-shirts and the subculture surrounding the rock band Phish. Miller's method is ideally suited to this study because she looked not only at the connection between subcultures and T-shirts but specifically at small batch, independently printed T-shirts, like the ones made by members of the IDF.
>
> Miller (2002) identified two points of connection between T-shirts and subculture identity: material expression of *values* and *coding*. Material expression, Miller contended, involves the display of actual physical objects which, among Phish Phans include things like hemp jewelry and clothing, "unstyled" hair, et cetera. These material expressions speak to particular values of the Phish Phan culture particularly an "easy going cooperative and communal" (p. 52) ethos.
>
> Miller's (2002) second point of connection is *coding* or "maps of meaning." Among Phish Phans this includes "an extensive vernacular linguistic register based on song titles, lyrics, and slang term for drugs." Coding is significant, Miller contended, because codes "allow group members to identify each other outside the primary location of the group activity" (p. 53–53).
>
> ## Analysis
>
> Now that we understand the two tenets of Miller's article we can apply these tenets to the IDF T-shirts. First, in terms of material expressions of a subculture's values, these T-shirts are obviously

Jordan's choice of topics demonstrates a lot of courage. The conflict between Israel and Palestine can be intense and arouse emotional responses in readers who strongly support one side or the other.

This choice, though, says something about Jordan's values as a researcher. He chose to focus on the use of violence against civilians and, while this is an important topic, it was not the only sort of T-shirt message to have been publicly criticized during this scandal. In this paper, Jordan did not look at T-shirts advocating sexual violence including pictures of bruised women with the slogan "Bet you got raped" (Blau, 2009, para. 3). How would this analysis differ if it was a feminist critique rather than racial / postcolonial perspective on the T-shirts?

(Continued)

material, something that they actually can put on to identify themselves. More than that however, they express a particular set of beliefs and values within groups of the IDF.

Although our sample is relatively small, at least one value seems to be consistent across a number of the IDF T-shirts: a willingness to defy conventional morality. For example, Blau (2009) quoted from an IDF soldier about one of the T-shirt slogans. The soldier responded, "It's a kid, so you've got a little more of a problem, morally, and also the target is smaller" (para. 17). The shirts boldly declare the wearer's allegiance to a value set which mocks the sentiment others might feel at shooting a pregnant woman or a child.

The shirts utilize a coding that distinguishes between insiders and outsiders. The IDF T-shirts utilize coding on two levels. On one level, the shirts themselves act as a code. The *New Zealand* (2009) herald noted that the shirts were made by groups who had bonded during basic training and other military courses. According to Blau (2009) the "One shot; two kills" design was developed by soldiers enrolled in the same snipers' course. So the shirts themselves define members of a group. The slogan "One shot; two kills" thus unites the members of that particular sniper group. Outsiders do not fully understand the origin or subtext of the codes.

Second, the shirts often make use of similar imagery and caricatures which demonstrate a continuity across the shirts. Although each is unique and developed by small groups of individuals, the similar images indicate that there is a shared "map of meaning" which unites members of the IDF. For example many of the images include a cross hair target, demonstrating a shared meaning across factions of the IDF.

Conclusion

The research question this analysis sought to answer was, does the IDF T-shirt scandal indicate the presence of a defined subculture within the Israeli

(Continued)

Defense Forces? Based on my analysis of the T-shirts, the answer is affirmative. There is both a material representation of values which define the group and a system of codes which distinguish between insiders and outsiders. The presence of both elements is strong evidence of a violent subculture within the IDF.

Extending from this conclusion, I would draw two critical conclusions. First, it is important to determine how "sub" this subculture is and second to realize that the IDF response to the scandal was insufficient to address the problem.

Having determined that the IDF has a violent subculture, we need to consider to what extent the "sub" culture is truly a "subculture" and not a reflection of the IDF or even military culture in general.

In his article "Literature as Equipment for Killing: Performance as Rhetoric in Military Training Camps" Jeff Parker Knight (1990) argued that learning these chants is part of "[t]he military training experience . . . designed as an instrument of secondary socialization, and is often viewed as a 'rite of passage'" which is calculated to "help to induce attitude changes in initiates" (p. 158). In other words, soldiers must be socialized to kill. The IDF T-shirts communicate a message of pro-civilian casualties that is being reinforced through the secondary socialization of military training.

Second, we need to recognize that the IDF leadership cannot address this problem simply by banning the T-shirts. Miller (2002) pointed out that although material expressions like T-shirts "may strengthen the subculture" and make members more identifiable to one another, "the social bond is formed once they open their mouths" (p. 56). Understood from this perspective, all that banning the T-shirts does is make the subculture less visible to outsiders. It does nothing to address the underlying values which define the culture.

The effects of that subculture are not invisible. According to the *New York Times*, On May 31st, 2010, IDF soldiers performed a raid on a humanitarian flotilla heading for blockaded Gaza. During this raid

(Continued)

the IDF fired upon the passengers, leaving nineteen dead and dozens hurt (Kershner, 2010). Given IDF's history of civilian causalities and because their actions can influence the current peace talks, a closer eye must be kept on the IDF.

This paper looks at the connection between T-shirts and subcultures. This is not one of those issues where we can just sit back, engage in an analysis and consider ourselves wiser for our efforts. When something as significant as peace in the Middle East can literally hinge upon the actions of a lone soldier and a single bullet, the values and the character of every soldier matter.

References

Blau, U. (2009, March 19). Dead Palestinian babies and bombed mosques – IDF fashion in 2009. *Haaretz*. Retrieved from www.haaretz.com.

Israeli soldiers spark outrage with "tasteless" sniper T-shirts. (2009, March 25). *The New Zealand Herald*. Retrieved from http://www.lexisnexis.com.

Kershner, I. (2010, May 31). Deadly Israeli raid draws condemnation. *The New York Times*. Retrieved from nytimes.com.

Knight, J. P. (1990). Literature as equipment for killing: Performance as rhetoric in military training camps. *Text and Performance Quarterly*, 10, 157–168.

Linn, V. (2007, February 13). History of the T-shirt. Pittsburgh Post-Gazette. Retrieved from www.post-gazette.com.

Miller, S. J. (2002). Phish phan pholklore: Identity and community through commodities in the Phish parking lot scene. *Miswestern Folklore*, 28, 42–60.

Ummah Protector. (2009, March 21). Response to "IDF T-shirt – pregnant Palestinian woman – 1 shot, 2 kills" [blog post]. Retrieved from www. mujahideenryder.net.

REFERENCES

Abrams, J., O'Connor, J., & Giles, H. (2002). Identity and intergroup communication. In W.B. Gudykunst & B. Mody (Eds.), *Handbook on international and intercultural communication* (pp. 225–240). Thousand Oaks, CA: Sage.

Adya, M., & Kaiser, K.M. (2005). Early determinants of women in the IT workforce: A model of girls' career choices. *Information Technology & People*, *18*, 230–259.

Afifi, A.A., & Weiner, J.L. (2004). Toward a theory of motivated information management. *Communication Theory*, *14*, 167–190.

Ahlstrom, D., & Wang, L.C. (2009). Groupthink and France's defeat in the 1940 campaign. *Journal of Management History*, *15*, 159–177.

Ajzen, I. (1991). The theory of planned behavior. *Organizational behavior and human decision processing*, *50*, 179–211.

Ajzen, I., & Fishbein, M. (1980). *Attitudes, personality, and behavior* (2nd ed.). Milton Keynes, UK: McGraw Hill.

Albert, S., Ashforth, B.E., & Dutton, J.E. (2000). Organizational identity and identification: Charting new waters and building new bridges. *Academy of Management Review*, *25*, 13–17.

Allen, J.L., Long, K.M., O'Mara, J., & Judd, B.B. (2003). Verbal and nonverbal orientations toward communication and the development of intracultural and intercultural relationships. *Journal of Intercultural Communication Research*, *32*, 129–160.

Althusser, L. (1989). Ideology and ideological state apparatuses. (B. Brewster, Trans.). In D. Latimer (Ed.) *Contemporary critical theory* (pp. 60–102). San Diego, CA: Harcourt Brace Jovanovich.

Altman, I. & Taylor, D. (1973). *Social penetration: The development of interpersonal relationships*. New York, NY: Rinehart & Winston.

Alvesson, M. (2004). Organizational culture and discourse. In D. Grant, C. Hardy, C. Oswisk, & L. Putnam (Eds.), *The SAGE handbook of organizational discourse* (pp. 317–335). London: Sage.

Amato, P.R. (2000). The consequences of divorce for adults and children. *Journal of Marriage and the Family*, *62*, 1269–1287.

Andersen, M.P. (1959). What is communication? *Journal of Communication*, *9*, 5.

Andersen, P.A. (1987). The trait debate: A critical examination of the individual differences paradigm in interpersonal communication. In D. Bervin & M. Voight (Eds.), *Progress in the communication sciences* (Vol. 8, pp. 47–82). Norwood, NJ: Ablex.

Andersen, P.A. (1991). When one cannot not communicate: A challenge to Motley's traditional communication postulates. *Communication Studies*, *42*, 309–325.

Andrews, K. R., Silk, K. S., Eneli, I. U. (2010). Parents as health promoters: A theory of planned behavior perspective on the prevention of childhood obesity. *Journal of Health Communication, 15*, 95–107.

Ansari, M. (1991). Iranians in America: Continuity and change. In V. Parrillo (Ed.), *Rethinking today's minorities* (pp. 119–144). Westport, CT: Greenwood Press.

Antony, M. G. (2010). On the spot: Seeking acceptance and expressing resistance through the bindi. *Journal of International and Intercultural Communication, 3*, 346–368.

Apker, J., Propp, K. M., & Zabava Ford, W. S. (2005). Negotiating status and identity tensions in healthcare team interactions: An exploration of nurse role dialectics. *Journal of Applied Communication Research, 33*, 93–115.

Appadurai, A. (1990). Disjuncture and difference in the global cultural economy. *Theory, Culture & Society, 7*, 295–310.

Aristotle. (1932). *The rhetoric of Aristotle* (L. Cooper, Trans.). New York, NY: D. Appleton-Century Company. Original work published Ca. 322 BCE.

Aristotle. (2007). *On rhetoric: A theory of civic discourse* (2nd ed.). (G. A. Kennedy, Trans.). New York, NY: Oxford University Press.

Arnett, J. J. (2002). The sounds of sex: Sex in teens' music and music videos. In J. D. Brown, J. R. Steele, & K. Walsh-Childers (Eds.), *Sexual teens, sexual media* (pp. 253–264). Mahwah, NJ: Lawrence Erlbaum Associates.

Arrow, H., Henry, K. B., Poole, M. S., Wheelan, S., & Moreland, R. (2005). Traces, trajectories, and timing. The temporal perspective on groups. In M. S. Poole & A. B. Hollingshead (Eds.), *Theories of small groups. Interdisciplinary perspectives* (pp. 313–368). Thousand Oaks, CA: Sage.

Arrow, H., McGrath, J. E., & Berdahl, J. L. (2000). *Small groups as complex systems: Formation, coordination, development, and adaptation.* Thousand Oaks, CA: Sage.

Ashcraft, K. L. (2005). Resistance through consent? Occupational identity, organizational form, and the maintenance of masculinity among commercial airline pilots. *Management Communication Quarterly, 19*, 67–90.

Aune, B. (1970). *Rationalism, empiricism and pragmatism: An introduction.* New York, NY: Random House.

Aust, P. J. (2004). Communicated values as indicators of organizational identity: A method for organizational assessment and its application in a case study. *Communication Studies, 55*, 515–534.

Babrow, A. S., & Mattson, M. (2003). Theorizing about health communication. In T. L. Thompson, A. M. Dorsey, K. I. Miller, R. Parrott (Eds.), *Handbook of health communication* (pp. 35–62). Mahwah, NJ: Lawrence Erlbaum.

Bae, H.-S., & Kang, S. (2008). The influence of viewing an entertainment-education program on cornea-donation intention: A test of the theory of planned behavior. *Health Communication, 23*, 87–95.

Baker, L. A., & Emery, R. E. (1993). When every relationship is above average: Perceptions and expectations of divorce at the time of marriage. *Law and Human Behavior, 17*, 439–450.

Baldwin, M. W. (1992). Relational schemas and the processing of social information. *Psychological Bulletin, 112*, 461–484.

Bandura, A. (1977). Self-efficacy: Toward a unifying theory of behavioral change. *Psychological Review, 84*, 191–215.

Bandura, A. (1986). *Social foundations of thought and action: A social cognitive theory.* Englewood Cliffs, NJ: Prentice Hall.

Bandura, A. (1997). *Self-efficacy: The exercise of control*. New York, NY: Freeman.

Bandura, A. (2002). Environmental sustainability by sociocognitive deceleration of population growth. In P. Schmuch & W. P. Schultz (Eds.), *Psychology of sustainable development* (pp. 209–238). Dordrecht, The Netherlands: Kluwer Academic.

Bandura, A., & Walters, R. H. (1963). *Social learning and personality development*. New York, NY: Holt, Rinehart & Winston.

Banerjee, S. C., & Greene, K. (2006). Analysis versus production: Adolescent cognitive and attitudinal responses to antismoking interventions. *Journal of Communication, 56*, 773–794.

Banerjee, S. C., & Greene, K. (2007). Antismoking initiatives: Effects of analysis versus production media literacy interventions on smoking-related attitude, norm, and behavioral intention. *Health Communication, 22*, 37–48.

Banks, A., & Banks, S. P. (1995). Cultural identity, resistance, and "good theory": Implications for intercultural communication theory from Gypsy culture. *Howard Journal of Communications, 6*, 146–163.

Barnlund, D. C. (1964). Toward a meaning centered philosophy of communication. *Journal of Communication, 12*, 197–211.

Barnlund, D. C. (1989). *Communicative styles of Japanese and Americans: Images and realities*. Belmont, CA: Wadsworth.

Baron, R. S. (2005). So right it's wrong: Groupthink and the ubiquitous nature of polarized group decision making. *Advances in Experimental Social Psychology, 37*, 219–253.

Bartel, C. A. (2001). Social comparisons in boundary-spanning work: Effects of community outreach on members' organizational identity and identification. *Administrative Science Quarterly, 46*, 379–414.

Bartholomew, K., & Horowitz, L. M. (1991). Attachment styles among young adults: A test of a four-category model. *Journal of Personality and Social Psychology, 61*, 226–244.

Baskerville, R. F. (2003). Hofstede never studied culture. *Accounting, Organizations and Society, 28*, 1–14.

Bateson, G. (1978). *Steps to an ecology of mind: Collected essays in anthropology, psychiatry, evolution and epistemology*. London, UK: Paladin.

Baumgardner, J., & A Richards. (2000). *Manifesta: Young women, feminism and the future*. New York, NY: Farrar, Straus and Giroux.

Baxter, L. A. (1990). Dialectical contradictions in relationship development. *Journal of Social and Personal Relationships, 7*, 69–88.

Baxter, L. A. (2004). A tale of two voices: Relational dialectics theory. *Journal of Family Communication, 4*, 181–192.

Baxter, L. A., & Montgomery, B. M. (1996). *Relating: Dialogues and dialectics*. New York, NY: Guilford.

Beebe, L. M., & Giles, H. (1984). Speech-accommodation theories: A discussion in terms of second-language acquisition. *International Journal of the Sociology of Language, 1984*(46), 5–32.

Beisecker, A. A. (1991). Interpersonal communication strategies to prevent drug abuse by health professionals and the elderly: Contributions of the Health Belief Model. *Health Communication, 3*, 241–250.

Bekus, N. (2014). Ethnic identity in post-Soviet Belarus: Ethnolinguistic survival as an argument in the political struggle. *Journal of Multilingual & Multicultural Development, 35*, 43–58.

Bem, D. J. (1967). Self-perception: An alternative interpretation of cognitive disso-nance phenomena. *Psychological Review*, 74, 183–200.

Bennis, W. G., & Shepard, H. A. (1975). A theory of group development. In G. S. Gibbard, J. J. Hartman, & R. D. Mann (Eds.), *Analysis of groups: Contributions to theory, research, and practice* (pp. 127–153). San Francisco, CA: Jossey-Bass.

Benoit, W. L. (1999). *Seeing spots: A Function Analysis of presidential television advertisements, 1953–1996.* Westport, CT: Praeger.

Benoit, W. L. (2007). *Communication in political campaigns.* New York, NY: Peter Lang.

Benoit, W. L., Klyukovski, A. A., McHale, J. P., & Airne, D. (2001). A fantasy theme analysis of political cartoons on the Clinton-Lewinsky-Starr Affair. *Critical Studies in Media Communication*, 18, 377–394.

Berelson, B., & Steiner, G. A. (1964). *Human behavior.* New York, NY: Harcourt Brace and World.

Berger, C. R., & Calabrese, R. (1975). Some explorations in initial interactions and beyond:

Toward a development theory of interpersonal communication. *Human Communica-tion Research*, 1, 99–112.

Bergman, A. A., & Connaughton, S. L. (2013). What is patient-centered care really? Voices of Hispanic prenatal patients. *Health Communication*, 28, 789–799.

Berlin, I. (1963). *Karl Marx: His life and environment.* New York, NY: Time, Inc.

Berry, J., & Kim, U. (1987). Acculturation and mental health. In P. Dasen, J. Berry, & N. Sartorious (Eds.), *Health and cross-cultural psychology* (pp. 35–58). Thousand Oaks, CA: Sage.

Berry, J., & Sam, D. (1997). Acculturation and adaptation. In J. Berry, M. Segall, & C. Kagitcibasi (Eds.), *Handbook of cross-cultural psychology* (2nd ed., Vol. 3.) (pp. 75–94). Boston, MA: Allyn and Bacon.

Bitzer, L. F. (1968). The rhetorical situation. *Philosophy and Rhetoric*, 1(1), 1–14.

Black, E. (1970). The second persona. *Quarterly Journal of Speech*, 56, 109–119.

Blake, R. R., & Mouton, J. S. (1964). *The managerial grid.* Houston, TX: Gulf.

Blumer, H. (1969). *Symbolic interactionism: Perspective and method.* Englewood Cliffs, NJ: Prentice Hall.

Blumer, J. G., & Katz, E. (1974). *The uses of mass communications: Current perspec-tives on gratifications research.* Beverly Hills, CA: Sage.

Boehm, C. (2000). *Hierarchy in the forest: The evolution of egalitarian behavior.* Cambridge, MA: Harvard University Press.

Bohnert, A. S. B., Zivin, K., Welsh, D. E., & Kilbourne, A. M. (2011). Ratings of patient–provider communication among veterans: Serious mental illnesses, sub-stance use disorders, and the moderating role of trust. *Health Communication*, 26, 267–274.

Boon, S. D., & Sulsky, L. M. (1997). Attributions of blame and forgiveness in romantic relationships: A policy-capturing study. *Journal of Social Behavior & Personality*, 12, 19–44.

Bormann, E. G. (1982). The symbolic convergence theory of communication: Applica-tions and implications for teachers and consultants. *Journal of Applied Commu-nication Research*, 10, 50–61.

Bormann, E. G. (1996). Symbolic convergence theory and communication in group decision making. In R. Y. Hirokawa & M. S. Poole (Eds.), *Communication and group decision making* (2nd ed., pp. 81–113). Thousand Oaks, CA: Sage.

Braithwaite, D. O., & Baxter, L. A. (1995). "I do" again: The relational dialectics of renewing marriage vows. *Journal of Social and Personal Relationships, 12,* 177–198.

Brandenburg, H. (2006). Party strategy and media bias: A quantitative analysis of the 2005 UK election campaign. *Journal of Elections, Public Opinion and Parties, 16,* 157–178.

Brann, M., & Sutton, M. L. (2009). The theory of planned behavior and college students' willingness to talk about smoking-related behavior. *Communication Research Reports, 26,* 198–207.

Brembeck, W. L., & Howell, W. A. (1952). *Persuasion.* Englewood Cliffs, NJ: Prentice Hall.

Bresnahan, M., Lee, S. Y., Smith, S. W., Shearman, S., Nebashi, R., Park, C. Y., & Yoo, J. (2007). A theory of planned behavior study of college students' intention to register as organ donors in Japan, Korea, and the United States. *Health Communication, 21,* 201–211.

Brett, J. M., Olekalns, M., Friedman, R., Goates, N., Anderson, C., & Lisco, C. C. (2007). Sticks and stones: Language, face, and online dispute resolution. *Academy of Management Journal, 50,* 85–99.

Brilliant, E., & Young, D. R. (2004). The changing identity of federated community service organizations. *Administration in Social Work, 28*(3/4), 23–46.

Brillstein, B., Folsey Jr., G., Sosna, D., & Weiss, R. K. (Producers), & Landis, J. (Director). (1908). *The Blues Brothers* [motion picture]. United States: Universal Pictures.

Brim, O., & Wheeler, S. (1966). *Socialization through the life cycle.* New York, NY: Wiley.

Briones, R., Nan, X., Madden, K., & Waks, L. (2012). When vaccines go viral: An analysis of HPV vaccine coverage on YouTube. *Health Communication, 27,* 478–485.

Brownie, J. (2012). Multilingualism and identity on Mussau. *International Journal of the Sociology of Language, 214,* 67–84.

Brownmiller, S. (1999). *In our time: Memoir of a revolution.* New York, NY: Dial P.

Buechler, S. (1990). *Women's movements in the United States: Woman suffrage, equal rights and beyond.* New Brunswick, NJ: Rutgers University Press.

Buenker, J. D., & Ratner, L. A. (1992). *Multiculturalism in the United States: A comparative guide to acculturation and ethnicity.* New York, NY: Greenwood Press

Bullis, C. (1993). Organizational socialization research: Enabling, constraining, and shifting perspectives. *Communication Monographs, 60,* 10–17.

Burgoon, M., & Ruffner, M. (1978). *Human communication.* New York, NY: Holt, Rinehart, & Winston.

Burke, K. (1945). *Grammar of motives.* New York: Prentice Hall.

Burke, K. (1966). *Language as symbolic action: Essays on life, literature, and method.* Berkeley, CA: University of California Press.

Burke, K. (1969a). *A grammar of motives* (California ed.). Berkeley, CA: University of California Press.

Burke, K. (1969b). *A rhetoric of motives* (California ed.). Berkeley, CA: University of California Press.

Burleson, B. R. (2003). The experience and effects of emotional support: What the study of cultural and gender differences can tell us about close relationships, emotion, and interpersonal communication. *Personal Relationships, 23,* 1–23.

Buss, D. M. (1989). Conflict between the sexes: Strategic interference and the evocation of anger and upset. *Journal of Personality and Social Psychology*, *56*, 735–747.

Butler, J. (1990). *Gender trouble: Feminism and the subversion of identity*. New York, NY: Routledge.

Butler, J. (1993). *Bodies that matter: On the discursive limits of sex*. New York, NY: Routledge.

Butler, J. (1997). *Excitable speech: A politics of the performative*. New York, NY: Routledge.

Cacioppo, J., Priester, J., & Bernston, G. (1993). Rudimentary determinants of attitudes: II. Arm flexion and extension have differential effects on attitudes. *Journal of Personality and Social Psychology*, *65*, 5–17.

Cahnman, W. J., Maier, J. B., Tarr, Z., & Marcus, J. T. (Eds.). (1995). *Weber and Töennies: Comparative sociology in historical perspective*. Piscataway, NJ: Transaction Publishers.

Cai, D., & Fink, E. (2002). Conflict style differences between individualists and collectivists. *Communication Monographs*, *69*, 67–87.

Cai, D., & Ni, L. (2005). *Anxiety and uncertainty management in an intercultural setting: The impact on organization-public relationships*. Paper presented in International Communication Association, New York, NY.

Campbell, K. K. (1989). *Man cannot speak for her: Volume 1: A critical study of early feminist rhetoric*. Westport, CT: Praeger.

Campbell, K. K. (1971). The rhetoric of women's liberation: An oxymoron. *Journal of Speech*, *59*, 74–86.

Campbell, K. K. (1999). The rhetoric of women's liberation: An oxymoron revisited. *Communication Studies*, *50*, 138–142.

Canary, D. J., & Messman, S. J. (2000). Relationship conflict. In C. Hendrick & S. S. Hendrick (Eds.), *Close relationships: A sourcebook* (pp. 261–270). Thousand Oaks, CA: Sage.

Carbaugh, D. (2007). Cultural discourse analysis: Communication practices and intercultural encounters. *Journal of Intercultural Communication Research*, *36*, 167–182.

Carroll, J. G. & McLeod, J. M. (1984). Public opinion de jour: An examination of the spiral of silence. *Public Opinion Quarterly*, *48*, 731–740.

Carruthers, P. (1992). *Human knowledge and human nature*. Oxford, UK: Oxford University Press.

Cartwright, D., & Zander, A. (1968). *Group dynamics: Research and theory*. New York: Harper & Row.

Cassata, D. M. (1977). Health communication theory and research: A definitional overview. In D. Nimmo (Ed.), *Communication yearbook 2* (pp. 495–503). New Brunswick, NJ: Transaction Books.

Casullo, A. (2003). *A priori knowledge and justification*. New York, NY: Oxford University Press.

Cawyer, C. S., & Friedrich, G. W. (1998). Organizational socialization: Processes for new communication faculty. *Communication Education*, *47*, 234–245.

Cegala, D. J., & Lenzmeier Broz, S. (2003). Provider and patient communication skills training. In T. L. Thompson, A. M. Dorsey, K. I. Miller, R. Parrott (Eds.),

Handbook of health communication (pp. 95–120). Mahwah, NJ: Lawrence Erlbaum.

Cenoz, J., & Valencia, J. F. (1993). Ethnolinguistic vitality, social networks and motivation in second language acquisition: Some data from the Basque country. *Language, Culture and Curriculum, 6,* 113–127.

Centers for Disease Control and Prevention (2008). Smoking-attributable mortality, years of potential life, lost, and productivity losses-United States, 2000–2004. *Morbidity and Mortality, Weekly Report, 57,* 1226–1228.

Chau, E. G., & Gudykunst, W. B. (1987). Conflict resolution styles in low – and = high context cultures. *Communication Research Reports, 4,* 32–37.

Chapman, A. H. (1976). *Harry Stack Sullivan: His life and his work.* New York, NY: Putnam.

Chen, G. M. (2011). Tweet this: A uses and gratifications perspective on how active Twitter use gratifies a need to connect with others. *Computers in Human Behavior, 27,* 755–762.

Chen, L. (2002). Communication in intercultural relationships. In W. B. Gudykunst & B. Mody (Eds.), *Handbook of international and intercultural communication* (2nd ed., pp. 241–257). Thousand Oaks, CA: Sage.

Chen, Y. (2006). The Twain have met!: Investigating crucial indicators for intercultural friendship levels between international students from four East Asian countries and US Americans. Paper presented in the International Communication Association, Dresden, Germany.

Chen, Y. (2010). *International students' communication with US faculty: A further examination of anxiety/uncertainty management (AUM) theory.* Paper presented in the conference of International Communication Association, Singapore.

Chen, Y.-W. & Nakazawa, M. (2012). Measuring patterns of self-disclosure in intercultural friendships: Adjusting differential item functioning using multiple-indicators, multiple-causes models. *Journal of Intercultural Communication Research, 41,* 131–151.

Cheney, G. (1991). *Rhetoric in an organizational society: Managing multiple identities.* Columbia, SC: University of South Carolina.

Cheney, G., & Christensen, L. T. (2001). Organizational identity. In F. M. Jablin & L. L. Putnam (Eds.), *The new handbook of organizational communication: Advances in theory, research, and methods* (pp. 231–269). Thousand Oaks, CA: Sage.

Cheney, G., Christensen, L. T., Zorn, T. E. Jr., & Ganesh, S. (2004). *Organizational communication in an age of globalization: Issues, reflections, practices.* Prospect Heights, IL: Waveland.

Chew, F., Palmer, S., & Kim, S. (1998). Testing the influence of the health belief model and a television program on nutrition behavior. *Health Communication, 10,* 227–245.

Chun, C. A., & Choi, J. M. (2003). The violence of assimilation and psychological well-being. In E. M. Kramer (Ed.), *The emerging monoculture* (pp. 75–84). New York, NY: Praeger.

Clark, E., McCann, T. V., Rowe, K., & Lazenbatt, A. (2004). Cognitive dissonance and undergraduate nursing students' knowledge of, and attitudes about, smoking. *Journal of Advanced Nursing, 46,* 586–594.

Cloud, D. L. (1999). The null persona: Race and the rhetoric of silence in the uprising '34. *Rhetoric & Public Affairs, 2,* 177–209.

Cloven, D. H., & Roloff, M. E. (1994). A developmental mode of decisions to withhold relational irritations in romantic relationships. *Personal Relationships*, *1*, 143–164.

Cohen, B. C. (1963). *The press and foreign policy*. Princeton, NJ: Princeton University Press.

Cohen, L., Manion, L., & Morrison, K. (2007). *Research methods in education 6th edition*. London, UK: Routledge.

Collins, N. L., & Read, S. J. (1990). Adult attachment, working models, and relationship quality in dating couples. *Journal of Personality and Social Psychology*, *58*, 644–663.

Condit, C. M. (1990). The birth of understanding: Chaste science and the harlots of the arts. *Communication Monographs*, *57*, 323–327.

Conklin, N. F., & Louire, M. A. (1983). *A host of tongues: Language communities in the United States*. New York, NY: Free Press.

Constine, J. (July 23, 2014). American users spend an average of 40 minutes per day on Facebook. *Techcrunch.com*. Retrieved from: http://techcrunch.com/2014/07/23/facebook-usage-time/.

Cooper, J., & Fazio, R. H. (1984). A new look at dissonance theory. In L. Berkowitz (Ed.), *Advances in experimental social psychology* (Vol. 17, pp. 229–266). New York, NY: Academic.

Corballis, M. C. (2002). *From hand to mouth: The origins of language*. Princeton, NJ: Princeton University Press.

Costello, D. E. (1977). Health communication theory and research: An overview. In B. D. Ruben (Ed.), *Communication yearbook 1* (pp. 557–568). New Brunswick, NK: Transaction Books.

Cragan, J. F., & Shields, D. C. (1992). The use of symbolic convergence theory in corporate strategic planning: A case study. *Journal of Applied Communication Research*, *20*, 199–218.

Cragan, J. F., & Wright, D. W. (1999). *Communication in small groups: Theory, process, skills* (5th ed.). Belmont, CA: Wadsworth.

Craig, R. T. (1989). Communication as a practical discipline. In B. Dervin, L. Grossberg, B. J. O'Keefe, & E. Wartella (Eds.), *Rethinking communication: Paradigm issues* (pp. 97–122). Newbury Park, CA: Sage.

Craig, T., & Tracy, K. (1995). Grounded practical theory: The case of intellectual discussion. *Communication Theory*, *5*, 248–272.

Crook, B. (2014). Teaching intercultural communication with "an idiot abroad." *Communication Teacher*, *28*, 9–13.

Croucher, S. M. (2006). The impact of external pressures on an ethnic community: The case of Montreal's Quarter Chinois and Muslim-French immigrants. *Journal of Intercultural Communication Research*, *35*, 235–252.

Croucher, S. M. (2009). How limiting linguistic freedoms influences the cultural adaptation process: An analysis of the French Muslim population. *Communication Quarterly*, *57*, 302–318. doi:10.1080/01463370903109929.

Croucher, S. M. (2011). Social networking and cultural adaptation: A theoretical model. *Journal of International and Intercultural Communication*, *4*, 259–264. doi:10.1080/17513057.2011.598046.

Croucher, S. M. (2013). Communication apprehension, self-perceived communication competence, and willingness to communicate: A French analysis. *Journal of International and Intercultural Communication*, *6*, 298–316. doi: 10.1080/17513057.2013.769615.

Croucher, S. M., Braziunaite, R., Homsey, D., Pillai, G., Saxena, J., Saldanha, A., Joshi, V., Jafri, I., Choudhary, P., Bose, L., & Agarwal, K. (2009). Organizational dissent and argumentativeness: A comparative analysis between American and Indian organizations. *Journal of Intercultural Communication Research, 38,* 175–192.

Croucher, S. M., & Cronn-Mills, D. (2015). *Understanding communication research methods: A theoretical and practical approach.* New York, NY: Routledge.

Croucher, S. M., Long, B. L., Meredith, M. J., Oommen, D., & Steele, E. L. (2009a). Factors predicting organizational identification with intercollegiate forensics teams. *Communication Education, 58,* 74–91.

Croucher, S. M., & Rahmani, D. (2015 in press). A longitudinal test of the effects of Facebook on cultural adaptation. *Journal of International and Intercultural Communication, 8,* TBD.

Croucher, S. M., Spencer, A. T., & McKee, C. (2014). Religion, religiosity, sex, and willingness to express political opinions: A spiral of silence analysis of the 2008 US Presidential Election. *Atlantic Journal of Communication, 22,* 111–123.

Cupach, W. R., & Metts, S. (1986). Accounts of relational dissolution: A comparison of marital and non-marital relationships. *Communication Monographs, 53,* 311–334.

Cutrona, C. E. (1996). *Social support in couples.* Thousand Oaks, CA: Sage.

Czaja, R., Manfredi, C., & Price, J. (2003). The determinants and consequences of information seeking among cancer patients. *Journal of Health Communication, 8,* 529–562.

Dailsay, F. S. (2012). The spiral of silence and conflict avoidance: Examining antecedents of opinion expression concerning the US military buildup in the Pacific island of Guam. *Communication Quarterly, 60,* 481–503.

Davison, B. J., Goldenberg, L., Gleave, M. E., & Denger, L. F. (2003). Provision of individualized information to men and their partners to facilitate treatment decision making in prostate cancer. *Oncology Nursing Forum, 20,* 107–114.

Deetz, S. (1994). The future of the discipline: The challenges, the research, and the social contribution. In S. A. Deetz (Ed.), *Communication yearbook 17* (pp. 565–600). Thousand Oaks, CA: Sage.

Deetz, S. A. (2001). Conceptual foundations. In F. M. Jablin & L. L. Putnam (Eds.), *The new handbook of organizational communication: Advances in theory, research, and methods* (pp. 3–46). Thousand Oaks, CA: Sage.

DeFleur, M. L. (1998). Where have all the milestones gone? The decline of significant research on the processes and effects of mass communication. *Mass Communication & Society, 1,* 85–98.

DeFleur, M. L., & Ball-Rokeach, S. (1989). *Theories of mass communication* (5th ed.). New York, NY: Longman.

DeLorme, D. E., Huh, J., & Reid, L. N. (2007). Seniors' perceptions of prescription drug information sources. *International Journal of Pharmaceutical and Healthcare Marketing, 1*(2), 107–127.

DeLorme, D. E., Huh, J., & Reid, L. N. (2011). Source selection in prescription drug information seeking and influence factors: Applying the comprehensive model of information seeking in an American context. *Journal of Health Communication, 16,* 766–787.

de Mul, J. (2004). *The tragedy of finitude: Dilthey's hermeneutics of life.* T. Burrett (Trans.). New Haven, CT: Yale UP.

de Oñate, M. L., & Amador, M. V. (2013). The intercultural component in Business English textbooks. *Iberica, 26,* 171–194.

Derlega, V. J., Winstead, B. A., Wong, P. T. P., & Greenspan, M. (1987). Self-disclosure and relationship development: An attributional analysis. In M. E. Roloff & G. R. Miller (Eds.), *Interpersonal processes: New directions in communication research* (pp. 172–187). Newbury Park, CA: Sage.

Deshpande, A., Menon, A., Perri, M. III, & Zinkhah, G. M. (2003). Direct-to-consumer advertising and its utility in health care decision making: A consumer perspective. *Journal of Health Communication, 9*, 499–513.

Diddi, A., & LaRose, R. (2006). Getting hooked on news: Uses and gratifications and the formation of new habits among college students in an Internet environment. *Journal of Broadcasting & Electronic Media, 50*, 193–210.

Dillard, J. P., & Pfau, M. (2002). Introduction. In J. P. Dillard & M. Pfau (Eds.), *The persuasion handbook: Developments in theory and practice* (pp. ix–xx). Thousand Oaks, CA: Sage.

Dimitroff, R. D., Schmidt, L. A., & Bond, T. D. (2005). Organizational behavior and disaster: A study of conflict at NASA. *Project Management Journal, 36*, 28–38.

Dindia, K. (1994). The intrapersonal-interpersonal dialectical process of self-disclosure, In S. Duck (Ed.), *Understanding relationship processes IV: The dynamics of relationships* (pp. 27–57). Newbury Park, CA: Sage.

Dion, K. L., & Dion, K. K. (1988). Romantic love: Individual and cultural perspectives. In R. J. Sternberg & M. L. Barnes (Eds.), *The psychology of love* (pp. 100–118). New Haven, CT: Yale University Press.

Dionne, K. Y. (2014, July 15). Why West African governments are struggling in response to Ebola. *The Washington Post Online.* Retrieved from: www.washingtonpost.com/blogs/monkey-cage/wp/2014/07/15/why-west-african-governments-are-struggling-in-response-to-ebola/.

Dixon, M. A., & Dougherty, S. D. (2010). Managing the multiple meanings of organizational culture in interdisciplinary collaboration and consulting. *Journal of Business Communication, 47*, 3–19.

Djerf-Pierre, M., & Wiebull, L. (2005). *Par condicio? Politisk partiskhet I italienska medier.* Stockhold, Sweden: Studieförbundet Näringsliv och Samhälle.

Dougherty, S. D., & Smythe, M. J. (2004). Sensemaking, organizational culture, and sexual harassment. *Journal of Applied Communication Research, 32*, 293–317.

Dubin, R. (1978). *Theory building* (Rev. ed.). New York, NY: Free Press.

Durkheim, E. (1938). *Rules of the sociological method.* (S. Solovay & J. Mueller, Trans.). G. Catilin (Ed.). Chicago, IL: University of Chicago Press.

Duronto, P. M., Nishida, T., & Nakayama, S. I. (2005). Uncertainty, anxiety, and avoidance in communication with strangers. *International Journal of Intercultural Relations, 29*, 549–560.

Dutta-Bergman, M. J. (2005). Developing a profile of consumer intention to seek out additional information beyond a doctor: The role of communicative and motivation variables. *Health Communication, 17*, 1–16.

Dyson, M. E. (2014, November 29). Where do we go after Ferguson? *The New York Times.* Retrieved from www.nytimes.com.

Eagleton, T. (2003). *After theory.* New York, NY: Penguin Books.

Eccles, J. S., & Barber, B. L. (1999). Student council, volunteering, basketball, or marching band: What kind of extracurricular involvement matters? *Journal of Adolescent Research, 14*, 10–43.

Echols, A. (2003). *Daring to be bad: Radical feminism in America, 1967–1975.* Minneapolis, MN: University of Minnesota Press.

Eisenberg, E.M., & Riley, P. (2001). Organizational culture. In F.W. Jablin & L. Putnam (Eds.), *The new handbook of organizational communication: Advances in theory, research, and methods* (pp. 291–322). Thousand Oaks, CA: Sage.

Eisenberg, I.N., & Wynn, D.R. (2003). *Working in groups: Communication principles and strategies* (3rd ed.). Boston, MA: Houghton Mifflin.

Englund, H., Gerdin, J., & Burns, J. (2011). 25 years of Giddens in accounting research: Achievements, limitations and the future. *Accounting, Organizations and Society, 36,* 494–513.

Esser, J.K., & Lindoerfer, J.L. (1989). Group think and the space shuttle Challenger accident: Towards a quantitative case analysis. *Journal of Behavioral Decision-Making, 2,* 167–177.

Fairhurst, G.T., & Putnam, L. (2004). Organizations as discursive constructions. *Communication Theory, 14,* 5–26.

Fay, M.J., & Kline, S.L. (2012). The influence of informal communication on organizational identification and commitment in the context of high-intensity telecommuting. *Southern Communication Journal, 77,* 61–76.

Feather, N.T. (1962). Cigarette smoking and lung cancer: A study of cognitive dissonance. *Australian Journal of Psychology, 14,* 55–64.

Festinger, L. (1957). *A theory of cognitive dissonance.* Stanford, CA: Stanford University Press.

Festinger, L., & Carlsmith, J.M. (1959). Cognitive consequences of forced compliance. *Journal of Abnormal and Social Psychology, 58,* 203–210.

Firestone, S. (2003). *The dialectic of sex: The case for feminist revolution.* New York, NY: Farrar, Straus and Giroux.

Fish, S. (2005, July 19). Intentional neglect. *New York Times.* A25.

Fishbein, M., & Ajzen, I. (1975). *Belief, attitude, intention, and behavior: An introduction to theory and research.* Reading, MA: Addison-Wesley.

Fisher, W.R. (1970). A motive view of communication. *Quarterly Journal of Speech, 56,* 131–139.

Fitch, K.L. (2006). Cultural persuadables. *Communication Theory, 13,* 100–123.

Fitzpatrick, M.A. (1977). A typological approach to communication in relationships. In B. Rubin (Ed.), *Communication yearbook 1* (pp. 263–275). Rutgers, NJ: Transaction Books.

Fitzpatrick, M.A. (1988). *Between husbands and wives.* Newbury Park, CA: Sage.

Foner, P.S. (Ed.). (1978). *Paul Robeson speaks: Writings, speeches, interviews 1918–1974.* New Royk, NY: Brunner/Mazel.

Ford, C.L., & Airhihenbuwa, C.O. (2010). Critical race theory, race equity, and public Health: Toward antiracism praxis. *American Journal of Public Health, 100*(S1), S30–S35.

Forward, G.L. (1999). Encountering the nonprofit organization: Clergy uncertainty and information-seeking during organizational entry. *Journal of Communication and Religion, 22,* 190–213.

Foss, K.A., & Foss, S.K. (1991). *Women speak: The eloquence of women's lives.* Prospect Heights, IL: Waveland.

Fost, J. (2013). The extended self, functional constancy, and personal identity. *Linguistic & Philosophical Investigations, 12,* 47–66.

Foucault, M. (1972). *The archaeology of knowledge & the discourse of language.* New York, NY: Pantheon Books.

Foucault, M. (1984). *The history of sexuality*. Paris, France: Éditions Gallimard.

Foucault, M. (1995). *Discipline and punish: The birth of the prison*. New York, NY: Vintage Books.

Foucault, M. (2005). *Archaeology of knowledge*. New York, NY: Routledge.

Fougère, M., & Moulettes, A. (2007). The construction of the modern west and the backward rest: Studying the discourse of Hofstede's *Culture's consequences*. *Journal of Multicultural Discourses, 2*, 1–19.

Frandsen, S. (2012). Organizational image, identification, and cynical distance: Prestigious professionals in a low-prestige organization. *Management Communication Quarterly, 26*, 351–376.

Freeman, J. (1971). *The women's liberation movement: Its origin, structures, and ideals*. Pittsburgh, PA: Know, Inc.

Friedan, B. (1997). *The feminine mystique*. New York, NY: W.W. Norton.

Freimuth, V. S., Stein, J. A., & Kean, T. J. (1989). *Searching for health information: The cancer information service model*. Philadelphia, PA: University of Pennsylvania Press.

Frey, L., & Sunwolf. (2005). The symbolic-interpretive perspective of group life. In M. S. Poole, & A. B. Hollingshead (Eds.), *Theories of small groups: Interdisciplinary perspectives* (pp. 185–240). Thousand Oaks, CA: Sage.

Froner, P. S. (Ed.). (1978). *Paul Robeson speaks: Writings, speeches, and interviews*. New York, NY: Brunner/Mazel Publishers.

Gadamer, H.-G. (2003). *Truth and method* (2nd revised ed.). New York: Continuum.

Gallagher, E. B., & Sias, P. M. (2009). The new employee as a source of uncertainty: Veteran employee information seeking about new hires. *Western Journal of Communication, 73*, 23–46.

Garcia, J. A. (1995). A multicultural America: living in a sea of diversity. In D. Harris (Ed.), *Multiculturalism from the margins: Non-dominant voices on difference and diversity* (pp. 29–38). Westport, CT: Greenwood Press.

Gareis, E. (2000). Intercultural friendship: Five case studies of German students in the USA. *Journal of Intercultural Studies, 21*, 67–91.

Garner, J. T. (2007). Give me liberty or give me (occupational) death: Organizational dissent and workplace freedom of speech. Paper presented at the International Communication Association Convention. San Francisco, CA.

Garner, J. T. (2009). When things go wrong at work: An exploration of organizational dissent messages. *Communication Studies, 60*, 197–218.

Garnett, B. R., Buelow, R., Franko, D. L., Becker, C., Rodgers, R. F., & Austin, S. B. (2014). The importance of campaign saliency as a predictor of attitude and behavior change: A pilot evaluation of social marketing campaign Fat Talk Free Week. *Health Communication, 29*, 984–995.

Gasper, P. (2010). Marxiam and the dialectic [Audio file]. Retrieved from: wearemany.org

Geertz, C. (1973). *The interpretation of cultures*. New York, NY: Basic Books.

Gibbons, F. X., Eggleston, T. J., & Benthin, A. C. (1997). Cognitive reactions to smoking relapse: The reciprocal relation between dissonance and self-esteem. *Journal of Personality and Social Psychology, 72*, 184–195.

Giddens, A. (1984). *The constitution of society: Outline of the theory of structuration*. Berkeley, CA: University of California Press.

Giles, H., & Johnson, P. (1987). Ethnolinguistic identity theory: A social psychological approach to language maintenance. *International Journal of the Sociology of Language, 68*, 69–99.

Gilpin, E. A., & Pierce, J. P. (1998). *Smoking initiation* (Vol. 12, Lesson 5). [Online]. Available from: http://chest-main.edoc.com/pccu/lesson5–12.html.

Glaser, S. R., Zamanou, S., & Hacker, K. (1987). Measuring and interpreting organizational culture. *Management Communication Quarterly, 1,* 173–198.

Goddard, S. A., & Torres, M. B. (2009). *Conflict, face, and disability: An exploratory study of the experiences of college students with disabilities.* Paper presented in International Communication Association, Chicago, US.

Goffman, E. (1963). *Behavior in public places: Notes on the social organization of gatherings.* New York, NY: Free Press.

Golden, A. G. (2013). The structuration of information and communication technologies and work–life interrelationships: Shared organizational and family rules and resources and implications for work in a high technology organization. *Communication Monographs, 80,* 101–123.

Gonzaga, G. C., Turner, R. A., Keltner, D., & Campos, B. (2006). Romantic love and sexual desire in close relationships. *Emotion, 6,* 163–179.

Gorden, W. I., & Infante, D. A. (1991). Test of a communication model of organizational commitment. *Communication Quarterly, 39,* 144–155.

Gordon, B. (2007, Spring). US competitiveness: The education imperative. *Issues in Science and Technology, 23,* 31–36.

Gottman, J. (1977). The effects of a modelling film on social isolation in preschool children a methodological investigation. *Journal of Abnormal Child Psychology, 5,* 69–78.

Gottman, J. M. (1993). The roles of conflict engagement, escalation, and avoidance in marital interaction: A longitudinal view of five types of couples. *Journal of Consulting and Clinical Psychology, 61,* 6–15.

Gottman, J. M., & Levenson, R. W. (2000). The timing of divorce: Predicting when a couple will divorce over a 14-year period. *Journal of Marriage and the Family, 62,* 737–745.

Gozenbach, W. J., King, C., & Jablonski, P. (1999). Homosexuals and the military: An analysis of the spiral of silence. *The Howard Journal of Communications, 10,* 281–296.

Griffin, R. J., Dunwoody, S., & Neuwirth, K. (1999). Proposed model of the relationship of information seeking and processing to the development of preventive behaviors. *Environmental Research Section, A80,* S230–S245.

Grigg, F., Fletcher, G. J. O., & Fitness, J. (1989). Spontaneous attributions in happy and unhappy dating relationships. *Journal of Social and Personal Relationships, 6,* 61–68.

Gronstedt, A. (2000). *The customer century: Lessons from world-class companies in integrating marketing and communications.* New York: Routledge.

Gudykunst, W. B. (Ed.). (1983). *International and Intercultural Communication Annual,* vol. VII. Beverly Hills, CA: Sage.

Gudykunst, W. B. (1985). A model of uncertainty reduction in intercultural encounters. *Journal of Language and Social Psychology, 4*(2), 79–98.

Gudykunst, W. B. (1989). Culture and the development of interpersonal relationships. In J. A. Anderson (Ed.), *Communication Yearbook* (Vol. 12, pp. 315–354). Newbury Park, CA: Sage.

Gudykunst, W. B. (1993). Toward a theory of effective interpersonal and intergroup communication: An anxiety/uncertainty management (AUM) perspective. In R. L. Wiseman & J. Koester (Eds.), *Intercultural communication theory* (pp. 33–71). Newbury Park, CA: Sage.

Gudykunst, W.B. (1998). Applying anxiety\uncertainty management (AUM) theory to intercultural adjustment training. *International Journal of Intercultural Relations, 22*, 227–250. doi:10.1016/S0147–1767(98)00005–4.

Gudykunst, W.B., & Hammer, M.R. (1988). Strangers and hosts: An uncertainty reduction based theory of intercultural adaptation. In Y.Y. Kim, & W.B. Gudykunst (Eds.), *Cross-cultural adaptation: Current approaches* (pp. 106–139). Newbury Park, CA: Sage.

Gudykunst, W.B., & Kim, Y.Y. (1997). *Communicating with strangers: an approach to intercultural communication* (3rd ed.). Boston, MA: McGraw Hill.

Gudykunst, W.B., & Kim, Y.Y. (2003). *Communicating with strangers: an approach to intercultural communication* (4th ed.). Boston, MA: McGraw Hill.

Gudykunst, W.B., & Nishida, T. (1978). The intercultural communication workshop: foundations, development and affects. *Communication, 7*, 72–92.

Gudykunst, W.B., & Nishida, T. (2001). Anxiety, uncertainty, and perceived effectiveness of communication across relationships and cultures. *International Journal of Intercultural Relations, 25*, 55–71.

Gudykunst, W.B., & Shapiro, R.B. (1997). Communication in everyday interpersonal and intergroup encounters. *International Journal of Intercultural Relations, 20*(1), 19–45.

Gunn, J. (2003). Refiguring fantasy: Imagination and its decline in US rhetorical studies. *Quarterly Journal of Speech, 89*, 41–59.

Guo, C. (2001). A review on consumer external search: Amount and determinants. *Journal of Business and Psychology, 15*, 505–519.

Hall, B.J. (1992). Theories of culture and communication. *Communication Theory, 2*, 50–70.

Hall, E.T. (1959). *The silent language.* New York, NY: Doubleday.

Hall, E.T. (1966). *The hidden dimension.* New York, NY: Doubleday.

Hall, E.T. (1976). *Beyond culture.* New York, NY: Doubleday.

Hammer, M.R., Wiseman, R.L., Rasmussen, J.L., & Bruschke, J.C. (1998). A test of anxiety/uncertainty management theory: The intercultural adaptation context. *Communication Quarterly, 46*, 309–326.

Harrell, J., & Linkugel, W.A. (1978). On rhetorical genre: An organizing perspective. *Philosophy & Rhetoric, 11*, 262–281.

Haslam, S.A., Postmes, T., & Ellemers, N. (2003). More than a metaphor: Organizational identity makes organizational life possible. *British Journal of Management, 14*, 357–369.

Hatch, M.J., & Schultz, M. (1997). Relations between organizational culture, identity, and image. *European Journal of Marketing, 31*, 356–365.

Heisler, J.M., & Ellis, J.B. (2008). Motherhood and the construction of "mommy identity": Messages about motherhood and face negotiation. *Communication Quarterly, 56*, 445–467.

Heracleous, L. (2013). The employment of structuration theory in organizational discourse: Exploring methodological challenges. *Management Communication Quarterly, 27*, 599–608.

Herat, M. (2014). Avoiding the reaper: Notions of death in Sri Lankan obituaries. *International Journal of Language Studies, 8*(3), 117–144.

Herzog, H. (1940). Professor quiz: A gratification study. In P.F. Lazarfel (Ed.), *Radio and the printed page* (pp. 64–93). New York, NY: Duell, Sloan and Pearce.

Hester, J.B., & Gibson, R. (2007). The agenda-setting function of national versus local media: A time-series analysis for the issue of same-sex marriage. *Mass Communication & Society, 10,* 299–317.

Hirokawa, R.Y. (1980). A comparative analysis of communication patterns within effective and ineffective decision-making groups. *Communication Monographs, 47,* 312–321.

Hirokawa, R.Y. (1982). Group communication and problem/solving effectiveness II: A critical review of inconsistent findings. *Communication Quarterly, 30,* 134–141.

Hirokawa, R.Y. (1985). Discussion procedures and decision-making performance: A test of a functional perspective. *Human Communication Research, 12,* 203–224.

Hirokawa, R.Y., & Pace, R. (1983). A descriptive investigation of the possible communication-based reasons for effective and ineffective group decision making. *Communication Monographs, 50,* 363–379.

Hirokawa, R.Y., & Rost, K.M. (1992). Effective group decision making in organizations: Field test of the vigilant interaction theory. *Management Communication Quarterly, 5,* 267–288.

Ho, S.Y., & Bodoff, D. (2014). The effects of web personalization on user attitude and behavior: An integration of the elaboration likelihood model and consumer search theory. *MIS Quarterly, 38,* 497–520.

Hobbes, T. (1981). *Leviathan.* In M. Curtis (Ed.), *The great political theories, volume 1* (pp. 329–349). New York, NY: Avon Books.

Hoben, J.B. (1954). English communication at Colgate re-examined. *Journal of Communication, 4,* 76–86.

Hocker, J., & Wilmot, W. (1991). *Interpersonal conflict* (3rd ed.). Dubuque, IA: Brown.

Hoffman, D.M. (1989). Self and culture revisited: Culture acquisition among Iranians in the United States. *Ethos, 17,* 32–49. doi: 10.1525/eth.1989.17.1.02a00020.

Hoffman, M.F., & Cowan, R.L. (2010). Be careful what you ask for: Structuration theory and work/life accommodation. *Communication Studies, 61,* 205–223.

Hofstede, G. (1980). *Culture's consequences: International differences in work-related values.* Beverly Hills, CA: Sage.

Hofstede, G. (2001). *Culture's consequences: Comparing values, behaviors, institutions and organizations across nations* (2nd ed.). Thousand Oaks, CA: Sage.

Hogg, M.A., & Terry, D.J. (2001). Social identity theory and organizational processes: In M.A. Hogg & D.J. Terry (Eds.), *Social identity processes in organizational contexts* (pp. 1–12). Philadelphia: Psychology Press.

Holder, T. (1996). Women in nontraditional occupations: Information-seeking during organizational entry. *The Journal of Business Communication, 33,* 9–26.

Honeycutt, J.M., & McCann, R.M. (2008). Predicting intrapersonal communication satisfaction on the basis of imagined interactions in the Pacific Rim. *Journal of Intercultural Communication Research, 37,* 25–42.

Hopmann, D.N., Elmelund-Praestekaer, Albaek, E., Vliegenthart, R., & de Vreese, C.H. (2012). Party media agenda-setting: How parties influence election news coverage. *Party Politics, 18,* 173–191.

Huston, T.L., & Vangelisti, A.L. (1991). Socioemotional behavior and satisfaction in marital relationships. *Journal of Personality and Social Psychology, 61,* 721–733.

Husserl, E. (1970). *The crisis of European sciences and transcendental phenomenology: An introduction to phenomenological philosophy*. Evanston, IL: Northwestern University Press.

Hyams, M. (2004). Hearing girls' silences: Thoughts on the politics and practices of a feminist method of group discussion, *Gender, Place & Culture: A Journal of Feminist Geography, 11*, 105–119.

Infante, D. A., & Rancer, A. S. (1982). A conceptualization and measure of argumentativeness. *Journal of Personality Assessment, 46*, 72–80.

Ingram, D., & Simon-Ingram, J. (1992). *Critical theory: The essential readings*. New York, NY: Paragon House.

internetlivestats (2014). Twitter usage statistics. Retrieved from: www.internetlivestats.com/twitter-statistics/#trend.

Ivanov, B., Parker, K. A., Pfau, M. (2012). The interaction effect of attitude base and multiple attacks on the effectiveness of inoculation. *Communication Research Reports, 29*, 1–11.

Iyengar, S., & Kinder, D. R. (1987). *News that matters*. Chicago, IL: University of Chicago Press.

Jablin, F. M. (1984). Assimilating new members into organizations. In R. N. Bostrom (Ed.), *Communication yearbook 8* (pp. 594–626). Beverly Hills, CA: Sage.

Jablin, F. M. (1985). An exploratory study of vocational organizational communication socialization. *Southern Speech Communication Journal, 50*, 261–282.

Jablin, F. M. (1990). Organizational communication. In G. L. Dahnke & G. W. Clatterbuck (Eds.), *Human communication: Theory and research* (pp. 156–182). Belmont, CA: Wadsworth.

Jablin, F. M. (2001). Organizational entry, assimilation, and disengagement/exit. In F. M. Jablin & L. L. Putnam (Eds.), *The new handbook of organizational communication: Advances in theory, research, and methods* (pp. 732–818). Thousand Oaks, CA: Sage.

Jacobson, N. S., Waldron, H., & Moore, D. (1980). Toward a behavioral profile of marital distress. *Journal of Consulting and Clinical Psychology, 48*, 696–703.

Janis, I. L. (1972). *Victims of groupthink*. Boston: Houghton Mifflin.

Janis, I. L. (1982). *Groupthink: Psychological studies of policy decisions* (2nd ed.). Boston: Houghton Mifflin.

Janis, I. L. (1985). Sources of error in strategic decision making. In J. M. Pennings (Ed.), *Organizational strategy and change* (pp. 157–197). San Francisco, CA: Jossey Bass.

Janz, N. K., & Becker, M. H. (1984). The health belief model: A decade later. *Health Education Quarterly, 11*, 1–47.

Jenson, J. (2002). Identifying the links: Social cohesion and culture. *Canadian Journal of Communication, 27*, 141–151.

Johnson, J. D. (1983). A test of a model of magazine exposure and appraisal in India. *Communication Monographs, 50*, 148–157.

Johnson, J. D. (1997). *Cancer-related information seeking*. Creskill, NJ: Hampton Press.

Johnson, J. D. (2003). On contexts of information seeking. *Information Processing and Management, 39*, 735–760.

Johnson, J. D., & Meischke, H. (1993). A comprehensive model of cancer-related information seeking applied to magazines. *Human Communication Research, 19*, 343–367.

Johnson, K. L., & Roloff, M. E. (1998). Serial arguing and relational quality: Determinants and consequences of perceived resolvability. *Communication Research*, 26, 327–343.

Johnson, R. E. (1968). Smoking the reduction of cognitive dissonance. *Journal of Personality and Social Psychology*, 9, 260–265.

Johnson Avery, E., & Kim, S. (2008). Preparing for pandemic while managing uncertainty: An analysis of the construction of fear and uncertainty in press releases of major health agencies. *Conference Papers – International Communication Association*, 1–26.

Jones, M. R., & Karsten, H. (2008). Giddens's structuration theory and information systems research. *MIS Quarterly*, 32, 127–157.

Joyce, N., & Harwood, J. (2014). Improving intergroup attitudes through televised vicarious intergroup contact: Social cognitive processing of ingroup and outgroup information. *Communication Research*, 41, 627–643.

Kalman, M. E., Monge, P., Fulk, J., & Heino, R. (2002). Motivations to resolve communication dilemmas in database-mediated collaboration. *Communication Research*, 29, 125–154.

Kassing, J. W. (1997). Articulating, antagonizing, and displacing: A model of employee dissent. *Communication Studies*, 48, 311–332.

Kassing, J. W. (1998). Development and validation of the Organizational Dissent Scale. *Management Communication Quarterly*, 12, 183–229.

Kassing, J. W. (2000a). Investigating the relationship between superior-subordinate relationship quality and employee dissent. *Communication Research Reports*, 17, 58–70.

Kassing, J. W. (2000b). Exploring the relationship between workplace freedom of speech, organizational identification, and employee dissent. *Communication Research Reports*, 17, 387–396.

Kassing, J. W. (2008). Consider this: A comparison of factors contributing to employees' expression of dissent. *Communication Quarterly*, 65, 342–355.

Kassing, J. W. (2011). *Dissent in organizations*. Cambridge: Polity.

Kassing, J. W., & Avtgis, T. A. (1999). Examining the relationship between organizational dissent and aggressive communication. *Management Communication Quarterly*, 13, 100–115.

Kassing, J. W., & McDowell, Z. (2008). Talk about fairness: Exploring the relationship between procedural justice and employee dissent. *Communication Research Reports*, 25, 1–10.

Katriel, T., & Philipsen, G. (1981). "What we need is communication": "Communication" as a cultural category in some American speech. *Communication Monographs*, 48, 301–317.

Katz, E., Blumler, J. G., & Gurevitch, M. (1974). Utilization of mass communication by the individual. In J. G. Blumler & E. Katz (Eds.), *The uses of mass communications: Current perspectives on gratifications research* (pp. 19–32). Beverly Hills, CA: Sage.

Kelly, G. A. (1981). From *lèse-majesté* to *lèse-nation*: Treason in eighteenth-century France. *Journal of the History of Ideas*, 42, 269–286.

Kelvin, P. (1970). *The bases of social power*. New York, NY: Holt, Rinehart, and Winston.

Keuth, H. (2005). *The philosophy of Karl Popper*. New York, NY: Cambridge University Press.

Keyton, J. (1999). Relational communication in groups. In L. R. Frey, D. S. Gouran, & M. S. Poole (Eds.), *The handbook of group communication theory and research* (pp. 192–222). Thousand Oaks, CA: Sage.

Keyton, J., Caputo, J. M., Ford, E. A., Fu, R., Leibowitz, S. A., Liu, T., & Wu, C. (2013). Investigating verbal workplace communication behaviors. *Journal of Business Communication, 50*, 152–169. doi:10.1177/0021943612474990.

Khakimova, L., Zhang, Y., & Hall, J. A. (2012). Conflict management styles: The role of ethnic identity and self-construal among young male Arabs and Americans. *Journal of Intercultural Communication Research, 41*, 37–57.

Kim, S.-H., Han, M., Choi, D.-H., & Kim, J.-N. (2012). Attribute agenda setting, priming and the media's influence on how to think about a controversial issue. *The International Communication Gazette, 74*, 43–59.

Kim, S.-H., Kim, H., & Oh, S.-H. (2014). Talking about genetically modified (GM) foods in South Korea: The role of the Internet in the spiral of silence process. *Mass Communication & Society, 17*, 713–732.

Kim, Y. Y. (1976). *Communication patterns of foreign immigrants in the process of acculturation: A survey among the Korean population in Chicago.* Unpublished dissertation, Northwestern University.

Kim, Y. Y. (1977). Communication patterns of foreign immigrants in the process of acculturation. *Human Communication Research, 4*(1), 66–77.

Kim, Y. Y. (1988). *Communication and cross-cultural adaptation: An integrative theory.* Boston, MA: Multilingual Matters.

Kim, Y. Y. (1989). Personal, social, and economic adaptation: The case of 1975–1979 arrivals in Illinois. In D. Haines (Ed.), *Refugees as immigrants: Survey research on Cambodians, Laotians, and Vietnamese in America* (pp. 86–104). Totowa, NJ: Rowman & Littlefield.

Kim, Y. Y. (1994). Intercultural personhood. In L. Samovar & R. Porter (Eds.), *Intercultural communication: A reader* (7th ed.). Belmont, CA: Wadsworth.

Kim, Y. Y. (1995). Cross-cultural adaptation: An integrative theory. In R. L. Wiseman (Ed.), *Intercultural communication theory* (pp. 170–193). Thousand Oaks, CA: Sage.

Kim, Y. Y. (2000). Mapping the domain of intercultural communication: An overview. In W. B. Gudykunst (Ed.), *Communication yearbook 24* (pp. 139–157). Thousand Oaks, CA: Sage.

Kim, Y. Y. (2001). *Becoming intercultural: An integrative theory of communication and cross-cultural adaptation.* Thousand Oaks, CA: Sage.

Kim, Y. Y. (2002). Adapting to an unfamiliar culture: An interdisciplinary overview. In W. B. Gudykunst, & B. Mody (Eds.), *Handbook of International and Intercultural Communication* (2nd ed.) (pp. 259–274). Thousand Oaks, CA: Sage.

Kim, Y. Y., & Gudykunst, W. B. (1988). *Cross-cultural adaptation: Current approaches.* Newbury Park, CA: Sage.

Kirby, E. L., & Krone, K. J. (2002). "The policy exists but you can't really use it": Communication and the structuration of work-family policies. *Journal of Applied Communication Research, 30*, 50–77.

Kirschbaum, K. (2012). Physician communication in the operating room: expanding application of face-negotiation theory to the health communication context. *Health Communication, 27*, 292–301.

Kistler, M., Boyce Rodgers, K., Power, T., Weintraub Austin, E., & Griner Hill, L. (2010). Adolescents and music media: Toward an involvement-mediational model of consumption and self-concept. *Journal of Research on Adolescence, 20,* 616–630.

Kitzmann, K. M., & Beech, B. M. (2006). Family-based interventions for pediatric obesity: Methodological and conceptual challenges from family psychology, *Journal of Family Psychology, 20,* 175–189.

Knapp. M. L. (1978). *Social intercourse: From greeting to goodbye.* Boston, MA: Allyn & Bacon.

Knapp. M. L. (1984). *Interpersonal communication and human relationships.* Boston, MA: Allyn & Bacon.

Knapp, M. L., Daly, J. A., Albada, K. F., & Miller, G. R. (2002). Background and current trends in the study of interpersonal communication. In M. L. Knapp & J. A. Daly (Eds.), *Handbook of interpersonal communication* (pp. 3–20). Thousand Oaks, CA: Sage.

Koenig Kellas, K., Bean, D., Cunningham, C., & Cheng, K. Y. (2008). The ex files: Trajectories, turning points, and adjustment in the development of post-dissolutional relationships. *Journal of Social and Personal Relationships, 25,* 23–50.

Koller, V. (2012). How to analyse collective identity in discourse-textual and contextual parameters. *Critical Approaches to Discourse Analysis across Disciplines, 5,* 19–38.

Koponen, J., Pyörälä, E., & Isotalus, P. (2010). Teaching interpersonal communication competence to medical students through theatre in education. *Communication Teacher, 24,* 211–214.

Koschmann, M. A. (2013). Human rights collaboration and the communicative practice of religious identity. *Journal of Communication & Religion, 36,* 107–133.

Kramer, E. M. (1998). The theory of cultural fusion. Paper delivered at the Nineteenth Annual Intercultural Education Society Convention. University of International Studies, Chiba, Japan.

Kramer, E. M. (2000). Cultural fusion and the defense of difference. *InterSections: The Journal of Global Communications & Culture,* 183–223.

Kramer, E. M. (2003). *Gaiatsu* and the cultural judo. In E. Kramer (Ed.), *The emerging monoculture* (pp. 1–32). New York, NY: Praeger.

Kramer, E. M. (2003a). Introduction: Assimilation and the model minority ideology. In E. M. Kramer (Ed.), *The emerging monoculture* (pp. xi–xxi). New York, NY: Praeger.

Kramer, R. M. (1998). Revisiting the Bay of Pigs and Vietnam decisions 25 years later: How well has the groupthink hypothesis stood the test of time? *Organizational Behavior and Human Decision Processes, 73,* 236–271.

Kudo, K. & Simkin, K. A. (2003). Intercultural friendship formation: The case of Japanese students at an Australian university. *Journal of Intercultural Studies, 24,* 91–114.

Kurdek, L. A. (1993). Predicting marital dissolution: A 5-year prospective longitudinal study of newlywed couples. *Journal of Personality and Social Psychology, 64,* 221–242.

Lakey, S. G., & Canary, D. J. (2002). Actor goal achievement and sensitivity to partner as critical factors in understanding interpersonal communication competence and conflict strategies. *Communication Monographs, 69,* 217–235.

Lammers, J. C., Atouba, Y. L., & Carlson, E. J. (2013). Which identities matter? A mixed-method study of group organizational, and professional identities and their relationship to burnout. *Management Communication Quarterly, 27,* 503–536.

LaRose, R., Lin, C.A., & Eastin, M.S. (2003). Unregulated Internet usage: Addiction, habit, or deficient self-regulation. *Media Psychology, 5*, 225–253.

Lazarsfeld, P.F., & Merton, R.K. (1948). Mass communication, popular taste and organized social action. In L. Bryson (Ed.), *Communication of ideas* (pp. 95–118). New York, NY: Harper.

Lee, A.A., Fredenburg, K., Belcher, D., & Cleveland, N. (1999). Gender differences in children's conception of competence and motivation in physical education. *Sport, Education & Society, 4*, 161–174.

Lee, D., & LaRose, R. (2007). A socio-cognitive model of video game usage. *Journal of Broadcasting & Electronic Media, 51*, 632–650.

Lee, H., & Len-Ríos, M.E. (2014). Defining obesity: second-level agenda setting attributes in black newspapers and general audience newspapers. *Journal of Health Communication, 19*, 1116–1129.

Lee, H.-R., Ebesu Hubbard, A.S., Kulp O'Riordan, C., & Kim, M.-S. (2006). Incorporating culture into the Theory of Planned Behavior: Predicting smoking cessation intentions among college students. *Asian Journal of Communication, 16*, 315–332.

Leeds-Hurwitz, W. (1990). Notes in the history of intercultural communication: The Foreign Service Institute and the mandate for intercultural training. *Quarterly Journal of Speech, 76*, 262–281.

Leonard, S.P. (2013). Phenomenology of speech in a cold place: The Polar Eskimo language as "lived experience." *International Journal of Language Studies, 7*, 151–174.

Levine, K.J., & Hoffner, C.A. (2006). Adolescents' conception of work: What is learned from different sources during anticipatory socialization. *Journal of Adolescent Research, 21*, 647–669.

Lim, S.S., Vadrevu, S., Chan, Y.H., & Basnyat, I. (2012). Facework on Facebook: The online publicness of juvenile delinquents and youths-at-risk. *Journal of Broadcasting & Electronic Media, 56*, 346–361.

Lin, J.-H. (2013). Identification matters: A moderated mediation model of media interactivity, character identification, and video game violence on aggression. *Journal of Communication, 63*, 682–702.

Lindlof, T.R., & Taylor, B.C. (2002). *Qualitative communication research methods* (2nd ed.). Thousand Oaks, CA: Sage.

Lipkin, M. (2010). The history of communication skills knowledge and training. In D.W. Kissane, B.D. Bultz, P.M. Butow, & I.G. Finlay (Eds.), *Handbook of communication in oncology and palliative care* (pp. 3–12). New York, NY: Oxford University Press.

Lippmann, W. (1922). *Public opinion.* New York, NY: Harcourt Brace.

Littlejohn, S.W. (1999). *Theories of human communication* (6th ed.). Belmont, CA: Wadsworth Publishing Company.

Lizzio, A., Wilson, K., & Hadaway, V. (2007). University students' perceptions of a fair learning environment: A social justice perspective. *Assessment & Evaluation in higher Education, 32*, 195–213.

Locke, J. (n.d.), The second treatise of government (B. Small, Ed.). Houston, TX: Communican. (Original work published 1690.)

Love, D.E., & Powers, W.G. (2002). Communicating under uncertainty: Interaction between Arab students and western instructors. *Journal of Intercultural Communication Research, 31*, 217–231.

Lustig, M.W., & Koester, J. (1999). *Intercultural competence: Interpersonal communication across cultures* (3rd ed.). New York: Longman.

Mägiste, E. (1988). Changes in the lateralization pattern of two immigrant groups in Sweden. In Y.Y. Kim, & W.B. Gudykunst (Eds.), *Cross-cultural adaptation: Current approaches* (pp. 233–251). Newbury Park, CA: Sage.

Maier, M. (2002). Ten years after a major malfunction . . . reflections on "the Challenger syndrome." *Journal of Management Inquiry, 11,* 282–292.

Marley, B. (1999). *Songs of Freedom* [CD]. New York, NY: Def Jam Music Group.

Marx, K. (1978). Capital, volume one. In R.C. Tucker (Ed.), *The Marx-Engels reader* (2nd ed.) (pp. 294–438). New York, NY: Norton.

Marx, K. (1978a). Contribution to the critique of Hegel's *Philosophy of Right*: Introduction. In R.C. Tucker (Ed.), *The Marx-Engels reader* (2nd ed.) (pp. 53–65). New York, NY: W.W. Norton & Company, Inc.

Marx, K. (1978b). For a ruthless criticism of everything existing. In R.C. Tucker (Ed.), *The Marx-Engels reader* (2nd ed.) (pp. 12–15). New York, NY: Norton.

Marx, K. (1978c). The German ideology. In R.C. Tucker (Ed.), *The Marx-Engles reader* (2nd ed.) (pp. 146–200). New York, NY: W.W. Norton & Company, Inc.

Marx, K. (1978d). Marx on the History of His Opinions. In R.C. Tucker (Ed.), *The Marx-Engels reader* (2nd ed.) (pp. 3–6). New York, NY: W.W. Norton & Company, Inc.

Mastekaasa, A. (1997). Marital dissolution as a stressor: Some evidence on psychological, physical, and behavioral changes during the preseparation period. *Journal of Divorce & Remarriage, 26,* 155–183.

Matthes, J., Morrison, K.R., Schemer, C. (2010). A spiral of silence for some: Attitude certainty and the expression of political minority opinions. *Communication Research, 37,* 774–800.

Matveev, A.V. (2004). Describing intercultural communication competence: In-depth interviews with American and Russian managers. *Qualitative Research Reports in Communication, 5,* 55–62.

Mazziotta, A., Mummendey, A., & Wright, S.C. (2011). Vicarious intergroup contact effects: Applying social-cognitive theory to intergroup contact research. *Group Processes & Intergroup Relations, 14,* 255–274.

McCombs, M.E. (2004). *Setting the agenda: The mass media and public opinion.* Cambridge, MA: Polity Press.

McCombs, M., & Shaw, D. (1972). The agenda setting function of mass media. *Public Opinion Quarterly, 36,* 176–185.

McCombs, M.E., Shaw, D.L., & Weaver, D. (Eds.) (1997). *Communication and democracy: Exploring the intellectual frontiers of agenda-setting theory.* Mahwah, NJ: Erlbaum.

McDonald, D.G., Glynn, C.J., Kim, S., Ostman, R.E. (2001). The spiral of silence in the 1948 Presidential Election. *Communication Research, 28,* 139–155.

McGee, M.C. (1975). In search of "the people": A rhetorical alternative. *Quarterly Journal of Speech, 61,* 235–249.

McGuire, W.J. (1964). Inducing resistance to persuasion: Some contemporary approaches. In L. Berkowitz (Ed.), *Advances in experimental social psychology* (Vol. 1, pp. 191–229). New York, NY: Academic Press.

McGuire, W.J. (1966). Persistence of the resistance to persuasion induced by various types of prior belief defenses. In C.W. Backman & P.F. Secord (Eds.), *Problems in social psychology* (pp. 128–135). New York, NY: McGraw Hill.

McKay-Semmler, Semmler, S.M., & Kim, Y.Y. (2014). Local news media cultivation of host receptivity in Plainstown. *Human Communication Research, 40,* 188–208.

McKay-Semmler, K., & Kim, Y.Y. (2014). Cross-cultural adaptation of Hispanic youth: A study of communication patterns, functional fitness, and psychological health. *Communication Monographs, 81,* 133–156.

McKerrow, R. (1989). Critical rhetoric: Theory and praxis. *Communication Monographs, 56,* 91–111.

McNamee, L.G. (2011). Faith-based organizational communication and its implications for member identity. *Journal of Applied Communication Research, 39,* 422–440.

McPhee, R.D. (2004). Text, agency and organization in the light of structuration theory. *Organization, 11,* 355–371.

McQuail, D. (2010). *McQuail's mass communication theory.* Thousand Oaks, CA: Sage.

McSweeney, B. (2002). Hofstede's model of national cultural differences and their consequences: A triumph of faith – a failure of analysis. *Human Relations, 55,* 89–118.

Medved, C.E., Brogan, S.M., McClanahan, A.M., Morris, J.F., & Shepherd, G.J. (2006). Family and work socializing communication: Messages, gender, and ideological implications. *Journal of Family Communication, 6,* 161–180.

Merino, M., & Tileagă, C. (2011). The construction of ethnic minority identity: A discursive psychological approach to ethnic self-definition in action. *Discourse & Society, 22,* 86–101.

Messersmith, A.S., Keyton, J., & Bisel, R.S. (2009). Teaching organizational culture. *Communication Teacher, 23*(2), 81–86.

Miller, A.N., & Samp, J.A. (2007). Planning intercultural interaction: Extending anxiety/uncertainty management theory. *Communication Research Reports, 24,* 87–95.

Miller, G.R. (1966). On defining communication: Another stab. *Journal of Communication, 16,* 88–98.

Miller, G.R. (1980). On being persuaded: Some basic distinctions. In M.E. Roloff & G.R. Miller (Eds.), *Persuasion: New directions in theory and research* (pp. 11–28). Beverly Hills, CA: Sage.

Miller, G.R. (1980 [2002]). On being persuaded: Some basic distinctions. In J.P. Dillard & M. Pfau (Eds.), *The persuasion handbook: Developments in theory and practice* (pp. 3–16). Thousand Oaks, CA: Sage.

Miller, G.R., & Burgoon, M. (1973). *New techniques of persuasion.* New York, NY: Harper & Row.

Miller, K. (2005). *Communication theories: Perspectives, processes, and contexts.* Boston: McGraw-Hill.

Miller, N.E., & Dollard, J. (1941). *Social learning and imitation.* New Haven, CT: Yale University Press.

Miniard, P., Bhatla, S., Lord, K., Dickson, P., & Unnava, H.R. (1991). Picture-based persuasion processes and the moderating role of involvement. *Journal of Consumer Research, 18,* 92–107.

Minugh, P.A., Rice, C., & Young, L. (1998). Gender, health beliefs, health behaviors, and alcohol consumption. *American Journal of Drug and Alcohol Abuse, 24,* 483–497.

Min-Sun, K. (2010). Intercultural communication in Asia: current state and future prospects. *Asian Journal of Communication, 20,* 166–180.

Mitchell, D.H., & Eckstein, D. (2009). Jury dynamics and decision-making: A prescription for groupthink. *International Journal of Academic Research, 1*(1), 163–169.

Moon, S. J. (2011). Attention, attitude, and behavior: Second-level agenda-setting effects as a mediator of media use and political participation. *Communication Research*, 40, 698–719.

Moorhead, G., Ference, R., & Neck, C. P. (1991). Group decision fiascoes continue: Space shuttle Challenger and a revised groupthink framework. *Human Relations*, 44, 539–550.

Moring, T., Husband, C., Lojander-Visapää, C., Vincze, L., Fomina, J., & Mänty, N. N. (2011). Media use and ethnolinguistic vitality in bilingual communities. *Journal of Multilingual & Multicultural Development*, 32, 169–186.

Morley, D. D., Shockley-Zalabak, P., & Cesaria, R. (1997). Organizational communication and culture: A study of 10 Italian high-technology companies. *The Journal of Business Communication*, 34, 253–268.

Morris, C. E. (2002). Pink herring & the fourth persona. *Quarterly Journal of Speech*, 88, 228–244.

Mosher, D. L. (1989). Threat to sexual freedom: Moralistic intolerance instills a spiral of silence. *The Journal of Sex Research*, 26, 492–509.

Motley, M. T. (1990). On whether one can(not) not communicate: An examination via traditional communication postulated. *Western Journal of Speech Communication*, 54, 1–20.

Moy, P., Domke, D., & Stamm, K. (2001). The spiral of silence and public opinion on affirmative action. *Journalism & Mass Communication Quarterly*, 78, 7–25.

Mumby, D. K. (2000). Common ground from the critical perspective: Overcoming binary oppositions. In S. R. Corman & M. S. Poole (Eds.), *Perspectives on organizational communication: Finding common ground* (pp. 68–86). New York, NY: Guilford.

Murphy, J. W., & Esposito, L. (2003). The hidden justification for assimilation, multiculturalism, and the prospects for democracy. In E. Kramer (Ed.), *The emerging monoculture* (pp. 1–32). New York, NY: Praeger.

Murphy, M., Glaswer, K., & Grundy, E. (1997). Marital status and long-term illness in Great Britain. *Journal of Marriage and the Family*, 59, 156–164.

Murray, S. L., Holmes, J. G., Griffin, D. W., Bellavia, G., & Rose, P. (2001). The mismeasure of love: How self-doubt contaminates relationship beliefs. *Personality and Social Psychology Bulletin*, 27, 423–436.

Myers, K. K., Jahn, J. L. S., Gailliard, B. M., & Stoltzfus, K. (2011). Vocational anticipatory socialization (VAS): A communicative model of adolescents' interests in STEM. *Management Communication Quarterly*, 25, 87–120.

Myers, K. K., & Oetzel, J. G. (2003). Exploring the dimensions of organizational assimilation: Creating and validating a measure. *Communication Quarterly*, 51, 438–457.

Nabi, R. L., & Clark, S. (2008). Exploring the limits of social cognitive theory: Why negatively reinforced behaviors on TV may be modeled anyway. *Journal of Communication*, 58, 407–427.

National Communication Association. (2014). Why study communication? Retrieved from: www.natcom.org/whystudycommunication/.

Neuliep, J. W. (2012). The relationship among intercultural communication apprehension, ethnocentrism, uncertainty reduction, and communication satisfaction during initial intercultural interaction: An extension of anxiety and uncertainty management (AUM) theory. *Journal of Intercultural Communication Research*, 41, 1–16.

Neuman, W. L. (2011). *Social research methods: Qualitative and quantitative approaches* (7th ed.). Boston, MA: Allyn & Bacon.

Nielsen (2014). Nielsen estimates more than 116 million TV homes in the US. Retrieved January 5, 2015 from: www.nielsen.com/us/en/insights/news/2014/nielsen-estimates-more-than-116-million-tv-homes-in-the-us.html.

Nijland, N., van Gemert-Pijnen, J., Boer, H., Steehouder, M. F., Seydel, E. R. (2008). Evaluation of Internet-based technology for supporting self-care: Problems encountered by patients and caregivers when using self-care applications. *Journal of Medical Internet Research*, 10(2), 3.

Nisbet, E. C., & Myers, T. A. (2010). Challenging the state: Transnational TV and political identity in the Middle East. *Political Communication*, 27, 347–366.

Nocella, G., Boecker, A., Hubbard, L., & Scarpa, R. (2012). Eliciting consumer preferences for certified animal-friendly foods: Can elements of the theory of planned behavior improve experiment analysis? *Psychology & Marketing*, 29, 850–868.

Noelle-Neumann, E. (1974). The spiral of silence a theory of public opinion. *Journal of Communication*, 24, 43–51.

Noelle-Neumann, E. (1977). Turbulences in the climate of opinion: Methodological applications of the spiral of silence theory. *Public Opinion Quarterly*, 41, 143–158.

Noelle-Neumann, E. (1979). Public opinion and the classic tradition: A re-evaluation. *Public Opinion Quarterly*, 43, 143–158.

Noelle-Neumann, E. (1984). *The spiral of silence—our social skin*, Chicago, IL: University of Chicago Press.

Noelle-Neumann, E. (1985). The spiral of silence: A response. In K. L. Sanders, L. L. Kaid, & D. Nimmo (Eds.) *Political communication yearbook 1984* (pp. 66–94), Carbondale, IL. Southern Illinois University Press.

Noelle-Neumann, E. (2004). The spiral of silence and the social nature of man. In L. L. Kaid (Ed). *Handbook of political communication research* (pp. 339–356). Mahwah, NJ. Lawrence Erlbaum Associates.

Novek, E. M. (2005). "Heaven, hell, and here": Understanding the impact of incarceration through a prison newspaper. *Critical Studies in Media Communication*, 22, 281–301.

Oakley, M. R. (2009). Agenda setting and state policy diffusion: The effects of media attention, state court decisions, and policy learning on fetal killing policy. *Social Science Quarterly*, 90, 164–178.

Oetzel, J. G. (1998). Explaining individual communication processes in homogeneous and heterogeneous groups through individualism-collectivism and self-construal. *Human Communication Research*, 25, 202–224.

Oetzel, J. G. (2001). Self-construals, communication processes, and group outcomes in homogeneous and heterogeneous groups. *Small Group Research*, 32, 19–54.

Oetzel, J. G., & Bolton-Oetzel, K. (1997). Exploring the relationship between self-construal and dimensions of group effectiveness. *Management Communication Quarterly*, 10, 289–315.

Oetzel, J., Meares, M., Myers, K. K., & Lara, E. (2003). Interpersonal conflict in organizations: Explaining conflict styles via face-negotiation theory. *Communication Research Reports*, 20, 106–115.

Oetzel, J. G., & Ting-Toomey, S. (2003). Face concerns in interpersonal conflict: A gross-cultural empirical test of the face negotiation theory. *Communication Research*, 30, 599–624.

Ogden, C. K., & Richards, I. A. (1927). *Meaning of meaning*. New York, NY: Harcourt, Brace & Company.

Oh, H., & Jasper, C. R. (2006). Processing of apparel advertisements: Application and extension of Elaboration Likelihood Model. *Clothing & Textiles Research Journal, 24,* 15–32.

Oh, Y., Koeske, G. F., & Sales, E. (2002). Acculturation, stress and depression symptoms among Korean immigrants in the United States. *Journal of Social Psychology, 142,* 511–530.

Oliver, R. L. (1997). *Satisfaction: A behavioral perspective on the consumer.* New York, NY: McGraw Hill.

Olsen, K., & Olsen, H. (2010). Language use, attitude, and linguistic identity among Palestinian students in East Jerusalem. *International Multilingual Research Journal, 4,* 31–54.

Orbe, M. P. & Harris, T. M. (2008). *Interracial communication: Theory into practice* (2nd ed.). Los Angeles, CA: Sage.

Orlitzky, M., & Hirokawa, R. Y. (2001). To err is human, to correct for it divine: A meta-analysis of research testing the functional theory of group decision-making effectiveness. *Small Group Research, 32,* 313–341.

Oshikawa, S. (1969). Can cognitive dissonance theory explain consumer behavior? *Journal of Marketing, 33,* 44–49.

Pacanowsky, M. E., & O'Donnell-Trujillo, N. (1982). Communication and organizational cultures. *The Western Journal of Communications, 46,* 115–130.

Palmgreen, P. (1984). Uses and gratifications: A theoretical perspective. In R. N. Bostrom (Ed.), *Communication yearbook 8* (pp. 20–55). Beverly Hills, CA: Sage.

Palmgreen, P., & Rayburn, J. D., II. (1979). Uses and gratifications and exposure to public television. *Communication Research, 6,* 155–180.

Palomares, N. A. (2009). It's not just your goal, but also who you know: How the cognitive associations among goals and relationships influence goal detection in social interaction. *Human Communication Research, 35,* 534–560.

Papageorgis, D., & McGuire, W. J. (1961). The generality of immunity to persuasion produced by pre-exposure to weakened counterarguments. *Journal of Abnormal and Social Psychology, 62,* 475–481.

Penchmann, C., & Reibling, E. T. (2000). Anti-smoking advertising campaigns targeting youth: Case studies from USA and Canada. *Tobacco Control, 9,* ii18–ii22.

Penelope, J. (1990). *Speaking freely: Unlearning the lies of the father's tongues.* New York, NY: Pergamon.

Petty, R. E., & Cacioppo, J. T. (1981). *Attitudes and persuasion: Classic and contemporary approaches.* Dubuque, IA: Brown.

Petty, R. E., & Cacioppo, J. T. (1984). The effects of involvement on responses to argument quantity and quality: Central and peripheral routes to persuasion. *Journal of Personality and Social Psychology, 46,* 69–81.

Petty, R. E., & Cacioppo, J. T. (1986). *Communication and persuasion: Central and peripheral routes to attitude change.* New York, NY: Springer-Verlag.

Petty, R. E., Cacioppo, J. T., & Schumann, D. (1983). Central and peripheral routes to advertising effectiveness: The moderating role of involvement. *Journal of Consumer Research, 10,* 135–146.

Petty, R. E., & Wegener, D. (1998). Attitude change: Multiple roles for persuasion variables. In D. Gilbert, S. Fiske, & G. Lindzey (Eds.), *The handbook of social psychology* (Vol. 1, pp. 323–390). Boston, MA: McGraw-Hill.

Petty, R. E., & Wegener, D. (1999). The elaboration likelihood model: Current status and controversies. In S. Chaiken & Y. Trope (Eds.), *Dual process theories in social psychology* (pp. 37–72). New York, NY: Guilford.

Pew Research Center (2010). Section 1: Watching, reading and listening to the news. Retrieved January 5, 2015 from: www.people-press.org/2010/09/12/section-1-watching-reading-and-listening-to-the-news/.

Pew Research Center (2014). Mobile technology fact sheet. Retrieved January 5, 2015 from: www.pewinternet.org/fact-sheets/mobile-technology-fact-sheet/.

Pfau, M. (1992). The potential of inoculation in promoting resistance to the effectiveness of comparative advertising messages. *Communication Quarterly, 40,* 26–44.

Pfau, M. (1995). Designing messages for behavioral inoculation. In E. Maibach & R. L. Parrott (Eds.), *Designing health messages: Approaches from communication theory and public health practice* (pp. 99–113). Thousand Oaks, CA: Sage.

Pfau, M. (1997). Inoculation model of resistance to influence. In G. A. Barnett & F. J. Boster (Eds.), *Progress in communication sciences: Advances in persuasion* (Vol. 13, pp. 133–171). Norwood, NJ: Ablex.

Pfau, M., & Burgoon, M. (1988). Inoculation in political campaign communication. *Human Communication Research, 15,* 91–111.

Pfau, M., Haigh, M. M., Sims, J., & Wigley, S. (2007). The influence of corporate front-group stealth campaigns. *Communication Research, 34,* 73–99.

Pfau, M., Holbert, R. L., Zubric, S. J., Pasha, N. H., & Lin, W. (2000). Role and influence of communication modality in the process of resistance to persuasion. *Media Psychology, 2,* 1–33.

Pfau, M., Kenski, H. C., Nitz, M., & Sorenson, J. (1990). Efficacy of inoculation strategies in promotion resistance to political attack messages: Application to direct mail. *Communication Monographs, 57,* 25–43.

Pfau, M., Tusing, K. J., Lee, W. P., Godbold, L. C., Koerner, A. F., Penaloza, L. J., Yang, V. S., & Hong, Y. (1997). Nuances in inoculation: The role of inoculation approach, receiver ego-involvement, and message processing disposition in resistance. *Communication Quarterly, 45,* 461–481.

Pfau, M., Van Bockern, S., & Kang, J. G. (1992). Use of inoculation to promote resistance to smoking initiation among adolescents. *Communication Monographs, 59,* 213–230.

Philipsen, G. (2000). Permission to speak the discourse of difference: A case study. *Research on Language and Social Interaction, 33,* 213–234.

Philipsen, G., & Albrecht, T. L. (1997). *Developing communication theories.* Albany, NY: State University of New York Press.

Phillips, D. C. (1987). *Philosophy, science and social inquiry: Contemporary methodological controversies in social science and related applied fields of research.* New York, NY: Pergamon.

Phinney, J. S., & Ong, A. D. (2007). Conceptualization and measurement of ethnic identity: Current status and future directions. *Journal of Counseling Psychology, 54,* 271–281.

Pincus, I. D. (1986). Communication satisfaction, job satisfaction and job performance. *Human Communication Research, 12,* 395–419.

Planalp, S. (1985). Relational schemata: A test of the alternative forms of relational knowledge as guides to communication. *Human Communication Research, 12,* 3–29.

Plato. (1961a). Gorgias. (W.D. Woodhead, Trans.). In E. Hamilton & H. Cairns (Eds.), *The collected dialogues of Plato including the letters* (pp. 229–307). Princeton, NJ: Princeton University Press.

Plato. (1961b). Socrates' defense (Apology) (H. Tredennick, Trans.). In E. Hamilton & H. Cairns (Eds.), *The collected dialogues of Plato including the letters* (pp. 3–26). Princeton, NJ: Princeton University Press.

Poole, M.S. (2013). Structuration research on group communication. *Management Communication Quarterly, 27,* 607–614.

Poole, M.S., Siebold, D.R., & McPhee, R.D. (1996). The structuration of group decisions. In R.Y. Hirokawa & M.S. Poole (Eds), *Communication and group decision making* (2nd ed., pp. 114–146). Thousand Oaks, CA: Sage.

Popper, K., & Eccles, J. (1974). Falsifiability and freedom. In F. Elders (Ed.), *Reflexive water: The basic concerns of mankind* (pp. 69–131). Ontario, Canada: Souvenir Press, Ltd.

Poster, M. (1989). *Critical theory and poststructuralism.* Ithaca, NY: Cornell University Press.

Powers, T.L., & Jack, E.P. (2013). The influence of cognitive dissonance on retail product returns. *Psychology & Marketing, 30,* 724–735.

Pratt, M.G., & Foreman, P.O. (2000). Classifying managerial responses to multiple organizational identities. *Academy of Management Review, 25,* 18–42.

Prentice, D.A., & Miller, D.T. (1996). Pluralistic ignorance and the perpetuation of social norms by unwitting actors. *Advances in Experimental Social Psychology,* 161–208.

Putnam, L.L., & Stohl, C. (1996). Bona fide groups: An alternative perspective for communication and small group decision making. In R.Y. Hirokawa & M.S. Poole (Eds), *Communication and group decision making* (2nd ed., pp. 179–214). Thousand Oaks, CA: Sage.

Putnam, L.L., Van Hoeven, S.A., & Bullis, C.A. (1991). The role of rituals and fantasy themes in teachers' bargaining. *Western Journal of Speech Communication, 55,* 85–103.

Pyszczynski, T.A., & Greenberg, J. (1981). Role of disconfirmed expectancies on the instigation of attributional processing. *Journal of Personality and Social Psychology, 40,* 31–38.

Quick, B.L. (2010). Applying the health belief model to examine news coverage regarding steroids in sports by ABC, CBS, and NBC between March 1990 and May 2008. *Health Communication, 25,* 247–257.

Raacke, J., & Bonds-Raacke, J. (2008). MySpace and Facebook: Applying the uses and gratifications theory to exploring friend-networking sites. *CyberPsychology & Behavior, 11,* 169–174.

Rabinow, P. (Ed.). (1984). *The Foucault reader.* New York, NY: Pantheon Books.

Rahim, M. (1983). A measure of styles of handling interpersonal conflict. *Academy of Management Journal, 26,* 368–376.

Rawlins, W.K. (1983). Negotiating close friendships: The dialectic of conjunctive freedoms. *Human Communication Research, 9,* 255–266.

Rawlins, W.K. (1989). A dialectical analysis of the tensions, functions and strategic challenges of communication in young adult friendships. In J.A. Anderson (Eds.), *Communication yearbook 12* (pp. 157–189). Newbury Park, CA: Sage.

Rawlins, W.K. (1992). *Friendship matters: Communication, dialectics, and the life course.* New York, NY: Aldine de Gruyter.

Reinsch, P. (2001). *Measuring immigrant integration: Diversity in a European city.* Aldershot, UK: Ashgate.

Rigotti, N.A., Lee, J.E., & Wechsler, H. (2000). US College students' use of tobacco products: Results of a national survey. *Journal of the American Medical Association, 9,* 699–705.

Rivera-Sánchez, M., & Lin, J. (2012). Understanding users' choice of competing browsers: An application of relative mechanism using the theory of planned behavior. *Online Journal of Communication & Media Technologies, 2,* 186–204.

Roddenberry, G., Menosky, J., & LaZebnik, P. (Writers), & Kolbe, W.W. (Director). (1991). Darmok [Television series episode]. *Star Trek: The Next Generation.* Los Angeles, CA: Paramount Studios.

Roethlisberger, F.J., & Dickson, W.J. (1939). *Management and the worker.* Cambridge, MA: Harvard University Press.

Rogers, E.M., Dearing, J.W., & Bergman, D. (1993). The anatomy of agenda setting research. *Journal of Communication, 43,* 68–84.

Rogers, E.M., Hart, W.B., & Miike, Y. (2002). Edward T. Hall and the history of intercultural communication: The United States and Japan. *Keio Communication Review, 24,* 3–26.

Rokeach, M. (1968). *Beliefs, attitudes, and values.* San Francisco, CA: Jossey-Bass.

Rokeach, M. (1973). *The nature of human values.* New York, NY: Free Press.

Rosenfeld, L.B., Richman, J.M., & May, S.K. (2004). Information adequacy, job satisfaction and organizational culture in a dispersed-network organization. *Journal of Applied Communication Research, 32,* 28–54.

Rosengren, K. (1974). Uses and gratifications: A paradigm outlined. In J. Blumler & E. Katz (Eds.), *The uses of mass communication: Current perspectives of gratifications research* (pp. 525–548). Mahwah, NJ: Lawrence Erlbaum.

Rosenstock, I.M. (1974). The health belief model and preventative health behavior. In M.H. Becker (Ed.), *The health belief model and personal health behavior* (pp. 27–59). Thorofare, NJ: Charles B. Slack.

Rosenstock, I.M. (1974a). The health belief model and preventative health behavior. *Health Education Monographs, 2,* 354–385.

Rothwell, J.D. (1992). *In mixed company: Small group communication.* Fort Worth: Harcourt Brace Jovanovich College Publishers.

Rowe-Whyte, A.M., O'Sullivan, P.B., & Hunt, S.K. (2003). *Immediacy on the web: Narrowing the digital divide.* Paper presented in the International Communication Association, San Diego, CA, USA. doi:ica_proceeding_12032.PDF.

Rubin, A.M. (1986). Uses, gratifications, and media effects research. In J. Bryant & D. Zillman (Eds.), *Perspectives on media effects* (pp. 281–301). Hillsdale, NJ: Erlbaum.

Rucker, D.E., & Petty, R.E. (2006). Increasing the effectiveness of communications to consumers: Recommendations based on elaboration likelihood and attitude certainty perspectives. *Journal of Public Policy & Marketing, 25,* 39–52.

Ruesch, J. (1957). Technology and social communication. In L. Thayer (Ed), *Communication theory and research* (pp. 452–481). Springfield, IL: Charles C Thomas.

Ruggiero, T.E. (2000). Uses and gratifications theory in the 21st century. *Mass Communication & Society, 3,* 3–37.

Sahlstein, E.M. (2004). Relating at a distance: Negotiating being together and being apart in long-distance relationships. *Journal of Social and Personal Relationships, 21,* 689–710.

Salazar, A. J., Hirokawa, R. Y., Propp, K. M., Julian, K. M., & Leatham, G. B. (1994). In search of true causes: Examination of the effect of group potential and group interaction on decision performance. *Human Communication Performance*, 20, 529–599.

Salmon, C. T., & Kline, F. G. (1985). The spiral of silence ten years later: An examination and evaluation. In K. L. Sanders, L. L. Kaid, & D. Nimmo (Eds). *Political communication yearbook 1984* (pp. 3–30). Carbondale, IL. Southern Illinois University Press.

Schafer, R. B., Keith, P. M., & Schafer, E. (1995). Predicting fats in diets of marital partners using the health belief model. *Journal of Behavioral Medicine*, 18, 419–433.

Schein, E. (1992). *Organizational culture and leadership* (2nd ed.). San Francisco, CA: Jossey-Bass.

Schein, E. (1999). *The corporate culture survival guide*. San Francisco, CA: Jossey-Bass.

Scheufele, D. A., & Tewksbury, D. (2007). Framing, agenda setting, and priming: The evolution of three media effects models. *Journal of Communication*, 57, 9–20.

Scholl, J. C., & Ragan, S. L. (2003). The use of humor in promoting positive provider–patient interactions in a hospital rehabilitation unit. *Health Communication*, 15, 319–330.

Schraffenberger, D. (2011). Karl Marx and the American Civil War. *International Socialist Review*, 80. Retrieved from: isreview.org

Scott, C. R. (2007). Communication and social identity theory: Existing and potential connections in organizational identification research. *Communication Studies*, 58, 123–138.

Segrin, C., & Nabi, R. L. (2002). Does television viewing cultivate unrealistic expectations about marriage? *Journal of Communication*, 52, 247–263.

Sha, B.-L. (2009). Exploring the connection between organizational identity and public relations behaviors: How symmetry trumps conversation in engendering organizational identification. *Journal of Public Relations Research*, 21, 295–317.

Shaw, D. L., & McCombs, M. E. (1977). *The emergence of American political issues: The agenda-setting function of the press*. St. Paul, MN: West.

Sheafer, T. (2007). How to evaluate it: The role of story-evaluative tone in agenda setting and priming. *Journal of Communication*, 57, 21–39.

Sheer, V. C., & Cline, R. J. (1995). Testing a model of information adequacy and uncertainty reduction in patient interactions. *Journal of Applied Communication Research*, 23, 44–59.

Showalter, E. (1971). *Women's liberation and literature*. New York, NY: Harcourt Brace Jovanovich.

Shuang, L. (2014). Becoming intercultural: Exposure to foreign cultures and intercultural competence. *China Media Research*, 10(3), 7–14.

Shuter, R. (2011). Introduction: New media across cultures—Prospect and promise. *Journal of International & Intercultural Communication*, 4, 241–245.

Shuter, R. (2012). Intercultural new media studies: The next frontier in intercultural communication. *Journal of Intercultural Communication Research*, 41, 219–237.

Shyman Sundar, S., & Limperos, A. M. (2013). Uses and grats 2.0: New gratifications for new media. *Journal of Broadcasting & Electronic Media*, 57, 504–525.

Sias, P., & Jablin, F. (1995). Differential superior-subordinate relations, perceptions of fairness, and coworker communication. *Human Communication Research*, 22, 5–38.

Signorini, P., Wiesemes, R., & Murphy, R. (2009). Developing alternative frameworks for exploring intercultural learning: A critique of Hofstede's cultural difference model. *Teaching in Higher Education*, *14*, 253–264. doi: 10.1080/1356251090 2898825.

Silverstein, M. (1979). Language structure and linguistic ideology. In P. R. Clyne, W. F. Hanks, & C. L. Hofbauer (Eds.), *The elements: A parasession on linguistic units and levels* (pp. 193–247). Chicago, IL: Chicago Linguistic Society.

Silverstein, M. (1985). Language and culture of gender. In E. Mertz & R. Parmentier (Eds.), *Semiotic Meditation* (pp. 23–47). Orlando, FL: Academic Press.

Simmel, G. (1950). *The sociology of Georg Simmel*. (K. H. Wolff, Ed. and Trans.). New York, NY: Free Press. (Original work published 1908).

Simmons, V. N., Webb, M. S., & Brandon, T. H. (2004). College-student smoking: An initial test of an experiential dissonance enhancing intervention. *Addictive Behaviors*, *29*, 1129–1136.

Simons, H. W. (1976). *Persuasion: Understanding, practice, and analysis*. Reading, MA: Addison-Wesley.

Slotter, E. B., Gardner, W. L., & Finkel, E. J. (2010). Who am I without you? The influence of romantic breakup on the self-concept. *Personality and Social Psychology Bulletin*, *36*, 147–160.

Smith, S. (1984). Groupthink and the hostage rescue mission. *British Journal of Political Science*, *15*, 453–458.

Song, I., LaRose, R., Eastin, M. S, & Lin, C. A. (2004). Internet gratifications and Internet addiction: On the uses and abuses of new media. *CyberPsychology & Behavior*, *7*, 384–394.

Sorenson, M. (1997). Maintenance of exercise behavior for individuals at risk for cardiovascular disease. *Perceptual and Motor Skills*, *85*(3 Pt. 1), 867–880.

Sowards, S. K., & Renegar, V. R. (2006). Reconceptualizing rhetorical activism in contemporary feminist contexts. *The Howard Journal of Communications*, *17*, 57–74.

Sowards, S. K., & Renegar, V. R. (2004). The rhetorical function of consciousness-raising in third wave feminism. *Communication Studies*, *55*, 535–552.

Sowell, T. (1994). *Race and culture: A world view*. New York, NY: Basic Books.

Spender, D. (1980). *Man made language*. London, UK: Routledge.

Spitzberg, B. H. (1988). Communication competence: Measures of perceived effectiveness. In C. Tardy (Ed.), *A handbook for the study of human communication* (pp. 67–105). Norwood, NJ: Ablex.

Spitzberg, B. H., & Cupach, W R. (1984). *Interpersonal communication competence*. Beverly Hills, CA: Sage.

Spivak, G. C. (1995). Ghostwriting. *Diacritics*, *25*, 65–84.

Stacks, D. W., & Andersen, P. A. (1989). The modular mind: Implications for intrapersonal communication. *Southern Communication Journal*, *54*, 273–293.

Staggers, S. M., Brann, M., & Maki, S. M. (2012). Let's talk about HPV: Examining college male perceptions of the HPV vaccine. *Qualitative Research Reports in Communication*, *13*, 28–36.

Stasser, G., & Titus, W. (1985). Pooling of unshared information in group decision making: Biased information sampling during discussion. *Journal of Personality and Social Psychology*, *48*, 1467–1478.

State of the Media. (2013). Audio: By the numbers. Retrieved January 5, 2015 from: www.stateofthemedia.org/2013/audio-digital-drives-listener-experience/audio-by-the-numbers/.

Stein, E. A., & Kellam, M. (2014). Programming presidential agendas: Partisan and media environments that lead presidents to fight crime and corruption. *Political Communication, 31*, 25–52.

Steiner, I. D. (1972). *Group process and productivity.* New York, NY: Academic Press.

Steinke, J. (2005). Cultural representations of gender and science: Portrayals of female scientists and engineers in popular films. *Science Communication, 27*, 27–63.

Stets, J. E. (1995). Modeling control in relationships. *Journal of Marriage and the Family, 57*, 489–501.

Stiff, J. B. (1986). Cognitive processing of persuasive message cues: A meta-analytic review of the effects of supporting information on attitudes. *Communication Monographs, 53*, 75–89.

Stiff, J. B. (1994). *Persuasive communication.* New York, NY: Guilford.

Stiff, J. B., & Boster, F. J. (1987). Cognitive processing: Additional thoughts and a reply to Petty, Kasmer, Haugtvedt, and Cacioppo. *Communication Monographs, 55*, 198–213.

Stone, J. F. (2002). Using symbolic convergence theory to discern and segment motives for enrolling in professional master's degree programs. *Communication Quarterly, 50*, 227–243.

Surra, C. A. (1985). Courtship types: Variations in interdependence between partners and social networks. *Journal of Personality and Social Psychology, 49*, 357–375.

Surra, C. A., Arizzi, P., & Asmussen, L. A. (1988). The association between reasons for commitment and the development and outcome of marital relationships. *Journal of Social and Personal Relationships, 5*, 47–63.

Sweeney, J. C., Hausknecht, D., & Soutar, G. N. (2000). Cognitive dissonance after purchase: A multidimensional scale. *Psychology & Marketing, 17*, 369–385.

Szabo, E. A., & Pfau, M. (2002). Nuances in inoculation: Theory and applications. In J. P. Dillard & M. Pfau (Eds.), *The persuasion handbook: Developments in theory and practice* (pp. 233–258). Thousand Oaks, CA: Sage.

Szalay, L. B., & Inn, A. (1988). Cross-cultural adaptation and diversity: Hispanic-Americans. In Y. Y. Kim, & W. B. Gudykunst (Eds.), *Cross-cultural adaptation: Current approaches* (pp. 212–232). Newbury Park, CA: Sage.

Taggart, H. M., & Connor, S. E. (1995). The relation of exercise habits to health beliefs and knowledge about osteoporosis. *Journal of the American College of Health, 44*(3), 127–130.

Tajfel, H., & Turner, J. C. (1979). An integrative theory of intergroup conflict. In W. C. Austin & S. Worchel (Eds.), *The social psychology of intergroup relations* (pp. 33–53). Monterey: Brooks/Cole.

Tam, K. Y., & Ho, S. Y. (2005). Web personalization as a persuasion strategy: An elaboration likelihood model perspective. *Information Systems Research, 16*, 271–291.

Tan, Y., & Weaver, D. H. (2007). Agenda-setting effects among the media, the public, and Congress, 1946–2004. *Journalism & Mass Communication Quarterly, 84*, 729–744.

Tan, Y., & Weaver, D. H. (2010). Media bias, public opinion, and policy liberalism from 1956 to 2004: A second-level agenda-setting study. *Mass Communication and Society, 13*, 412–434.

Taylor, D. G. (1982). Pluralistic ignorance and the spiral of silence: A formal analysis. *Public Opinion Quarterly, 46*, 311–335.

Taylor, J. (1993). *Rethinking the theory of organizational communication: How to read an organization.* Norwood, NJ: Ablex.

Taylor, D. & Altman, I. (1987). Communication in interpersonal relationships: Social penetration theory. In M.E. Roloff & G.R. Miller (Eds.), *Interpersonal processes: New directions in communication research* (pp. 257–277). Newbury Park, CA: Sage.

The American College Dictionary. (1964). New York, NY: Random House.

Therborn, G. (1980). *The ideology of power and the power of ideology.* New York, NY: Verso.

Therkelsen, A.R. (2011). Encounters with philanthropic information: Cognitive dissonance and implications for the social sector. *Voluntas, 22,* 518–545.

Thibaut, J.W., & Kelly, H.H. (1959). *The social psychology of groups.* New York, NY: John Wiley.

Thompson, T.L. (1984). The invisible helping hand: The role of communication in the health and social service professions. *Communication Quarterly, 32,* 148–163.

Tien Vu, Guo, L., & McCombs, M.E. (2014). Exploring "the world outside and the pictures in our heads": A network agenda-setting study. *Journalism & Mass Communication Quarterly, 91,* 669–686.

Ting-Toomey, S. (1985). Toward a theory of conflict and culture. In W.B. Gudykunst, L.P. Stewart, & S. Ting-Toomey (Eds.), *Communication, culture, and organizational processes* (pp. 71–86). Beverly Hills, CA: Sage.

Ting-Toomey, S. (1993). Communicative resourcefulness: An identity negotiation perspective. In R.L. Wiseman & J. Koester (Eds.), *Intercultural communication competence* (pp. 72–111). Newbury Park, CA: Sage.

Ting-Toomey, S., & Kurogi, A. (1998). Facework competence in intercultural conflict: An updated face-negotiation theory. *Journal of Intercultural Relations, 22,* 187–225. doi:10.1016/S0147–1767(98)00004–2.

Ting-Toomey, S., Oetzel, J.G., & Yee-Jung, K. (2001). Self-construal types and conflict management styles. *Communication Reports, 14*(2), 87–104.

Toller, P.W. (2005). Negotiation of dialectical contradictions by parents who have experienced the death of a child. *Journal of Applied Communication Research, 33,* 46–66.

Tolstedt, B.E. & Stokes, J.P. (1984). Self-disclosure, intimacy, and the depenetration process. *Journal of Personality and Social Psychology, 46,* 84–90.

Tompkins, P.K. (1967). Organizational communication: A state-of-the-art review: In G. Richetto (Ed.). *Conference on organizational communication* (pp. 4–26). Huntsville, AL: NASA.

Trifiletti, L.B., Gielen, A.C., Sleet, D.A., & Hopkins, K. (2005). Behavioral and social science theories and models: Are they used in unintentional injury prevention research? *Health Education Research, 20,* 298–307.

Trobst, K.K., Collins, R.L., & Embree, J.M. (1994). The role of emotion in social support provision: Gender, empathy and expression of distress. *Journal of Social and Personal Relationships, 11,* 45–62.

Underation, C. (2012). Seeding the vision: Symbolic convergence theory and Aimee Semple McPherson. *Atlantic Journal of Communication, 20,* 274–289.

UNICEF, Communication for Development. (2014). *Ebola and C4D.* Retrieved from: www.unicef.org/cbsc/index_73157.html.

van Praag, P., & van der Eijk, C. (1998). News content and effects in an historic campaign. *Political Communication, 15,* 165–183.

Van Der Werf, M. (2000). Georgetown's growing pains: Eager applicants, troubled finances. *Chronicle of Higher Education, 46*(21), A38–A40.

Vangelisti, A.L. (1988). Adolescent socialization into the workplace: A synthesis and critique of current literature. *Youth & Society, 19*, 460–484.

Vangelisti, A.L., & Daly, J.A. (1997). Gender differences in standards for romantic relationships. *Personal Relationships, 4*, 203–219.

Vatz, R.E. (1973). The myth of the rhetorical situation. *Philosophy and Rhetoric, 6*, 154–161.

Vincze, L., & Freynet, N. (2014). Objective vitality as moderator of ethnolinguistic identity gratifications. *Communication Research Reports, 31*, 117–123.

Vincze, L., & Holley, P. (2013). Making news between cultures: Ethnolinguistic identity and journalism in four minority language daily newspapers. *Communication Reports, 26*, 61–72.

Wachowski, A., & Wachowski, L. (Directors). (1999). *The Matrix* [DVD]. United States: Warner Bros. Home Video.

Waipeng, L., Detenber, B., Willnat, L., Aday, S., & Graf, J. (2004) A Cross-cultural Test of the Spiral of Silence Theory in Singapore and the United States. *Asian Journal of Communication, 14*(2), 205–226.

Waipeng, L., Willnat, L., & Detenber, B.H. (2004). Individual-level predictors of public outspokenness: A test of the spiral of silence theory in Singapore. *International Journal of Public Opinion Research, 14*, 391–412.

Waldeck, J.H., Seibold, D.R., & Flanigan, A.J. (2004). Organizational assimilation and communication technology use. *Communication Monographs, 71*, 161–183.

Wander, P.C. (1984). The third persona: An ideological turn in rhetorical theory. *Central States Speech Journal, 35*, 197–216.

Ward Sr., M. (2010). "I was saved at an early age": An ethnography of fundamentalist speech and cultural performance. *Journal of Communication and Religion, 33*, 108–144.

Waters, R.D. (2009). Examining the role of cognitive dissonance in crisis fundraising. *Public Relations Review, 35*, 139–143.

Waters, R.D., & Tindall, N.T.J. (2011). Exploring the impact of American news coverage on crisis fundraising: Using media theory to explicate a new model of fundraising communication. *Journal of Nonprofit & Public Sector Marketing, 23*, 20–40.

Watson, K. (2005). Queer theory. *Group Analysis, 38*(1), 67–81.

Watzlawick, P., Beavin, J.H., & Jackson, D.D. (1967). *Pragmatics of human communication*. New York, NY: Norton.

Weaver, D.H. (1996). What voters learn from media. *The Annals of the American Academy of Political and Social Sciences, 546*, 34–47.

Weaver, D.H., McCombs, M., & Shaw, D.L. (2004). Agenda-setting research: Issues, attributes, and influences. In L.L. Kaid (Ed.), *Handbook of political communication research* (pp. 257–282). Mahwah, NJ: Lawrence Erlbaum Associates.

Weaver, W. (1949). Recent contributions to the mathematical theory of communication. In C. Shannon & W. Weaver, *The mathematical theory of communication*. Urbana, IL: University of Illinois Press.

Weber, M. (1991). The nature of social action. In W.G. Runciman (Ed.), *Weber selections in translation* (pp. 7–32). Cambridge, UK: Cambridge University Press.

Wei, P.-S., & Lu, H.-P. (2014). Why do people play mobile social games? An examination of network externalities and of uses and gratifications. *Internet Research, 24*, 313–331.

Wheeless, L. R., & Grotz, J. (1976). Conceptualization and measurement of reported self-disclosure. *Human Communication Research, 3,* 250–257.

Whorf, B. L. (1940). Linguistics as an exact science. In J. B. Carrol (Ed.). (1956). *Language, thought and reality: Selected writings of Benjamin Lee Whorf* (pp. 220–232). Cambridge, MA: MIT Press.

Williams, D. (2002). Structure and competition in the US home video game industry. *The International Journal of Media Management, 4,* 41–54.

Williams, E. A., & Connaughton, S. L. (2012). Expressions of identifications: The nature of talk and identity tensions among organizational members in a struggling organization. *Communication Studies, 63,* 457–481.

Wimmer, R. D., & Dominick, J. R. (1994). *Mass media research: An introduction.* Belmont, CA: Wadsworth.

Wiseman, R. L. (2002). Intercultural communication competence. In W. B. Gudykunst & B. Mody (Eds.), *Handbook of international and intercultural communication* (2nd ed.) (pp. 207–224). Thousand Oaks, CA: Sage.

Witmer, D. F. (1997). Communication and recovery: Structuration as an ontological approach to organizational culture. *Communication Monographs, 64,* 324–349.

Witte, K. (1992). Putting the fear back into fear appeals: The extended parallel process model. *Communication Monographs, 59,* 329–349.

Wood, J. (2008). *Gendered lives: Communication, gender, and culture* (8th ed.). Boston, MA: Cengage Learning.

Wright, L. (1999, July). The Stonewall riots 1969: A turning point in the struggle for gay and lesbian liberation. *Socialist Alternative.* Retrieved from www.socialist alternative.org.

Xiao, J. J., Tang, C., Serido, J., & Shim, S. (2011). Antecedents and consequences of risky behavior among college students: Application and extension of the theory of planned behavior. *Journal of Public Policy & Marketing, 30,* 239–245.

Yoo, W., Kwon, M.-W., & Pfeiffer, L. J. (2013). Influence of communication on colorectal cancer screening: Revisiting the health belief model. *Journal of Communication in Healthcare, 6,* 35–43.

Yuan, Y., Fulk, J., Shumate, M., Monge, P. R., Bryant, J. A., Matsaganis, M. (2005). Individual participation in organizational information commons. The impact of team level social influence and technology-specific competence. *Human Communication Research, 31,* 212–240.

Zhang, Q., Ting-Toomey, S., & Oetzel, J. G. (2014). Linking emotion to the conflict face-negotiation theory: A US–China investigation of the mediating effects of anger, compassion, and guilt in interpersonal conflict. *Human Communication Research, 40,* 373–395.

Zhu, J. H., & Blood, D. (1997). Media agenda-setting theory: Telling the public what to think about. In D. P. Cushman & G. Kovacic (Eds.), *Emerging theories of human communication* (pp. 88–114). Albany, NY: University of New York Press.

Zhu, J.-H., Watt, J. H., Snyder, L. B., Yan, J., & Jiang, Y. (1993). Public issue priority formation: Media agenda-setting and social interaction. *Journal of Communication, 43,* 8–29.

Zimmerman, F. J., Oritz, S. E., Christakis, D. A., Elkun, D. (2012). The value of social cognitive theory to reducing preschool TV viewing: A pilot randomized trial. *Preventive Medicine, 54,* 212–218.

IMAGE CREDITS

INDEX

Note: 'F' after a page number indicates a figure.

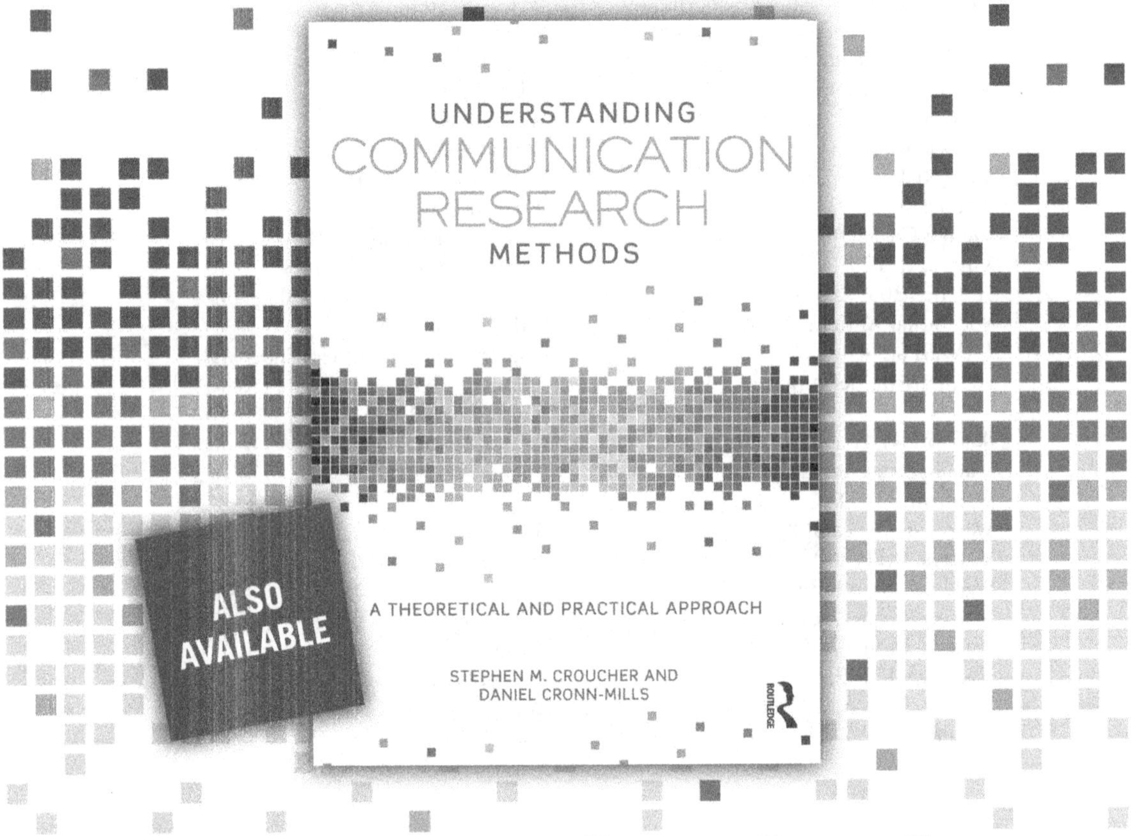